THE MACARTHUR NEW TESTAMENT COMMENTARY

MATTHEW 16-23

John MacArthur Jr.

MOODY PRESS/CHICAGO

© 1988 by
THE MOODY BIBLE INSTITUTE
OF CHICAGO

Library of Congress Cataloging in Publication Data

MacArthur, John, 1939-
    Matthew 16-23 / John MacArthur, Jr.
        p.   cm. — (The MacArthur New Testament commentary)
    Bibliography: p.
    Includes indexes.
    ISBN 0-8024-0764-1
    1. Bible. N.T.   Matthew XVI-XXIII—Commentaries.   I. Title.
II. Series: MacArthur, John, 1939-   MacArthur New Testament
commentary.
BS2575.3.M244 1988
266'.2077—dc19   88-8440
                                                                              CIP

Printed in the United States of America

To Felix Martin del Campo, Jr., who expresses his friendship to me through loving service

Contents

Preface

It continues to be a rewarding divine communion for me to preach expositionally through the New Testament. My goal is always to have deep fellowship with the Lord in the understanding of His Word, and out of that experience to explain to His people what a passage means. In the words of Nehemiah 8:8, I strive "to give the sense" of it so they may truly hear God speak and, in so doing, may respond to Him.

Obviously, God's people need to understand Him, which demands knowing His Word of truth (2 Tim. 2:15) and allowing that Word to dwell in us richly (Col. 3:16). The dominant thrust of my ministry, therefore, is to help make God's living Word alive to His people. It is a refreshing adventure.

This New Testament commentary series reflects this objective of explaining and applying Scripture. Some commentaries are primarily linguistic, others are mostly theological, and some are mainly homiletical. This one is basically explanatory, or expository. It is not linguistically technical, but deals with linguistics when that seems helpful to proper interpretation. It is not theologically expansive, but focuses on the major doctrines in each text and on how they relate to the whole of Scripture. It is not primarily homiletical, although each unit of thought is generally treated as one chapter, with a clear outline and logical flow of thought. Most truths are illustrated and applied with other Scripture. After establishing the context of a passage, I have tried to follow closely the writer's development and reasoning.

My prayer is that each reader will fully understand what the Holy Spirit is saying through this part of His Word, so that His revelation may lodge in the minds of believers and bring greater obedience and faithfulness—to the glory of our great God.

The Blind Who Will Never See
(16:1-4)

And the Pharisees and Sadducees came up, and testing Him asked Him to show them a sign from heaven. But He answered and said to them, "When it is evening, you say, 'It will be fair weather, for the sky is red.' And in the morning, 'There will be a storm today, for the sky is red and threatening.' Do you know how to discern the appearance of the sky, but cannot discern the signs of the times? An evil and adulterous generation seeks after a sign; and a sign will not be given it, except the sign of Jonah." And He left them, and went away. (16:1-4)

Good eyesight is a marvelous blessing, and in order to see better, Americans spend some five billion dollars a year on eye care. About seven percent of the population is considered legally blind. In many parts of the world, of course, the percentage of blind people is much higher.

It is even more significant that, since the fall of Adam, every person on earth has been born spiritually blind. They fall into two categories: those who will never see and know God and those who, by the grace of God and the illumination of the Holy Spirit, are enabled to see and to have intimate fellowship with Him. The deciding factor is how a person is related to Jesus Christ. The person who rejects the Savior remains forever blind; the person who confesses Him as Lord is given spiritual sight as well as spiritual life. Unfortunately, men do not universally have the desire for spiritual sight that they do for physical. The vast majority do not know they are spiritually blind and do not care. Even when offered sight, many refuse it.

Jesus "was the true light which, coming into the world, enlightens every man. He was in the world, and the world was made through Him, and the world did not know Him. He came to His own, and those who were His own did not receive Him" (John 1:9-11). Paul declares that, although "since the creation of the world [God's] invisible attributes, His eternal power and divine nature, have been clearly seen, being understood through what has been made," rebellious mankind "did not honor Him as God, or give thanks; but they became futile in their speculations, and their foolish heart was darkened" (Rom. 1:20-21). Even with evidence of God plainly before them, unregenerate men refuse to see Him. Their eyes reject the evidence because their hearts reject the One who gives it.

"A natural man does not accept the things of the Spirit of God," Paul explains; "for they are foolishness to him, and he cannot understand them, because they are spiritually appraised" (1 Cor. 2:14). Unredeemed men are "darkened in their understanding, excluded from the life of God, because of the ignorance that is in them, because of the hardness of their heart" (Eph. 4:18).

The Old Testament writers also testified to men's natural spiritual blindness. The wicked "do not know nor do they understand," wrote the psalmist; "they walk about in darkness" (Ps. 82:5). The same writer confessed that before he came to know God he "was senseless and ignorant, . . . like a beast before Thee" (Ps. 73:22). We learn from Proverbs that "the way of the wicked is like darkness; they do not know over what they stumble" (Prov. 4:19). Because of their sin and rebelliousness, Jeremiah described God's chosen nation of Israel as "foolish and senseless people, who have eyes, but see not; who have ears, but hear not" (Jer. 5:21). Micah described Israel's pagan enemies as those who "do not know the thoughts of the Lord, and they do not understand His purpose" (Mic. 4:12).

Three things contribute to man's spiritual blindness. The first is sin. When God's own Son came to earth as the light of the world, "men loved the darkness rather than the light; for their deeds were evil" (John 3:19). The second contributor to spiritual blindness is Satan. As "the god of this world [he] has blinded the minds of the unbelieving, that they might not see the light of the gospel of the glory of Christ, who is the image of God" (2 Cor. 4:4). The third contributor is God's sovereign judgment. When, because of their sin and their allegiance to Satan, men persistently reject God's light, He judicially confirms them in their self-chosen darkness. Of those in Jerusalem who rejected Him, Jesus declared, "If you had known in this day, even you, the things which make for peace! But now they have been hidden from your eyes" (Luke 19:42).

Through the seven parables of Matthew 13 Jesus describes the characteristics of the age between His rejection and His coming again to establish His millennial kingdom. Those parables present "the mysteries of the kingdom," truths not revealed in the Old Testament but given only to those who during this age trust in Jesus Christ for salvation (13:11). The singular purpose of those particular parables was to teach that the mystery time, which has now lasted some 2,000 years, is a time of both belief and of unbelief, of receiving and of rejecting.

Following the seven parables, Jesus presented eight illustrations (Matt. 13:53—16:12), six of which focus on His rejection and two on His acceptance. History verifies that rejection of Jesus has been vastly greater than reception of Him, just as those parables and illustrations indicate.

The gospel accounts make clear that, beginning with the ministry of John the Baptist, the most vocal and determined rejection of Christ and His gospel was by the Jewish religious leaders, especially the influential and powerful **Pharisees and Sadducees.**

The events of Matthew 16 began just after the Lord crossed the Sea of Galilee from the Gentile area of Decapolis, where He had miraculously fed "four thousand men, besides women and children," and came to the Jewish "region of Magadan," on the western shore (Matt. 15:32-39). The exact location of Magadan, which Mark refers to as Dalmanutha (8:10), is unknown, but Jesus' opponents came there as soon as they heard He had arrived.

In 16:1-4, Matthew records Jesus' final invitation to those religious leaders; and by their persistent rejection of Him they confirmed themselves as among the spiritually blind who steadfastly refuse to see. In this brief passage we see four characteristics of those whose spiritual blindness will never end: they seek darkness, they curse the light, they regress still deeper into darkness, and finally they are abandoned by God.

They Seek Darkness

The first characteristic is seen in the fact that **the Pharisees and Sadducees came up** to Jesus together. Although they ordinarily criticized and despised each other, the two religious groups found common cause in their opposition to Jesus. They were bound together by their love of spiritual darkness.

For the most part, the **Sadducees** were aristocratic, and they traditionally boasted the high priests and chief priests among their numbers. Many of them made fortunes operating the lucrative Temple concessions of money changing and selling of sacrificial animals. **The Pharisees,** on the other hand, were generally from the working class, and many of them, like Paul (Acts 18:3), made their living from a trade. Scribes and priests were found in both parties (see Matt. 3:7; 15:12; 21:15; 23:2-36; Mark 2:16; 3:6; Luke 7:30; 16:14; John 7:32; 8:3-6; 9:40-41).

The Pharisees were the more conservative and fundamental, but they held rabbinic tradition to be of equal authority with Scripture (see Matt. 15:2, 6). They were strongly separatistic, continuing the zealous protection of Judaism from Gentile influence that was begun several centuries earlier by the Hasidim in their resistance to the Hellenization campaigns of Antiochus Epiphanes.

The **Sadducees,** on the other hand, cared nothing for rabbinic tradition and had no compunction about making religious, cultural, or political compromises. Their cardinal principle was expediency. Although they claimed to believe Scripture, their interpretations were so spiritualized that all significant meaning was lost. They were thoroughly liberal and materialistic, not believing in angels, immortality, resurrection of the dead, or anything else supernatural.

Once when Paul was brought before the Sanhedrin he capitalized on the great doctrinal differences between the two groups by identifying himself as a Pharisee and affirming his belief in the resurrection. When he did so, "there arose a dissension between the Pharisees and Sadducees; and the assembly was divided. For the Sadducees say that there is no resurrection, nor an angel, nor a spirit; but the Pharisees acknowledge them all. And there arose a great uproar; and some of the scribes of the Pharisaic party stood up and began to argue heatedly, saying, 'We find nothing wrong with this man; suppose a spirit or an angel has spoken to him?'" (Acts 23:6-9).

Matthew's use of a single article (**the**) suggests that **the Pharisees** were the main group, with **Sadducees** intermingled among them; and from Mark 8:11 we learn that the Pharisees took the lead in confronting Jesus. Those "blind guides of the blind" (Matt. 15:14) enlisted the support of men who, if anything, were more spiritually blind than themselves. Instead of coming to Jesus for spiritual sight, they confirmed their love of blindness by making league with other ungodly men against Him. The ritualists and the rationalists joined forces on the basis of mutual contempt for Jesus. That is always the way of those who are willfully, sinfully blind. Their common trust is in themselves and in their own good works, and therefore their common enemy is God and His sovereign grace.

THEY CURSE THE LIGHT

A second characteristic of the willfully blind is the other side of the first: they curse the light. The person who is content in his spiritual blindness has no use for spiritual light, because it intrudes into his darkness and exposes his sin. "And this is the judgment," Jesus said, "that the light is come into the world, and men loved the darkness rather than the light; for their deeds were evil. For everyone who does evil hates the light, and does not come to the light, lest his deeds should be exposed. But he who practices the truth comes to the light, that his deeds may be manifested as having been wrought in God" (John 3:19-21). The Pharisees and Sadducees did not come to Jesus in hope of finding truth for themselves but in hope of finding falsehood in Him. Therefore, **testing Him,** they **asked Him to show them a sign from heaven.**

They did not expect Jesus to perform such **a sign,** and if He had given them one, their unbelief would have remained just as strong. They had already seen sign after sign, the miraculous nature of which was irrefutable. They did not deny His supernatural power but refused to recognize it as being from God, having even accused Him of working as an agent of Satan (Matt. 12:24).

Popular Jewish superstition held that demons could perform earthly miracles but that only God could perform heavenly ones. **From heaven** indicates the desire to see a miraculous **sign** in the sky. The Pharisees and Sadducees demanded a miracle they thought was beyond Jesus, hoping to prove that His power, and therefore His message, were not divine. He would be publicly discredited, and they would be vindicated.

In their blindness they could not see that Jesus Himself was **a sign from heaven.** Nor could they see that they themselves were helping to fulfill that sign. As the godly Simeon held the infant Jesus in his arms he prophesied, "Behold, this Child is appointed for the fall and rise of many in Israel, and for a sign to be opposed" (Luke 2:34). Because the unbelieving religious leaders refused to recognize God's supreme Sign, His only Son, they could not accept His lesser signs, despite the evidence they saw with their own eyes. Physical sight is of no help to spiritual blindness, and had those leaders seen a hundred more miracles a hundred times more dramatic, they would simply have been driven to deeper darkness—as their rejection of the miracle of Jesus' resurrection proved. As Abraham said of the brothers in the story of the rich man and Lazarus, "If they do not listen to Moses and the Prophets, neither will they be persuaded if someone rises from the dead" (Luke 16:31). Like Pharaoh before Moses, the more they saw God's power demonstrated, the more they hardened their hearts against Him (Ex. 7-11). Heavenly signs would come in the future (Matt. 24:29-30; Luke 21:11, 25; Acts 2:19; Rev. 15:1), but they would signal the very end.

If a person's heart is set on darkness, when the light comes he curses it. Proudly confessing that very disposition, the French atheist Voltaire declared, "Even if a miracle should be wrought in the open marketplace before a thousand sober witnesses, I would rather mistrust my senses than admit a miracle." Unbelief will always find a way to reject the truth, even to the point of denying the undeniable.

The liberal theologian does not prefer the speculations of philosophy or psychology because these are more provable or persuasive than the truths of Scripture but because he prefers man's wisdom to God's. And, contrary to his claim, the agnostic does not refuse to believe because he *cannot* know about God but because he *will not* know about Him. The person who turns to rationalism, evolution, skepticism, or simply to himself for meaning and purpose does not do so because of lack of evidence about God and Christ but in spite of it. The person who turns to man-made religion does not do so because no light about the true God is available but because he despises that light and that God.

Men turn to acts of penance, to self-affliction, to confessionals, and to every other human resource to try to expiate particular sins; but they refuse to deal with the root in their hearts, their basic sinful nature with which they do not want to part.

Knowing that the true intent of the Pharisees' and Sadducees' demand for a heavenly sign was to discredit Him, Jesus **answered and said to them, "When it is evening, you say, 'It will be fair weather, for the sky is red.' And in the morning, 'There will be a storm today, for the sky is red and threatening.'"** Those sayings correspond to the age-old mariner's ditty, "Red sky at night, sailor's delight. Red sky in the morning, sailor's warning." From many years of observation men learned that a red sky in the evening is usually followed by good weather, whereas a red sky in the morning is often followed by a storm. The religious leaders who confronted Jesus accepted the reliability of that folk meteorology without question.

"Do you know how to discern the appearance of the sky," Jesus asked them, **"but cannot discern the signs of the times?"** Both the Pharisees and Sadducees were proud of their religious heritage and considered themselves experts on the things of God. But despite their religious training and positions, their primitive and limited knowledge of weather was far superior to their knowledge of God. "Your sensitivity to weather," Jesus said in effect, "makes a mockery of your insensitivity to God's kingdom. You have no idea of what God is doing in the world. You are oblivious to **the times** in which you are privileged to live, the very times of redemption by God's own Son, before whom you now stand." It was the beginning of the messianic age that Jews had long hoped for, but those Jewish leaders did not recognize it. They were better weathermen than biblical scholars (cf. Luke 12:54-56). They were "blind guides of the blind" (Matt. 15:14). In Matthew 23, Jesus labeled them blind guides (vv. 16, 24) and blind fools (v. 17).

Modern society also has many people with great insight and discernment about the things of the world but who have no comprehension of the things of God. Experts are able to predict whether the stock market will go up or down, whether gold and silver will become more or less valuable, and whether the dollar will become stronger or weaker. Others can predict the direction of interest rates, fashions, the real estate market, and of import/export ratios. Others can predict trends in education, sociology, morality, and government. But our society is short of those who know what God's plan for the world is and that it is still the "last time," the time of the Messiah. What it means to be a citizen of His kingdom escapes them.

In answer to the disciples' question about "the sign of [His] coming, and of the end of the age," Jesus said, "You will be hearing of wars and rumors of wars; . . . nation will rise against nation, and kingdom against kingdom, and in various places there will be famines and earthquakes. . . . And many false prophets will arise, and will mislead many. And because lawlessness is increased, most people's love will grow cold" (Matt. 24:3, 6-7, 11-12).

Those signs that Jesus will return abound in our day. No period of history has experienced more wars or been so preoccupied with the prospect of war as our own. With unprecedented surpluses of food in some parts of the world, other parts still experience devastating famines. Cults and false religions of every sort are proliferating even in countries that have been nominally Christian for hundreds of years. The spirit of lawlessness and self-will is rampant.

Paul declared, "The mystery of lawlessness is already at work; only he who now restrains will do so until he is taken out of the way. And then that lawless one will be revealed whom the Lord will slay with the breath of His mouth and bring to an end by the appearance of His coming" (2 Thess. 2:7-8). The apostle explained to

Timothy that "the Spirit explicitly says that in later times some will fall away from the faith, paying attention to deceitful spirits and doctrines of demons" (1 Tim. 4:1). Peter wrote of the great apostasy, false teaching, heresies, mockery, and denial of Christ's return that would characterize the last days (2 Pet. 2:1-3; 3:3-4).

Ezekiel predicted that in the end times God would restore His chosen people to the land He had promised them (Ezek. 34:11-31); and in our present generation that promise has begun to be fulfilled with the reestablishment of the state of Israel. The same prophet wrote of a hostile power from the north that would attack Israel (Ezek. 38); and Russia's great military might, geography, atheism, and anti-Semitism make that nation a prime prospect for being that hostile power.

Scripture also declares that the end times will be characterized by great concern for world unity, world government, world economics, and world religion (see Dan. 2; 7; Rev. 13; 17-18). The world is looking for stability and security and is ripe for the unifying role of a world leader who can stop wars and bring an end to political, economic, and social chaos—the role that one day will be filled by the antichrist.

All of those signs that mark the end times are characteristic of our day. There can be no doubt that we live near the end of the age, and the concern of believers should be for what the Bible says rather than for what men say and for what God is doing rather than for what men are doing.

THEY REGRESS DEEPER INTO SIN

A third characteristic of the spiritually blind who will never see is that they continue to regress deeper and deeper into darkness. They become more and more hardened and blinded, and the very things they suppose make them more pleasing to God drive them further from Him.

Jesus knew the true motive of the Pharisees and Sadducees was to entrap Him, not to be convinced of His messiahship. He also knew that another sign, no matter how astonishing, would not convince them about that which they were determined to reject. It was for this reason He spoke to them in parables, as indicated in Matthew 13:13-15. He would not capitulate to their hypocritical and wicked demand. **"An evil and adulterous generation seeks after a sign,"** He told them; **"and a sign will not be given it, except the sign of Jonah."**

The sign of Jonah was the final sign Jesus gave to the world, the sign of His victory over sin, death, and Satan through His resurrection. As He had declared to a group of scribes and Pharisees on an earlier occasion, "Just as Jonah was three days and three nights in the belly of the sea monster, so shall the Son of Man be three days and three nights in the heart of the earth. The men of Nineveh shall stand up with this generation at the judgment, and shall condemn it because they repented at the preaching of Jonah; and behold, something greater than Jonah is here" (Matt. 12:39-41; for further explanation, see the author's commentary volume *Matthew 8-15*).

That **sign,** too, would be rejected by the Jewish religious leaders. When they heard of Jesus' resurrection, they bribed the soldiers who guarded His tomb to say that His body was stolen by His disciples (Matt. 28:11-15).

THEY ARE ABANDONED BY GOD

The fourth characteristic of those who persist in their love of darkness and rejection of the light is that they are finally abandoned by God, given over by Him to their lusts, impurities, degrading passions, and depraved minds (Rom. 1:24, 26, 28). That which is willful, sinful, and satanic blindness becomes God's sovereign blindness.

Because the unbelieving Pharisees and Sadducees would not have Him as Lord and Savior, Jesus **left them and went away.** *Kataleipō* (**left**) means to leave behind, and it often carried the idea of forsaking or abandoning (see 2 Pet. 2:15).

That event marked an important transition in Jesus' ministry. Henceforth the Lord spent most of His time with His disciples and little time with the crowds or religious leaders. He turned **away** from those who rejected Him and focused His attention on His own. He gave no more arguments or signs for unbelievers, only additional truth for those who believed.

The Blind Who Are Made to See
(16:5-12)

And the disciples came to the other side and had forgotten to take bread. And Jesus said to them, "Watch out and beware of the leaven of the Pharisees and Sadducees." And they began to discuss among themselves, saying, "It is because we took no bread." But Jesus, aware of this, said, "You men of little faith, why do you discuss among yourselves that you have no bread? Do you not yet understand or remember the five loaves of the five thousand, and how many baskets you took up? Or the seven loaves of the four thousand, and how many large baskets you took up? How is it that you do not understand that I did not speak to you concerning bread? But beware of the leaven of the Pharisees and Sadducees." Then they understood that He did not say to beware of the leaven of bread, but of the teaching of the Pharisees and Sadducees. (16:5-12)

When he was a college student, Thomas Steward accidentally jabbed himself in the eye with a knife, causing permanent blindness in that eye. Fearing that the good eye might be harmed, the doctor recommended removal of the damaged eye. As Thomas was recovering from the anesthetic, however, it was discovered that the surgeon had removed the wrong eye, thereby plunging the young man into total blindness.

Undaunted by the tragedy, Thomas determined to continue his law study at McGill University in Montreal, Canada. He completed the course at the top of his class, and his brother William was second. For four years William not only had pursued his own studies in law but had acted as his brother's eyes, accompanying him to classes, reading the assigned material to him, and writing his tests and papers. Understandably, Thomas's gratitude to his brother was unbounded, because without that help, his own degree and career in law would have been impossible.

Far worse than physical blindness is the reality that every person has been afflicted with spiritual blindness because of sin, and without the help of God through the work of His Son, Jesus Christ, spiritual life and sight remain forever impossible.

The famous seventeenth-century English philosopher Thomas Hobbes was totally godless and anti-Christian. When he was about to die it is said that he loudly declared, "I am about to take a leap into the dark." The truth was that he had been deep in darkness all his life.

The French philosopher Voltaire openly mocked God and was especially antagonistic against Christianity. When he felt he was near death, he was overcome with grief and despair. But instead of asking his believing friends to lead him to Christ, he gathered them together and told them bitterly, "Begone! Begone! It is you that have brought me to my present condition. Leave me, I say. Begone! What a wretched glory is this which you have produced for me." Having something of a change of mind, he later hoped to allay his anguish by making a written recantation of his unbelief. For two months he alternated between railing against God and calling on the name of Christ. But his heart was too long hardened and had become impervious to God's love and light. Among his last words were, "I die abandoned by God and man."

It is no wonder that Jesus frequently referred to hell as "outer darkness" (Matt. 8:12; 22:13; 25:30), because it is the eternal perpetuation of the spiritual darkness that unbelieving man refuses to forsake while he is on earth. Matthew 16:1-4 pictures spiritually blind persons who will never see, epitomized by the unbelieving Pharisees and Sadducees who refused to receive the light and life that Jesus offered.

In contrast, verses 5-12 give a picture of the spiritually blind who, by God's sovereign grace, are made to see. The four characteristics of these persons are the reverse sides of the characteristics of the blind who will never see: they seek the light, curse the darkness, receive still greater light, and are taught by the Lord.

THEY SEEK THE LIGHT

The disciples stood at a crossroads as they decided whether or not to hold on to the system in which they were reared and identify themselves with the Pharisees and Sadducees, whom they had been trained to respect and honor. The Pharisees were the recognized interpreters of the Jewish law and traditions, and the Sadducees were the religious aristocracy, which customarily included the high priest and the chief priests.

But the Twelve did not hesitate in following Jesus, and when He crossed back to the eastern, Gentile side of the Sea of Galilee, they **came to the other side** with Him. They genuinely sought God's light, and they knew Jesus was Himself that light. Through Jeremiah, the Lord had promised, "You will seek Me and find Me, when you search for Me with all your heart. And I will be found by you" (Jer. 29:13-14). The disciples had seeking hearts, and God honored His promise to lead them to Himself.

As He stood teaching in the Temple one day, Jesus declared to the disciples along with the unbelieving scribes and Pharisees, "I am the light of the world; he who follows Me shall not walk in the darkness, but shall have the light of life" (John 8:12). The disciples believed that truth, and they knew that, as God's light, He not only was to be seen but followed. They knew the Messiah would come "as a light to the nations" (Isa. 42:6) and, as David had proclaimed, would indeed *be* their "light and [their] salvation" (Ps. 27:1). Jesus was the light that illumined their darkness, and, though often stumbling and misunderstanding, they genuinely sought to follow Him.

But not everyone who became interested in Jesus was faithful to follow Him. When they began to realize the true nature of His message and the cost of discipleship, many superficial disciples "withdrew, and were not walking with Him anymore" (John 6:66).

But the true believers knew they would never be able to have spiritual sight apart from the gracious work of God on their behalf through Jesus Christ. Some of them perhaps prayed with the psalmist, "Open my eyes, that I may behold wonderful things from Thy law. . . . Teach me, O Lord, the way of Thy statutes, . . . Incline my heart to Thy testimonies, . . . Thy hands made me and fashioned me; give me understanding, that I may learn Thy commandments" (Ps. 119:18, 33, 36, 73).

THEY CURSE THE DARKNESS

Because they sought God's light, the true disciples also, in effect, cursed Satan's darkness. They had hungry hearts for God's light and truth and were eager learners. They turned their backs on the willfully blind and corrupt Pharisees and Sadducees, who led their followers into deeper and deeper darkness and made them even more wicked than themselves (see Matt. 23:15). When Jesus asked "the twelve, 'You do not want to go away also, do you?' Simon Peter answered Him, 'Lord, to whom shall we go? You have words of eternal life. And we have believed and have come to know that You are the Holy One of God'" (John 6:67-69).

They were as naturally blind as the Pharisees and Sadducees, but unlike those unbelieving religious leaders, the Twelve recognized their blindness and came to Jesus for help.

THEY RECEIVE STILL GREATER LIGHT

As soon as the disciples arrived at **the other side** with Jesus, they realized they **had forgotten to take bread** with them. They had left hurriedly after the confrontation with the Pharisees and Sadducees (vv. 1-4), and on the sparsely populated northeastern **side** of the Sea of Galilee they were possibly many miles from a place where they could buy food. Mark reports that they "did not have more than one loaf in the boat with them" (Mark 8:14), far from enough to feed thirteen men even one meal.

Despite Jesus' divine teaching, His perfect example, and His great miracles, the disciples still thought and functioned primarily on the physical level. When they became hungry after rowing to the other side of the lake, their thoughts did not turn to Jesus' provision but to their own lack. As He frequently did, the Lord took their extremity as a divine opportunity to teach His truth.

That is an apt example of how Christians should disciple other Christians, walking alongside them and helping them interpret life's struggles, perplexities, problems, and opportunities in light of spiritual truth and resources. Christian maturity is learning to live day by day by the light of God's Word and in His provision.

Knowing the disciples' concern over their lack of food, **Jesus said to them, "Watch out and beware of the leaven of the Pharisees and Sadducees."** The imperative **watch out** is from *horaō*, which has the basic meaning of seeing clearly or taking notice of. "Open your eyes," Jesus was saying, "and pay close attention to **the leaven of the Pharisees and Sadducees.** Don't be concerned about bread but about what is truly important. In the present situation, what is important is the spiritual danger of **the Pharisees and Sadducees."**

Christ was only months from the cross, and He had much more to teach the disciples and they had much more to learn. One day without food was of no consequence. But like believers in all ages, the disciples were caught up in the physical and temporal. Their spiritual vision was limited, and their spiritual attention span was short.

Because the disciples' thoughts were on physical food they missed the spiritual warning, so that when Jesus mentioned leaven **they began to discuss among themselves, saying, "It is because we took no bread."** Perhaps they thought Jesus was concerned that they might buy some **bread** to eat that was baked by a Pharisee or sold by a Sadducee and that it would therefore somehow be defiled. But such things were of no consequence to Jesus, as the Twelve should have known from what He repeatedly said and did. Only a short while before, He had made plain that it is "not what enters into the mouth [that] defiles the man" (Matt. 15:11). Jesus was not the least concerned about whether the earthly bread they ate came from a Pharisee or a Sadducee, a Jew or a Gentile. Such matters have absolutely no bearing on spirituality and godliness and were not in His mind when He spoke that warning.

The disciples were confused about what Jesus meant because their earthly orientation was a great barrier to spiritual vision. Their response revealed again how much they needed divine help in understanding, prompting the Lord to say to them what He had said numerous times before: **"You men of little faith"** (cf. Matt. 6:30; 8:26; 14:31). They did not fail to understand because of limited information or limited intellectual ability but because of limited **faith.**

"**Why do you discuss among yourselves that you have no bread?**" "You should know that I am not speaking about the fact that we **have no bread**," He said in effect. "**Do you not yet understand or remember the five loaves of the five thousand, and how many baskets you took up? Or the seven loaves of the four thousand, and how many large baskets you took up? How is it that you do not understand that I did not speak to you concerning bread?**" "If I were concerned about our having bread, I would simply create some Myself," He implied, "just as I did when I fed **the five thousand** in Jewish territory, where twelve baskets were left over (see John 6:1-14), and **the four thousand** in Gentile territory, where seven baskets remained (see Matt. 15:32-39). Have you forgotten those occasions so soon?"

When believers live on the level of spiritual trust and obedience, God makes provision for their physical needs. In the Sermon on the Mount Jesus cautioned, "Do not be anxious then, saying, 'What shall we eat?' or 'What shall we drink?' or 'With what shall we clothe ourselves?' For all these things the Gentiles eagerly seek; for your heavenly Father knows that you need all these things. But seek first His kingdom and His righteousness; and all these things shall be added to you" (Matt. 6:31-33). "He who supplies seed to the sower and bread for food," Paul assured the Corinthians, "will supply and multiply your seed for sowing and increase the harvest of your righteousness" (2 Cor. 9:10).

The Twelve needed to heed the counsel Paul would one day give the church at Philippi: "Finally, brethren, whatever is true, whatever is honorable, whatever is right, whatever is pure, whatever is lovely, whatever is of good repute, if there is any excellence and if anything worthy of praise, let your mind dwell on these things" (Phil. 4:8; cf. Col. 3:2). The Christian needs constant exposure to the Word of God and constant illumination by the Spirit of God. Only God's Word and Spirit can raise him above the cares, concerns, perplexities, and confusion that are the inevitable heritage of life that is viewed and lived purely in the human dimension.

Jesus was grieved that the Twelve, after so much clear teaching and so many miraculous manifestations, were still living by human rather than by divine sight. But He was patient with them, as He always is with His own, and He knew they could not comprehend without divine illumination.

He then repeated the warning (cf. v. 8): "**Beware of the leaven of the Pharisees and Sadducees.**" **Leaven** made bread rise before baking and was used in much the same way yeast is used today. But the only method ancient peoples had for reproducing yeast was to save a small piece of unbaked dough, which was later used to start fermentation in the next batch of bread.

Because a small piece of leaven was able to cause a relatively large amount of dough to rise, the term was often used figuratively to represent any sort of influence—usually, but not inherently, a harmful influence, as seen in its use in Matthew 13:33. When the Israelites were led out of bondage in Egypt, the Lord did not allow them to take any leavened bread with them, symbolically representing His intention that the people take no influence of pagan Egypt with them into the Promised Land. Israel was to start life afresh, with no contaminating influence from the wicked, ungodly land of her oppression.

It was the spiritually contaminating influence of the **Pharisees and Sadducees** that Jesus here uses **leaven** to represent. **"Beware of** their influence," the Lord was saying. "Their way of thinking and living has no part in My kingdom or its righteousness."

On another occasion Jesus explained that **the leaven of the Pharisees** was hypocrisy (Luke 12:1). Their particular form of ungodliness was characterized by religious phoniness, external purity without internal righteousness. The legalism, formalism, and ritualism they cherished so dearly were a cover for spiritual uncleanness and deadness. "Woe to you, scribes and Pharisees, hypocrites!" Jesus told them. "For you are like whitewashed tombs which on the outside appear beautiful, but inside they are full of dead men's bones and all uncleanness" (Matt. 23:27). And their hypocrisy adversely permeated the whole religious scene in Israel.

The **leaven of the . . . Sadducees,** on the other hand, was religious liberalism. To them, religion was primarily a means to earthly, temporal ends. They did not believe in angels, miracles, the resurrection, an afterlife, or anything else supernatural (see Acts 23:8). They were thoroughly materialistic and rationalistic, and they, too, had an adverse permeating influence with many.

Both types of **leaven** are enemies of the gospel. They corrupt God's truth and God's people. "Don't let either the legalism of the Pharisees or the liberalism of the Sadducees influence you," Jesus was saying. False doctrine is always a danger, no matter what its form, and it should be shunned and rejected by the believer wherever and however it is encountered.

The Galatian church was threatened by the legalistic perversions of the Judaizers, who insisted that observance of circumcision and the Mosaic law be added to the finished work of Christ. To them Paul declared, "This is the only thing I want to find out from you: did you receive the Spirit by the works of the Law, or by hearing with faith? Are you so foolish? Having begun by the Spirit, are you now being perfected by the flesh?" (Gal. 3:2-3). The Colossian church, on the other hand, was threatened by religious rationalism and liberalism. To those believers Paul wrote, "See to it that no one takes you captive through philosophy and empty deception, according to the tradition of men, according to the elementary principles of the world, rather than according to Christ" (Col. 2:8).

False doctrine is never to be trifled with or minimized. Jude warns that when a believer seeks to help deliver someone from a false system he should go about it as if he were snatching a brand from the fire (Jude 23). To get too close to a cult or pagan religion is to risk being burned.

THEY ARE TAUGHT BY THE LORD

Because the Twelve received His light, God gave them still greater light. Jesus explained that He was not talking about physical bread but was warning them to **beware of the leaven of the Pharisees and Sadducees.** By the Lord's sovereign and gracious illumination, **then they understood that He did not say to beware**

of the leaven of bread, but of the teaching of the Pharisees and Sadducees.

Jesus' continual desire during His earthly ministry was to teach those who trusted in Him, the apostles in particular. Even after He rose from the grave He continued to teach during the forty days before His ascension (Acts 1:3). He had already provided for the continuation of His teaching after the ascension: "The Helper, the Holy Spirit, whom the Father will send in My name, He will teach you all things, and bring to your remembrance all that I said to you" (John 14:26). A short while later He told His disciples, "I have many more things to say to you, but you cannot bear them now. But when He, the Spirit of truth, comes, He will guide you into all the truth; for He will not speak on His own initiative, but whatever He hears, He will speak; and He will disclose to you what is to come. He shall glorify Me; for He shall take of Mine, and shall disclose it to you. All things that the Father has are Mine; therefore I said, that He takes of Mine, and will disclose it to you" (John 16:12-15).

Not only is the believer given God's own Word to study and believe but is given His indwelling Spirit to illumine and interpret the Word. A vital part of the Holy Spirit's present ministry is to elucidate God's Word and apply it to the hearts and lives of those who belong to Christ. John assured his Christian readers, "You have an anointing from the Holy One, and you all know. . . . And as for you, the anointing which you received from Him abides in you, and you have no need for anyone to teach you; but as His anointing teaches you about all things, and is true and is not a lie, and just as it has taught you, you abide in Him" (1 John 2:20, 27).

Paul declared to the Corinthian believers, "My message and my preaching were not in persuasive words of wisdom, but in demonstration of the Spirit and of power, that your faith should not rest on the wisdom of men, but on the power of God" (1 Cor. 2:4-5). Writing as God's apostle, Paul's word was God's Word, not human wisdom but divine. "For our gospel did not come to you in word only," he explained to the Thessalonians, "but also in power and in the Holy Spirit and with full conviction" (1 Thess. 1:5).

When on a previous occasion the disciples had asked Jesus, "'Why do You speak to them [the multitudes] in parables?' . . . He answered and said to them, 'To you it has been granted to know the mysteries of the kingdom of heaven, but to them it has not been granted'" (Matt. 13:10-11). The majority of the people who heard Jesus teach and preach had no desire for the things of God, and therefore what He said made no sense to them. "While seeing they do not see," Jesus explained; "and while hearing they do not hear, nor do they understand. . . . For the heart of this people has become dull, and with their ears they scarcely hear, and they have closed their eyes lest they should see with their eyes, and hear with their ears, and understand with their heart and return, and I should heal them" (vv. 13, 15). But to the Twelve Jesus then said, "Blessed are your eyes, because they see; and your ears, because they hear" (v. 16). The difference was not in the innate ability of the disciples but in their willingness to be taught by God. They, too, were spiritually blind, but through their faith the Lord enabled them to see.

"Things which eye has not seen and ear has not heard, and which have not entered the heart of man, all that God has prepared for those who love Him," Paul wrote, quoting Isaiah. "For to us God revealed them through the Spirit; for the Spirit searches all things, even the depths of God. . . . Now we have received, not the spirit of the world, but the Spirit who is from God, that we might know the things freely given to us by God" (1 Cor. 2:9-10, 12; cf. Isa. 64:4; 65:17).

As the believer studies God's Word and allows God's Spirit to interpret and apply it, he is divinely enabled to understand even the deep things of God. Though utterly blind in his natural mind and spirit, by God's gracious provision he is given knowledge and understanding of the most important truths in the universe. As with the two disciples to whom Jesus appeared on the Emmaus road, a Christian's heart should burn with wonder and glory as the Lord makes His truth come alive (see Luke 24:32).

The story is told of a blind French girl who was given a copy of the gospel of Mark in braille. As she read and reread the book, she came to have faith in Christ, and the book became more precious with each reading. She read it so much that she developed callouses on her fingers that eventually prevented her from feeling the raised dots. She was so determined to read God's Word that she peeled the skin off the tips of her fingers to make them more sensitive, but in doing so she permanently damaged the nerves. Devastated, she picked up the book to kiss it farewell, only to discover that her lips were even more sensitive than her fingers.

God will always find a way to feed the heart that hungers for His truth.

The famous American revolutionary hero Ethan Allen was an avowed atheist and wrote a book denying the deity of Christ. When his devout Christian wife died, the daughter was torn between the ways of her parents. Some years after her mother died, the daughter was also struck with a terminal illness. As she lay dying, she said to her father, "You will bury me by the side of Mother, for that was her dying request. But Father, you and Mother have never agreed on religion. Mother often spoke to me of the blessed Savior who died for us all, and she used to pray for both you and me that the Savior might be our Friend and that we might all see Him when He sits enthroned in His glory." Looking desperately into her father's eyes, she pleaded, "I don't feel I can go into death alone. Tell me whom I shall follow, you or Mother? Shall I reject Christ as you've taught me, or shall I accept Him, as Mother wanted me to do?" Deeply moved and heartbroken, her father replied, "My child, cling to your Mother's Savior. She was right. And I, too, shall try to follow you to that blessed place."

Only through Christ are the blind made to see.

The Supreme
Confession
(16:13-17)

3

Now when Jesus came into the district of Caesarea Philippi, He began asking His disciples, saying, "Who do people say that the Son of Man is?" And they said, "Some say John the Baptist; and others, Elijah; but still others, Jeremiah, or one of the prophets." He said to them, "But who do you say that I am?" And Simon Peter answered and said, "Thou art the Christ, the Son of the living God." And Jesus answered and said to him, "Blessed are you, Simon Barjona, because flesh and blood did not reveal this to you, but My Father who is in heaven." (16:13-17)

This passage represents the climax of Jesus' teaching ministry. It was, in effect, the apostles' final examination, consisting of but one question, the ultimate question that every human being must face: Who is Jesus Christ? A person's answer is of the most monumental importance, because on it hinges his eternal destiny. It is a question that no one can escape or avoid. Every soul, as it were, will be pinned against the wall of eternity and forced to answer that question.

For some two and a half years Jesus had been moving to this moment—teaching and reteaching, affirming and reaffirming, demonstrating and redemonstrating, building and rebuilding the truth of who He was in order to establish it completely and securely in the minds and hearts of the Twelve.

During the previous several months the Lord had largely shunned the crowds and the Jewish leaders. His few encounters with them were brief and terse. The misguided multitudes wanted to make Him their political deliverer from the military bondage of Rome and the capricious ambitions of Herod. The scribes, Pharisees, and Sadducees were, for the most part, thoroughly convinced He was a threat to their religious system and were determined to be rid of Him, if necessary by taking His life.

As He spent more and more time alone with the Twelve, Jesus went more often into Gentile territory and stayed longer. He withdrew to the fringes of Palestine in order to be free of the misguided and fickle adulation of the multitudes and the growing hostility of the Jewish religious leaders.

THE SETTING

Now when Jesus came into the district of Caesarea Philippi, (16:13*a*)

The city of **Caesarea Philippi** was originally named Paneas (or Panias), after the Greek god Pan, who, according to pagan mythology, was born in a nearby cave. Caesar Augustus had given the region to Herod the Great, who built a temple in Paneas in honor of the emperor. Herod's son, Philip the tetrarch, inherited the land, greatly enlarged the city, and renamed it after Caesar. He added the name **Philippi** both to gain honor for himself and to distinguish this **Caesarea** from the one on the Mediterranean coast west of Jerusalem.

Caesarea Philippi was located some 25 miles northeast of the Sea of Galilee and 40 miles southwest of Damascus, on a beautiful plateau near the headwaters of the Jordan River. A few miles to the north, snow-covered Mount Hermon rose to a height of more than 9,000 feet above sea level. On clear days the majestic mountain can easily be seen from northern Galilee towns such as Capernaum, Cana, and Nazareth.

Caesarea Philippi was but a few miles from the ancient Jewish city of Dan, which for centuries had been considered the northernmost boundary of the Promised Land, the southernmost being Beersheba (see Judg. 20:1; 1 Chron. 21:2). On the north it was the last outpost of Israel and had always been especially susceptible to pagan influence.

The location offered Jesus and the disciples welcome relief from the hot Galilean lowlands and from the pressure of the Jewish leaders and the threat from Herod Antipas.

From Luke 9:18 we learn that Jesus posed His all-important question to the disciples just after He had spent time praying alone, and from Mark 8:27 that the group had not yet arrived in the city of **Caesarea Philippi** proper but were passing through some of the villages on the outskirts. At this crossroads of heathenism and Judaism Jesus left a time of intimate fellowship with His heavenly Father and confronted His disciples with the question that every person and every religion must one day answer.

THE EXAMINATION

He began asking His disciples, saying, "Who do people say that the Son of Man is?" And they said, "Some say John the Baptist; and others, Elijah; but still others, Jeremiah, or one of the prophets." He said to them, "But who do you say that I am?" (16:13b-15)

Son of Man was Jesus' most common designation of Himself and is used of Him some eighty times in the New Testament. It was clearly recognized by Jews as a title of the Messiah (see Dan. 7:13); but because it emphasized His humanness, many Jews preferred not to use it. No doubt it was for that reason that Jesus *did* prefer it—to focus on the humiliation and submission of His first coming and His work of sacrificial, substitutionary atonement.

Jesus' priority ministry in the world was to reveal Himself, to teach and to demonstrate who He was. **He** therefore **began** the examination by **asking His disciples, . . . "Who do people say that the Son of Man is?"** The **people** to whom the Lord referred were the Jews, God's chosen people, to whom the Messiah was sent first (Rom. 1:16; cf. John 4:22).

It was not that Jesus was unaware of what the **people** were saying about Him but that He wanted the Twelve to think carefully about those popular perceptions. He was not concerned about the opinions of the unbelieving and hypocritical scribes and Pharisees, some of whom had even accused Him of being in league with Satan (Matt. 10:25; 12:24). He was rather **asking** about the thoughts of those who looked on Him positively, although uncertainly, and who recognized Him to be more than an ordinary religious leader. After hearing His teaching and witnessing His miracles, what was their final verdict about Jesus, **the Son of Man?**

"Some say John the Baptist," the Twelve replied. Perhaps following the frightened assessment of Herod the tetrarch (Matt. 14:1-2), some of the Jews believed Jesus was a reincarnated **John the Baptist,** come back from the grave to continue his ministry of announcing the Messiah. Like Herod, those people recognized that Jesus' miraculous power was unexplainable on a human basis.

Others believed Jesus was a reincarnated **Elijah,** considered by most Jews to be the supreme Old Testament prophet, whom the Lord was to send again "before the coming of the great and terrible day of the Lord" (Mal. 4:5). In modern Jewish Passover celebrations an empty chair is reserved at the table for **Elijah,** in the hope of his one day coming to announce the Messiah's arrival.

Still others said Jesus was **Jeremiah,** another of the most revered prophets. In the apocryphal book of 2 Maccabees (2:4-8), Jeremiah is said to have taken the Ark of the Covenant and the altar of incense out of the Temple and hidden them on Mount Nebo in order to preserve them from desecration and destruction by the Babylonians. Some Jews thought that before the Messiah returned to establish His kingdom, Jeremiah would return to earth and restore the Ark and the altar to their proper places in the Temple. The same apocryphal book pictures a white-bearded Jeremiah handing a golden sword to the great Jewish hero Judas Maccabaeus to use in overthrowing the Greeks (15:12-16).

Some of the people perhaps saw in Jesus something of the character and message of John the Baptist. Some saw in Him the fire and intensity of Elijah; and still others saw in Him the lament and grief of Jeremiah. In all three of those identities, however, Jesus was thought to be only the Messiah's forerunner, who had come back to life with God-given miraculous powers.

The rest of the people who recognized Jesus' uniqueness did not speculate about His particular identity but simply considered Him to be **one of the prophets** who was "risen again" (see Luke 9:19).

In each instance the people considered Jesus to be a forerunner of the Messiah but not the Messiah Himself. They could not deny His supernatural power, but they would not accept Him as Messiah and Savior. They came as close to God's ultimate truth as they could without fully recognizing and accepting it.

Since Jesus' day, much of the world has similarly wanted to speak highly of Him without recognizing His deity and lordship. Pilate said, "I find no guilt in this man" (Luke 23:4). Napoleon said, "I know men, and Jesus was no mere man." Diderot referred to Jesus as "the unsurpassed," Strauss, the German rationalist, as "the highest model of religion," John Stuart Mill as "the guide of humanity," the French atheist Renan as "the greatest among the sons of men," Theodore Parker as "a youth with God in His heart," and Robert Owens as "the irreproachable one." Some in our own day have called Him the ultimate Superstar. But all those titles and descriptions fall short of identifying Jesus as He fully is—the Messiah, God in human flesh.

After the disciples reported what the multitudes were saying about Him, Jesus then asked, **"But who do you say that I am?"** The Twelve knew that most of the people's views of Jesus were inadequate. Now they had to answer for themselves.

THE CONFESSION

And Simon Peter answered and said, "Thou art the Christ, the Son of the living God." (16:16)

As usual (see, e.g., Matt. 15:15; 19:27; John 6:68), **Simon Peter** was the spokesman, "the director of the apostolic choir," as Chrysostom called him. Also as usual, his comments were brief, emphatic, and decisive: **"Thou art the Christ, the Son of the living God." Christ** is the Greek equivalent of the Hebrew *Messiah*, God's predicted and long-awaited deliverer of Israel, the supreme "Anointed One," the coming High Priest, King, Prophet, and Savior. Without hesitation **Peter** declared Jesus to be the Messiah, whereas the multitudes of Jews believed Him to be only the Messiah's precursor.

On first meeting Jesus, Andrew had excitedly proclaimed Him to be the Messiah, and Nathaniel had called Him "the Son of God . . . the King of Israel" (John 1:41, 49). The disciples knew that John the Baptist had borne witness that

Jesus "is the Son of God" (John 1:34), and the longer they stayed with Him, the more evidence they had of His divine nature, power, and authority.

Like their fellow Jews, however, they had been taught to expect a conquering and reigning Messiah who would deliver God's people from their enemies and establish forever His righteous kingdom on earth. And when Jesus refused to use His miraculous power for His own benefit or to oppose the Roman oppressors, the disciples wondered if they were right about Jesus' identity. His humility, meekness, and subservience were in total contrast to their preconceived views of the Messiah. That the Messiah would be ridiculed with impunity, not to mention persecuted and executed, was inconceivable. When Jesus spoke of His going away and coming back, Thomas doubtlessly echoed the consternation of all the disciples when he said, "Lord, we do not know where You are going, how do we know the way?" (John 14:5).

It was similar bewilderment that caused John the Baptist to question his earlier affirmation of Jesus' messiahship. "When John in prison heard of the works of Christ, he sent word by his disciples, and said to Him, 'Are you the Expected One, or shall we look for someone else?'" (Matt. 11:1-3). Jesus' miracles were clear evidence of His messiahship, but His failure to use those powers to overthrow Rome and establish His earthly kingdom brought Jesus' identity into question even with the godly, Spirit-filled John.

Like John the Baptist, the Twelve fluctuated between moments of great faith and of grave doubt. They could proclaim with deep conviction, "Lord, to whom shall we go? You have words of eternal life. And we have believed and have come to know that You are the Holy One of God" (John 6:68-69). They could also display remarkable lack of faith and discernment, even after witnessing hundreds of healings and dramatic demonstrations of supernatural power (see Matt. 8:26; 14:31; 16:8). They were sometimes strong in faith and sometimes weak. Jesus frequently spoke of their "little faith."

Now, at last, the truth of Jesus' divinity and messiahship was established in their minds beyond question. They would still experience times of weakness and confusion about what Jesus said and did, but they would no longer doubt who it was who said and did them. He was indeed **the Christ, the Son of the living God**. God's own Spirit had now imbedded the truth indelibly in their hearts.

It took two and a half years for them to come to this place of confession, through the struggles and hatred of the Jewish religious leaders, the mounting fickleness and rejection of the people, and their own confusion about what the Messiah had come to do. But without question they now knew He was the fulfiller of their hopes, the source of their salvation, the desire of the nations.

On behalf of all the apostles, Peter not only confessed Jesus as the Messiah, **the Christ**, but as **the Son of the living God**. The Son of Man (v. 13) was also **the Son of . . . God**, the Creator of the universe and all that is in it. He was the true and real **God**, not a mythological figment such as Pan or a mortal "deity" such as caesar—both of whom had shrines in Caesarea Philippi. The disciples' Lord was **Son of the living God**.

As evidenced by numerous things the Twelve later said and did, they did not at this time have a full comprehension of the Trinity or even of the full nature and work of **Christ**. But they knew Jesus was truly **the Christ** and that He was truly divine, **the Son of the living God**. **Son** reflects the idea of oneness in essence, because a son is one in nature with his father. So Jesus Christ was one in nature with God the Father (cf. John 5:17-18; 10:30-33).

THE RESULT

And Jesus answered and said to him, "Blessed are you, Simon Barjona, (16:17a)

Those who truly confess that Jesus is God, which is to confess Him as Lord and Savior (1 John 4:14-15), are divinely and eternally **blessed**. They are "blessed . . . with every spiritual blessing in the heavenly places in Christ," chosen "in Him before the foundation of the world . . . [to] be holy and blameless before Him," and "in love [are] predestined . . . to adoption as sons through Jesus Christ to Himself" (Eph. 1:3-5). God pours out all His supernatural resources on those who come to Him through faith in His Son, because through Him they become God's own children.

Emphasizing Peter's human inadequacy, Jesus called him by his original family name, **Simon Barjona**, the second part of the name being an Aramaic term that meant son of Jonah (or John).

THE SOURCE

because flesh and blood did not reveal this to you, but My Father who is in heaven." (16:17b)

The disciples were not finally convinced of Jesus' messiahship and divinity because of His teaching or His miracles, amazing as those were. Those things alone were not sufficient to convince the Twelve, just as they were not sufficient to convince the thousands of other people who heard the same truth and witnessed the same miracles but failed to accept and follow the one who taught and performed them. Man's human capabilities, here represented by the metonym **flesh and blood**, cannot bring understanding of the things of God (cf. 1 Cor. 2:14). The **Father** Himself must **reveal** them and bring understanding of His Son to human minds.

From the gospel accounts it seems clear that the **Father** disclosed the Son primarily through the Son Himself. There is no record or intimation that any divine revelation was given to the Twelve during Jesus' earthly ministry other than that given through Jesus Himself. As the light of Jesus' teaching and the significance of His miraculous power began to dawn on them, the Spirit opened their minds to see

Him as the Messiah, the Son of the living God.

Jesus had made many astounding claims about Himself. He declared that He Himself had come to fulfill the law and the prophets (Matt. 5:17) and that in the last days many people will address Him as Lord (7:22). He said, "I am the living bread that came down out of heaven; if anyone eats of this bread, he shall live forever" (John 6:51), and, "I am the door; if anyone enters through Me, he shall be saved" (10:9; cf. 14:6).

Jesus had also performed astounding miracles. He had turned ordinary water into the highest quality wine (John 2:6-11), healed multiplied thousands of every sort of disease (see, e.g., Matt. 4:24; 8:16; 9:35), and even quieted a raging storm with a word (Matt. 8:26).

Perhaps the greatest testimony to Jesus' messiahship, however, was His claim to be Lord of the Sabbath (Matt. 12:8), a claim that for a Jew of His day could only have been interpreted as presumption of deity. The Sabbath, which has the basic meaning of rest or cessation, was the center of Jewish life. Not only their week but their entire calendar of feasts and holy days was built on the concept of sabbath. The seventh day of the week (Ex. 20:11) and every other sabbath observance was a time of rest and worship. The book of Leviticus mentions nine sabbath-based festivals, which included the weekly Sabbath (Lev. 23:3); the Passover (vv. 4-8); the feast of first fruits (vv. 9-14); Pentecost (vv. 15-22); the feast of trumpets (vv. 23-25); the Day of Atonement, Yom Kippur (vv. 26-32); the feast of tabernacles (vv. 33-44); the sabbatical year (25:2-7); and the year of jubilee (vv. 8-55), when, every fiftieth year, all slaves were freed and all land restored to its original owners.

All of those sabbath observances were pictures of the final and eternal rest of the children of God, the time when Messiah would come to earth to set His people free and establish His divine kingdom. Every time a Jew celebrated a sabbath he was reminded that some day he and all his fellow Jews would be released from all bondage—whether the bondage of political oppression, the bondage of continual sacrifices, or the bondage of labor to make a living. The entire sabbath system pointed to the true, perfect, and eternal rest that Messiah would bring to His people.

For Jesus to claim that He fulfilled the prophecy of Isaiah 61:1-2, as He did in the synagogue in Nazareth (Luke 4:18-21), was unmistakably to claim messiahship. For Him to present Himself as the source of rest (Matt. 11:28) was to present Himself as the source of holiness, and to claim lordship over the Sabbath (Matt. 12:8) was to claim lordship over everything.

Because Jesus is Himself God's perfect sabbath rest and the source of true holiness, believers have no more reason to observe the seventh day of the week or any other special day. "For we who have believed enter that rest, just as He has said. . . . There remains therefore a Sabbath rest for the people of God. For the one who has entered His rest has himself also rested from his works, as God did from His" (Heb. 4:3, 9-10). "Therefore let no one act as your judge in regard to food or drink or in respect to a festival or a new moon or a Sabbath day," Paul wrote. Such things "are a mere shadow of what is to come; but the substance belongs to Christ" (Col. 2:16-17).

The command to keep the Sabbath day is the only one of the Ten Commandments that the New Testament does not require of Christians. By His grace, Jesus Christ gives every believer in Him a jubilee liberation that is perfect, final, and eternal. A Christian therefore does not violate the Sabbath when he works on the Lord's Day but when he persists in self-righteous works in the presumptuous hope of adding to what the Savior has already accomplished.

"All things have been handed over to Me by My Father," Jesus had explained on an earlier occasion; "and no one knows the Son, except the Father; nor does anyone know the Father, except the Son, and anyone to whom the Son wills to reveal Him" (Matt. 11:27).

As with the disciples, when people today confess Jesus Christ as Lord and Savior and fellowship with Him through His Word, the Spirit opens their minds and hearts to more and more of His truth and power. "Faith comes from hearing, and hearing by the word of Christ," Paul declared (Rom. 10:17). As we continue to gaze into His glory we are transformed into His image (see Rom. 8:29; 1 Cor. 15:49; Col. 3:10).

The Church That Christ Builds
(16:18-20)

4

"And I also say to you that you are Peter, and upon this rock I will build My church; and the gates of Hades shall not overpower it. I will give you the keys of the kingdom of heaven; and whatever you shall bind on earth shall be bound in heaven, and whatever you shall loose on earth shall be loosed in heaven." Then He warned the disciples that they should tell no one that He was the Christ. (16:18-20)

Throughout history, philosophers have speculated on the reason for man's existence, the purpose and meaning of human life. Many ancient Greeks believed that life is cyclical, continually repeating itself in endless circles, going nowhere with no purpose. To many modern thinkers, life is just as pointless and futile. In his inaugural address as president of Cambridge University, Dr. G. N. Clark said, "There is no secret and no plan in history to be discovered." The French novelist and critic André Maurois wrote, "The universe is indifferent. Who created it? Why are we here on this puny mud heap spinning in infinite space? I have not the slightest idea, and I am quite convinced that no one has." Jean-Paul Sartré, the famous existentialist philosopher, maintained that man exists in a watertight compartment as an utterly isolated individual in the midst of a purposeless universe.

The French molecular biologist Jacques Monod declared that man's existence is due to the chance collision between minuscule particles of nucleic acid and proteins in a vast "prebiotic soup." According to such cynical views, man is alone in the vast universe, out of which he accidentally emerged by chance. Francis Schaeffer observed that, according to such thinking, "man is the product of the impersonal plus time plus chance." Although many of its advocates would deny it, humanistic, evolutionary philosophy must inevitably conclude that there is no real difference between a man and a tree, and that therefore killing a man is no different than chopping down a tree.

In illustration of this point one needs merely to read the ideas of Peter Singer, present patriarch of the equal rights for animals movement, who believes that farmers who raise animals for food should be jailed. He writes: "We should reject the doctrine that places the lives of members of our own species [humans] above the lives of members of other species [animals]. Some members of other species are persons; some members of our own species are not. . . . Killing say a chimpanzee is worse than the killing of a gravely defective human who is not a person." Singer identifies nonpersons as the retarded and handicapped (*Practical Ethics* [Cambridge: Cambridge U., 1979], pp. 97, 73).

In light of such shallow, hopeless, and increasingly popular views of mankind, it is no wonder that many young people demand total license in their life-styles and willingly become entrapped in the seductive webs of drugs, sexual promiscuity, perversion, meaningless violence, and lawlessness. If men are only animals and there is no meaning or purpose to life beyond mere existing, then nothing is wrong and everything is permissible.

When men see no ultimate and eternal reason for their existence and no accountability to God, they see no reason for anything else, including law, morality, or religion. Their only motive for self-restraint is fear of criticism by their peers or of being caught and punished by civil authorities. Their ultimate standard is hedonism, the desire to get everything out of life you can, while you can and in whatever way you can.

The Bible, however, makes clear that there is divine and eternal value and meaning to human life and that God revealed His high purpose to men. Despite men's spiritual darkness caused by the Fall, "that which is known about God is evident within them; for God made it evident to them. For since the creation of the world His invisible attributes, His eternal power and divine nature, have been clearly seen, being understood through what has been made" (Rom. 1:19-20). In the same letter Paul declares that "from Him and through Him and to Him are all things. To Him be the glory forever" (11:36).

The universe was created by God, and man was made in God's image in order to glorify Himself. All things were made *by* Him and *for* Him, Paul declared (Col. 1:16). That is the reason for human existence. And if the ultimate purpose of mankind is to glorify God, it should not seem strange that God is collecting for Himself a redeemed assembly of people who will forever be the praise of His glory (see Eph. 1:6; 3:21). That is the theme of redemptive history. Because He is a worthy God and deserving of glory, the Lord has made men who are able to give Him glory and who will reflect eternally the majesty and splendor of His glorious being. From out of the rebels who now populate the world, God is calling a redeemed church that will forever be privileged to render Him glory (see Rev. 4:6-11; 5:9-14). To be a part of that is to fulfill man's reason for existence.

As both the Maker and Redeemer of mankind, Jesus Christ is the supreme and sovereign architect of history. All the other notables of history, whether righteous and godly or wicked and rebellious, are no more than players in the great drama that Christ has written and now directs. As someone has said, history is "His story."

The background of Jesus' teaching in the present passage, however, was not cynical Greek or Roman philosophy but the God-given Jewish religion that had been humanly perverted. Jesus was speaking to those who from their earliest years had been taught to anticipate the coming of the Lord's Anointed—the Messiah, the Christ. But their expectations, though partly scriptural, were distorted by the traditional interpretations of the rabbis and scribes over the previous several centuries. They knew the Messiah would bring righteousness and truth, but they also believed that He would militarily conquer and destroy their oppressors and usher in a kingdom of everlasting peace and prosperity for God's chosen people.

As the disciples walked with Jesus through the outskirts of Caesarea Philippi (see Matt. 16:13), they knew they were in a type of self-imposed exile. The Jewish leaders were becoming more and more adamant in their opposition to Jesus and the multitudes were becoming more and more skeptical and disillusioned.

The disciples shared much of that disillusionment, because they, too, wondered why, if Jesus were truly the Messiah, He refused to overthrow Rome and establish His own earthly kingdom. Despite Jesus' obvious supernatural powers and His claims of divine authority, He was less influential and respected among the people now than when He first began His ministry. And instead of being the conquering King's vice-regents, the Twelve were still a nondescript band of nobodies who were beginning to share Jesus' rejection.

A short while later, Jesus would paint an even darker picture for them as He "began to show His disciples that He must go to Jerusalem, and suffer many things from the elders and chief priests and scribes, and be killed" (v. 21). That the Messiah should be rejected by His own people was unbelievable enough; that He should be executed by them, or by anyone else, was incomprehensible. The bad news became still worse when Jesus declared that every true disciple of His must "deny himself, and take up his cross, and follow Me" (v. 24).

But before revealing those heartrending truths, He assured the Twelve that His program was on schedule, that He was indeed in control, and that they had every reason to continue their unreserved trust in Him. What they saw on the surface did not reflect the reality of what God was doing. Just as the Lord sought to bolster the confidence of His people in Egypt while He was preparing to deliver them, and just as He has continued to bolster the confidence of believers in every age while they are enduring trials and hardships on His behalf, He now sought to convince the Twelve that they had no reason to doubt or despair. The Lord here gives a message of great hope to the maligned, beleaguered, rejected, persecuted, and ignoble people of God in every age. In the end there is glorious purpose and victory, because they belong to the indomitable and eternal church that Jesus Christ Himself is building.

In Matthew 16:18-20 Jesus points up at least seven features and characteristics of the church that He builds. He speaks of its foundation, its certainty, its intimacy, its identity and continuity, its invincibility, its authority, and its spirituality.

First, Jesus set forth the foundation of the Church: **And I also say to you that you are Peter, and upon this rock I will build My church.**

For more than fifteen hundred years the Roman Catholic church has maintained that this passage teaches the church was built on the person of **Peter,** who became the first pope and bishop of Rome and from whom the Catholic papacy has since descended. Because of this supposed divinely ordained apostolic succession, the pope is considered to be the supreme and authoritative representative of Christ on earth. When a pope speaks ex cathedra, that is, in his official capacity as head of the church, he is said to speak with divine authority equal to that of God in Scripture.

Such an interpretation, however, is presumptuous and unbiblical, because the rest of the New Testament makes abundantly clear that Christ alone is the foundation and only head of His church.

Peter is from *petros,* a masculine form of the Greek word for small stone, whereas **rock** is from *petra,* a different form of the same basic word, referring to a rocky mountain or peak. Perhaps the most popular interpretation is therefore that Jesus was comparing **Peter,** a small stone, to the great mountainous **rock** on which He would build His church. The antecedent of **rock** is taken to be Peter's divinely inspired confession of Jesus as "the Christ, the Son of the living God" (vv. 16-17).

That interpretation is faithful to the Greek text and has much to commend it, but it seems more likely that, in light of other New Testament passages, that was not Jesus' point. In his letter to Ephesus Paul says that God's household is "built upon the foundation of the apostles and prophets, Christ Jesus Himself being the corner stone" (Eph. 2:20). In all four gospel accounts Peter is clearly the leading apostle, and he remains so through Acts 10. He was most often the Twelve's spokesman during Jesus' earthly ministry (see, e.g., Matt. 15:15; 19:27; John 6:68), and he was the chief preacher, leader, and worker of miracles in the early years of the church (see, e.g., Acts 1:15-22; 2:14-40; 3:4-6, 12-26; 5:3-10, 15, 29).

It therefore seems that in the present passage Jesus addressed Peter as representative of the Twelve. In light of that interpretation, the use of the two different forms of the Greek for **rock** would be explained by the masculine *petros* being used of Peter as an individual man and *petra* being used of him as the representative of the larger group.

It was not on the apostles themselves, much less on Peter as an individual, that Christ built His church, but on the apostles as His uniquely appointed, endowed, and inspired teachers of the gospel. The early church did not give homage to the apostles as persons, or to their office or titles, but to their doctrine, "continually devoting themselves to the apostles' teaching" (Acts 2:42). When the Jews outside the Temple were astonished at the healing of the crippled man, Peter quickly warned them not to credit him with the miracle, saying, "Men of Israel, why do you marvel at this, or why do you gaze at us, as if by our own power or piety we had made him walk?" (Acts 3:12). Although it was he alone who commanded the man to walk (v. 6), Peter replied to the crowd in John's behalf as well as his own.

Because they participated with the apostles in proclaiming the authoritative gospel of Jesus Christ, the prophets of the early church were also part of the church's foundation (Eph. 2:20). In fact, as Martin Luther observed, "All who agree with the confession of Peter [in Matt. 16:16] are Peters themselves setting a sure foundation." The Lord is still building His church with "living stones, . . . built up as a spiritual house for a holy priesthood, to offer up spiritual sacrifices acceptable to God through Jesus Christ" (1 Pet. 2:5).

Therefore, whether one interprets Matthew 16:18 as referring to Peter as a small stone placed on the mountainous stone of his confession of Christ or as referring to his being one with the rest of the Twelve in his confession, the basic truth is the same: The foundation of the church is the revelation of God given through His apostles, and the Lord of the church is the cornerstone of that foundation. Because it is His Word that the apostles taught and that the faithful church has always taught, Jesus Christ Himself is the true foundation, the living Word to whom the written Word bears witness (John 5:39). And "No man," Paul says—not even an apostle—"can lay a foundation other than the one which is laid, which is Jesus Christ" (1 Cor. 3:11). The Lord builds the church on the truth of Himself, and because His people are inseparable from Him they are inseparable from His truth. And because the apostles were endowed with His truth in a unique way, by their preaching of that truth they were the foundation of His church in a unique way.

That the Lord did not establish His church on the supremacy of Peter and his supposed papal successors was made clear a short while after Peter's great confession. When the disciples asked Jesus who was greatest in the kingdom of heaven, He replied by placing a small child before them and saying, "Whoever then humbles himself as this child, he is the greatest in the kingdom of heaven" (Matt. 18:1-4). Had the Twelve understood Jesus' teaching about the **rock** and the keys of the kingdom (Matt. 16:18-19) as referring exclusively to Peter, they would hardly have asked who was greatest in the kingdom. Or, had they forgotten or misunderstood Jesus' previous teaching, He would have answered by naming Peter as the greatest and probably would also have chided them for not remembering or believing what He had already taught (cf. Matt. 14:31; 26:24; John 14:9).

A short while after that, the mother of James and John asked Jesus to give her sons the chief places of honor in His kingdom, one on His left and the other on His right (Matt. 20:20-21). We learn from Mark 10:35-37 that James and John were themselves directly involved in the request, one they would never have made had they understood Peter to have been given primacy as Christ's successor. Or, as with the previous incident, had James and John misunderstood His teaching about the foundation **rock** of the church and the keys of the kingdom, Jesus would have taken the occasion to restate and underscore Peter's supremacy.

Although Peter recognized himself as an apostle (see, e.g., 1 Pet. 1:1; 2 Pet. 1:1), he never claimed a superior title, rank, or privilege over the other apostles. He even referred to himself as a "fellow elder" (1 Pet. 5:1) and as "a bond-servant" of Christ (2 Pet. 1:1). Far from claiming honor and homage for himself, he soberly warns his fellow elders to guard against lording it over those under their pastoral care (1 Pet. 5:3). The only glory he claimed for himself was that which is shared by all believers and which is yet "to be revealed, . . . when the Chief Shepherd appears" (vv. 1, 4).

Second, Jesus pointed up the certainty of the church, declaring, **"I will build My church."** As Peter had just confessed, Jesus is the Son of God; and God cannot lie or be mistaken. Therefore, because Jesus said, **"I will build My church,"** it will be built. It is the divine promise of the divine Savior.

In using the future tense, Jesus was not saying, as some contend, that He had not built His church in the past. The idea is that He would continue to build His church just as He had always done. As will be discussed below, **church** is used here in a general, nontechnical sense and does not indicate the distinct body of believers that first came into existence at Pentecost.

Jesus was not emphasizing the time of His building but its certainty. No matter how liberal, fanatical, ritualistic, apathetic, or apostate its outward adherents may be, and no matter how decadent the rest of the world may become, Christ **will build** His **church.** Therefore, no matter how oppressive and hopeless their outward circumstances may appear from a human perspective, God's people belong to a cause that cannot fail.

Several years ago a man traveled across the United States interviewing pastors in a number of large evangelical churches. He concluded that wherever there is great growth there is a corresponding great desire on the part of the church leadership to build the church. Perhaps the man misinterpreted some of the responses given to him, or perhaps the pastors did not express their objectives in the best of terms. In any case, however, no leader in Christ's church should have the desire to build it himself. Christ declared that He alone builds the church, and no matter how well intentioned he may be, anyone else who attempts to build it is competing with, not serving, the Lord.

I once visited a church at which the pastor pointed to a certain man and said, "He is one of my converts." "That's wonderful," I replied. "When did he come to the Lord?" "I didn't say he was the Lord's convert," the pastor explained. "I said he was one of mine."

By human reason, persuasiveness, and diligence it is possible to win converts to an organization, a cause, a personality, and to many other things. But it is totally impossible to win a convert to the spiritual church of Jesus Christ apart from the sovereign God's own Word and Spirit. Human effort can produce only human results. God alone can produce divine results.

When he studies and is obedient to the Word, and when he walks in the Spirit and produces the fruit of the Spirit, a believer can be sure he is living where Christ is building His **church.** It is not faithful believers who build Christ's church, but Christ who builds His church through faithful believers. Wherever His people are committed to His kingdom and His righteousness the Lord builds His church. If believers in one place become cold or disobedient, Christ does not stop building but simply starts work somewhere else. His true church is always "under construction."

Jesus said, "All that the Father gives Me shall come to Me" (John 6:37). At Pentecost, Peter declared that from among both Jews and Gentiles, Christ builds into His church "as many as the Lord our God shall call to Himself" (Acts 2:39). It was not the apostles but the Lord Himself who "was adding to their number day by day those who were being saved" (v. 47; cf. 11:24). When the Gentiles of Pisidian Antioch heard the preaching of Paul and Barnabas, "they began rejoicing and glorifying the word of the Lord; and as many as had been appointed to eternal life believed. And the word of the Lord was being spread through the whole region" (Acts 13:48-49). That preaching, true and faithful as it was, was not capable by itself of winning converts to Christ. Only those whom He had sovereignly chosen for salvation and who believed the truth of His Word were saved.

The New Testament is replete with commands and guidelines for believers' attitudes and conduct. It gives direction for selecting godly men and women to serve in the church. It gives abundant instruction for righteous living, for prayer, and for acceptable worship. Many of the Lord's blessings are contingent on His people's obedience and trust. But the most sincere and diligent efforts to fulfill those commands and standards are useless apart from Christ's own divine provision and control. He desires and He uses the faithful work of those who belong to Him; but only He builds His church, the church that He loves and for whom He "gave Himself up, . . . that He might sanctify her, having cleansed her by the washing of water with the word, that He might present to Himself the church in all her glory, having no spot or wrinkle or any such thing; but that she should be holy and blameless" (Eph. 5:25-27). Men are able to build human, earthly, physical organizations, but they cannot build the eternal, spiritual church.

Third, Jesus alluded to the intimacy of the fellowship of believers. "It is **My church**," He said. As Architect, Builder, Owner, and Lord of His **church,** Jesus Christ assures His followers that they are His personal possession and eternally have His divine love and care. They are His Body, "purchased with His own blood" (Acts 20:28), and are one with Him in a marvelous, holy intimacy. "The one who joins himself to the Lord is one spirit with Him" (1 Cor. 6:17). Christ is not ashamed to call them "brethren" (Heb. 2:11) and "God is not ashamed to be called their God" (Heb. 11:16). That is why when men attack God's people they attack God Himself. When Jesus confronted Paul (then known as Saul) on the Damascus road, He asked, "Saul, Saul, why are you persecuting Me?" (Acts 9:4). By persecuting Christians (see 8:3; 9:1-2) Saul had been persecuting Christ.

God has always identified Himself with His people and jealously guarded them as His own. He several times referred to His chosen people Israel as the apple, or pupil, of His eye. Through the prophet Zechariah He declared to them, "He who touches you, touches the apple of His eye" (Zech. 2:8; cf. Deut. 32:10; Ps. 17:8; Prov. 7:2). The front part of the eye, the cornea, is the most sensitive exposed part of the human body. God was therefore saying that to harm Israel was to poke a finger in His own eye. To harm God's people is to harm God Himself, and to cause them pain is to cause Him pain.

Fourth, Jesus emphasized the identity and continuity of His people. They are His **church**. The word *ekklēsia* (**church**) literally means "the called out ones" and was used as a general and nontechnical term for any officially assembled group of people. It was often used of civic gatherings such as town meetings, where important announcements were made and community issues were debated. That is the sense in which Stephen used *ekklēsia* in Acts 7:38 to refer to "the congregation" of Israel called out by Moses in the wilderness (cf. Ex. 19:17). Luke used it of a riotous mob ("assembly") incited by the Ephesian silversmiths against Paul (Acts 19:32, 41).

Matthew 16:18 contains the first use of *ekklēsia* in the New Testament, and Jesus here gives it no qualifying explanation. Therefore the apostles could not have understood it in any way but its most common and general sense. The epistles use the term in a more distinct and specialized way and give instructions for its proper functioning and for its leadership. But at Caesarea Philippi, Jesus' use of *ekklēsia* could only have carried the idea of "assembly," "community," or "congregation." If He spoke in Aramaic, as is probable, He would have used the term *qāhāl* (taken directly from the Hebrew), which means an invited gathering, and was commonly used of synagogue meetings. In fact, the word *synagogue* itself originally referred to any gathering or congregation of people. Only during the Babylonian exile did Jews begin using it to denote their formal and organized place of religious activity and worship. And only after the Day of Pentecost did the term *ekklēsia* take on a new and technical significance in reference to the distinct redeemed community built on the work of Christ by the Holy Spirit's coming.

In describing the inhabitants of heaven, the writer of Hebrews speaks of "the general assembly and church of the first-born" (Heb. 12:23), referring to the redeemed saints of all ages. That seems to be the sense in which Christ uses **church** in Matthew 16:18, as a synonym for citizens of His eternal kingdom, to which He refers in the following verse. The Lord does not build His kingdom apart from His church or His church apart from His kingdom.

Fifth, Jesus spoke of the invincibility of the church, which **the gates of Hades shall not overpower.**

The gates of Hades has often been interpreted as representing the evil forces of Satan attacking the church of Jesus Christ. But **gates** are not instruments of warfare. Their purpose is not to conquer but to protect those behind them from being conquered, or, in the case of a prison, to keep them from escaping. And **Hades,** which corresponds to the Hebrew *sheol,* refers here to the abode of the dead, not to eternal hell.

When the terms **gates** and **Hades** are properly understood, it becomes clear that Jesus was declaring that death has no power to hold God's redeemed people captive. Its **gates** are not strong enough to **overpower** (*katischuō*, to have mastery over) and keep imprisoned the church of God, whose Lord has conquered sin and death on her behalf (Rom. 8:2; cf. Acts 2:24). Because "death no longer is master over Him" (Rom. 6:9), it is no longer master over those who belong to Him. "Because I live," Jesus said, "you shall live also" (John 14:19). Satan now has the power of death, and he continually uses that power in his futile attempt to destroy Christ's church. But Christ's ultimate victory over Satan's power of death is so certain that the writer of Hebrews speaks of it in the past tense: "Since then the children share in flesh and blood, He Himself likewise also partook of the same, that through death He might render powerless him who had the power of death, that is, the devil" (Heb. 2:14; cf. Rev. 1:18).

It is that great truth of which Peter spoke at Pentecost, declaring that "God raised [Christ] up again, putting an end to the agony of death, since it was impossible for Him to be held in its power" (Acts 2:24). It is the truth about which Paul wrote to the Corinthian believers who were wavering in their belief in the resurrection. He declared, "Death is swallowed up in victory," and then asked, "O death, where is your victory? O death, where is your sting? The sting of death is sin, and the power of sin is the law; but thanks be to God, who gives us the victory through our Lord Jesus Christ" (1 Cor. 15:54-57).

In light of what He was about to teach them concerning His own death and resurrection and their own willingness to deny themselves and take up their crosses and follow Him (Matt. 16:21-24), Jesus now assured the Twelve, and all believers who would ever come to Him, that **the gates of Hades,** the chains of death itself, could never permanently **overpower** them and hold them captive.

Sixth, Jesus spoke about the authority of the church. **"I will give you the keys of the kingdom of heaven,"** He said; **"and whatever you shall bind on earth shall be bound in heaven, and whatever you shall loose on earth shall be loosed in heaven."**

The Lord was still addressing Peter as representative of the Twelve, telling him that **whatever you shall bind,** that is, forbid, **on earth shall be bound in heaven** and that **whatever you shall loose,** that is, permit, **on earth shall be loosed in heaven.** He told Peter and the Twelve, and by extension all other believers, that they had the astounding authority to declare what is divinely forbidden or permitted **on earth!**

Shortly after His resurrection Jesus told the disciples, "If you forgive the sins of any, their sins have been forgiven them; if you retain the sins of any, they have been retained" (John 20:23). In giving instruction for church discipline to all His people, Jesus said that, if a sinning believer refuses to turn from his sin after being counselled privately and even after being rebuked by the entire congregation, the church not only is permitted but obligated to treat the unrepentant member "as a Gentile and a tax-gatherer" (Matt. 18:15-17). He then said to the church as a whole what He earlier had said to Peter and to the other apostles: "Truly I say to you, whatever you shall bind on earth shall be bound in heaven; and whatever you loose on earth shall be loosed in heaven" (v. 18). In other words, a duly constituted body of believers has the right to tell an unrepentant brother that he is out of line with God's Word and has no right to fellowship with God's people.

Christians have such authority because they have the truth of God's authoritative Word by which to judge. The source of the church's authority is not in itself, anymore than the source of the apostles' authority was in themselves or even in their office, exalted as it was. Christians can authoritatively declare what is acceptable to God or forbidden by Him because they have His Word. Christians do not *determine* what is right or wrong, forgiven or unforgiven. Rather, on the basis of God's own Word, they recognize and proclaim what God has already determined to be right or wrong, forgiven or unforgiven. When they judge on the basis of God's Word, they can be certain their judgment corresponds with the judgment of **heaven.**

If a person declares himself to be an atheist, or to be anything other than a believer in and lover of the Lord Jesus Christ, Christians can say to that person with absolute certainty, "You are under God's judgment and condemned to hell," because that is what Scripture teaches. If, on the other hand, a person testifies that he has trusted Christ as his saving Lord, Christians can say to him with equal certainty, "If what you say is true, then your sins are forgiven, you are a child of God, and your eternal destiny is heaven." The authority of the church lies in the fact that it has heaven's word on everything "pertaining to life and godliness, through the true knowledge of Him who called us by His own glory and excellence" (2 Pet. 1:3). When believers are in agreement with God's Word, God is in agreement with them. Believers can declare a person's spiritual state with divinely granted authority by comparing that person to the Word of God.

Finally, Jesus reminds the disciples that His church is a *spiritual* reality, as **He warned** them **that they should tell no one that He was the Christ.** Most Jews, including the disciples, expected the Messiah to come as a conquering King, as a military and political leader to set them free from Rome, not as a Savior to set them free from sin. The people's expectations were so warped and selfishly misguided that to **tell** them that Jesus **was the Christ** would be to cast pearls before swine (see Matt. 7:6).

Jesus declared to Pilate, "My kingdom is not of this world. If My kingdom were of this world, then My servants would be fighting, that I might not be delivered up to the Jews; but as it is, My kingdom is not of this realm" (John 18:36). When Christians mix their faith with politics and various humanitarian causes, they run the risk of losing their spiritual focus and their spiritual power. Although human government is divinely ordained by God (Rom. 13:1-7; Titus 3:1; 1 Pet. 2:13), the state is no more to be an instrument of the church's program than the church is to be an instrument of the state's.

Like the kingdom of God, the church is "righteousness and peace and joy in the Holy Spirit. For he who in this way serves Christ is acceptable to God" (Rom. 14:17-18).

This great teaching of our Lord only introduces the subject of the church, which from Acts on dominates the rest of the New Testament.

Offending Christ
(16:21-23)

5

From that time Jesus Christ began to show His disciples that He must go to Jerusalem, and suffer many things from the elders and chief priests and scribes, and be killed, and be raised up on the third day. And Peter took Him aside and began to rebuke Him, saying, "God forbid it, Lord! This shall never happen to You." But He turned and said to Peter, "Get behind Me, Satan! You are a stumbling block to Me; for you are not setting your mind on God's interests, but man's. (16:21-23)

Throughout its pages the Bible contrasts God's view of things with man's. Perhaps the strongest and best-known declaration of that contrast is found in Isaiah: "'My thoughts are not your thoughts, neither are your ways My ways,' declares the Lord. 'For as the heavens are higher than the earth, so are My ways higher than your ways, and My thoughts than your thoughts'" (Isa. 55:8-9). "There is a way which seems right to a man," Solomon tells us, "but its end is the way of death" (Prov. 14:12). The psalmist wrote, "How great are Thy works, O Lord! Thy thoughts are very deep. A senseless man has no knowledge; nor does a stupid man understand this" (Ps. 92:5-6).

When the Lord refused David the privilege of building the Temple because he was a military man, a man of blood, He nevertheless promised David an eternal heritage of the throne of Israel, on which the Messiah Himself would some day sit and reign. In awe and deep gratitude David exclaimed, "Thou art great, O Lord God; for there is none like Thee, and there is no God besides Thee. . . . Thou art God, and Thy words are truth" (2 Sam. 7:22, 28).

When Peter rebuked Jesus for declaring that He must be crucified in Jerusalem by the Jewish leaders there, he either forgot or ignored that great truth. Peter had just proclaimed Jesus as being "the Christ, the Son of the living God" (Matt. 16:16); yet when Jesus made a statement that did not fit Peter's ideas about the Messiah, the apostle held to his way above the Lord's and found himself contradicting the Son of God he had just confessed.

By this time Peter had been a believer for some while, so that the lessons drawn from this passage are therefore primarily for believers. Not even Christians can know and understand God's ways except through a proper understanding of and submission to His Word and the illumination of His Spirit. When believers insist on their own way above God's, then, like Peter, they become an offense and a stumbling block.

It is likely that both in his confession and his rebuke of Christ, Peter also reflected the perspective of the other eleven. They shared Peter's belief that Jesus was the divine Messiah and they likely shared his confidence that the Messiah could hardly be rejected by His own people, much less put to death by them. Jesus had just assured them that He Himself was building His church, which not even death could overcome, and that through the divine Scripture they had heavenly authority to declare what is acceptable and not acceptable to Him (vv. 18-19). Jesus then "warned the disciples that they should tell no one that He was the Christ" (v. 20), not only because the Jewish people and their leaders had false notions about the Messiah but because the Twelve still shared many of those false notions. The idea of the Messiah suffering on a cross was anathema to Jews and a massive stumbling block to their faith in Jesus (1 Cor. 1:23).

From that time seems to be a transition phrase Matthew used to indicate a significant change in Jesus' ministry. He used the same phrase in 4:17 to mark the beginning of the Lord's public ministry to Israel. He now uses it to mark the beginning of His private ministry to the Twelve. The first phase was primarily public, with some occasional private instruction. The second was primarily private, with some occasional public instruction.

The Plan of God

Jesus Christ began to show His disciples that He must go to Jerusalem, and suffer many things from the elders and chief priests and scribes, and be killed, and be raised up on the third day. (16:21)

At this time **Jesus Christ began to show His disciples** some deeper and more difficult truths about His divine plan and work. It was not that He had said nothing previously about His rejection and crucifixion. In veiled ways He had spoken of His impending death, saying that "the Son of Man [would] be three days and three nights in the heart of the earth" (Matt. 12:40) and had declared to the Jewish leaders in Jerusalem, "Destroy this temple, and in three days I will raise it up" (John 2:19). He would continue to speak of His burial (John 12:7) and to explain that the Son of Man would rise from the dead after He had suffered at the hands of His enemies (see, e.g., 17:9, 12, 22-23).

The **must** of which Jesus spoke was not that of human devotion to a great ideal but a divine imperative and absolute necessity. God had no backup or alternate plan. This **must** came thundering out of eternity. It was the essential, unalterable plan of God set in motion before the foundation of the world.

Four things made that plan necessary. First was human sin, for which the Messiah had to give His life as the penalty in man's stead, as "a ransom for many" (Matt. 20:28). Second was the divine requirement that, "without shedding of blood there is no forgiveness" (Heb. 9:22). Third was the divine decree of God's sovereign foreknowledge (Rom. 8:29; Eph. 1:4-5), and fourth was the prophetic promise that the Messiah must die (see Pss. 16; 22; Isa. 53). God's plan is not subject to change. It can only be believed or rejected, never altered.

In verse 21 Jesus mentions four stages or phases of that divine plan which He had come to fulfill, four things **that He must** do before it would be completed.

The first **must** was for Him to **go to Jerusalem.** Had Jesus chosen any road but the one to Jerusalem, He could not have become the Savior of mankind, no matter how many more people He healed or how much more truth He taught. He had to go to the city of sacrifices and become the Passover Lamb, offering Himself "once for all" (Heb. 7:27).

When Jesus spoke of going to **Jerusalem,** He was in Caesarea Philippi, as far from Jerusalem as He could be and still remain in Palestine. After a brief stay in that remote northern city, He and the disciples would move down again through Galilee and Samaria to **Jerusalem,** where the Twelve began to fear that death by stoning at the hands of the hostile Jewish leaders awaited Jesus and probably them as well (John 11:16). At that point the disciples saw such a possibility not as the fulfilling of the plan of God but as the hindrance or even destruction of it.

Even when He was in Galilee, it was the Jewish leaders from Jerusalem who gave Jesus the most opposition (see Matt. 15:1-2). The hypocritical, self-righteous Judaism that flourished in Jerusalem could not stand Jesus, because He exposed their wickedness and ungodliness and rejected their cherished, man-made traditions (see vv. 3-9). But the Jewish leaders in Jerusalem would not have to seek Him out or hunt Him down like a fugitive. He would go there entirely of His own volition and in His own time. "I lay down My life that I may take it again," He declared. "No one has taken it away from Me, but I lay it down on My own initiative. I have authority to lay it down, and I have authority to take it up again" (John 10:17-18). He told Pilate, "You would have no authority over Me, unless it had been given you from above" (John 19:11).

The name **Jerusalem** means "foundation of peace," although at few times in its long history has that description been fitting. The city is located 33 miles east of the Mediterranean Sea and 14 miles west of the Dead Sea, elevated on a plateau some 2,500 feet above sea level. When first mentioned in Scripture it was known as Salem, whose king was Melchizedek, "a priest of God Most High" (Gen. 14:18) and a picture of Christ, who was "designated by God as a high priest according to the order of Melchizedek" (Heb. 5:10). It was on Mount Moriah, which was near Salem, that Abraham offered Isaac as a sacrifice to the Lord (Gen. 22:2). At the time David was made king, Jerusalem was in the hands of the Jebusites, and one of the first acts of the new monarch was to conquer the city and name it after himself (2 Sam. 5:5-9). Three months later he brought the Ark of the Covenant there and Jerusalem became the city where the Lord Himself symbolically dwelled. It was in Jerusalem that David's son, Solomon, built the Temple, and the city therefore became the central place for Jewish worship.

Jerusalem was alternately lost and recaptured by the Jews, but it never lost its identity in their minds and hearts as the city of God. When they were led into captivity to Babylon, the psalmist cried, "If I forget you, O Jerusalem, may my right hand forget her skill. May my tongue cleave to the roof of my mouth, if I do not remember you, if I do not exalt Jerusalem above my chief joy" (Ps. 137:5-6).

But when Jesus came to earth, **Jerusalem** was far from living up to its title of the city of God. During the first Passover of His ministry, Jesus took a whip and cleansed the Temple of the defiling money changers and merchants of sacrificial animals (John 2:13-16). During the next Passover, He violated the revered Sabbath traditions that the rabbis had devised, and the Jewish leaders tried to kill Him for it (5:16-18). During the third Passover, He deliberately stayed away because of the hatred of Him there. Later, when He attended the Feast of Booths, the Jewish leaders again tried to arrest Him and have Him put to death (7:1-19, 44-45; cf. 8:59).

Because of its rejection of Jesus, **Jerusalem** was given a new and pagan name, "the great city which mystically is called Sodom and Egypt, where also their Lord was crucified" (Rev. 11:8). In A.D. 70 God used the Roman army to destroy the city, which would not again be under Jewish control until 1,900 years later, when the modern state of Israel came into being in 1948. One day the city will deserve the name Jerusalem, because "it will come about in that day that living waters will flow out of Jerusalem, . . . [it] will rise and remain on its site from Benjamin's Gate as far as the place of the First Gate to the Corner Gate, and from the Tower of Hananel to the king's wine presses. And people will live in it, and there will be no more curse, for Jerusalem will dwell in security" (Zech. 14:8, 10-11).

It was in the divine plan that Messiah should die in **Jerusalem,** the divinely ordained place of sacrifice, and therefore, Jesus said, "I must journey on today and tomorrow and the next day; for it cannot be that a prophet should perish outside of Jerusalem" (Luke 13:33).

The second **must** in God's great plan was that His Son, the Messiah, would **suffer many things from the elders and chief priests and scribes.** Those three groups of religious leaders comprised the Sanhedrin, the Jewish high council, whose headquarters was in Jerusalem. **The elders** were primarily the leaders of the various tribes scattered throughout Israel. The **chief priests** were largely Sadducees, and the **scribes** were largely Pharisees. Because of their unbelief and rejection, as well as their political power, Jesus would **suffer many things** at the hands of those men.

The third **must** in God's plan was that Jesus **be killed.** The Greek word behind **killed** was not used of legal executions, and in this context the meaning is that of murder. Jesus was not legally tried or proved guilty of any wrongdoing but was sentenced to death on the false and vindictive charges of the Jewish leaders, who were determined to be rid of Him at any cost. It was in God's plan that at the hand of man He was to be murdered (Acts 2:22-23).

The fourth and last **must** was that Jesus would **be raised up on the third day.** But because of their great distress at hearing the first three imperatives, it is likely the disciples failed to hear this one at all. Yet it was this truth that made the others bearable. This was the truth of victory that would conquer those seeming defeats. This was the **must** of triumph and glory.

Peter's reply (v. 22) makes clear that he and his fellow disciples had not really heard Jesus' words about His being **raised up on the third day,** any more than they had really heard Him say that "the gates of Hades," that is, death, would not overcome His church (v. 18). They had seen Him raise the daughter of Jairus and the son of the widow of Nain. But if He Himself were to die, they probably reasoned, who would raise Him? How could a dead Messiah deliver and rule His people?

THE PRESUMPTION OF PETER

And Peter took Him aside and began to rebuke Him, saying, "God forbid it, Lord! This shall never happen to You." (16:22)

Because what Jesus had just said was so utterly contrary to what he himself strongly believed, **Peter** brashly **took Him aside and began to rebuke Him.**

Yet it was more than brashness that caused Peter to do such a thing. What he did also gave testimony to Jesus' humanness. Had He been a mystical and demanding Lord of the kind the Jews expected the Messiah to be, Peter would never have dared address Him as he did here and on many other occasions. Despite Peter's arrogant presumption, it is comforting to realize that Jesus was his close friend as well as his Lord. Peter showed no fear in speaking this rebuke to Jesus, demonstrating the reality of their intimate relationship as men.

Christians who are quick to rebuke Peter for such incredible presumption should be honest in recognizing that they, too, have in effect contradicted the Lord at times. The believer who complains about his sufferings and trials and asks, "Why me, Lord?" shares in Peter's presumption. It is easy to accept God's blessings, but not His testings. It is easy to accept prosperity and health as part of God's plan for us, but not hardship and sickness. When joy comes to us, that seems to be our proper lot as a child of God, but when sorrow comes we are inclined to doubt our heavenly Father's wisdom and love.

Rebuke translates the same word (*epitimaō*) Matthew used of Jesus' warning the disciples to tell no one He was the Christ (v. 20). The word carried the idea of authoritative judgment, normally used by an official or leader against someone under his jurisdiction. The present infinitive form suggests that Peter made the rebuke repeatedly.

Perhaps Peter's presumption came out of the officiousness that sometimes comes with age, or out of his being the acknowledged leader of the apostles. It was to him that Jesus had just declared the Father had given special revelation (v. 17), and Peter may now have considered himself a spokesman for God. Or perhaps the response was simply typical of Peter's self-confident personality. Certainly his deep love for and dependence on the Savior made the thought of His death a fearful prospect, so that both love and fear entered into Peter's response. In any case, his sinful pride led him to place his own understanding above Christ's.

God forbid it translates a Hebrew colloquialism that literally meant, "gracious to you" or "merciful to you" and was understood to mean something such as "God be gracious to you" or "May God in His mercy spare you this." In the context of Peter's rebuke, the phrase is here translated in its most negative connotation, **God forbid it.** Consequently, Peter's addressing Jesus as **Lord** rings hollow, because Peter was placing his own human will above the divine will of Christ.

To reinforce his rebuke, Peter said, **"This shall never happen to You,"** completely contradicting what Jesus had just declared was necessary. Because he could not understand or accept the idea of a humiliated, abused, and crucified Messiah, Peter rejected God's plan for redemption. The wisdom of the best of men is typically antagonistic to the wisdom of God.

THE PROTEST OF CHRIST

But He turned and said to Peter, "Get behind Me, Satan! You are a stumbling block to me; (16:23a)

It would be hard to imagine anything that would have shocked Peter more than those words of Jesus. On the surface, Peter's intention not only seems honorable but loving and compassionate. He did not want his Lord and Friend to die. He could not even bear the idea of Jesus suffering. Even Peter's more selfish motives are understandable. For several years he and the rest of the Twelve had become completely dependent on Jesus, not only for teaching and guidance but for food, tax money, and virtually everything else. Without Him, they would be a ship with no rudder.

As one commentator has observed, Peter "could hardly have understood that by his attempt to dissuade Jesus from the cross he was placing arrows in the bow of Satan to be shot at his beloved Savior."

But when Peter rebuked Him for even considering the idea of going to His death, the Lord must have looked the disciple straight in the eye as **He turned and said to Peter, "Get behind Me, Satan."** It was a stinging, devastating response that must have shaken Peter to the core of his being. Before Peter had a chance to finish his objections, Jesus abruptly cut him off and accused him of being the mouthpiece for His adversary, **Satan.**

Jesus had spoken almost the same words to Satan himself after the temptations in the wilderness (Matt. 4:10). And although Satan left, we learn from Luke's parallel account that "he departed from Him until an opportune time" (Luke 4:13). He continued to tempt Jesus throughout His ministry in every way he could. Now he put into Peter's mind the same idea He had tried to put into Jesus': "God's plan is too difficult and demanding. Give Your allegiance to me and your life will be immeasurably better. My way is superior to God's."

That is basically what Peter was saying to Jesus: "My way is better than Yours and the Father's." The same apostle who had just confessed Jesus as the Messiah and Son of God (v. 16) now contradicted Him. The one whom the Father had just inspired to give that confession (v. 17) was now "inspired" by Satan.

If such a thing could happen to Peter, it can happen to any believer. The same Christian who extols the plan of God can be lured into extolling the plan of Satan. When he follows his own wisdom instead of the Spirit's, the same one who has strongly taken the side of God can find himself unwittingly taking the side of Satan.

Jesus knew that **Satan** had as surely put the rebuke in Peter's mind as the Father had put the confession there. Whether by obsession, oppression, or simply by supernatural influence, Satan managed to prompt Peter to oppose Christ's way and try to lure Jesus into disobeying God's will. The text does not explain the means of the temptation, only its source. And because he succumbed, Peter found himself opposing the plan of God in the same way the devil had opposed it in the wilderness. Before he realized what he was doing, he found himself speaking for Satan rather than for God. In trying to defend Christ on the basis of his own understanding, he found himself standing against Christ.

Satan knew that the way of the cross was the way of his own defeat, and he therefore opposed the cross with all his being. And it is because they are spiritual children of the devil (John 8:44) that unbelievers consider the cross of Christ to be a foolish stumbling block (1 Cor. 1:18, 23). Satan knows that the cross is the place of men's deliverance from his dominion of sin and death, the only path from his kingdom of darkness to God's kingdom of light. After Christ died on the cross, Satan tried to keep Him dead; but the grave had no power over Him, just as it would have no power over His church (Matt. 16:18), the redeemed fellowship of those who put their trust in Him.

The temptation to avoid the cross was a real temptation to Christ, because He knew the cross meant inconceivable agony to Him. He knew what the agony would be in taking all the consequences of the world's sin upon Himself and what a horror it would be to be separated from His heavenly Father even for a few hours. That is why in the Garden of Gethsemane He sweat drops of blood and prayed, "Father, if Thou art willing, remove this cup from Me" (Luke 22:42-44).

Because Peter had taken the side of Satan, he became **a stumbling block** to

Christ. **Stumbling block** is from *skandalon,* a word originally used of an animal trap, in particular the part where the bait was placed. The term eventually came to be used of luring a person into captivity or destruction. Satan was using Peter to set a trap for Jesus.

THE PRINCIPLES FOR US

for you are not setting your mind on God's interests, but man's." (16:23b)

Jesus here gives the reason Peter fell into Satan's trap and found himself trying to lure his Lord into it as well: he was **not setting** his **mind on God's interests, but man's.** Because he is fallen and sinful, **man's** ways are not the Lord's, his **interests** are not **God's.**

Because Peter was reasoning from his own finite and sinful mind, he found himself siding with Satan and opposing God. When he trusted in his own perspective, he could no longer see God's. Because he did not continue to submit to the leading of the Father (see v. 17), he lost the Father's perspective. In his human wisdom he could not fathom why his Lord, the Messiah, had to "go to Jerusalem, and suffer many things from the elders and chief priests and scribes, and be killed" (v. 21). He was thinking like an unredeemed, fleshly man and found himself becoming "hostile toward God" (Rom. 8:7).

When believers focus on their present pain or potential distress rather than on the Lord who has allowed that pain, they are easy prey for Satan's traps and can even become his traps for ensnaring others. James therefore says, "Consider it all joy, my brethren, when you encounter various trials, knowing that the testing of your faith produces endurance. And let endurance have its perfect result, that you may be perfect and complete, lacking in nothing" (James 1:2-4). "Blessed is a man who perseveres under trial," he goes on to say; "for once he has been approved, he will receive the crown of life, which the Lord has promised to those who love Him" (v. 12).

From Peter's rebuke and Jesus' counter rebuke, Christians can learn two important lessons. The first is that God's way of salvation does not correspond to men's. His kind of Messiah is not man's kind. Therefore the person who insists on his own kind of Savior and on coming to God on his own terms finds himself opposing God and moving away from Him. Men's ways never lead to God.

Men cannot have Christ on their own terms. To reject the way of the cross is to reject Christ, no matter how much He may be professed and praised.

Although he failed totally on that occasion in Caesarea Philippi, Peter came to understand and love the way of the cross. That was the way he preached at Pentecost and throughout his ministry. He would one day write with great conviction and joy that Christ "Himself bore our sins in His body on the cross, that we might die to sin and live to righteousness; for by His wounds you were healed" (1 Pet. 2:24).

The second important lesson is that there is pain in God's refining process. As Jesus went on to explain in the next verse, He calls His disciples to share His suffering and His cross. They are called to deny themselves and take up their own crosses as they follow Him (Matt. 16:24). Their is no crossless obedience to Christ.

To make spiritual gold of His children, the Father must burn off the sinful dross. Of His redeemed remnant He says, "I will . . . refine them as silver is refined, and test them as gold is tested. They will call on My name, and I will answer them; I will say, 'They are My people,' and they will say, 'The Lord is my God'" (Zech. 13:9).

Someone has written,

> Man judgeth man in ignorance,
>   he seeth but in part;
> Our trust is in our Maker, God,
>   Who searcheth every heart;
> And every wrong and every woe,
>   when put beneath our feet,
> As stepping-stones may help us on
>   to His high mercy-seat.
> Then teach us still to smile, O Lord,
>   though sharp the stones may be,
> Remembering that they bring us near
>   to Thee, dear Lord, to Thee!

Winning by Losing: the Paradox of Discipleship

6

(16:24-27)

Then Jesus said to His disciples, "If anyone wishes to come after Me, let him deny himself, and take up his cross, and follow Me. For whoever wishes to save his life shall lose it; but whoever loses his life for My sake shall find it. For what will a man be profited, if he gains the whole world, and forfeits his soul? Or what will a man give in exchange for his soul? For the Son of Man is going to come in the glory of His Father with His angels; and will then recompense every man according to his deeds." (16:24-27)

This passage sets forth the heart of Christian discipleship and it strikes a death blow to the self-centered false gospels that are so popular in contemporary Christianity. It leaves no room for the gospel of getting, in which God is considered a type of utilitarian genie who jumps to provide a believer's every whim. It closes the door to the gospel of health and wealth, which asserts that if a believer is not healthy and prosperous he has simply not exercised his divine rights or else does not have enough faith to claim his blessings. It undermines the gospel of self-esteem, self-love, and high self-image, which appeals to man's natural narcissism and prostitutes the spirit of humble brokenness and repentance that marks the gospel of the cross.

To come to Jesus Christ is to receive and to keep on receiving forever. But Jesus, through His direct instruction during His earthly ministry and through His apostles in the rest of the New Testament, repeatedly makes clear that there must be a cross before the crown, suffering before glory, sacrifice before reward. The heart of Christian discipleship is giving before gaining, losing before winning.

This was not the first time Jesus spoke of the high cost of discipleship. He had said, "He who loves father or mother more than Me is not worthy of Me; and he who loves son or daughter more than Me is not worthy of Me. And he who does not take his cross and follow after Me is not worthy of Me. He who has found his life shall lose it, and he who has lost his life for My sake shall find it" (Matt. 10:37-39; cf. Luke 14:26-27). He had told the wealthy young man in Perea, "One thing you lack: go and sell all you possess, and give to the poor, and you shall have treasure in heaven; and come, follow Me" (Mark 10:21). To the Greeks who asked to see Him, Jesus said, "Truly, truly, I say to you, unless a grain of wheat falls into the earth and dies, it remains by itself alone; but if it dies, it bears much fruit. He who loves his life loses it; and he who hates his life in this world shall keep it to life eternal" (John 12:24-25).

But those teachings ran contrary to the popular Judaism of Jesus' day, just as they run contrary to much popular quasi-Christianity today. Like most of their fellow Jews, the Twelve expected the Messiah to throw off the Roman yoke, dethrone the Herods, and establish God's earthly kingdom in all its glory. It was therefore difficult to reconcile Jesus' teachings about humility, sacrifice, and self-giving with that view. Jesus did not act like the regal Messiah they expected, and He forbade them to act like vice-regents of such a mythical Messiah. Yet they knew Jesus' miracles and His teaching could not be explained humanly, and by the work of God in their hearts they had finally come to recognize that He was indeed the Messiah (Matt. 16:16). The whole picture did not yet fit together for them.

Particularly as Peter's brash reply to Jesus makes clear (v. 22), they were not yet willing to accept the idea of the Messiah's rejection, suffering, and death. Nor were they yet convinced that the way of discipleship involved those same great costs. Jesus therefore repeated the lesson many times and in many forms. They were not yet thinking like God thinks but still like fallen men think, because their minds were not "on God's interests, but man's" (v. 23).

They did not accept the truism that it is impossible for God, whether incarnate in His Son or living in the hearts of believers, to come into the midst of an anti-God society without there being hostility, reproach, and oppression. When holiness meets unholiness, a violent reaction is inevitable. "And indeed, all who desire to live godly in Christ Jesus will be persecuted," Paul said (2 Tim. 3:12).

THE PRINCIPLE

Then Jesus said to His disciples, "If anyone wishes to come after Me, let him deny himself, and take up his cross, and follow Me. (16:24)

When **Jesus said to His disciples,** "**If anyone wishes to come after Me,**" they were doubtless reminded of the time He had called each of them. Some two and a half years earlier they had left families, friends, occupations, and everything else in order to follow Jesus.

To unbelievers among the multitudes who were present on that occasion (see Mark 8:34), Jesus' words **come after Me** applied to the initial surrender of the new birth, when a person comes to Christ for salvation and the old life of sin is exchanged for a new life of righteousness. To the believers there, including the Twelve, **come after Me** reiterated the call to the life of daily obedience to Christ.

It is sadly possible for believers to lose the first love they had when they received Christ as saving Lord and surrendered all they were and had to Him (see Rev. 2:4). It is a constant temptation to want to take back what was given up and to reclaim what was forsaken. It is not impossible to again place one's own will above God's and to take back rights that were relinquished to Him. It is especially tempting to compromise our commitment when the cost becomes high. But the fact that believers sometimes succumb to disobedience does not alter the truth that the character of a true disciple is manifest in obedience. Although imperfect obedience is inevitable because of the unredeemed flesh, the basic desire and life-direction of the true Christian is obedience to the Lord.

Discipleship is on God's terms, just as coming to Him is on His terms. The Lord here reminds us that the key discipleship principle of winning by losing involves self-denial, cross-bearing, and loyal obedience.

The first requirement of discipleship is self-denial. A person who is not willing to **deny himself** cannot claim to be a disciple of Jesus Christ. **Deny** is from *aparneomai*, which means to completely disown, to utterly separate oneself from someone. It is the word Jesus used to describe Peter's denial of Him while He was being questioned by the high priest (Matt. 26:34). Each time he was confronted about his relationship to Jesus, Peter more vehemently denied knowing Him (vv. 70, 72, 74). He disowned his Master before the world.

That is exactly the kind of denial a believer is to make in regard to **himself.** He is to utterly disown himself, to refuse to acknowledge the self of the old man. Jesus' words here could be paraphrased, "Let him refuse any association or companionship with **himself.**" Self-denial not only characterizes a person when he comes in saving faith to Christ but also as he lives as a faithful disciple of Christ.

The self to which Jesus refers is not one's personal identity as a distinct individual. Every person is a unique creation of God, and the heavenly Father knows each of His children by name. He has every believer's name "recorded in heaven" (Luke 10:20). The self of which Jesus is speaking is rather the natural, sinful, rebellious, unredeemed self that is at the center of every fallen person and that can even reclaim temporary control over a Christian. It is the fleshly body, the "old self, which is being corrupted in accordance with the lusts of deceit" (Eph. 4:22) and is yet to be redeemed in glorification (cf. Rom. 8:23). To deny that self is to confess with Paul, "I know that nothing good dwells in me, that is, in my flesh" (Rom. 7:18).

To deny that self is to have the sincere, genuine conviction that one has nothing in his humanness to commend himself before God, nothing worthwhile to offer Him at all.

The believer is made acceptable before God when he trusts in Jesus Christ, and he stands before the Lord in perfect righteousness, clothed in "the new self, which in the likeness of God has been created in righteousness and holiness of the truth" (Eph. 4:24). But as Paul also declared, even after salvation a believer has no more goodness in *himself*, "that is, in [his] flesh," than he had before salvation. To deny self is to "make no provision for the flesh" (Rom. 13:14) and to "put no confidence in [it]" (Phil. 3:3). To deny self is to subject oneself entirely to the lordship and resources of Jesus Christ, in utter rejection of self-will and self-sufficiency.

Jesus proclaimed that the first requirement for entering the kingdom is to be "poor in spirit" (Matt. 5:3), to have the spirit of utter poverty in regard to one's own goodness, righteousness, worth, and merit. It is to humbly recognize one's spiritual destitution. It is only the person who realizes how poor he is who will ever know the riches of Christ. It is only the person who realizes how sinful and damned he is who will ever come to know how precious the forgiveness of God is. "The Lord is near to the brokenhearted, and saves those who are crushed in spirit" (Ps. 34:18). It is the broken and contrite heart that God loves and will never despise (Ps. 51:17). It is not the self-righteous and self-satisfied but the penitent and humble whom God saves. It was not the proud Pharisee who had such a high image of himself, but the brokenhearted tax collector who asked God for mercy, who Jesus said "went down to his house justified" (Luke 18:14).

The whole purpose of the Old Testament, reflected pointedly in the law of Moses, was to show man how spiritually and morally destitute and powerless he is in himself. The law was not meant to show men how they could work their way into God's favor but to show them how impossible it is to live up to God's holy standards by their own resources.

Arthur Pink wrote, "Growth in grace is growth downward; it is the forming of a lower estimate of ourselves; it is a deepening realization of our nothingness; it is a heartfelt recognition that we are not worthy of the least of God's mercies."

To be saved calls for a sinner to deny self so as to "consider the members of [his] earthly body as dead to immorality, impurity, passion, evil desire, and greed, which amounts to idolatry" (Col. 3:5). It is to "lay aside the old self, which is being corrupted in accordance with the lusts of deceit, and . . . be renewed in the spirit of [one's] mind" (Eph. 4:22-23).

The second requirement of discipleship is to **take up** one's **cross**. This idea has profound meaning which must be understood. Taking up one's **cross** is not some mystical level of selfless "deeper spiritual life" that only the religious elite can hope to achieve. Nor is it the common trials and hardships that all persons experience sometime in life. A cross is not having an unsaved husband, nagging wife, or domineering mother-in-law. Nor is it having a physical handicap or suffering from an incurable disease. To **take up** one's **cross** is simply to be willing to pay any price for Christ's sake. It is the willingness to endure shame, embarrassment, reproach, rejection, persecution, and even martyrdom for His sake.

To the people of Jesus' day the **cross** was a very concrete and vivid reality. It was the instrument of execution reserved for Rome's worst enemies. It was a symbol of the torture and death that awaited those who dared raise a hand against Roman authority. Not many years before Jesus and the disciples came to Caesarea Philippi, 100 men had been crucified in the area. A century earlier, Alexander Janneus had crucified 800 Jewish rebels at Jerusalem, and after the revolt that followed the death of Herod the Great, 2,000 Jews were crucified by the Roman proconsul Varus. Crucifixions on a smaller scale were a common sight, and it has been estimated that perhaps some 30,000 occurred under Roman authority during the lifetime of Christ.

When the disciples and the crowd heard Jesus speak of taking up the **cross,** there was nothing mystical to them about the idea. They immediately pictured a poor, condemned soul walking along the road carrying (which is an accurate translation of *airō,* meaning "to raise, bear, or carry") the instrument of his execution on his own back. A man who took **up his cross** began his death march, carrying the very beam on which he would hang.

For a disciple of Christ to **take up** his **cross** is for him to be willing to start on a death march. To be a disciple of Jesus Christ is to be willing, in His service, to suffer the indignities, the pain, and even the death of a condemned criminal.

Obviously the extent of suffering and persecution varies from believer to believer, from time to time, and from place to place. Not all the apostles were martyred, but all of them were willing to be martyred. Not every disciple is called on to be martyred, but every disciple is commanded to be willing to be martyred. "Beloved," Peter wrote to his fellow believers, "do not be surprised at the fiery ordeal among you, which comes upon you for your testing, as though some strange thing were happening to you; but to the degree that you share the sufferings of Christ, keep on rejoicing; so that also at the revelation of His glory, you may rejoice with exultation. If you are reviled for the name of Christ, you are blessed, because the Spirit of glory and of God rests upon you" (1 Pet. 4:12-14).

To come to Jesus Christ for salvation is not to raise a hand or sign a card, although such things may sometimes play a part. To come to Jesus Christ is to come to the end of self and sin and to become so desirous of Christ and His righteousness that one will make any sacrifice for Him.

Jesus had earlier said, "Do not think that I came to bring peace on the earth; I did not come to bring peace, but a sword. For I came to set a man against his father, and a daughter against her mother, and a daughter-in-law against her mother-in-law; and a man's enemies will be the members of his household" (Matt. 10:34-36). He had also said, "A disciple is not above his teacher, nor a slave above his master. . . . If they have called the head of the house Beelzebul, how much more the members of his household!" (vv. 24-25). Christ was now in effect saying to His disciples that if He, their Lord, would have to "suffer many things . . . and be killed"

(Matt. 16:21), how could they expect to escape the same treatment?

The **cross** represents suffering that is ours because of our relationship to Christ. As Jesus moved unwaveringly toward Jerusalem, the place of execution where He "must go" (v. 21), He had already taken up His cross and was beginning to bear on His back the sins of the whole world. And in His train, millions of disciples, all with their own crosses, have since borne reproach with Him.

Christ does not call disciples to Himself to make their lives easy and prosperous, but to make them holy and productive. Willingness to **take up his cross** is the mark of the true disciple. As the hymnist wrote, "Must Jesus bear the cross alone, and all the world go free? No, there's a cross for everyone, and there's a cross for me." Those who make initial confessions of their desire to follow Jesus Christ, but refuse to accept hardship or persecution, are characterized as the false, fruitless souls who are like rocky soil with no depth. They wither and die under threat of the reproach of Christ (Matt. 13:20-21). Many people want a "no-cost" discipleship, but Christ offers no such option.

The third requirement of discipleship is loyal obedience. Only after a person denies himself and takes up his cross, Jesus said, is he prepared to **follow Me.** True discipleship is submission to the lordship of Christ that becomes a pattern of life. "The one who says he abides in Him ought himself to walk in the same manner as He walked" (1 John 2:6). "Not everyone who says to Me, 'Lord, Lord,' will enter the kingdom of heaven," Jesus declared; "but he who does the will of My Father who is in heaven" (Matt. 7:21). To continue in His Word is to be His true disciple (John 8:31).

Paul calls salvation the "obedience of faith" (Rom. 1:5; 16:26). Peter describes God's sovereign saving work in a life as "the sanctifying work of the Spirit, that you may obey Jesus Christ and be sprinkled with His blood" (1 Pet. 1:2). Obviously, obedience is an integral feature in salvation and is as characteristic of a believer as is the sanctifying work of the Holy Spirit and the sacrificial saving work of the Son. Peter told the Jewish Sanhedrin that the Holy Spirit is given only to those who obey God (Acts 5:32), and since every believer has the Holy Spirit (Rom. 8:9), every believer is also characterized by obedience to God as a pattern of life.

"If anyone serves Me," Jesus said, "let him follow Me; and where I am, there shall My servant also be; if anyone serves Me, the Father will honor him" (John 12:26).

THE PARADOX

For whoever wishes to save his life shall lose it; but whoever loses his life for My sake shall find it. For what will a man be profited, if he gains the whole world, and forfeits his soul? Or what will a man give in exchange for his soul? (16:25-26)

Life and **soul** are here synonymous with each other and with the self (v. 24). All three words represent the inner person, the "real you."

What may here seem to be a complex and contradictory idea is really quite simple. The Lord is saying that **whoever** lives only **to save his** earthly, physical **life,** his ease and comfort and acceptance by the world, will **lose** his opportunity for eternal **life.** But **whoever is willing to give up his** earthly, worldly life and to suffer and die, if necessary, for Christ's sake, will **find** eternal life. Every person has a choice. He can "go for it" now and lose it forever; or he can forsake it now and gain it forever.

Jesus also identified the false believer who makes initial gestures of following the gospel, but will not let go of the world and all its trinkets, as bad soil full of weeds that choke out true spiritual life (Matt. 13:22).

The true disciple is willing to pay whatever price faithfulness to the Lord requires. The price may mean suffering martyrdom as Paul did or enduring physical exhaustion and illness in Christ's service as Epaphroditus did. Whatever the particulars of a believer's cross-bearing may be, it requires the willingness to abandon safety, security, personal resources, health, friends, job, and even life.

The story is told of a plantation slave in the old South who was always happy and singing. No matter what happened to him, his joy was always abounding. One day his master asked him, "What have you got that makes you so happy?"

The slave replied, "I love the Lord Jesus Christ. He has forgiven my sin and put a song in my heart."

"Well, how do I get what you have?" his master asked.

"You go and put on your best Sunday suit and you come down here and work in the mud with us and you can have it," came the reply.

"I would never do that," the owner retorted indignantly as he rode off in a huff.

Some weeks later, the master asked the same question and was given the same answer. A few weeks later, he came a third time and said, "Now be straight with me. What do I have to do to have what you have?"

"Just what I've told you the other times," came the answer.

In desperation, the owner said, "All right, I'll do it."

"Now you don't have to do it," the slave said. "You only had to be willing."

It is not that a disciple has to be a martyr, but that he is willing to be a martyr if faithfulness to Christ demands it.

Jesus reinforced the paradox by adding, **"For what will a man be profited, if he gains the whole world, and forfeits his soul? Or what will a man give in exchange for his soul?"** Here is the ultimate hyperbole. "Imagine, if you can," Jesus was saying, "what it would be like to somehow possess **the whole world.** Of what lasting benefit would that be, if in gaining it you forfeited your **soul,** your eternal life?" Such a person would be a walking dead man who temporarily owned everything but who faced an eternity in hell rather than in heaven.

"Or," Jesus continued, **"what** could possibly be worth having during this lifetime, if to gain it you would have to **exchange** your **soul?"** To gain every possession possible in this world and yet be without Christ is to be bankrupt forever. But to abandon everything in this world for the sake of Christ is to be rich forever (cf. Matt. 6:19-21).

The Parousia

For the Son of Man is going to come in the glory of His Father with His angels; and will then recompense every man according to his deeds. (16:27)

Parousia is a noun form of the Greek verb behind **to come** and is often used to refer to Christ's second coming, of which this is the first mention in the New Testament.

A day of judgment is coming, Jesus reminded the disciples and the multitude. The Father "has given all judgment to the Son" (John 5:22), and when **the Son of Man,** who is also the Son of God, comes **in the glory of His Father with His angels** (an event further described in Matt. 24-25), He **will then recompense every man according to his deeds.** Christ's holy **angels** are the instruments of His service and His judgment, and when He comes to earth again they will come with Him, to raise "those who did the good deeds to a resurrection of life" and "those who committed the evil deeds to a resurrection of judgment" (John 5:29).

That general truth had been proclaimed long before by the psalmist: "Thou dost recompense a man according to his work," the psalmist declared (Ps. 62:12). It was also echoed by Paul in his letter to the church at Rome. In 2:5-8, he is specific:

> But because of your stubbornness and unrepentant heart you are storing up wrath for yourself in the day of wrath and revelation of the righteous judgment of God, who will render to every man according to his deeds: to those who by perseverance in doing good seek for glory and honor and immortality, eternal life; but to those who are selfishly ambitious and do not obey the truth, but obey unrighteousness, wrath and indignation.

"Each one of us," the apostle later wrote, "shall give account of himself to God" (Rom. 14:12). Matthew 25 records the Lord's teaching about the judgment of the nations. They, too, will be judged by their works (vv. 31-46).

As the Lord reviews the life of each person who has ever lived, He will say, as it were, "There is a believer. I can tell by his works, because they are the product of My Holy Spirit. There is an unbeliever, as I can also tell by his works, because they are the product of the flesh." It is not that works save, but that they are the product of salvation. James teaches that the only kind of faith that saves is the kind that results in righteous behavior (James 2:14-26; cf. Eph. 2:10).

Those whose works are pleasing to the Lord are those who, by God's sovereign grace and power, have trusted in Christ as saving Lord, while denying self, taking up their crosses, and following Him. They will receive everlasting life and all the blessings of heaven. Those whose works are rejected by the Lord are those who put their hope and trust in the ephemeral things of this life. They will receive eternal damnation and all the torments of hell.

The call to salvation is a call to discipleship as described in this passage. When God saves, He produces this kind of follower.

Promise and Warning Concerning the Second Coming (16:27-28)

7

"For the Son of Man is going to come in the glory of His Father with His angels; and will then recompense every man according to his deeds. Truly I say to you, there are some of those who are standing here who shall not taste death until they see the Son of Man coming in His kingdom." (16:27-28)

Although the Old Testament contains more than 1,500 prophecies of the coming of the Messiah, the Christ, it was not revealed clearly to the saints of that era that His coming would be in two separate stages, thousands of years apart. The first stage would be characterized by suffering and sacrifice for sin, and the second by conquest and splendor. The central focus of the New Testament is on Christ's first coming, but the second coming is also mentioned or alluded to once in every 25 verses, a total of some 320 times.

The Old Testament references to a suffering Messiah and Redeemer were frequently rationalized away by Jewish interpreters or spiritualized to the point of insignificance. In the minds of most Jews in Jesus' day, the Messiah was to come but once, as the conquering King of the earth.

Therefore as Jesus moved closer to His time of suffering, He continued to prepare His disciples for what they all but refused to believe: that He, the divine Son of Man and the Messiah, rather than conquering His enemies and establishing His eternal kingdom on earth at that time, would first have to die at the hands of those enemies.

Matthew 16:27—17:6 contains one of the great highlights of the Lord's ministry on earth. It looks ahead to His coming that second and last time, the time of His return in exaltation and glory, when all His enemies will indeed be placed under His feet and He will establish the long-hoped-for eternal kingdom. As He introduces this teaching (16:27-28), Jesus gives a promise, a warning, and then a repeat of the promise.

The Promise

For the Son of Man is going to come in the glory of His Father with His angels; (16:27*a*)

Jesus referred to Himself as **the Son of Man** more than by any other designation. The name reflects His humanness and His incarnation, of His fully identifying Himself with mankind as one of their own, and in this prophetic context the ancient title has especially rich significance.

In his vision of the four beasts, Daniel looked, as it were, across the entire history of mankind and saw its awesome climax. "I kept looking until thrones were set up," he says, "and the Ancient of Days took His seat; His vesture was like white snow, and the hair of His head like pure wool. His throne was ablaze with flames, its wheels were a burning fire." It was a scene of God, "the Ancient of Days," sitting on His throne of judgment. His white garments speak of His perfect purity and holiness, His pure wool hair speaks of His perfect wisdom, and the burning wheels speak of His sovereign authority. The "river of fire . . . flowing and coming out from before Him" portrays His consuming, purging divine judgment. With "thousands upon thousands . . . attending Him, and myriads upon myriads . . . standing before Him," the court of divine judgment convened and "the books were opened" (Dan. 7:9-10).

After the beast, the supreme satanic world leader and the Antichrist, is destroyed, Daniel sees "One like a Son of Man," who "came up to the Ancient of Days and was presented before Him. And to Him was given dominion, glory and a kingdom, that all the peoples, nations, and men of every language might serve Him. His dominion is an everlasting dominion which will not pass away; and His kingdom is one which will not be destroyed" (vv. 11-14).

It was about that time of fateful judgment that Jesus was here speaking to the disciples, who desperately needed a word of encouragement. Recently they had heard much of pain but little of gain, much of suffering but little of glory, much of the cross but little of the crown. Jesus therefore assured them that He was indeed the **Son of Man** whom Daniel saw **come in the glory of His Father with His** thousands upon thousands and myriads upon myriads of holy **angels** to receive the kingdom and execute judgment.

Here was Jesus' first specific revelation to His disciples of His second coming.

After just telling them that He was God in human flesh, that He was the promised Messiah, that He would build a kingdom that nothing could hinder or destroy—but that He first had to be rejected, killed, and rise from the dead—He now informed them that He will one day return in great glory and righteous judgment to establish His throne.

In Scripture, the word **glory** is often used to represent the totality of God's nature, character, and attributes. When He came to earth as a man, Jesus' deity was veiled (cf. Phil. 2:6-8), and there was nothing in His human appearance to mark Him as being different from other men (cf. Isa. 53:2). That very fact made it difficult for many Jews to acknowledge Him as the Messiah, whose divine power and glory they thought would be immediately manifest. But that was not God's plan.

When Moses asked God, "I pray Thee, show me Thy glory!" the Lord replied, "I Myself will make all My goodness pass before you, and will proclaim the name of the Lord before you; and I will be gracious to whom I will be gracious, and will show compassion on whom I will show compassion" (Ex. 33:18-19). To witness God's attributes is to have a glimpse of His **glory**, all that the fullness of His *name* implies.

During the Olivet discourse, only a few days before His arrest and crucifixion, Jesus spoke again of His coming. "But immediately after the tribulation of those days the sun will be darkened," He said, "and the moon will not give its light, and the stars will fall from the sky, and the powers of the heavens will be shaken, and then the sign of the Son of Man will appear in the sky, and then all the tribes of the earth will mourn, and they will see the Son of Man coming on the clouds of the sky with power and great glory. And He will send forth His angels with a great trumpet and they will gather together His elect from the four winds, from one end of the sky to the other" (Matt. 24:29-31). He will then come in blazing, unveiled **glory**, and the entire earth will be filled with that **glory**, just as in Isaiah's vision (Isa. 6:3; cf. Ps. 72:19).

The message that the Messiah would come in **glory** was not new. It was perhaps the messianic truth with which the Jews of that day were most familiar. Jesus now affirmed and gave a more complete perspective to that truth, a truth His disciples thought was being contradicted and frustrated both by His rejection by the Jewish leaders and by His own failure to assert His divine power and glory.

In *Son of Man to Thee I Cry,* an old and out-of-print hymn by an unknown author, we find these lovely truths:

> He who wept above the grave,
> He who stilled the raging wave,
> Meek to suffer, strong to save,
> He shall come in glory!

> He who sorrow's pathway trod,
> He that every good bestowed—
> Son of Man and Son of God—
> He shall come in glory.

He who bled with scourging sore,
Thorns and scarlet meekly wore,
He who every sorrow bore—
He shall come in glory.

Monarch of the smitten cheek,
Scorn of Jew and scorn of Greek,
Priest and King, divinely meek—
He shall come in glory.

He who died to set us free,
He who lives and loves e'en me,
He who comes whom I shall see, Jesus only—only He—
He shall reign in glory!

For those who know and love the Lord Jesus Christ, His return in **glory** is a comforting and thrilling promise that fills them with great hope and anticipation. Like the saints under the heavenly altar (Rev. 6:9-10), they wonder how long the Lord will allow the world to go its sinful way before intervening in sovereign power and bringing righteousness, equity, and justice to the world. They wonder with the psalmist, "How long, O God, will the adversary revile, and the enemy spurn Thy name?" (Ps. 74:10; cf. 35:17). In response to Jesus' promise, "Yes, I am coming quickly," they pray with John, "Amen. Come, Lord Jesus" (Rev. 22:20).

At this point in Jesus' ministry the disciples especially needed a word of hope from their Lord. He had just told them of His impending suffering and death and of the demanding conditions of true discipleship, of taking up one's own cross and of giving up one's own life in order to save it (Matt. 16:21-25). Perhaps for the first time it was becoming clear to them that the way of Christ is the way of self-denial, sacrifice, rejection, persecution, and quite possibly martyrdom. It was beginning to dawn on them that the way of Christ is the way of willing obedience at any price. It is saying no to ease, comfort, money, and pleasure and of saying yes to pain, struggle, persecution, and spiritual warfare for His sake.

The Warning

and will then recompense every man according to his deeds. (16:27b)

At His glorious coming Jesus also **will then recompense every man according to his deeds.** The believer looks forward to the second coming in the hope of sharing His Lord's glory, whereas the unbeliever can look forward to it only in the fear of being condemned under the Lord's judgment. **Every man** here is comprehensive!

In light of that twofold prospect, the Lord's return is bittersweet for believers who are sensitive and loving. Like John as he tasted the little book he took from the angel's hand (Rev. 10:10), they think of the second coming as "sweet as honey" regarding their own destiny but "bitter" regarding the destiny of the myriad lost souls who will have nothing of Christ. It was perhaps that truth that prompted Paul to declare, "Therefore knowing the fear of the Lord, we persuade men" (2 Cor. 5:11).

In speaking here of His recompensing **every man according to his deeds,** Jesus was speaking in general terms about the second coming, not about a specific event or element within it. He was simply pointing out that it will be a time of glory and reward for those who belong to Him and a time of judgment and punishment for those who do not. His coming will resolve the destiny of **every man** (cf. John 5:25-29).

On the day of judgment **every man** will be judged on the basis of his **deeds.** It is not that **deeds** are the means of salvation, which is by grace through faith alone. But a person's outward **deeds** are the surest evidence of his inward spiritual condition. People are best known by their fruits, Jesus said (Matt. 7:16). James declared that "faith, if it has no works, is dead" (James 2:17).

Righteous **deeds** are not the source of salvation, but they are the objective verification that it has occurred. Jesus declared, "Not everyone who says to Me, 'Lord, Lord,' will enter the kingdom of heaven; but he who does the will of My Father who is in heaven" (Matt. 7:21). Paul told the Corinthian believers in his first letter to them, "Each man's work will become evident; for the day will show it, because it is to be revealed with fire; and the fire itself will test the quality of each man's work" (1 Cor. 3:13). In his second letter to them he said, "For we must all appear before the judgment seat of Christ, that each one may be recompensed for his deeds in the body, according to what he has done, whether good or bad" (2 Cor. 5:10). To the church at Thyatira the Lord Himself declared, "I will give to each one of you according to your deeds" (Rev. 2:23; cf. 20:13).

Among the last words of Scripture is Jesus' declaration, "Behold, I am coming quickly, and My reward is with Me, to render to every man according to what he has done" (Rev. 22:12). Throughout the New Testament it is repeatedly made clear that "each one of us shall give account of himself to God" (Rom. 14:12), who "will render to every man according to his deeds: to those who by perseverance in doing good seek for glory and honor and immortality, eternal life; but to those who are selfishly ambitious and do not obey the truth, but obey unrighteousness, wrath and indignation. There will be tribulation and distress for every soul of man who does evil, . . . but glory and honor and peace to every man who does good" (Rom. 2:6-10).

No genuinely righteous works can be manifest in the life of an unbeliever, because he has no indwelling Holy Spirit to produce them and no godly new nature through which the holiness of the Spirit can be expressed. The life of the believer, on the other hand, is characterized by righteous works, because he has God's own life and Spirit within him as the source and power for those works. A person who has no evidence of righteous behavior in his life has no basis for assurance of salvation, no matter how long and vocally he may have professed being a Christian.

Yet the honest, humble believer knows that, no matter how faithfully he studies and obeys God's Word and has fellowship with Him in prayer, he still falls far short of the Lord's perfect righteousness. But he also knows that, "If we confess our sins, He is faithful and righteous to forgive us our sins and to cleanse us from all unrighteousness" (1 John 1:9). He knows that, by God's gracious Spirit continuing to work through him, even such confession is verification of his genuineness. His life is sure to produce more fruit that is pleasing to God, fruit for which the Lord will say, "Well done, good and faithful slave, . . . enter into the joy of your master" (Matt. 25:21). Because a believer has given his life to Jesus Christ, His own Spirit produces in us works that are worthy of God's reward. For the believer, therefore, the truth that the Lord **will then recompense every man according to his deeds** is a wonderful promise.

For unbelievers, however, that truth is a dire warning, because at Christ's judgment seat they will have no acceptable **deeds** to present to the Lord as evidence of salvation. Many professed Christians will say to the Lord "on that day, 'Lord, Lord, did we not prophesy in Your name, and in Your name cast out demons, and in Your name perform many miracles?' And then [Christ] will declare to them, 'I never knew you; depart from Me, you who practice lawlessness'" (Matt. 7:22-23).

For the unsaved, that day will be one of unrelieved fear as they finally realize that the good works on which they had been relying to make them right with God were nothing more than filthy garments (cf. Isa. 64:6) that leave them totally unfit to stand before the righteous King and Judge. The term Isaiah uses in that passage (usually translated "filthy rags" or "filthy garment") literally means menstrual cloth, a graphic figure used to represent the best that human goodness can produce. At Jesus' second coming, Paul warns, He will deal out "retribution to those who do not know God and to those who do not obey the gospel of our Lord Jesus. And these will pay the penalty of eternal destruction, away from the presence of the Lord and from the glory of His power, when He comes to be glorified in His saints on that day" (2 Thess. 1:8-10).

For all men there will be a day of accounting, a day of reckoning. For the cross-bearing, obedient Christian it will be a day of great rejoicing and glory, because he will have evidence that the life of God is within him by faith in Jesus Christ. But for the unrepentant, Christ-rejecting sinner, it will be a day of great terror and torment, because he will have had no evidence of divine life.

THE PROMISE REPEATED

Truly I say to you, there are some of those who are standing here who shall not taste death until they see the Son of Man coming in His kingdom. (16:28)

In light of Jesus' growing opposition by the Jewish religious leaders and His predictions of impending suffering and death, it was no doubt with some skepticism that the disciples heard their Lord's promise of one day returning in glory. "If we were so confused about His first coming," they may have reasoned, "why should we get our hopes up about a second coming of which we know so little?" All they seemed sure of at the present time was that their Lord's work appeared to be an utter failure, that He was facing imminent death, and that He had commanded them to willingly accept the same fate. Therefore, understanding the disciples' bewilderment and weak faith, Jesus repeated the promise, adding that **"some of those who are standing here . . . shall not taste death until they see the Son of Man coming in His kingdom."**

Taste death was a common Jewish expression that referred to drinking the cup of death, in other words, to dying. Jesus assured the Twelve that, before death, some of them would see Him **coming in His kingdom.**

Because all the Twelve have long been dead and Jesus still has not returned after nearly 2,000 years, many people have stumbled over this text. But because Jesus was incapable either of lying or of being mistaken, it should be obvious He was not saying that some of them would not physically die before His actual second coming.

To understand correctly what Jesus meant, it is first of all helpful to know that *basileia* (**kingdom**) was often used as a metonym to mean "royal majesty" or "regal splendor"—in much the same way that *scepter* has long been used figuratively to represent royal power and authority. Used in that way, *basileia* would refer to a manifestation of Jesus' kingliness rather than to His literal earthly reign. His promise could therefore be translated, **"until they see the Son of Man coming in His** kingly splendor."

At the beginning of his Pentecost sermon Peter quotes an extensive passage from the prophet Joel (Acts 2:28-32), a passage that specifically relates to events that "shall be in the last days" (Acts 2:17; cf. Joel 2:28). Referring to the dramatic events that had just occurred on the Day of Pentecost, Peter said, "This is what was spoken of through the prophet Joel" (Acts 2:16). Yet it is obvious that all of those events did not transpire at Pentecost. God's Spirit was not poured out on all mankind; there were no "signs on the earth beneath, blood, and fire, and vapor of smoke"; and the sun was not "turned into darkness" or "the moon into blood" (Acts 2:17-21). The events of that day, wondrous as they were, did not signal the second coming. The day of Pentecost was not "in the last days" of which Joel spoke.

Nevertheless, the Pentecost events were a glimpse and foretaste of the last days, as Peter declares in verse 16. The "noise like a violent, rushing wind" that "filled the whole house where they [the 120 believers who had gathered for prayer] were sitting," the appearance of "tongues as of fire" that "rested on each one of them," and their being filled with the Spirit and enabled "to speak with other tongues, as the Spirit was giving them utterance" (2:2-4) were foreshadows of the Lord's second coming glory. To some extent, *all* of Jesus' divine teaching and miracles and the teaching and miracles of the apostles were a glimpse of the kind of phenomena that will characterize that future glory. They were a taste of "the good word of God and the powers of the age to come" (Heb. 6:5) that countless thousands, unbelievers as well as believers, had been privileged to hear and see.

Yet it seems that Jesus' promise to the Twelve about seeing **the Son of Man coming in His kingdom** was more definite and immediate than those general glimpses.

It was not uncommon for Old Testament prophecies to combine a prediction of a far distant event with a prediction of one in the near future, with the earlier even prefiguring the latter. Such prophecies would thereby have near as well as distant fulfillments. The fulfillment of the near prophecy served to verify the reliability of the distant one. It seems reasonable, therefore, to assume that Jesus verified the reliability of His second coming prophecy by giving a glimpse of His second coming glory to **some** of the disciples before they would **taste death**.

In light of that interpretation—and because in all three gospel accounts the promise of seeing His glory is given immediately preceding the account of the transfiguration (see Mark 9:1-8; Luke 9:27-36) and, as mentioned above, *basileia* can be translated "royal splendor"—it seems that Jesus must here have been referring specifically to His unique and awesome transfiguration before Peter, James, and John only six days later (see 17:1). Those three disciples were the **some** among the Twelve who would not die until, in a most miraculous preview, they would **see the Son of Man coming in His kingdom**.

Preview of the Second Coming
(17:1-13)

And six days later Jesus took with Him Peter and James and John his brother, and brought them up to a high mountain by themselves. And He was transfigured before them; and His face shone like the sun, and His garments became as white as light. And behold, Moses and Elijah appeared to them, talking with Him. And Peter answered and said to Jesus, "Lord, it is good for us to be here; if You wish, I will make three tabernacles here, one for You, and one for Moses, and one for Elijah." While he was still speaking, behold, a bright cloud overshadowed them; and behold, a voice out of the cloud, saying, "This is My beloved Son, with whom I am well-pleased; listen to Him!" And when the disciples heard this, they fell on their faces and were much afraid. And Jesus came to them and touched them and said, "Arise, and do not be afraid." And lifting up their eyes, they saw no one, except Jesus Himself alone.

And as they were coming down from the mountain, Jesus commanded them, saying, "Tell the vision to no one until the Son of Man has risen from the dead." And His disciples asked Him, saying, "Why then do the scribes say that Elijah must come first?" And He answered and said, "Elijah is coming and will restore all things; but I say to you, that Elijah already came, and they did not recognize him, but did to him whatever they wished. So also the Son of Man is going to suffer at their hands." Then the disciples understood that He had spoken to them about John the Baptist. (17:1-13)

As noted at the end of the previous chapter, the preview of His glory that Jesus promised some of the disciples would experience before they died (16:28) doubtlessly referred to His transfiguration, the event related in the present text.

Six days after the promise was given it was fulfilled. The fact that Luke says it was "some eight days later" (9:28) simply indicates that he was speaking in inclusive terms, unlike Matthew and Mark (9:2). Whereas those writers referred to the **six** intervening days between the prediction and the fulfillment, Luke also included the days on which those events occurred.

Peter and James and John his brother were the most intimate disciples of Jesus, constituting, with Peter's brother Andrew, the Lord's inner circle. (See vol. 2 in this commentary series [*Matthew 8–15*], p. 136). It is therefore not surprising that it was these three men whom He **brought . . . up to a high mountain by themselves.**

Four reasons seem to suggest themselves for Jesus' taking only these three with Him to witness His transfiguration. First, they would be reliable witnesses of His manifested glory, able to confirm the event to the other disciples and to the rest of the church. According to Deuteronomy 19:15, "on the evidence of two or three witnesses a matter shall be confirmed." The Lord's promised display of His kingdom glory (Matt. 16:27-28) would be confirmed by the testimony of these three trustworthy witnesses.

Second, these three men were probably chosen because of their intimacy with Jesus. They were with Him the most and understood Him the best, and they frequently accompanied Him when He went away for times of intense fellowship with His heavenly Father (Mark 5:37; 14:33). It was fitting that those who would most intimately share His suffering and sorrow would also most intimately share in witnessing His glory.

Third, as the acknowledged spokesmen among the Twelve, the ones whose word was most respected, these three men could most reliably and convincingly articulate what they witnessed on the mountain.

The fourth possible reason is negative. If all twelve disciples had seen the transfiguration, or if all of them plus the crowds that had been with them in upper Galilee were to have seen Jesus transfigured, the entire region could quickly have been in turmoil. The people may have run down the hillside and into the surrounding towns babbling uncontrollably about what they had seen. The accounts doubtlessly would have varied greatly and been embellished with each retelling, and Jesus could have been pressured even more forcefully to become the political and military deliverer the people expected the Messiah to be (see John 6:15; 12:12-19).

The particular **high mountain** is not identified, but it was apparently somewhere near and to the south of Caesarea Philippi, on the route to Capernaum and eventually Jerusalem (see Matt. 16:13, 21; 17:24).

We learn from Luke 9:32 that, as in the Garden (Matt. 26:40-45), these three disciples could not stay awake, despite the momentousness of the experience. It was "from sorrow" that they slept in the Garden (Luke 22:45), and it was perhaps for the same reason that they slept on the mountain top. Sleep can be a form of escape, a way of temporarily forgetting problems and anxieties. Depression accelerates weariness. It is likely that the promise Jesus made a few days earlier was too vague and indefinite to bolster their spirits after learning of His impending suffering and death and His call for them to be willing to suffer and die in His service (16:21-25). They slept the sleep of frustration and depression. It was not until Moses and Elijah appeared that the three "became fully awake . . . and saw His glory and the two men standing with Him" (Luke 9:32*b*).

In the events that followed are found five powerful confirmations, or proofs, that Jesus was indeed the predicted Son of Man, the Messiah, the divine King of glory. First is the transformation of the Son (Matt. 17:2); second is the testimony of the saints (vv. 3-4); third is the terror of the Father (vv. 5-6); fourth is what may be called the tapestry of the scene (vv. 7-9); and fifth is the tie with Jesus' forerunner, John the Baptist (vv. 10-13). The first three are given during the transfiguration, and the last two are given just afterward.

THE TRANSFORMATION OF THE SON

And He was transfigured before them; and His face shone like the sun, and His garments became as white as light. (17:2)

Was transfigured is from *metamorphoō*, which has the basic meaning of changing into another form and is the term from which we get *metamorphosis*. Because no further description is given, all we know of the change is that, during this brief display of divine glory, Jesus' **face shone like the sun, and His garments became as white as light.** The Jesus who had been living for over thirty years in ordinary human form was now partially seen in the blazing effulgence of God (cf. Heb. 1:1-3). From within Himself, in a way that defies full description, much less full explanation, Jesus' divine glory was manifested **before** Peter, James, and John.

Here is the greatest confirmation of His deity yet in the life of Jesus. Here, more than on any other occasion, Jesus revealed Himself as He truly is, the Son of God. As the divine glory radiated from **His face,** it illumined even **His garments,** which **became as white as light,** in supernatural testimony to His spiritual splendor. As with the Shekinah manifestations of the Old Testament, God here portrayed Himself to human eyes in a form of **light** so dazzling and overwhelming that it could barely be withstood.

The **light** portrayed Jesus' glory and majesty, as Peter testified years later in his second epistle: "For when He received honor and glory from the Father, such an utterance as this was made to Him by the Majestic Glory, 'This is My beloved Son with whom I am well-pleased'" (2 Pet. 1:17). The experience of seeing Christ's glory must have been a major contributor to the second coming's becoming a dominant theme of Peter's preaching and writing. The message of his two epistles might be summarized as: "Fellow believers, don't worry about your pain, your hardship, your testing, your persecution, your sacrifice. Jesus is coming! That's all that really matters." John later testified that "we beheld His glory, glory as of the only begotten from the Father, full of grace and truth" (John 1:14). We have no record of James's testimony to this event, because he was martyred in the very early days of the church, the first apostle to give his life for Christ (Acts 12:2; cf. Mark 10:39). As best they could with human eyes, these three men had seen the essence of God shine forth from Jesus.

That awesome experience was but a foretaste of the day in which "the Son of Man is going to come in the glory of His Father with His angels" (Matt. 16:27). On that day, "all the tribes of the earth will mourn, and they will see the Son of Man coming on the clouds of the sky with power and great glory" (Matt. 24:30). And "when the Son of Man comes in His glory, and all the angels with Him, then He will sit on His glorious throne" (25:31). In his vision on Patmos, John saw the returning Christ as "one like a son of man, clothed in a robe reaching to the feet, and girded across His breast with a golden girdle. And His head and His hair were white like white wool, like snow; and His eyes were like a flame of fire; and His feet were like burnished bronze, when it has been caused to glow in a furnace, and His voice was like the sound of many waters. And in His right hand He held seven stars; and out of His mouth came a sharp two-edged sword; and His face was like the sun shining in its strength" (Rev. 1:13-16).

In His human form Jesus Christ was veiled, but when He comes again to earth He will come in His full divine majesty and glory, a glimpse of which Peter, James, and John witnessed on the mountain. There could henceforth be no doubt in their minds that He was God incarnate, and there should have been no doubt that He would come some day in the fullness of glory.

The Testimony of the Saints

And behold, Moses and Elijah appeared to them, talking with Him. And Peter answered and said to Jesus, "Lord, it is good for us to be here; if You wish, I will make three tabernacles here, one for You, and one for Moses, and one for Elijah." (17:3-4)

As the three disciples watched in amazement, **Moses and Elijah** also **appeared to them,** shrouded in the Lord's glory (Luke 9:31). The testimony of those two Old Testament saints was a second confirmation of Jesus' deity.

Why, we may wonder, were these two men chosen out of the many godly Old Testament believers who might have been chosen? Why, for instance, did God not present Abraham, the father of the Hebrew people and of all the faithful? Why was not David selected, the one from whose throne Jesus would one day reign? Why was Isaiah or Jeremiah or Ezekiel or one of the other prophets not chosen? Scripture gives no explanation, but it seems that, more than any others, Moses and Elijah typified the Old Testament man of God.

Moses was synonymous with the Old Covenant, which the Lord gave through him. The Jewish Scriptures were often referred to as Moses and the prophets, and the Old Testament law was often called the law of Moses. Reared in the court of Pharaoh, exiled to the fields and flocks of Midian to learn humility and become a servant of God, and then chosen by the Lord to lead His people out of bondage and to give them His law and lead them to the borders of the Promised Land, **Moses** was supremely God's man. Besides the Lord Himself, he was arguably the greatest leader in human history. He led an estimated two million rebellious, faithless people out of Egypt and into the wilderness, where they wandered together for forty years while God raised up a more obedient and manageable generation. Before the people of Israel had formal prophets, Moses was a kind of prophet, bringing them God's word. Before they had formal priests, he was a kind of priest, mediating between them and God. And before they had formal kings, he was a kind of king, ruling them in God's name.

Perhaps the only other Old Testament man who could have stood with Moses was **Elijah.** Moses was the great law giver, and Elijah was the great defender of the law. This prophet was zeal personified, a godly man of unmatched courage, boldness, and fearlessness. He had a heart for God, he walked with God, and, more than any other Old Testament saint, he was the instrument of God's miracle-working power. He was the preeminent prophet of God, and to the Jews the most romantic Old Testament personality.

As no others, **Moses and Elijah** represented the Old Testament, the law and the prophets. And as no others, they could give human testimony to Christ's divine majesty and glory. By their presence together, they affirmed, in effect: "This is the One of whom we testified, the One in whose power we ministered, and the One in whom everything we said and did has meaning. Everything we spoke, accomplished, and hoped for is fulfilled in Him."

From Luke we learn that these two great saints were talking with Jesus "of His departure which He was about to accomplish at Jerusalem" (9:31). They were not simply standing there, passively reflecting on the Lord's glory, but were talking with Him as friend to Friend about His departure, His imminent sacrifice, which was the supreme objective and work of His earthly ministry. "Departure" is from the Greek term from which we get *exodus.* Just as the Exodus out of Egypt under Moses led God's people out of the bondage of slavery, the "exodus" of Jesus out of the grave would lead believers out of the bondage of sin. This would be accomplished, as Luke reports, at Jerusalem.

It was significant that the discussion was about Christ's saving work through His death, because that was the central work of His ministry, yet the truth the disciples found most difficult to accept. **Moses and Elijah** not only gave confirmation of Jesus' divine glory but of His divine plan. Their supernatural testimony no doubt later gave the apostles added conviction and courage as they proclaimed that Jesus was "delivered up by the predetermined plan and foreknowledge of God" (Acts 2:23). "Jesus is the predicted Savior and King," they were affirming before the three apostles, "and His divine plan is on schedule."

Jesus' death and resurrection were an inescapable part of that plan, without which redemption from sin would have been impossible. He was infinitely more than a good man whose example shows other men the way to God. He Himself was God, and it was by His atoning sacrifice as a substitute for men that He Himself brings those who trust in Him to God. No man can come to God by following Jesus' example, because no man could offer a sufficient sacrifice even for his own sins, much less for the sins of the whole world. It was therefore imperative for the disciples to understand that Jesus' coming the first time to die and rise again was as much a part of the divine plan as His coming again in glory.

As Moses and Elijah "were parting from Him" (Luke 9:33a), **Peter answered and said to Jesus, "Lord, it is good for us to be here; if You wish, I will make three tabernacles here, one for You, and one for Moses, and one for Elijah."**

Luke gives the additional information that **Peter** spoke "not realizing what he was saying" (9:33b). Peter completely failed to comprehend the significance of Jesus' glory or of Moses' and Elijah's testimony. Seemingly oblivious to the affirmation that Jesus must go to Jerusalem to die and that the glory they now witnessed was but a preview of the full glory in which He would in the future come again, in his combined bewilderment and fear Peter could think of nothing but making **three tabernacles** with his own hands in which Jesus and the two Old Testament witnesses could dwell.

We can only guess at Peter's motive for making the suggestion, except that he obviously was content to remain with the Lord on the mountain top. He had no interest in Jesus' going to Jerusalem or in His coming again. He wanted the Lord to stay, not leave and return. He especially did not want Him to leave by way of death (Matt. 16:22). As usual, he was caught up in his own plans and will rather than the Lord's. Although he prefaced his suggestion with **if You wish**, Peter probably assumed Jesus would approve.

New Testament chronologists have determined that the Jewish month in which the transfiguration took place was Tishri (October), the sixth month before Passover and therefore six months before Jesus' crucifixion. During this month the Jews celebrated the feast of Tabernacles, or Booths, and it is possible that at this very time the feast was being observed In Jerusalem. During a period of seven days the people lived in small shelters, or booths, made of boughs, symbolizing the temporary dwellings of their forefathers in the wilderness. It was a memorial to God's preserving His chosen and redeemed people (see Lev. 23:33-44).

Zechariah predicted that during the Millennium, when "the Lord will be king over all the earth; in that day the Lord will be the only one, and His name the only one. Then it will come about that any who are left of all the nations that went against Jerusalem will go up from year to year to worship the King, the Lord of hosts, and to celebrate the Feast of Booths" (Zech. 14:9, 16). That is the only week-long Old Testament festival that will be celebrated during the millennial reign of Christ. The feast of Tabernacles will be remembered every year for a thousand years as a picture of God's deliverance and preservation of His people.

The feast's being close at hand may therefore have caused Peter to suggest building the **three tabernacles** on the mountain. That possibility is even more likely in light of the fact that this festival commemorated the Exodus from slavery in Egypt and the wilderness wanderings of Israel under Moses. As noted above, Moses and Elijah were talking with Jesus "of His departure," or exodus (Luke 9:31), the soon-coming and infinitely greater deliverance of believing mankind from sin. How appropriate then, Peter may have thought, to celebrate the feast in that sacred place, not only in the presence of Moses himself but in the presence of the even greater Deliverer whom Moses foreshadowed and of whom Elijah was to be the forerunner.

Peter's idea was not so much wrong as foolish. He was foolish in perhaps thinking that Jesus might not have to die after all, that there was now opportunity to fulfill His mission by avoiding the cross and therefore avoiding the need of later returning. Peter was also foolish in placing Moses and Elijah, great as they were, on the same level as Christ by wanting to build **tabernacles** for all three of them. As previously noted, when Peter made this suggestion, Moses and Elijah were already departing (Luke 9:33). They knew their mission was temporary and their testimony to Christ was now completed. In their ministries they had merely proclaimed the word of the law and the prophets. But Jesus Christ, the living Word, was both the giver and the perfect fulfillment of the law and prophets, whose purpose was to point men to Himself (see Rom. 8:3; 10:4; Gal. 3:24). Leaving Christ in unchallenged supremacy, Moses and Elijah faded away so that the sole remaining object of adoration was the glorious Lord Himself. Once their testimony to Him was finished, they would not stay and risk detracting from Him.

THE TERROR OF THE FATHER

While he was still speaking, behold, a bright cloud overshadowed them; and behold, a voice out of the cloud, saying, "This is My beloved Son, with whom I am well-pleased; listen to Him!" And when the disciples heard this, they fell on their faces and were much afraid. (17:5-6)

A third confirmation of Jesus' deity was the terror caused by the intervention of the Father while Peter **was still speaking.** Through the form of **a bright cloud** God **overshadowed** the three disciples and spoke to them in **a voice out of the cloud.** To the testimony of the transfiguration itself and the testimony of the two Old Testament saints was now added the surprising testimony of God the Father.

Throughout the wilderness wanderings of Israel the Lord manifested Himself through "a pillar of cloud by day to lead them on the way" (Ex. 13:21; Num. 9:17; Deut. 1:33). Isaiah predicted that "when the Lord has washed away the filth of the daughters of Zion, and purged the bloodshed of Jerusalem from her midst, by the spirit of judgment and the spirit of burning, then the Lord will create over the whole area of Mount Zion and over her assemblies a cloud by day, even smoke, and the brightness of a flaming fire by night; for over all the glory will be a canopy" (Isa. 4:4-5). In his vision of the last days John "looked and behold, a white cloud, and sitting on the cloud was one like a son of man, having a golden crown on His head, and a sharp sickle in His hand. And another angel came out of the temple, crying out with a loud voice to Him who sat on the cloud, 'Put in your sickle and reap, because the hour to reap has come, because the harvest of the earth is ripe.' And He who sat on the cloud swung His sickle over the earth; and the earth was reaped" (Rev. 14:14-16).

Out of such **a bright cloud** the Father **overshadowed** Peter, James, and John, and spoke to them in an audible **voice, . . . saying, "This is My beloved Son, with whom I am well-pleased; listen to Him!"** The Father spoke almost identical words at Jesus' baptism (Matt. 3:17), and during Jesus' last week in Jerusalem—but a few days before His betrayal, arrest, and crucifixion—the Father again publicly and directly declared His approval of the Son (John 12:28).

In calling Jesus His **Son,** the Father declared Him to be of identical nature and essence with Himself (cf. John 5:17-20; 8:19, 42; 10:30, 36-38). Scripture frequently refers to believers as children of God, but they are adopted children, brought into the heavenly family only through the miracle of His grace (Rom. 8:15, 23; Gal. 4:5; Eph. 1:5). Jesus is the essence of divine nature, as the apostles repeatedly emphasize (see Rom. 1:1-4; 2 Cor. 1:3; Gal. 1:3; Eph. 1:3; Col. 1:3; 1 Pet. 1:3; 1 John 1:3; 2 John 3).

In calling Jesus His **beloved Son**, the Father declared not only a relationship of divine nature but a relationship of divine love. They had a relationship of mutual love, commitment, and identification in every way.

In saying, **"with whom I am well-pleased,"** the Father declared His approval with everything the **Son** was, said, and did. Everything about Jesus was in perfect accord with the Father's will and plan. Compare John 5:19; 8:29; 10:37-38; 12:49-50.

Then, directly addressing the three disciples, perhaps Peter in particular, God said, **"Listen to Him!"** He was saying, in effect, "If My Son tells you He must go to Jerusalem to suffer and die, believe Him. If He tells you He will be raised up on the third day, believe Him. If He tells you to take up your own cross and follow Him, that is what you are to do. If He says He will come again in glory, then believe Him and live accordingly."

The outspoken, brash Peter and his two companions now knew they stood in the awesome presence of Almighty God. As would be expected, **when the disciples heard this, they fell on their faces and were much afraid.** Peter was probably so utterly traumatized that he promptly forgot about his presumptuous suggestion to build the three tabernacles.

The combined awareness of the Lord's grace and His majesty, His love and His justice, His friendship and His lordship should cause a kind of spiritual tension in every believer. On the one hand he rejoices in his loving fellowship with the Lord because of His gracious kindness, and on the other hand he has reverential fear as he contemplates His awesome holiness and righteousness. As the believer walks in obedience to God, he experiences the comfort of His presence. But as he walks in disobedience, he should feel the terror of that same presence. Proverbs declares that spiritual wisdom begins with the fear of God (Prov. 9:10).

Sinful men in the presence of a holy God always want to hide. Before the Fall, Adam and Eve had uninterrupted fellowship with God, but after they sinned the relationship was vastly changed. When "they heard the sound of the Lord God walking in the garden in the cool of the day, . . . the man and his wife hid themselves from the presence of the Lord God among the trees of the garden" (Gen. 3:8). When Isaiah beheld the divine majesty and glory that surrounded the heavenly throne, he cried out in great fear, "Woe is me, for I am ruined! Because I am a man of unclean lips, and I live among a people of unclean lips; for my eyes have seen the King, the Lord of hosts" (Isa. 6:5). As he stood in the presence of perfect holiness, the sense of his own utter sinfulness overwhelmed him. Daniel was likewise terrified when the Lord spoke directly to him after his vision of the ram, goat, and little horn (Dan. 8:15-17).

THE TAPESTRY OF THE SCENE

And Jesus came to them and touched them and said, "Arise, and do not be afraid." And lifting up their eyes, they saw no one, except Jesus Himself alone.

And as they were coming down from the mountain, Jesus commanded them, saying, "Tell the vision to no one until the Son of Man has risen from the dead." (17:7-9)

The fourth confirmation of Jesus' deity was the entire tapestry of the scene that gave testimony to Christ's majestic power and royal splendor. It was less specific and dramatic than the first three, but in its own way was impressive.

Jesus was still the center of the scene, just as He will be at His second coming. He was standing on a high mountain, much as when He returns to earth, when "His feet will stand on the Mount of Olives, which is in front of Jerusalem on the east" (Zech. 14:4). When He comes, He will come *with* His saints (1 Thess. 3:13; Jude 14), just as here He is accompanied by Moses and Elijah, saints of the Old Covenant. And when He comes, He will also come *to* His saints (2 Thess. 1:10; Rev. 21:3-7), ministering to His own people, just as now He ministered to Peter, James, and John.

Another interesting aspect of the scene is the fact that, whereas Moses died, Elijah did not, having been carried to heaven by a whirlwind (2 Kings 2:11). Moses therefore represented the saints who will have died by the time Jesus returns, and Elijah those who will have been raptured.

Symbolically, the mountain is there. The people with whom He comes are there. The people to whom He comes are there. And both the saints who have died and the saints who have been translated are there.

Jesus' first actions and words after His mighty display of splendor were those of gentle, loving care. Knowing the great fear of His three beloved companions, **Jesus came to them and touched them and said, "Arise, and do not be afraid."** As they hesitatingly lifted **up their eyes**, it must have been a great relief to see **no one, except Jesus Himself alone.**

The impressions of the experience were now indelibly inscribed in their minds. They could testify with certainty and boldness that Jesus had indeed manifested Himself in glory before some of them had tasted death (16:28). Some thirty years later, Peter would write, "We did not follow cleverly devised tales when we made known to you the power and coming of our Lord Jesus Christ, but we were eyewitnesses of His majesty. For when He received honor and glory from God the Father, such an utterance as this was made to Him by the Majestic Glory, 'This is My beloved Son with whom I am well-pleased'—and we ourselves heard this utterance made from heaven when we were with Him on the holy mountain" (2 Pet. 1:16-18).

As they saw **Jesus . . . alone,** the disciples realized they had witnessed a preview of the Lord's second coming glory. And once they regained their composure, they must have had a strong and understandable desire to run down and report their astounding experience to the other disciples and to anyone else who would listen. But **as they were coming down from the mountain, Jesus commanded them, saying, "Tell the vision to no one until the Son of Man has risen from the dead."** How extremely difficult it must have been to keep **the vision** to themselves.

Just as Jesus had told the Twelve that "they should tell no one that He was the Christ" (16:20), He now told the three to tell no one of His manifestation of glory. The Christ that most Jews of that day were expecting was not the Christ who had come. Instead of coming to conquer, He had come to die. Instead of coming in divine glory, He came in humble meekness. And instead of coming to deliver the Jews from political bondage, He came to deliver from sin's bondage all men who would trust in Him.

For the people to have learned then about the experience on the mount would, as already mentioned, only have incited them to try as they did on other occasions (John 6:15; 12:12-19) to make Jesus into a king of their own kind to fulfill their immediate selfish and worldly expectations. But when they would hear the story after **the Son of Man** had **risen from the dead,** it would be clear that He had not come to conquer the Romans but to conquer death.

THE TIE WITH THE FORERUNNER

And His disciples asked Him, saying, "Why then do the scribes say that Elijah must come first?" And He answered and said, "Elijah is coming and will restore all things; but I say to you, that Elijah already came, and they did not recognize him, but did to him whatever they wished. So also the Son of Man is going to suffer at their hands." Then the disciples understood that He had spoken to them about John the Baptist. (17:10-13)

The fifth and final confirmation of Jesus' deity is seen in His messianic relationship to John the Baptist.

Having just seen Elijah on the mountain, a natural question for Jesus' **disciples** was, **"Why then do the scribes say that Elijah must come first?"** That particular teaching of **the scribes** was not based simply on rabbinical tradition but on scriptural teaching. Through Malachi the Lord declared, "Behold, I am going to send you Elijah the prophet before the coming of the great and terrible day of the Lord. And he will restore the hearts of the fathers to their children, and the hearts of the children to their fathers, lest I come and smite the land with a curse" (Mal. 4:5-6).

The prediction that the actual Old Testament person of Elijah would be the forerunner of the Messiah and His judgment was well-known to Jews of Jesus' day. Therefore, as Peter, James, and John came down the mountainside with the Lord, they could not have helped wondering how the appearance of Elijah they had just witnessed fit in with Malachi's prophecy. "If You are the Messiah, as you have declared and we have believed," they asked, in effect, "why did Elijah not appear *before* You began Your ministry?"

It was doubtlessly that same concern that many of the Jewish leaders used to justify rejecting Jesus' messiahship. And it was probably Malachi's prophecy that caused some people to think that Jesus was Elijah rather than the Messiah (Matt. 16:14). "Despite His great miracles," they may have reasoned, "Jesus cannot be the Messiah, because Elijah has not yet come. So He must Himself be Elijah."

That misunderstanding was made easier by the many embellishments that **the scribes** and their fellow rabbis had made to the prophecy of Malachi. Like many Bible interpreters throughout the ages, including many in our own day, they liked to "fill in the blanks," as it were, where a Bible prediction was not as clear and detailed as they would have liked. Consequently, they taught that Elijah would come again as a mighty miracle-working reformer who would bring order out of chaos and holiness out of unholiness. They maintained that when the Messiah arrived, the world, or at least Israel, would be morally and spiritually prepared for Him, and He would execute swift judgment and establish the kingdom for Israel.

Like all teaching that is only partly based on Scripture, theirs was, for that reason, all the more misleading. Jesus responded by first acknowledging the partial truth, saying, **"Elijah is coming and will restore all things."** There is an **Elijah** who is yet to come; and when he arrives, he **will restore all things,** just as Malachi prophesied. **"But I say to you,"** Jesus went on to explain, **"that Elijah already came, and they did not recognize him, but did to him whatever they wished. So also the Son of Man is going to suffer at their hands."** Then the disciples understood that He had spoken to them about John the Baptist.

The Elijah prophesied by Malachi was not to be a reincarnation of the ancient prophet. Rather, as the angel of the Lord told Zacharias regarding his son, **John the Baptist,** the prophesied forerunner would come "in the spirit and power of Elijah" (Luke 1:17). **John** would not be the ancient prophet come back to earth but would minister in much the same style and power as had Elijah. In that way, as Jesus had told the disciples at least once before, "[John] is Elijah, who was to come" (Matt. 11:14).

Why then, some wonder, did **John** himself disclaim being Elijah? When the priests and Levites from Jerusalem asked him, "'Are you Elijah?' . . . he said, 'I am not'" (John 1:21). He denied being Elijah because, though he knew of the prophecy of Luke 1, like Jesus, he realized the question was about a literal, reincarnated Elijah. And, though John did not share Jesus' omniscience, he doubtlessly also realized that the questioning of the priests and Levites originated from unbelief, not sincere faith. They were not interested in learning the truth but of finding a way to discredit John, just as they would later seek ways to discredit the One whose way he came to prepare.

The Jewish leaders' false motives and ungodliness became even more evident when **they did not recognize** John as the prophesied Elijah **but did to him whatever they wished.** They imprisoned and beheaded him. Therefore, whatever John's answer to the Jerusalem priests and Levites might have been, they would ultimately have rejected him because they hated John, and their hearts were opposed to God and His truth. Those who reject God inevitably reject His messengers.

The full wickedness of the Jewish leaders was manifested, however, when they rejected and persecuted **the Son of Man** Himself, who soon would **suffer at their hands.** Because they rejected the restoration work of Messiah's Elijah-like precursor and then rejected the Messiah Himself, the messianic kingdom was postponed.

In the last days, the Lord will send still another like Elijah, and the Messiah Himself will return, this time to establish His eternal kingdom in power, righteousness, and glory.

The Power of Faith
(17:14-21)

And when they came to the multitude, a man came up to Him, falling on his knees before Him, and saying, "Lord, have mercy on my son, for he is a lunatic, and is very ill; for he often falls into the fire, and often into the water. And I brought him to Your disciples, and they could not cure him." And Jesus answered and said, "O unbelieving and perverted generation, how long shall I be with you? How long shall I put up with you? Bring him here to Me." And Jesus rebuked him, and the demon came out of him, and the boy was cured at once.

Then the disciples came to Jesus privately and said, "Why could we not cast it out?" And He said to them, "Because of the littleness of your faith; for truly I say to you, if you have faith as a mustard seed, you shall say to this mountain, 'Move from here to there,' and it shall move; and nothing shall be impossible to you. [But this kind does not go out except by prayer and fasting.]" (17:14-21)

Matthew 17:14 marks the beginning of a special period of instruction by Jesus to the Twelve that continues through chapter 20. Having given them a revelation of His person as King and of His program for the kingdom, He now gives them further principles for living in the kingdom. The first is the foundational principle of faith. Just as spiritual life must be received by faith, so also it is to be lived by faith.

Scripture gives continual testimony to the power of faith in God in the lives of believers. It was faith in God's power that caused young Caleb to look at the land of Canaan with its giants and report to Moses, "We should by all means go up and take possession of it, for we shall surely overcome it" (Num. 13:30). It was faith in God's care that enabled Job to say of Him in the midst of personal disaster, "Though He slay me, I will hope in Him" (Job 13:15). It was faith in God's protection that enabled Shadrach, Meshach, and Abednego to stand at the edge of the fiery furnace and declare to King Nebuchadnezzar, "Our God whom we serve is able to deliver us from the furnace of blazing fire; and He will deliver us out of your hand, O king. But even if He does not, let it be known to you, O king, that we are not going to serve your gods or worship the golden image that you have set up" (Dan. 3:17-18). It was faith in God's protection that enabled Daniel to continue faithfully worshiping God, even though it meant being thrown into the lion's den (Dan. 6:10). It was faith in Jesus to forgive her sins that brought spiritual deliverance to the woman who entered the Pharisee's house and washed Jesus' feet with her tears and dried them with her hair (Luke 7:37-50).

From Hebrews 11 we learn that "by faith Abel offered to God a better sacrifice than Cain" (v. 4), that "by faith Enoch was taken up so that he should not see death" (v. 5), that "by faith Noah . . . prepared an ark . . . and became an heir of the righteousness which is according to faith" (v.7), and that "by faith Abraham, when he was called, obeyed, . . . went out, . . . [and] lived as an alien in the land of promise, . . . for he was looking for the city which has foundations, whose architect and builder is God" (vv. 8-10). The rest of that chapter names a host of other Old Testament saints who "gained approval through their faith" (v. 39). In view of "so great a cloud of witnesses surrounding us," the writer continues, "let us also lay aside every encumbrance, and the sin which so easily entangles us, and let us run with endurance the race that is set before us, fixing our eyes on Jesus, the author and perfecter of faith" (12:1-2).

It is not surprising, therefore, that the first lesson Jesus taught the disciples after He returned from the mount of transfiguration was a lesson about faith. Peter, James, and John had just had a glimpse of the power and majesty of the Lord Jesus Christ (Matt. 17:2), which Paul may have been referring to when he spoke of "the glory of God in the face of Christ" (2 Cor. 4:6). But now the disciples were brought face to face with their own *lack* of power, which was due directly, Jesus told them, to their lack of faith.

For this lesson, the scene shifts dramatically from the mountain of glory to the valley of despair. From the dazzling majesty of the unveiled Christ in the presence of Moses, Elijah, and God the Father, in a glorious preview of the Lord's second coming, Jesus and the three disciples descended into the reality of the sin-cursed world at its worst.

The Lord used the first tragic situation He encountered after the transfiguration as a living illustration of a principle He wanted to teach. Within this story can be seen four key elements: the pleading of the father (Matt. 17:14-15), the powerlessness of the followers (v. 16), the perversion of the faithless (vv. 17-18), and the power of faith (vv. 19-21).

THE PLEADING OF THE FATHER

And when they came to the multitude, a man came up to Him, falling on his knees before Him, and saying, "Lord, have mercy on my son, for he is a lunatic, and is very ill; for he often falls into the fire, and often into the water. (17:14-15)

From the second gospel we learn that **the multitude** included some scribes, the Jewish legal experts, who were arguing with the nine disciples who had remained below, and that as soon as the crowd saw Jesus coming, "they were amazed, and began running up to greet Him" (Mark 9:14-15).

From somewhere within **the multitude, a man came up to** Jesus, and fell **on his knees before Him.** From that posture of humility and reverence, the man said, **"Lord, have mercy on my son, for he is a lunatic, and is very ill; for he often falls into the fire, and often into the water."** We do not know how much the father meant by calling Jesus **Lord,** but at the least he recognized Him as a man of God who was endowed with divine power to heal. He fully believed that Jesus could bring sanity and wholeness to his **son,** his "only boy" (Luke 9:38), who had had this terrible affliction since childhood (Mark 9:21). Though the father may not have realized it at the time, he was about to bring *his* only beloved **son** into the presence of *God's* only beloved Son.

Have mercy translates the aorist imperative of *eleeō*, which means to demonstrate sympathy and compassion. In his deep anguish, the father pleaded with Jesus to have compassion on his **son** and restore him to health.

Like the Greek term it translates, **lunatic** literally refers to something related to the moon (lunar). It is the idea seen in the word *moonstruck*, an expression based on the ancient belief that mental illness or madness was caused by the influence of the moon. The Greek word was used to describe what we now understand to be various nervous disorders, including epilepsy, that cause convulsions.

This particular boy was **very ill**, indicating that his condition was unusually serious. It was so severe, the father explained, that **he often falls into the fire, and often into the water.** Open fires were common, as were many open bodies of water, such as pools or wells. Because the boy had actually fallen **into the fire** many times, he must have carried burn scars that added to his unattractiveness and probable ostracism. He was also in constant danger of drowning by falling **into the water.** The father or some other member of the family probably had to stay near the boy at all times, never knowing when a seizure might occur.

The father sensed what Jesus verified, that the boy's affliction was not simply physiological or mental but demonic. When he brought him to Jesus, he described his son as being "possessed with a spirit which makes him mute" (Mark 9:17). In addition to having seizures, the boy was unable to speak and was apparently deaf as well (see v. 25). The demon was exceptionally violent. Whenever the "spirit seizes him," the father said, "he suddenly screams, and it throws him into a convulsion with foaming at the mouth, and as it mauls him, it scarcely leaves him" (Luke 9:39).

Every unsaved person is subject to the control of Satan, "the prince of the power of the air" (Eph. 2:2), and the more a person willfully sins and rejects God, the more he leaves himself open to Satan's influence. But there is no indication that this boy's demonic affliction was due to any unusual moral or spiritual wrongdoing on his part or on the part of his parents. For his own reasons, Satan caused the demon to torment this particular child.

THE POWERLESSNESS OF THE FOLLOWERS

And I brought him to Your disciples, and they could not cure him." (17:16)

While Jesus had been on the mountain with Peter, James, and John, the man had **brought** his demon-possessed boy to the other **disciples** for healing, but **they could not cure him.**

In light of their previous commissioning, empowering, and experience, it seems strange that the **disciples** now failed where once they had succeeded. About a year earlier, Jesus had sent the Twelve out to minister "to the lost sheep of the house of Israel. And as you go," He said, "preach, saying, 'The kingdom of heaven is at hand.' Heal the sick, raise the dead, cleanse the lepers, cast out demons" (Matt. 10:6-8; cf. Mark 3:15). Perhaps to their own surprise, the disciples were highly successful "in casting out many demons and were anointing with oil many sick people and healing them" (Mark 6:13).

What had gone wrong or changed? Their failure now was not due to the fact that Jesus was not with them, because He was not with them on those earlier occasions, either. They still had Jesus' promise and His power, yet **they could not cure** the boy. The explanation for their failure is therefore obvious. They failed to appropriate the power available to them.

With increasing frustration and anguish, the father understandably despaired of help from the disciples and turned to Jesus Himself.

Throughout the history of the church, the faithlessness, weakness, and indifference of Christians has caused many seeking unbelievers to despair of help from God's people. Sometimes, like the father in this story, they turn to the Lord Himself.

THE PERVERSION OF THE FAITHLESS

And Jesus answered and said, "O unbelieving and perverted generation, how long shall I be with you? How long shall I put up with you? Bring him

here to Me." And Jesus rebuked him, and the demon came out of him, and the boy was cured at once. (17:17-18)

The disciples' faithless impotence not only grieved the boy's father but Jesus as well. Speaking to the disciples and to the multitude rather than to the man who had just confronted Him, **Jesus answered and said, "O unbelieving and perverted generation, how long shall I be with you? How long shall I put up with you?"**

Here Jesus gives a rare glimpse into the depths of His divine heart and soul. Having been accustomed from eternity past to having the angels instantly do His bidding, He was grieved at the blindness and faithlessness of God's people Israel, especially His disciples, whom He had personally chosen, taught, and endowed with unique power and authority.

The entire **generation** of Jews was faithless, represented on this occasion by the multitude, the disciples, and the self-righteous scribes who were there to entrap and discredit the Lord if they could. Even the father's faith was not complete, as he himself confessed: "I do believe; help my unbelief" (Mark 9:24).

The people not only were **unbelieving** but **perverted. Perverted** is from *diastrephō,* which has the basic idea of twisting or bending out of shape. The term was frequently used to describe a piece of pottery that a careless craftsman had misshaped or that had somehow become distorted before being fired in the oven.

Although many of His listeners doubtlessly were also morally **perverted,** Jesus was here speaking primarily of the spiritual perversion that is inevitable in those who are **unbelieving.** Any person who does not genuinely trust God cannot escape having a distorted view of Him and His will.

"How long shall I be with You? How long shall I put up with you?" the Lord said, perhaps as much to Himself as to them. No doubt He was becoming increasingly anxious to return to His heavenly Father, with whom He had just experienced a unique time of fellowship on the mountain. In His humanness, He must have been tempted to doubt whether His soon-coming suffering and death would be worthwhile. "If they do not trust You while You are with them," Satan may have whispered in Jesus' ear, "how do You expect them to trust You after You have returned to heaven?"

The thrill-seeking crowds followed Jesus for the personal benefit of His healing and out of curiosity. The gloating Jewish leaders followed Him in order to convict Him of a capital crime. And although the disciples knew He was the promised Christ (Matt. 16:16), they were frequently confused about the meaning of His teaching and work.

But Jesus would not vary from His divine mission nor succumb to Satan's temptation to despair. He was on earth to do His Father's business, from which nothing would deter Him. He therefore said to the father, **"Bring him here to Me."**

When **Jesus rebuked him, . . . the demon** had no choice but to come **out of him.** But before he departed, the evil spirit made a last attempt to destroy the boy, "crying out and throwing him into terrible convulsions; . . . and the boy became so much like a corpse that most of them said, 'He is dead!'" (Mark 9:26; cf. Luke 9:42).

The demon knew his efforts were hopeless, because, like the demon who tormented the man of Gadara (Mark 5:7) and the one who attacked the seven sons of Sceva (Acts 19:15), he recognized the divine identity of Jesus. He was compelled to obey the Son of God.

As soon as the demon was gone, **the boy was cured at once.** While the child was still in the death-like stupor in which the demon left him, "Jesus took him by the hand and raised him; and he got up" (Mark 9:27). He could now play like other boys, with no fear of suddenly being thrown into a fire to be burned or into water to be drowned. He would have no more seizures, no more foaming at the mouth or grinding of his teeth.

Although Jesus already had successfully cast out countless demons (see Matt. 4:24; 8:16, 32; 9:33; 12:22), Luke reports that on this occasion, the crowds "were all amazed at the greatness of God" (Luke 9:43). "Greatness" is from *megaleiotēs,* which refers to great splendor or magnificence. It is the word used by Peter to describe the divine majesty of which he, James, and John were eyewitnesses at the transfiguration. It was perhaps with that glory in mind that Luke here used the term to describe the crowd's amazement. Unknowingly, they, too, had had a small glimpse of the kind of majesty and splendor the Lord would reveal at His second coming.

THE POWER OF FAITH

Then the disciples came to Jesus privately and said, "Why could we not cast it out?" And He said to them, "Because of the littleness of your faith; for truly I say to you, if you have faith as a mustard seed, you shall say to this mountain, 'Move from here to there,' and it shall move; and nothing shall be impossible to you. [But this kind does not go out except by prayer and fasting.]" (17:19-21)

Jesus' purpose in the miracle went beyond the healing of the demonized boy, important as that was. The healing not only brought health to the boy and great joy to his father, but glory to God. But for **the disciples** the important lesson of that event was yet to be learned.

It is not surprising that they questioned **Jesus privately**—in a house, Mark tells us (9:28), perhaps the home of one of the disciples. They were embarrassed at their own failure and were perplexed as to **why** they themselves **could . . . not cast it out.** Why was He able to accomplish with a word what they had not been able to accomplish with great effort? "You commissioned and empowered us to heal and to cast out demons," they said, in effect. "And we have been successful before. Why did we fail this time?" They probably went about the act of casting out the demon in the same way they had on earlier occasions. They probably invoked the

Lord's name, commanded the demon to leave, and awaited his departure. But this time nothing happened.

"The reason should be obvious," Jesus implied. "You failed **because of the littleness of your faith.**" It was not because of total lack of faith but **because of . . . littleness of . . . faith** that they were powerless. They had saving faith, which they could not lose. And they had trusting faith to some degree, or they would not have attempted to heal the boy. But they lacked sufficient faith to employ the power Jesus had given to them.

Having **littleness of . . . faith** was a somewhat typical condition of the disciples. Soon after Jesus called them into His service, they sat among the crowd on the mountainside whom He charged with being anxious because of their little faith in God to provide for their physical needs (Matt. 6:25-34). When during the fierce storm on the Sea of Galilee they despaired of their lives, Jesus rebuked them before He rebuked the waves, saying "Why are you timid, you men of little faith?" (8:26). When Peter started to walk on the water but became afraid and began sinking, "Jesus stretched out His hand and took hold of him, and said to him, 'O you of little faith, why did you doubt?'" (14:31). Shortly before healing the demonized boy, Jesus had again charged the disciples with having little faith in not expecting Him to be able to feed the multitude near Magadan (16:8).

Those incidents illustrate that little faith is the kind of faith that believes in God when you have something in your hand, when His provision is already made. When things were going well with the disciples and everything seemed under control, they found it easy to trust their Lord. But as soon as circumstances became uncertain or threatening, their faith withered. Their faith was like the faith of most believers in all ages. When they are healthy and have the necessities of life, their faith is great and strong, but when they are in need, their faith is small and gives way to doubt.

Great faith trusts God when there is nothing in the cupboard to eat and no money to buy food. Great faith trusts in God when health is gone, work is gone, reputation is gone, or family is gone. Great faith trusts God while the windstorm is still howling and persecution continues.

The Lord was giving the disciples a sample of what their lives would be like once He had returned to heaven, when they could no longer see Him or touch Him or talk with Him in the way they were used to doing. He was also teaching them persistence. We do not know how often they tried to cast the demon out of the boy, but at some point they gave up. When Jesus first sent the disciples out, their success at healing and casting out demons was immediate. But Jesus had not promised that that would always be the case. The Twelve had to learn that, unlike the Lord's power, theirs was not inherent in themselves. It came only from Him, by His divine provision and will.

It is encouraging to realize that even the apostles, with their unique calling and miraculous gifts, always had to rely on Jesus to minister effectively. To strengthen their faith and sense of dependence, the Lord sometimes made them wait—just as He often does with believers today. To help strengthen our faith, He may sometimes make us wait a long time for an answer to prayer. Just as an athlete grows stronger by gradually lifting heavier weights or by running longer distances, so a believer grows stronger in faith by facing ever-increasing challenges that expose his own weakness and drive him to the Lord.

Continuing the lesson on faith, Jesus said, **"For truly I say to you, if you have faith as a mustard seed, you shall say to this mountain, 'Move from here to there,' and it shall move; and nothing shall be impossible to you."**

Jesus seems to contradict Himself, first rebuking the disciples for having small faith and then telling them that even the smallest faith can move mountains. But as He made clear in the parable of the mustard seed, the seed does not represent littleness as such but rather littleness that grows into greatness. "When it is full grown," He explained, "it is larger than the garden plants, and becomes a tree" (Matt. 13:32). Small faith can accomplish great things only if, like **a mustard seed**, it grows into something greater than it was. Only when small faith grows into great faith can it move a **mountain.**

Mustard seed faith is persistent faith. It continues to grow and become productive because it never gives up. It is the sort of faith exercised by the importunate man who kept knocking on his neighbor's door late at night until he got a response. "I tell you," Jesus said, that "even though he will not get up and give him anything because he is his friend, yet because of his persistence he will get up and give him as much as he needs" (Luke 11:8). Jesus also illustrated **mustard seed** faith in the parable of the oppressed widow, a parable He gave specifically "to show that at all times [the disciples] ought to pray and not to lose heart" (Luke 18:1). When the widow would not take no for an answer, the godless, indifferent judge finally gave her "legal protection, lest," he said, "by continually coming she wear me out" (v. 5). "Hear what the unrighteous judge said," Jesus went on to explain; "now shall not God bring about justice for His elect, who cry to Him day and night, and will He delay long over them? I tell you that He will bring about justice for them speedily" (vv. 6-8).

It must also be clearly understood that Jesus was not talking about moving a literal **mountain.** Neither the apostles nor the Lord Himself ever performed such a feat—nor has anyone else in the nearly 2,000-year history of the church. That would have been the sort of grand but pointless miracle the scribes and Pharisees expected of the Messiah but which Jesus refused to perform (Matt. 12:38-39).

The expression "able to move mountains" was a common figure of speech in that day that represented the ability to surmount great obstacles. As William Barclay has observed,

> A great teacher, who could really expound and interpret Scripture and who could explain and resolve difficulties, was regularly known as an *uprooter* or even a *pulverizer* of mountains. To tear up, to uproot, to pulverize mountains were all regular phrases for removing difficulties. Jesus never meant this to be taken physically and literally. After all, the ordinary man seldom finds any necessity to remove a mountain. What He meant was: "If you have faith

enough, all difficulties can be solved, and even the hardest task can be accomplished. Faith in God is the instrument that allows men to remove the hills of difficulty which block their path. (*The Gospel of Matthew* [Philadelphia: Westminster, 1959], pp. 184-85)

Jesus was talking figuratively about mountain-size difficulties, such as the nine disciples had just experienced in not being able to cure the demonized boy.

The promise **nothing shall be impossible to you** is conditional, valid only within the framework of God's will. Mountain-moving faith is not faith in oneself, much less faith in faith, but faith in God. It is not faith itself, no matter how great, that moves mountains, but the God in whom the faith is grounded. Faith has only as much power as its object. When Jesus said to the Samaritan leper and the blind man of Jericho, "your faith has made you well" (Luke 17:19; 18:42), He did not mean that their faith in itself healed them. That would mean they healed themselves, which, of course, they did not do.

Jesus' point was that **"nothing shall be impossible to you** when you prayerfully and persistently trust in Me." The disciples could not heal the demonized boy, even though they had Jesus' commission and promised power, because they did not persist in dependent prayer.

Throughout the ages believers often have failed to receive God's promised joy, freedom, forgiveness, guidance, fruitfulness, protection, wisdom, and countless other blessings simply because, like those disciples, they have not persisted in prayer.

"This kind of demon **does not go out except by prayer,"** Jesus declared. Although that phrase is not found in the best manuscripts of Matthew (indicated by brackets in some versions), it is a genuine saying of Jesus and is found in Mark's account (9:29), from which an early scribe probably picked it up and added it to Matthew. However, the last two words of the verse, **and fasting,** are not found in the best manuscripts of any gospel.

Jesus' emphasis was clearly on **prayer.** As James wrote some years later, "The effective prayer of a righteous man can accomplish much" (James 5:16). Dedicated, fervent, passionate, persistent prayer gets results, because such prayer is honored by God.

During one point of his ministry, the nineteenth-century Christian leader George Mueller began to pray for five personal friends. It was not until five years later that the first one of them came to Christ. After five more years, two more of them became Christians, and after twenty-five years the fourth man was saved. He prayed for the fifth friend until the time of his death, a few months after which the last friend came to salvation. For that friend George Mueller had prayed more than fifty years!

The Believer as a Citizen

(17:22-27)

10

And while they were gathering together in Galilee, Jesus said to them, "The Son of Man is going to be delivered into the hands of men; and they will kill Him, and He will be raised on the third day." And they were deeply grieved.

And when they had come to Capernaum, those who collected the two-drachma tax came to Peter, and said, "Does your teacher not pay the two-drachma tax?" He said, "Yes." And when he came into the house, Jesus spoke to him first, saying, "What do you think, Simon? From whom do the kings of the earth collect customs or poll-tax, from their sons or from strangers?" And upon his saying, "From strangers," Jesus said to him, "Consequently the sons are exempt. But, lest we give them offense, go to the sea, and throw in a hook, and take the first fish that comes up; and when you open its mouth, you will find a stater. Take that and give it to them for you and Me." (17:22-27)

In the last several decades many religious political action groups have arisen, including a number that claim to speak for evangelical Christianity. Some of the groups are highly critical of certain laws, policies, and court decisions. Some even specifically endorse and campaign for candidates they think would support Christian values in government.

Other evangelicals believe that, beyond voting, Christians should shy away from political and government involvement as much as possible, leaving the running of secular government to the secular world. The only legitimate work of the church, they believe, is to preach the gospel and faithfully live by its standards.

The New Testament certainly makes clear that a believer's primary citizenship is not in this world. Paul charged the church at Philippi, "Brethren, join in following my example, and observe those who walk according to the pattern you have in us. For many walk, of whom I often told you, and now tell you even weeping, that they are enemies of the cross of Christ, whose end is destruction, whose god is their appetite, and whose glory is in their shame, who set their minds on earthly things." In contrast to such people, he goes on to say, "our citizenship is in heaven, from which also we eagerly wait for a Savior, the Lord Jesus Christ; who will transform the body of our humble state into conformity with the body of His glory, by the exertion of the power that He has even to subject all things to Himself" (Phil. 3:17-21). To the Ephesian Christians Paul wrote, "You are fellow citizens with the saints, and are of God's household" (Eph. 2:19). The writer of Hebrews says to believers, "You have come to Mount Zion and to the city of the living God, the heavenly Jerusalem, and to myriads of angels, to the general assembly and church of the first-born who are enrolled in heaven" (Heb. 12:22-23).

How then, some Christians argue, can those who have such a glorious heavenly heritage contaminate themselves by becoming involved in the earthly affairs of unbelieving society and government? Their attempt to appeal to the Bible for support leads them to such queries as the following: Did not Paul teach that believers are "to be blameless and innocent, children of God above reproach in the midst of a crooked and perverse generation, among whom [they] appear as lights in the world" (Phil. 2:15)? Did not both Paul and Isaiah command believers in God's name, "'Come out from their midst and be separate,' says the Lord. 'And do not touch what is unclean'" (2 Cor. 6:17; cf. Isa. 52:11)? Did not John declare, "If anyone loves the world, the love of the Father is not in him" (1 John 2:15)? And did not James say "that friendship with the world is hostility toward God" and that "whoever wishes to be a friend of the world makes himself an enemy of God" (James 4:4)?

In light of such passages, some Christians have opted out of any government involvement, including paying taxes. Because they not only are citizens of God's kingdom but members of His family, they argue, why should they participate in a sinful human society that, for the most part, never takes God into account, tramples on His standards of righteousness, blasphemes His name, and often even denies His existence?

Such advocacy forces the believer to ask what is the Christian's reasonable relationship to human society and to governmental authority in particular? That is the issue, specifically in regard to the basic duty required by government, that of paying taxes, which Jesus confronts in Matthew 17:24-27. But before He gave that lesson to Peter, the Lord again told the Twelve of His coming death and resurrection.

After the brief ministry in Caesarea Philippi (16:13) and the manifestation of His second coming glory before Peter, James, and John on the mount of transfiguration

(17:1-8), Jesus and His disciples **were gathering together in Galilee.** The exact location is not mentioned, but it was probably just northwest of Capernaum (see v. 24).

It should be noted that as He entered the last six months of His public ministry, Jesus spent less and less time with the multitudes and more and more time alone with the disciples, giving them intense further instruction about the principles of His kingdom. Interjected throughout those teachings were periodic reminders of His imminent suffering, death, and resurrection, which He here mentions to them for the third time (see Matt. 16:21; 17:12).

While He was still meeting with the disciples privately (17:19), **Jesus said to them, "The Son of Man is going to be delivered into the hands of men; and they will kill Him, and He will be raised on the third day."**

Jesus was neither helpless nor passive in going to the cross. "When the days were approaching for His ascension, . . . He resolutely set His face to go to Jerusalem" (Luke 9:51; cf. 13:22). As He later explained, He willingly accepted the cross in order that "all things which are written through the prophets about the Son of Man will be accomplished" (18:31). He willingly laid down His life (John 10:15, 17), which no one could have taken from Him without His consent. "No one has taken it away from Me," He said, "but I lay it down on My own initiative. I have authority to lay it down, and I have authority to take it up again" (v. 18).

But in His willingness to give His life a ransom for many, Jesus submitted Himself both to the evil plans of men and to the gracious and righteous plan of His heavenly Father (see Acts 2:22-23). Because of His willing submission to wicked men, He was **going to be delivered,** by the treachery of Judas, **into the hands of men.** Also because of His willing submission to wicked men, **they** (the Jewish and Roman leaders) would **kill Him.** But because of His willing submission to His righteous heavenly Father, He would **be raised on the third day.**

Mark reports that the disciples "did not understand this statement, and they were afraid to ask Him" (9:32). Because they still could not comprehend the full reality and significance of Jesus' promised resurrection—partly because they were stunned by the prospect of His promised suffering and death—the disciples **were deeply grieved.** After having just witnessed Jesus' resplendent glory at the transfiguration, Peter, James, and John were perhaps even more **deeply grieved** than the others in hearing again of Jesus' death.

The disciples also may have taken Jesus' reference to **the third day** as merely figurative and, like Martha concerning Lazarus, were thinking only of "the resurrection on the last day" (John 11:24). They believed in the resurrection of both the righteous and the wicked as predicted by the Lord through Daniel (Dan. 12:2), but that far away prospect was of little comfort to them now.

Jesus understood their slow comprehension (cf. Luke 24:25) as well as their small faith (Matt. 17:20) and realized that they needed repeated reminders, especially about truths that not only were hard to understand but painful to accept. They needed to be prepared for the reality that their Lord was soon going to be taken from them by death and that before He died He would suffer and be tormented.

They also needed assurance that His suffering and death were in God's plan, that those events, horrible as they were, would not interrupt, much less destroy, the Messiah's work. That was, in fact, the ultimate work He came to accomplish, without which His other divine work—His teaching and miracles—would have left men better informed and in better health but still lost and eternally condemned in their sin. The crucifixion did not catch Jesus or His heavenly Father by surprise; it was the reason the Father sent Him to earth and that He willingly came. "For this purpose," He said, "I came to this hour" (John 12:27).

After Jesus gave the Twelve that third prediction of His death and resurrection, He gave Peter a private object lesson in the believer's obligation to human government. In spite of what that hostile leadership would do to the Lord Jesus, the disciples had a certain obligation to it.

THE PAYMENT DEMANDED

And when they had come to Capernaum, those who collected the two-drachma tax came to Peter, and said, "Does your teacher not pay the two-drachma tax?" He said, "Yes." (17:24-25a)

Shortly after Jesus and the disciples **had come to Capernaum,** perhaps even as they entered the city, those **who collected the two-drachma tax** singled out **Peter.** He not only was a resident of the city but was known to be the leading member of Jesus' disciples. It is likely Jesus was staying at Peter's house and that the other disciples had gone elsewhere to lodge, since only those two are mentioned here.

The two-drachma tax was a government-approved tax that the Romans allowed the Jewish religious leaders to collect for the operation of the Jerusalem Temple.

When the Tabernacle was first built in the wilderness, God provided for its maintenance and operation through the yearly assessment of every male twenty years old and over for a half shekel. "The rich shall not pay more, and the poor shall not pay less than the half shekel, when you give the contribution to the Lord to make atonement for yourselves." The money was to be used "for the service of the tent of meeting, that it may be a memorial for the sons of Israel before the Lord" (Ex. 30:11-16). When the Temple replaced the Tabernacle, the same assessment continued, although it was temporarily reduced to a third of a shekel by Nehemiah because the former exiles in Babylon were so poor when they returned to Judah (Neh. 10:32).

Two-drachma tax translates the single Greek word *didrachma,* which means simply "two drachmas," or "double drachma." Although there was no two-drachma coin in circulation, the term *didrachma* was commonly used in reference to the Jewish Temple tax because two drachmas were equivalent to the required half shekel, which amounted to about two days' wages for the average worker.

The ancient Jewish historian Josephus reported that, after Titus destroyed Jerusalem and the Temple in A.D. 70, the emperor Vespasian decreed that Jews throughout the Roman Empire would continue to be assessed the two-drachma tax in order to maintain the pagan temple of Jupiter Capitolinus. The tax was imposed as a calculated, vindictive reminder both to Jews and to the rest of the world of the high cost of opposing Rome.

Because the Jewish Temple tax was to be paid by the time of Passover, collectors were sent throughout Palestine a month or so in advance. It was such tax collectors, rather than the Roman-appointed *publicani* ("publicans"), who **came to Peter, and said, "Does your teacher not pay the two-drachma tax?"**

The phrasing of the question suggests that the collectors, perhaps under instruction from Jewish leaders in Jerusalem, intended to challenge Jesus on the issue of paying the tax. Because He claimed to be the Messiah, they reasoned, He might consider Himself exempt. If He did, that would be yet another charge they could make against Him.

Peter did not have to ask his **teacher** for the answer, because he knew Jesus had always paid taxes, whether assessed by Rome or by the Jewish leaders. He therefore simply **said, "Yes."**

THE PRINCIPLE DISCUSSED

And when he came into the house, Jesus spoke to him first, saying, "What do you think, Simon? From whom do the kings of the earth collect customs or poll-tax, from their sons or from strangers?" And upon his saying, "From strangers," Jesus said to him, "Consequently the sons are exempt. But, lest we give them offense, (17:25b-27a)

When Peter **came into the house** to tell Jesus about his confrontation with the collectors, **Jesus spoke to him first.** In His omniscience He already knew what they had said and that Peter was thinking about it.

We are not specifically told what Peter's thoughts were, but from Jesus' comments it seems reasonable to infer that he was wondering why Jesus, the Messiah and Son of God, would condescend to pay taxes to those over whom He was eternally sovereign.

Using a method of teaching common in that day and beneficial in any day, Jesus answered Peter's unspoken question by first asking a question Himself. Addressing Peter by his original family name, Jesus said, **"What do you think, Simon? From whom do the kings of the earth collect customs or poll-tax, from their sons or from strangers?"**

With few exceptions, all ancient governments were autocratic, with power centered in one individual who passed on his royal legacy to his heirs. Whether called pharaoh, emperor, or other such titles, all supreme rulers were included in the term **kings,** and they all assessed taxes to support their families as well as their governments. The two basic types of taxes were **customs** (levied on goods) and the **poll-tax** (levied on individuals).

His question was rhetorical, and the answer was obvious. It would not make sense for a father to collect money from his **sons** who were dependent on him. To assess them would be to assess himself. In this context **strangers** is a general term referring to those outside the king's family, specifically his subjects.

When Peter answered, "**From strangers,**" **Jesus** stated the corollary truth: "**Consequently, the sons are exempt.**" In the human governments of that day, the rulers' families, represented by **the sons,** were **exempt** from taxation.

Had Jesus ended the lesson at that point, Christians would have a basis for arguing that they, too, as fellow heirs with Christ and children of God, should be exempt from human taxation. They could even argue that, as His children, they were not even obligated to support God's work.

If there was any tax that Jesus was not obligated to pay it would have been the Temple tax. He was the One whom the Temple was built to honor and to whom its sacrifices and offerings were made. He was Lord of all the earth but supremely Lord of the Temple. Jesus called the Temple His "Father's house" (Luke 2:49; John 2:16) and declared Himself to be greater than the Temple (Matt. 12:6). He had every right to refuse paying the Temple tax, just as He had every right to refuse being humiliated and persecuted. But when He willingly emptied Himself of His divine glory, "taking the form of a bond-servant, and being made in the likeness of men" (Phil. 2:7), He also willingly relinquished the rights and prerogatives belonging to that glory.

"**Lest we give them offense,**" Jesus told Peter, the tax was to be paid. Clearly implied was the idea that it was not only to be paid in full but paid willingly and without argument.

Regardless of how unjust a tax is assessed or how blasphemously or irresponsibly it is spent, it is to be paid. If the Son of God claimed no exemption for Himself in paying taxes to the "den of thieves" run by the wicked, false teachers and leaders of Israel, how much less can His followers claim exemption for themselves? And if He was concerned about not giving **offense** to unbelievers over that issue, how much more should His followers have such concern?

THE PROVISION DELIVERED

go to the sea, and throw in a hook, and take the first fish that comes up; and when you open its mouth, you will find a stater. Take that and give it to them for you and Me. " (17:27*b*)

There is no evidence that at any other time Jesus provided tax money through a miracle. On this occasion, however, the miracle reinforced the point that He was the Son of God and had the right with perfect impunity to refuse to pay the tax had He so chosen. He agreed to pay it entirely of His own divine volition.

Peter was instructed to **go to the sea,** apparently to any place he might choose on the shore of the Sea of Galilee, **throw in a hook,** apparently unbaited, **and take the first fish that comes up.** Then **"when you open its mouth,"** Jesus assured the disciple, **"you will find a stater. Take that and give it to them for you and Me."**

Because there was no two-drachma coin, it was customary for two Jewish men to pay the tax together, using **a stater,** which was equal to two *didrachma.* The coin Peter found in the fish's mouth was the exact amount needed to pay the tax for Jesus and himself.

Although this tax was for the support of the Temple services, it is certain that the hypocritical and corrupt Jewish leaders misappropriated a large part of what was collected. It is even more certain that the taxes Jesus paid to Rome were used for many ungodly and immoral purposes. Most of the Roman tax collectors were traitors to their own people, and the taxes they extorted from their fellow countrymen not only were excessive and unjust but were used to support the occupying army, the pagan rulers, and even pagan religions.

The general principle derived from this account is clear. A believer is obligated to fulfill his duties as a citizen of this world. Although his ultimate and eternal citizenship is in heaven and the governments of men are all in varying degrees of corruption, while he remains on earth he is also under obligation to human government. Except when it would cause him to disobey God directly, he is bound by divine law to be subject to human law.

When Peter wrote his first epistle he no doubt still vividly remembered the miraculous provision of the stater in the fish's mouth and the teaching of Jesus that accompanied the miracle. In the second chapter of that epistle he declares to believers, "You are a chosen race, a royal priesthood, a holy nation, a people for God's own possession, that you may proclaim the excellencies of Him who has called you out of darkness into His marvelous light" (1 Pet. 2:9).

Peter reminds his Christian readers that they are elected by God to be His own people and to minister as His priests to the unbelieving world around them. They are uniquely the Lord's possession, His children, and citizens of His divine kingdom, with their assignment on earth being to fulfill a divine mission. Having previously been a people of no consequence, they are now the people of God. Having previously been apart from God's mercy, they now live under His abundant mercy (v. 10). Because of that high standing, Peter says, "I urge you as aliens and strangers to abstain from fleshly lusts, which wage war against the soul. Keep your behavior excellent among the Gentiles, so that in the thing in which they slander you as evildoers, they may on account of your good deeds, as they observe them, glorify God in the day of visitation" (vv. 11-12).

Regarding the same issue, and in spite of the godlessness of Rome and the claim to deity by Caesar, Paul wrote, "Let every person be in subjection to the governing authorities. For there is no authority except from God, and those which exist are established by God. Therefore he who resists authority has opposed the ordinance of God; and they who have opposed will receive condemnation upon themselves. . . . For because of this you also pay taxes, for rulers are servants of God, devoting themselves to this very thing. Render to *all* what is due them: tax to whom tax is due; custom to whom custom; fear to whom fear; honor to whom honor" (Rom. 13:1-2, 5-7; italics added).

Believers are to submit themselves "for the Lord's sake to every human institution, whether to a king as the one in authority, or to governors as sent by him for the punishment of evildoers and the praise of those who do right" (1 Pet. 2:13-14). The key to the command is that it is obeyed "for the Lord's sake." It is not that every human law and ruler is godly and just. Most of them are not and make no claim to be. But the institution and operation of government are ordained by God for social order, and as a testimony to Him, human government is to be respected and obeyed by His people even when it is unjust.

Obedience to civil law and government is not to be done with reluctance or condescension but willingly, "not only because of wrath, but also for conscience's sake" (Rom. 13:5). Christians should have an attitude of genuine respect for human government, not because it is always deserving of respect but because that is the will of their Lord, who instituted it for man's benefit.

The people to whom Paul and Peter wrote were experiencing increased persecution and oppression at the hands of Rome. Yet the apostles told them not only to be loyal and law-abiding citizens but helpful citizens as well.

The early church did not start an insurrection against Rome or a campaign against slavery, wicked and cruel as both those were. In fact, the Holy Spirit took the words of slavery (slave, bond-slave, bondage, servant, etc.) and made them the symbols of Christian dedication and submission. In His omniscient providence God also used the pagan Romans to spread the Greek language, a universal language used to record His Word and carry it to the ends of the known world of that day. God used them to build a system of roads over which His messengers could easily travel as they carried the good news throughout the empire. And God used the Pax Romana, or Roman peace, to allow those messengers to travel in relative safety.

As Peter declared early in his ministry, there are obvious limits to a believer's submission to human authority. When he and John had been charged by the Jewish authorities in Jerusalem not to preach the gospel, the two men responded, "Whether it is right in the sight of God to give heed to you rather than to God, you be the judge; for we cannot stop speaking what we have seen and heard" (Acts 4:19-20; cf. 5:28-29). Many believers in the early church lost their freedom, their possessions, and even their lives because they refused to offer incense to Caesar. They would honor him as a human leader, but they would not worship him as a god.

The Christian's first obligation is to obey God, and when His law is directly opposed by men's laws, God's law must prevail. The Christian, for example, has no right to lie, steal, commit murder, or worship a false god, no matter what the dictates of a human government might be and no matter what the consequences for disobedience might be.

Nor is it that a Christian has no right to help change unjust laws and governments when he has opportunity to do so. But in a democratic society especially, the major injustices and evils within it are never primarily the result of poor government or poor laws, bad as those might be. When the people have no respect for law, God's or men's, and when their standards and motives revolve around their own selfish interests, no government can be stable or provide justice and order. Even the most godly and moral leaders cannot infuse morality into an immoral society. It is futile to work at changing evil laws and removing evil leaders without changing the evil hearts of those whom the laws try to control and the leaders try to rule.

Even slaves are to be submissive to their masters, Peter declared, "with all respect, not only to those who are good and gentle, but also to those who are unreasonable. For this finds favor, if for the sake of conscience toward God a man bears up under sorrows when suffering unjustly" (1 Pet. 2:18-19). Just as with a submissive wife who desires to win her unbelieving husband to Christ (3:1-2), effective witnessing begins with submission.

The supreme example of godly submission is Jesus Christ, who "suffered for you, leaving you an example for you to follow in His steps, who committed no sin, nor was any deceit found in His mouth; and while being reviled, He did not revile in return; while suffering, He uttered no threats, but kept entrusting Himself to Him who judges righteously" (1 Pet. 2:21-23). Jesus submitted to suffering He did not deserve from those who had no right to judge Him in the first place. He committed no sin, outwardly or inwardly, yet He submitted to corrupt and sinful authorities, both religious and political. He took unjust abuse in order that He might better win men to Himself, and He is the example for everyone who calls Him Lord.

The Christian's being a citizen of God's kingdom does not exempt him from responsibility to human kingdoms. In fact His being a citizen of God's kingdom gives him a special obligation to human kingdoms, because those, too, belong to God and are ordained by Him.

By being a good citizen the believer shows love for his fellow men, even those who are lost and unjust. By being a good citizen he shows respect for God-ordained human government, even when its leaders are ungodly, corrupt, and oppressive. By being a good citizen he shows that he loves God as well as his country and his fellow citizens. In the light of such testimony the onlooking world is compelled to consider the power that makes such love possible.

Entering the Kingdom
(18:1-4)

11

At that time the disciples came to Jesus, saying, "Who then is greatest in the kingdom of heaven?" And He called a child to Himself and set him before them, and said, "Truly I say to you, unless you are converted and become like children, you shall not enter the kingdom of heaven. Whoever then humbles himself as this child, he is the greatest in the kingdom of heaven." (18:1-4)

Scripture describes and identifies the people of God by many names. But more frequently than anything else we are called children—children of promise, children of the day, children of the light, beloved children, dear children, and children of God.

As believers we can rejoice in the wonderful truth that, through Christ, we have become God's own children, adopted through grace. Consequently, we bear the image of God's family and are joint heirs with Jesus Christ of everything God possesses. We enjoy God's love, care, protection, power, and other resources in abundance for all eternity.

But there is another side to our being children, and in Scripture believers are also referred to as children in the sense that we are incomplete, weak, dependent, undeveloped, unskilled, vulnerable, and immature.

Matthew 18 focuses on those immature, unperfected, childlike qualities that believers demonstrate as they mutually develop into conformity to the fullness of the stature of Jesus Christ.

This chapter is a single discourse or sermon by our Lord on the specific theme of the childlikeness of the believer, speaking directly to the reality that we are spiritual children with all the weaknesses that childhood implies. It is also essential to see that the chapter teaches the church, as a group of spiritually unperfected children, how to get along with each other. It is no exaggeration to say that this is the single greatest discourse our Lord ever gave on life among the redeemed people in His church. Sadly, because it has been largely misinterpreted, its profound riches often have been lost. We shall attempt to recover these truths that are so vital, powerful, and needed by the church in every age and place.

The first lesson in this masterful sermon is that everyone who enters the kingdom does so as a child (vv. 1-4). Jesus then teaches that all of us in the kingdom must be treated as children (vv. 5-9), cared for as children (vv. 10-14), disciplined as children (vv. 15-20), and forgiven as children (vv. 21-35).

The setting for the sermon is indicated by the phrase **at that time**, which refers to a period soon after Jesus told Peter to go to the Sea of Galilee and retrieve the coin from the fish's mouth (17:27). While Peter was paying the tax with the coin or, more likely, just after he returned, the rest of **the disciples came to Jesus,** possibly at Peter's house in Capernaum.

The two scenes are closely connected in time and in thought. On the same day the disciples received the lesson on being citizens of the world they were given a series of lessons on the issues related to being children of God.

The Lord's teaching was prompted by the disciples themselves, who asked Him a very selfish question that betrayed their sinful ambitions. We learn from Mark and Luke that the question, **Who then is greatest in the kingdom of heaven?** resulted from an argument the Twelve had been having among themselves "as to which of them might be the greatest" (Luke 9:46; cf. Mark 9:34). Although He omnisciently knew what had happened, Jesus asked, "What were you discussing on the way?" They were so ashamed of their attitude and conversation that "they kept silent" (Mark 9:33-34).

Their embarrassed reticence shows they knew that what they had been doing was inconsistent with what their Master had been teaching on humility. But the fact that they nevertheless were arguing about their relative ranks in the kingdom shows they were making little effort to apply what they had been taught. They were as proud, self-seeking, self-sufficient, and ambitious as ever. In light of what they had been discussing and the way they phrased the question to Jesus, it is obvious they expected Him to name one of them as the **greatest.**

Just as they had heard but not really accepted what Jesus had been teaching about humility, they also had heard but not really accepted what He had been teaching about the **kingdom.** Much like those to whom Isaiah was sent to preach (Isa. 6:9), the disciples listened but did not perceive and looked but did not understand. They obviously still expected Jesus soon to set up an earthly kingdom, and each of them was hoping to have a high rank in that dominion. They were especially competitive about being number one.

Perhaps it was earlier that same day (see 17:22-23) that Jesus had told them (for the third time) about His impending suffering and death. Although they did not fully understand what He was saying to them (Mark 9:32), they should have sensed its gravity. And even though they were afraid to ask Jesus what He meant (v. 32b), it would seem they would have been discussing *that* issue rather than which of them was to be the greatest. They were so caught up in their own desire for prestige, glory, and personal aggrandizement that they were impervious to much of what Jesus said—even about His suffering, death, and resurrection. They demonstrated no concept of humility, very little compassion, and certainly no willingness to take up their own crosses and follow Christ to death as they had been taught (Matt. 10:38-39; 16:24-26).

Several months after this lesson in Capernaum, their selfish ambition was still very much evident. Probably at her sons' instigation, the mother of James and John asked Jesus, "Command that in Your kingdom these two sons of mine may sit, one on Your right and one on Your left" (Matt. 20:20-21). The other disciples were indignant at the two brothers, but their indignation was not righteous but envious (v. 24).

It must have been especially painful to Jesus that, just as on the occasion recorded in chapter 18, this self-seeking request came immediately after He had predicted His suffering and death (20:19). There is no indication of sympathy, consolation, or grief concerning what their Lord was about to endure on their behalf and on the behalf of all the world. And on the night before He died, while He was eating the Last Supper with them, they were still arguing about their own greatness (Luke 22:24). Their insensitivity and selfishness is thus demonstrated as all the more sinful because it occurred at times when Jesus was speaking of His own suffering and death.

The rest of the disciples may have been jealous of Peter, knowing that he was the most intimate with Jesus and was always their chief spokesman. Peter was one of the three privileged to witness Jesus' transfiguration, and only Peter had walked on the water or had his Temple tax miraculously provided. But it was also only Peter who had been told by Jesus, "Get behind Me, Satan" (Matt. 16:23), and perhaps the other disciples thought the number one position was not yet finalized.

The teaching here is desperately needed in the church today, where selfish ambition is widespread and obligation to perform our duty to fellow children of God is routinely ignored.

Like all of us, the disciples needed repeated lessons in humility, and here Jesus used a child as His illustration. **And He called a child to Himself and set him before them.**

Paidion identifies a very young **child,** sometimes even an infant. This particular **child** was perhaps a toddler, just old enough to run to Jesus when **He called** him **to Himself.** Because the group was likely in Peter's house, the **child** may have belonged to Peter's family and already been well known to Jesus. In any case, he readily responded and allowed himself to be taken up into Jesus' arms (Mark 9:36). Jesus loved children and they loved Him, and as He sat before the disciples holding this small child in His arms, He had a beautiful setting in which to teach them profound lessons about the childlikeness of believers.

The essence of the first lesson is in verse three: **Truly I say to you, unless you are converted and become like children, you shall not enter the kingdom of heaven.** That is an absolute and far-reaching requirement of ultimate importance. Entrance into Christ's kingdom demands childlikeness. There is no other way to receive the grace of salvation than as a child.

The kingdom of heaven, a phrase Matthew uses some 32 times, is synonymous with the kingdom of God. It had become common for Jews at the end of the Old Testament era, and especially during the intertestamental period, to substitute out of reverence the word *heaven* for the Hebrew tetragrammaton (YHWH), God's covenant name (often rendered as Yahweh, or Jehovah). Used in that way, **heaven** was simply another way of saying *God.* Both phrases refer to the rule of God, **kingdom of heaven** emphasizing the sphere and character of His rule, and kingdom of God emphatically pointing to the ruler Himself. God rules His kingdom with heavenly principles and heavenly blessings and in heavenly power, majesty, and glory. Entering the kingdom means coming under the sovereign rule of God.

Our Lord is talking directly about entering God's kingdom by faith, through salvation that will result in future millennial blessing and eternal glory. The phrase "enter the kingdom of heaven" is used three times in the book of Matthew (see also 7:21; 19:23-24) and in each case refers to personal salvation. It is the same experience as entering into life (18:8) and entering into the joy of the Lord (25:21).

The fact that a person must **enter the kingdom** assumes he is born outside of it under the rule of Satan and that he is not naturally a heavenly citizen under the rule of God. The purpose of the gospel is to show men how they may **enter the kingdom** and become its citizens, moving from the kingdom of darkness to the kingdom of God's beloved Son (Col. 1:13). It is God's desire to have men come into His kingdom, and He does not wish "for any to perish but for all to come to repentance" (2 Pet. 3:9). The purpose of Christ's ministry and the ministries of John the Baptist and the apostles was to call people to the kingdom. That is still the supreme task of the church.

The central focus of Matthew's gospel is to draw men and women into the kingdom through faith in Jesus Christ, and that is doubtlessly one of the reasons the Holy Spirit placed this book at the beginning of the New Testament. Throughout his gospel, Matthew carefully and systematically presents the components of genuine belief.

The first component presented for entering the kingdom is repentance. The message of John the Baptist was, "Repent, for the kingdom of heaven is at hand" (3:2), and it was with that identical message that the Lord began His own ministry (4:17). The initial call for entering the kingdom was a call for people to recognize and repent of their sin, which involves genuine desire to turn away from it. This repentance is not a human work but a divine gift that only God can grant (see 2 Tim. 2:25).

A second component of the faith that grants entrance to the kingdom is the recognition of spiritual bankruptcy. That, too, is a work of God, not man, because it is the Holy Spirit who convicts of sin (John 16:8-11). The Beatitudes begin with a call to humility, expressed there as poverty of spirit (Matt. 5:3). The person who genuinely wants to enter God's kingdom sees himself as utterly unworthy and undeserving. His awareness of his sin brings guilt and frustration over his inadequacy to remove it. He knows that he cannot himself cleanse his sin and that he has nothing to offer God that could merit forgiveness for it. The Greek term behind "poor in spirit" refers to a beggar who has absolutely no resources of his own. Because the repentant and bankrupt person is deeply aware of his sin, he mourns over it (v. 4); because he has no righteousness of his own, he hungers and thirsts for God's righteousness (v. 6); and because he cannot himself cleanse his sin, he longs for the purity of heart (v. 8) that only God can provide.

A third component of the faith that allows entering the kingdom is meekness, which is closely related to the sense of having nothing of value to offer God. Because of his sense of personal unworthiness, the humble and meek person neither claims nor demands anything of glory for himself. He is committed to fight for God's causes, not his own.

The one who enters God's kingdom also will have a desire and capacity to be obedient. "Not everyone who says to Me, 'Lord, Lord,' will enter the kingdom of heaven," Jesus declared, "but he who does the will of My Father who is in heaven" (Matt. 7:21). Entering God's kingdom is more than simply expressing the wish to be in it and having the conviction that Jesus is its Lord. The sovereign, saving God will produce in the soul a personal submission to Jesus as Lord and a new heart longing to obey His commands. The person who is unwilling to leave the things of the world for the things of the Lord has no genuine desire for salvation (8:19-22). Coming into the **kingdom** assumes by the very term that one comes under the rule of the Lord of that kingdom.

When Jesus called people to follow Him, He was calling them to salvation (cf. Matt. 19:21). The new birth makes people followers of Jesus. It would be more consistent with the method of our Lord if, instead of asking people to "make a decision for Christ," modern evangelists would call them to turn from sin to follow the Lord's leadership and turn over to Him the rule of their lives.

The one who enters God's kingdom also is willing to make public confession of his desire to follow the Lord. "Everyone therefore who shall confess Me before men," Jesus said, "I will also confess him before My Father who is in heaven. But whoever shall deny Me before men, I will also deny him before My Father who is in heaven" (10:32-33).

The one who enters God's kingdom is aware of his need to be self-denying. Jesus said, "He who does not take his cross and follow after Me is not worthy of Me. He who has found his life shall lose it, and he who has lost his life for My sake shall find it" (10:38-39).

Further in Matthew's presentation of the faith that saves is the component of persistence. The Canaanite woman with the demon-possessed daughter did not give up when Jesus at first ignored her, when the disciples wanted to send her away, or even when Jesus reminded her that she was not an Israelite, one of God's chosen people. She was willing to take even the Lord's leftovers and would not give up until He had met her need. In response to her childlike persistence, Jesus said, "O woman, your faith is great; be it done for you as you wish" (15:28).

All of these components of the faith that God grants for salvation can be summed up in the first lesson Jesus teaches—the lesson of humility.

It is impossible to miss the fact that this teaching is directed at the disciples and implies they needed to hear and accept it. And from the argument among them that prompted this lesson from Jesus, it is obvious they were not living according to His standard of humility. They were manifesting pride and self-seeking. It may be that some of them were not yet in the kingdom (certainly this invitation was pertinent to the power-hungry, money-hungry Judas), and those who were in the kingdom had allowed their fallen flesh to dominate their attitudes. This makes the important statement that even though our hearts are in line with these principles of genuine saving faith at the time God graciously grants it to us, we fall often and easily to the power of sin that is still in us.

As He took the young child in His arms and held him up before the disciples, the Lord gathered up all those elements of salvation: **"Truly I say to you, unless you are converted and become like children, you shall not enter the kingdom of heaven."**

The phrase **are converted** translates an aorist passive of *strephō*, which elsewhere in the New Testament is always translated with an idea of "turning" or "turning around." It means to make an about face and go in the opposite direction. Peter used a form of the term twice in his message shortly after Pentecost, as he called his hearers to "repent therefore and return, that your sins may be wiped away" and declared of Jesus that "God raised up His Servant, and sent Him to bless you by turning every one of you from your wicked ways" (Acts 3:19, 26). The term is used repeatedly in the book of Acts to speak of conversion (11:21; 15:19; 26:18, 20). Paul used the word when speaking of the Thessalonian believers, who had turned "to God from idols to serve a living and true God" (1 Thess. 1:9).

Conversion is the other half of repentance. Repentance is being sorry for sin and turning away from it; conversion is the expression of will that fully turns from sin to the Lord. Psalm 51:13 alludes to these two halves of the turning when it declares, "and sinners will be converted to Thee." Jesus' use here of the passive voice indicates that the disciples could not be **converted** from sin to righteousness by their own efforts but needed someone else to turn them around. Although the response of a person's will is required, only God has the power to convert.

To be **converted** requires people to **become like children,** Jesus explained. A little child is simple, dependent, helpless, unaffected, unpretentious, unambitious. Children are not sinless or naturally unselfish, and they display their fallen nature from the earliest age. But they are nevertheless naive and unassuming, trusting of others and without ambition for grandeur and greatness.

"It is the person who **humbles himself as this child,**" Jesus declared, "who **is greatest in the kingdom of heaven.**" The verb behind **humbles** is *tapeinoō,* which has the literal meaning of making low. In God's eyes, the one who lowers himself is the one who is elevated; the one who genuinely considers himself to be the least is the one God considers to be **the greatest.** "The greatest among you shall be your servant," Jesus told the self-righteous Pharisees. "And whoever exalts himself shall be humbled; and whoever humbles himself shall be exalted" (Matt. 23:11-12). The person who is not willing to humble himself as Jesus "humbled Himself" (Phil. 2:8) will have no place in Jesus' **kingdom.** For self-righteous Jews who exalted themselves so highly as to think God was pleased with them for their own goodness, this was a shattering blow.

But Jesus makes clear that you rise higher in His kingdom as you go lower. The great Lutheran commentator R. C. H. Lenski has written, "He who thinks of making no claims shall have all that others claim and by claiming cannot obtain. . . . Only an empty vessel can God fill with his gifts. And the emptier we are of anything that is due to ourselves, the more can God pour into these vessels his eternal riches, honors, and glories" (*The Interpretation of St. Matthew's Gospel* [Minneapolis: Augsburg, 1943], 683).

A little **child** makes no claims of worthiness or greatness. He simply submits to the care of his parents and others who love him, relying on them for all that he needs. He knows he cannot meet his own needs and has no resources to stay alive. That is the kind of humble submissiveness that results in greatness in God's eyes and in His **kingdom.**

A number of years ago I ministered to a group of black schools in the south. At one rural elementary school, I presented a simple message about God's love and the unique and lovely person of Jesus Christ, who especially loved children and died as a sacrifice for them on the cross to pay the punishment for all our sins. At the end of the message I asked, "How many of you would like to have Jesus live in your heart and forgive all your sin and desire to follow such a wonderful Lord and Savior and have Him take you to heaven some day?" To my amazement, every one of the one hundred or so hands in the room immediately went up. There was no skepticism, no doubting, no hesitation, no looking around to see how their friends would react. When the invitation was asked for, the heart of each one of those children was ready to respond positively to the claims of Jesus Christ. To be sure that they understood the commitment they were making, I asked, "Now how many of you are willing to let Jesus control your life and to obey whatever He says?" Again, every hand went up.

God knew the intent of their hearts and what that simple affirmation meant as a step toward Him. But what I saw was the illustration of saving faith. None of those children felt adequate in himself or so perfect as not to recognize sin and the need of forgiveness. None was reluctant to give his life to One who was so lovely and gracious and could provide all they would need in time and eternity. Nor were they reluctant to do what He asked them in obedience.

That is the kind of unpretentious, nonhypocritical, humble, childlike faith Jesus was talking about. That sort of response to His Son is **the greatest** in God's sight. **The greatest in the kingdom of heaven** is the one who is humble, unaffected, genuinely sincere, undemanding, nonself-centered, receptive to whatever God offers, and eagerly obedient to whatever He commands.

The popular "gospels" that propagate self-fulfillment and personal success are the antithesis of the gospel of Jesus Christ. They are a mockery of New Testament Christianity and strike at the heart of salvation and of Christian living. The Lord made no provision for the elevation of self, but rather declared unequivocally that the person who, on his own terms, "has found his life shall lose it" (Matt. 10:39). The way of self is the way of disqualification from the kingdom. Those who glorify self not only will not be great in the kingdom but will never enter it.

James presents an invitation to salvation that unarguably reiterates what our Lord demands in this passage of Matthew:

> But He gives a greater grace. Therefore it says, "God is opposed to the proud, but gives grace to the humble." Submit therefore to God. Resist the devil and he will flee from you. Draw near to God and He will draw near to you. Cleanse your hands, you sinners; and purify your hearts, you double-minded. Be miserable and mourn and weep; let your laughter be turned into mourning, and your joy to gloom. Humble yourselves in the presence of the Lord, and He will exalt you. (James 4:6-10)

The Danger of Causing a Christian to Sin

12

(18:5-9)

"And whoever receives one such child in My name receives Me; but whoever causes one of these little ones who believe in Me to stumble, it is better for him that a heavy millstone be hung around his neck, and that he be drowned in the depth of the sea.

"Woe to the world because of its stumbling blocks! For it is inevitable that stumbling blocks come; but woe to that man through whom the stumbling block comes! And if your hand or your foot causes you to stumble, cut it off and throw it from you; it is better for you to enter life crippled or lame, than having two hands or two feet, to be cast into the eternal fire. And if your eye causes you to stumble, pluck it out, and throw it from you. It is better for you to enter life with one eye, than having two eyes, to be cast into the fiery hell. (18:5-9)

I have four children who are precious to me. I love them deeply and am zealous for their welfare, especially their spiritual welfare. My deepest desire is that they continually grow into Christlikeness, conforming to the mind and will of the Lord. I feel an almost painful sense of responsibility and commitment to protect my children from every form of harm and danger. From time to time, when people and influences have come into their lives that I know would be harmful to them, I have done my best to shield them from those dangers. As any normal parent, I have great appreciation for those who help my children and great indignation for those who harm them.

Most parents are more grateful for what is done on behalf of and for the benefit of their children than for anything that could be done for themselves. Likewise, most parents find it easier to forgive an offense against themselves than one against their child. Parents are grateful to friends, teachers, and others who encourage, support, and build up their children. They are incensed, however, by a young man who makes their daughter pregnant, a supposed friend who induces their son to try drugs, or an unbelieving professor who tries to lead their son or daughter away from their Christian faith.

God is the perfect model of this kind of parental concern, because He has always been deeply concerned about the way His children are treated. It is of utmost importance to Him that they be protected and nurtured. He therefore promises blessing to those who treat His children well and gives dire warning to those who cause them harm.

This attitude of God toward His children goes all the way back to when He first called out a nation for Himself from the loins of Abraham and said of him and his descendants, "I will bless those who bless you, and the one who curses you I will curse" (Gen. 12:3). The Lord has always demanded good treatment of His people, commanding unbelievers to treat them well and commanding them to treat each other well.

As Jesus continued to hold the young child in His arms, He taught a lesson about mutual caring among His children.

THE PRINCIPLE

And whoever receives one such child in My name receives Me; (18:5)

The basic truth of that verse is that it is impossible to separate Christ from His people and that, consequently, whatever affects believers, affects Him. Specifically, **whoever receives** a **child** of God in Christ's **name receives** Christ.

As is clear from the context, Jesus was using the **child** He held in His arms only as an illustration. **One such child** identifies the specific child being referred to in the context. This can only mean the one who spiritually becomes a little child, as described in verses 3-4. Jesus was not speaking of the toddler himself but was using him to represent the children of God. That physical **child** symbolized the spiritual **child** of God, who becomes childlike in his faith and who humbly accepts the gospel and is converted (v. 3). Such converted people are the "little ones who believe in Me," Jesus explained (v. 6). And no matter how lowly, unsophisticated, immature, or weak a believer is, he must be treated as the precious **child** of God he truly is. There is solidarity and unity between the Lord and all who share His life by the indwelling Holy Spirit.

Christianity is not a system of religion but a redeemed people who are united with God, one with Him through His Son, Jesus Christ. Christians not only follow Jesus' teachings but Jesus Himself and are totally and intimately identified with Him. He is the Head and they are the Body (1 Cor. 12:27); He is the Vine and they are the branches (John 15:5); He is the Bridegroom and they are the bride (Rev. 21:2, 9).

In profound terms, Jesus affirmed this amazing reality to His disciples, "The one who listens to you listens to Me, and the one who rejects you rejects Me; and the one who rejects Me rejects the One who sent Me" (Luke 10:16; cf. John 13:20). When Saul was persecuting Christians, the Lord confronted him on the Damascus Road with the words, "Saul, Saul, why are you persecuting Me?" (Acts 9:4). In his first letter to the Corinthian church, Paul negatively confirmed the oneness between Christ and each believer when he strongly rebuked them for sexual immorality involving prostitutes. It was spiritually defiling in a unique way, because it made Christ Himself a kind of participant in the sin. Because the believer is spiritually united with Christ, when he sexually unites himself with a prostitute he involves the Lord in his sin. "Do you not know that your bodies are members of Christ?" the apostle asked. "Shall I then take away the members of Christ and make them members of a harlot? May it never be!" (1 Cor. 6:15). It is not that Christ Himself is made impure by the impurity of His followers but that His name is stained. He is not personally contaminated by believers' sins any more than sunlight in contaminated by shining on a garbage dump. But His name is maligned and His work is hindered when His people sin, just as His heart is blessed when His people are received.

Receives is from *dechomai*, which means to deliberately and readily take something or someone to oneself. The term was often used of welcoming honored guests and meeting their needs with special attention and kindness. Jesus' primary point here is that the way a person, believer or unbeliever, treats Christians is the way he treats Jesus Christ. When anyone welcomes with an open heart a Christian as an honored guest and friend, he welcomes Christ as his guest and friend. When he treats any Christian with tenderness and kindness, he treats Christ in the same way.

Our Lord emphatically taught this unity between Himself and His people when He said, "When the Son of Man comes in His glory, and all the angels with Him," Jesus said, "then He will sit on His glorious throne." After placing believers, the sheep, on His right and unbelievers, the goats, on the left,

the King will say to those on His right, "Come, you who are blessed of My Father, inherit the kingdom prepared for you from the foundation of the world. For I was hungry, and you gave Me something to eat; I was thirsty, and you gave Me drink; I was a stranger, and you invited Me in; naked, and you clothed Me; I was sick, and you visited Me; I was in prison, and you came to Me." Then the righteous will answer Him, saying, "Lord, when did we see You hungry, and feed You, or thirsty, and give You drink? And when did we see You a stranger, and invite You in, or naked, and clothe You? And when did we see You sick, or in prison, and come to You?" And the King will answer and say to them, "Truly I say to you, to the extent that you did it to one of these brothers of Mine, even the least of them, you did it to Me." (Matt. 25:31-40)

Believers are to receive one another with tenderness, care, kindness, and love, opening up their hearts to welcome fellow believers no matter who they are. In so doing, they embrace the Lord Christ who lives in them. We are to care for each other like precious children. What a vital message to the church!

The Peril

but whoever causes one of these little ones who believe in Me to stumble, it is better for him that a heavy millstone be hung around his neck, and that he be drowned in the depth of the sea.
"Woe to the world because of its stumbling blocks! For it is inevitable that stumbling blocks come; but woe to that man through whom the stumbling block comes! (18:6-7)

Next Jesus presents the negative side of the previously mentioned truth: When a person mistreats a Christian he mistreats Christ. This side of the truth also applies to believers and unbelievers. Whether the person is the worst persecuting pagan who causes harm to a Christian or whether he is a believer who causes harm to a fellow Christian, the result is the same: Christ Himself is attacked.

It is obvious that our Lord is not referring to physical but to spiritual children. The phrase **these little ones who believe in Me** makes clear that He has in mind the children He had just spoken of in the phrase "one such child" (v. 5), which refers to the children mentioned in verses 3-4.

Jesus is speaking of moral and spiritual stumbling, that is, of sinning. The verb *skandalizō* (**to stumble**) literally means "to cause to fall," and the Lord is therefore speaking of enticing, trapping, or influencing a believer in any way that leads him into sin or in any way makes it easier for him to sin. A person who is responsible for causing a Christian to sin commits an offense against Christ Himself as well as against the Christian.

In the most vivid and sobering language indicating the seriousness of such an act against one of God's children, Jesus declared that a person who does such a thing would be better off dying a terrible death. It would be **better for him,** in fact, **that a heavy millstone be hung around his neck, and that he be drowned in the depth of the sea.**

Heavy millstone translates *mulos onikos,* which refers to the large upper millstone that was turned in a grinding process by a donkey and often weighed hundreds of pounds. The Romans sometimes practiced this form of execution by tying a heavy stone around a criminal's neck and dropping him overboard in deep water. Such a pagan form of execution was unimaginably horrible to Jews, perhaps in some respects more fearful even than crucifixion. Yet Jesus said that suffering such a terrifying death would be better than causing even one of His people to sin.

The thought must have been especially sobering to the disciples, because they had just been indulging in a heated argument over who was the greatest in the kingdom of heaven. The dispute doubtlessly caused everyone's anger and resentment to rise, as one after the other gave reasons he was due the honor. The Twelve not only were sinning because of their own pride and boasting but also because they were inciting each other to envy, jealousy, and anger.

Every believer is a child of God and, like all children, needs protection, care, and understanding. It is an enormous crime to harm even one of them by leading him to sin. To ruin the character of a saint or to retard his spiritual growth is heinous in God's sight, because it amounts to attacking His beloved Son, Jesus Christ.

Zechariah declared that whoever harms God's people Israel "touches the apple of His eye" (Zech. 2:8). "The apple of the eye" was an ancient figure for the cornea, the most delicate and sensitive exposed part of the body. The idea is that whoever harms God's people pokes his finger in God's eye, causing serious irritation to the Sovereign.

One of the reasons the Bible speaks so forcefully against false teachers is that they not only believe and practice evil but also lure others, including God's saints, into their wicked beliefs and practices. People in the church who live ungodly lives and lure others into their sinful ways are sticking their finger in God's eye, as it were, and would be better off dead. How we treat fellow believers in the church is a matter of immense importance, and to lead them into sin, thus irritating Almighty God, is unthinkable.

There are many ways persons can be caused to **stumble** into sin. The most obvious way is by directly tempting them to sin, and Satan and the world can use even believers to tempt other believers to sin.

Eve provides the first and classic example of one who directly tempted another person to sin. After succumbing to Satan's temptation herself she immediately seduced Adam into joining her in disobeying God. Aaron, the first high priest of Israel, caused the whole nation to sin by molding and then worshiping the golden calf while Moses was on Mount Sinai receiving the commandments from God. King Jeroboam was so flagrant in leading Israel into idolatry that his name became a byword for idolatrous rebellion against God. He was the supremely sinful king who set an example of wickedness into which other sinful kings followed and to whom they were thus compared by being described as walking "in the sins of Jeroboam" (see, e.g., 1 Kings 16:31; 2 Kings 3:3; 17:22).

Jesus charged the Jewish leaders not only with being hypocritical and sinful themselves but with leading others into sin through their man-made traditions. Although they were not guilty of adultery in the sense of having an extramarital affair, many of them became adulterers themselves and promoted adultery by others through their tradition of permitting a husband to divorce his wife without legitimate cause. Whoever "divorces his wife, except for the cause of unchastity," Jesus declared, "makes her commit adultery; and whoever marries a divorced woman commits adultery" (Matt. 5:32).

The church at Pergamum was indicted by the Lord because it tolerated members who held "the teaching of Balaam, who kept teaching Balak to put a stumbling block before the sons of Israel, to eat things sacrificed to idols, and to commit acts of immorality" (Rev. 2:14). The church at Thyatira had a similar sin, the toleration of "the woman Jezebel, who calls herself a prophetess, and she teaches and leads My bond-servants astray, so that they commit acts of immorality and eat things sacrificed to idols" (2:20). Both churches tolerated the teaching of false doctrine and the practice of wicked standards of living.

A husband today may suggest to his wife, "Let's add this deduction to our income tax return. It really doesn't qualify, but no one will ever know, and besides everyone else does it." In doing that he commits a double sin by inducing his wife to join him in the fraudulence. A person may talk a co-worker into joining him in inflating company expense reports and pocketing the difference. That person, too, commits the double sin Jesus is warning against here. A man may seduce a Christian woman or lead her to watch immoral entertainment while on a date.

Those examples and many more would qualify as ways of leading a child of God to sin. It is amazing how reluctant we are to expose our physical children to evil and how eager we are to protect them. But frequently we are not as eager to protect all other children in the Lord's family.

God's children can also be caused to stumble indirectly. That is the broad category of danger about which Paul specifically warns parents, saying, "Do not provoke your children to anger" (Eph. 6:4). By such things as showing favoritism, demanding unrealistic achievements, being critical, overprotective, or overpermissive, parents can frustrate and exasperate their children and drive them to angry reactions that are emotionally and even spiritually damaging. Not allowing children to make their own mistakes now and then, neglecting them (sometimes because of church commitments), and showing little interest in their opinions and concerns can bring the same tragic result. In rebelling against their parents' attitudes and practices in such matters as those, children often rebel against their parents' beliefs and moral standards as well, siding against them on virtually every issue simply to vent their resentment and assert their independence. Spouses, friends, co-workers, and fellow church members can also be indirectly caused to stumble into sin by being treated in insensitive, unloving, and unkind ways.

A third manner of causing God's children to stumble is through sinful example. Without having a word said to them, believers can be led into sinful attitudes and practices simply by following the bad example of others. Here again, parents need to be on guard, because they are continually setting examples, both good and bad, for their children to follow.

The story is told of an alcoholic father who stole out of the house one winter night to go to his favorite tavern. He had not gone far when he heard a soft crunching noise in the snow behind him. He turned around to see his five-year-old boy a few yards behind him. When he asked his son what he was doing, the boy replied, "I'm trying to follow in your footsteps, Dad." According to the story, the man never took another drink.

Timothy succeeded Paul as leader of the church at Ephesus, and in the first letter to his successor the apostle admonished him that "in speech, conduct, love, faith and purity" he was to show himself "an example of those who believe" (1 Tim. 4:12). A church leader—whether pastor, youth worker, Sunday school teacher, or whatever—cannot escape being an example that, for better or worse, consciously or unconsciously, is going to be followed by those given into his care.

Even when a person himself is not sinning, it is possible for him to lead others into sin. By carelessly flaunting one's liberty in Christ by participating in an activity that is not itself a sin and is perfectly appropriate for a strong Christian, it is possible to cause weaker brothers and sisters **to stumble.** If they follow the mature believer's example while still being convicted in their own immature consciences that the practice is wrong, they are led into sin. Although the practice itself may not be sinful, it becomes sinful for the weaker Christian because it is done against what he believes to be right, and therefore against his conscience.

Many believers in the early church came out of strict Judaism, in which the eating of pork in any form was forbidden. They were also used to observing numerous holy days, especially the Sabbath. After becoming Christians it was difficult to break with those Old Covenant ceremonial regulations that had been instilled in them as required by God, and many could not bring themselves to eat pork or to work on the Sabbath. Many other believers, on the other hand, came out of rank paganism, where demonic practices and the worst sorts of immorality were integral parts of their religion. For them, anything associated with those pagan rites was abhorrent and repulsive, and to eat a piece of meat that had once been offered on a pagan altar was unthinkable.

That is the issue Paul fully covers in Romans 14 and 1 Corinthians 8 (see the volume *1 Corinthians* in this commentary series), an issue compounded by judgmental self-righteousness on both sides. The Gentile believers criticized weaker Jewish believers for still refusing to touch pork or do any work at all on the Sabbath, emphasizing the truth that, in Christ, they had been freed from such ceremonial restrictions. The Jewish believers criticized weaker Gentile believers for refusing to eat meat offered to pagan idols, emphasizing the truth that they now knew those pagan deities were not gods at all and that, in any case, the meat itself could not be spiritually or morally contaminating.

The important concern, Paul told both sides, was neither eating or not eating certain foods nor observing or not observing certain days. More important by far were the consciences of their fellow believers. As long as someone believes a practice is wrong, for him it *is* wrong, because his intent is to do wrong, even though the practice might not be wrong in itself. Until his conscience grows to the place where he can honestly accept doing it, the practice should be avoided. Not only that, but those who do not share that particular inhibition should respect those who have it. Otherwise they may cause their brother to commit sin by going against his conscience. In fact, the stronger Christian should himself refrain from the practice if doing so would help protect the conscience of a weaker believer. In summary Paul says, "All things indeed are clean, but they are evil for the man who eats and gives offense. It is good not to eat meat or to drink wine, or to do anything by which your brother stumbles. The faith which you have, have as your own conviction before God. Happy is he who does not condemn himself in what he approves. But he who doubts is condemned if he eats, because his eating is not from faith; and whatever is not from faith is sin" (Rom. 14:20-23; cf. 1 Cor. 8:1-13).

A weak Christian who is continually offered an activity that offends his conscience is likely either eventually to go along and do what he believes is wrong, and thus reveal a motive of disobedience and thereby go against his conscience, or to overreact against the activity and go deeper into legalism. In either case, he is caused **to stumble** spiritually, and anyone who contributes to his stumbling, Jesus says, would be better off dead.

Just as many in the last days will be surprised that they had served the Lord through serving His people, many others will be surprised that they had opposed the Lord by *not* serving His people. To the unbelieving goats on His left the Lord will say,

> "Depart from Me, accursed ones, into the eternal fire which has been prepared for the devil and his angels; for I was hungry, and you gave Me nothing to eat; I was thirsty, and you gave Me nothing to drink; I was a stranger, and you did not invite Me in; naked, and you did not clothe Me; sick, and in prison, and you did not visit Me." Then they themselves also will answer, saying, "Lord, when did we see You hungry, or thirsty, or a stranger, or naked, or sick, or in prison, and did not take care of You?" Then He will answer them, saying, "Truly I say to you, to the extent that you did not do it to one of the least of these, you did not do it to Me." And these will go away into eternal punishment. (Matt. 25:41-46)

It is even possible to cause someone **to stumble** into sin by failing to lead them into righteousness. That may, in fact, be the most common way in which believers contribute to other believers' sin. To keep God's truth and goodness to ourselves and not share our spiritual insights and experiences is to withhold from others what can help them grow. It is tragic that many believers starve for spiritual food while living in a Christian family and attending an evangelical church.

Throughout the New Testament, believers are admonished to encourage each other in righteousness. They are called "to stimulate one another to love and good deeds" (Heb. 10:24). God leads His people away from sin and to righteousness, and that is what every Christian should seek for himself and for his fellow Christians. In His model prayer, Jesus calls us to ask our heavenly Father "not [to] lead us into temptation," knowing that He would never do such a thing, because it is His supreme desire to "deliver us from evil" (Matt. 6:13). James assures us that "God cannot be tempted by evil, and He Himself does not tempt anyone" (James 1:13). The person who lives a godly life follows God's example. Like God, he never leads others into sin but helps protect them from it and builds them up in holiness.

Instead of inducing others to sin, we should induce them to grow in righteousness. Instead of misusing our liberty for our own satisfaction, we should be willing to restrict our liberty whenever so doing might help a weaker brother. Instead of setting an evil example, we should set a Christlike example. Instead of provoking others to the point of anger and rebellion, we should stimulate them to love and good works.

William Barclay tells the story of an old man on his deathbed who was terribly distraught. When asked what was bothering him, he replied, "When we were boys at play, one day at a crossroads we reversed a signpost, and I've never ceased to wonder how many people were sent in the wrong direction by what we did." Such acts go on all the time in the life of the church as believers send other believers signals that lead them on the road to sin. This is extremely serious. Just how serious is seen in the next verse.

"Woe to the world because of its stumbling blocks!" Jesus went on to warn. **"For it is inevitable that stumbling blocks come; but woe to that man through whom the stumbling block comes!"**

Woe was a word of cursing and condemnation. **The world** is under God's curse not only because of its own sinfulness but because of the spiritual and moral **stumbling blocks** it puts in the paths of His children. There seems to be no end of books, magazines, movies, TV programs, and commonly accepted practices and attitudes to mislead and corrupt those who belong to God. The world is constantly setting sin traps, and its favorite victims are God's children.

That is characteristic of the world's fallenness, and **it is inevitable that** such **stumbling blocks come** and continue to come until the Lord returns. **But woe to that man through whom the stumbling block comes!** Jesus had already established the gravity of that offense by declaring it would be better for the guilty person to have been thrown into the sea and drowned. Better off dead than to lead one of the Lord's little ones astray. Now He adds that such offenses bring the judgment of God.

One of the young men in our church handicapped ministry came to me one Sunday and said he had done a bad thing. "I got drunk," he explained remorsefully. Upon questioning him, I discovered that, as a prank, his brother and some friends had forced alcoholic beverages down his throat until he was drunk. But the worst tragedy was not his drunkenness but the guilt he was made to suffer. He thought he was responsible for becoming drunk and had asked Jesus for forgiveness, but he was so ashamed that he wondered if the Lord would forgive him. I assured him that Jesus fully understood and had forgiven him, though, of course, the guilt was not his at all. And those who *were* guilty for his drunkenness and stricken conscience were in danger of God's judgment.

THE PREVENTION

And if your hand or your foot causes you to stumble, cut it off and throw it from you; it is better for you to enter life crippled or lame, than having two hands or two feet, to be cast into the eternal fire. And if your eye causes you

to stumble, pluck it out, and throw it from you. It is better for you to enter life with one eye, than having two eyes, to be cast into the fiery hell. (18:8-9)

The Lord is obviously speaking figuratively, because no part of our physical bodies causes us to sin, and removing any part of it would not keep us from sinning. The point was that a person should do whatever is necessary, no matter how extreme and painful it might be, to keep from sinning himself or to keep from causing others to sin. Nothing is worth keeping if, in any way, it leads to sin. And the implication here is that there is overcoming grace available for victory over temptation and sin.

This is a repetition, with slight alteration, of the exhortation our Lord gave in Matthew 5:29-30. In 5:29-30, the reference is to the right eye and then the hand and foot, whereas here it is reversed and no mention is made of which eye. And whereas 5:29-30 refers to hell, here Jesus adds the terms *fire* to show the nature of hell and *everlasting life* to show the contrast to hell. All those details fade when we focus on the intent of the words. My own comments on the Matthew 5:29-30 text are repeated here:

> Here Jesus points the way to deliverance from heart sin. At first His advice seems incongruous with what He has just been saying. If the problem is in the heart, what good is plucking out an eye or cutting off a hand? If the right eye were lost, the left would continue to look lustfully, and if the right hand were cut off, the left would still remain to carry on sinful acts.
>
> Obviously, Jesus is speaking figuratively of those things, physical or otherwise, that cause us to be tempted or make us more susceptible to temptation. In Jewish culture, the right eye and right hand represented a person's best and most precious faculties. The right eye represented one's best vision, and the right hand one's best skills. Jesus' point is that we should be willing to give up whatever is necessary, even the most cherished things we possess, if doing that will help protect us from evil. Nothing is so valuable as to be worth preserving at the expense of righteousness. This strong message is obviously not to be interpreted in a wooden, literal way so that the Lord appears to be advocating mutilation. Mutilation will not cleanse the heart. The intent of these words is simply to call for dramatic severing of the sinful impulses in us which push us to evil action (cf. Matt. 18:8-9; John F. MacArthur, *Matthew 1-7*, The MacArthur New Testament Commentary [Chicago: Moody, 1985], p. 304.)

If any habit, situation, relationship, or anything else **causes you to stumble,** Jesus said, it should be permanently forsaken. Great danger often requires drastic measures. Even if a sacrifice causes a person to be figuratively **crippled** and to be blind in **one eye**—financially, socially, professionally, or in any other way—that is infinitely better than being **cast into the eternal fire** of **hell.**

This almost proverbial statement is a general exhortation calling for drastic action against sin. Although only unbelievers are in danger of hell, believers can understand from this statement the seriousness of sin and of leading others to sin. The best prevention against causing others to sin is making whatever sacrifice is necessary to protect *oneself* from sin. "I buffet my body and make it my slave," Paul said, "lest possibly, after I have preached to others, I myself should be disqualified" (1 Cor. 9:27). The person who deals decisively with his own temptations and sins will be in the least danger of causing others to sin. If he is genuinely and humbly concerned that he himself not **stumble** spiritually, he will also be prepared and motivated to help others not to stumble.

The Care of God's Children

(18:10-14)

13

See that you do not despise one of these little ones, for I say to you, that their angels in heaven continually behold the face of My Father who is in heaven. [For the Son of Man has come to save that which was lost.] What do you think? If any man has a hundred sheep, and one of them has gone astray, does he not leave the ninety-nine on the mountains and go and search for the one that is straying? And if it turns out that he finds it, truly I say to you, he rejoices over it more than over the ninety-nine which have not gone astray. Thus it is not the will of your Father who is in heaven that one of these little ones perish. (18:10-14)

An essential element in understanding the redemptive plan of God is the truth that only those who come to Him through Christ in childlike faith can enter His kingdom. Only those whom the Lord humbles in complete dependence on Him will become His children and therefore joint heirs with Jesus Christ (Matt. 18:4; Rom. 8:17; Eph. 1:11-14). That is why, as Paul points out to the Corinthians, the church does not include "many wise according to the flesh, not many mighty, not many noble; but God has chosen the foolish things of the world to shame the wise, and God has chosen the weak things of the world to shame the things which are strong" (1 Cor. 1:26-27). It is not that those who have great fame, high position, wealth, intellect, or other human status or achievement *cannot* come to God but that, because of their worldly recognition and power, they are often inclined to think they have no need of Him.

The "wise according to the flesh" to whom Paul refers are the intelligentsia, those whose learning is far above that of the average person. The "mighty" includes those who have political, military, or financial power and who thereby exercise control over the lives of many other people. The "noble" are the social elite, those who have inherited or achieved elevated social status. Feeling proud, superior, and self-satisfied, most such people feel no need for God, especially if coming to Him would demand childlike humility and surrendering confidence in their human abilities, accomplishments, and positions.

It is tragic that many Christians are eager to win the rich, famous, and powerful to Christ, not so much for the Lord's sake or for those persons' own sakes as for the supposed boon their testimonies would give to the cause of evangelism. Yet it is not a person's human greatness but his spiritual humility that the Lord honors and blesses. It is God's power alone that draws and wins men to Himself, and the human instruments He desires to use in that work are not the great but the humble. A human witness who attracts attention to himself draws attention away from Christ.

Until a person is willing to become one of Christ's **little ones** (Matt. 18:6, 10, 14), he can have no part in God's kingdom or God's work. That is why "the base things of the world and the despised, God has chosen, the things that are not, that He might nullify the things that are, that no man should boast before God" (1 Cor. 1:28-29). And that is why, as Isaiah prophesied, God anointed Jesus "to preach the gospel to the poor, . . . to proclaim release to the captives, and recovery of sight to the blind, to set free those who are downtrodden" (Luke 4:18; cf. Isa. 61:1). It is not that the outcasts of the world—represented by the poor, the captive, the blind, and the downtrodden—are the only ones who have need of the gospel but that they are often the ones who are most willing to recognize their need.

As He continues to teach the disciples about caring for one another as believers, the Lord first states the rule and then the reasons for the rule.

The Rule

See that you do not despise one of these little ones; (18:10*a*)

As explained in the previous chapter, **little ones** does not refer to physical children but to Christians, those who believe in Christ (v. 6). The young toddler whom Jesus perhaps still held in His arms (see v. 2) was a visual illustration of God's spiritual children.

See that you do not despise is a warning, a negative command that strongly implies God's displeasure with disobedience of it. The Greek use of the negative with a subjunctive verb intensifies the prohibition. Jesus had already made clear the seriousness of mistreating any of God's **little ones:** It would be better for a person who commits such an offense to have "a heavy millstone . . . hung around his neck, and that he be drowned in the depth of the sea" (v. 6).

Despise is from *kataphroneō,* which has the literal meaning of thinking down on. To **despise** someone is to look down on him as inferior and not worth consideration or care. It is to disdain a person and treat him with contempt as being worthless. To **despise one of these little ones** is therefore to treat one of God's own precious and beloved children with disdain and contempt.

Little ones included the Twelve themselves. And in the context of what had just happened, Jesus was telling them that their bickering about who was greatest in the kingdom was a form of despising God's **little ones**, in this case each other. When one of them pushed himself up, it was at the expense of pushing the others down. Instead of their proud, self-seeking attitudes that created jealousy, envy, and resentment, they should have been showing concern for each other's welfare. They should have been building others up rather than themselves.

Paul exhorted the Philippian believers:

> Make my joy complete by being of the same mind, maintaining the same love, united in spirit, intent on one purpose. Do nothing from selfish or empty conceit, but with humility of mind let each of you regard one another as more important than himself; do not merely look out for your own personal interests, but also for the interests of others. Have this attitude in yourselves which was also in Christ Jesus, who, although He existed in the form of God, did not regard equality with God a thing to be grasped, but emptied Himself, taking the form of a bond-servant, and being made in the likeness of men. And being found in appearance as a man, He humbled Himself by becoming obedient to the point of death, even death on a cross. (Phil. 2:2-8)

It is natural for the world to resent Christians and to look down on them. But it is not acceptable for Christians to look at each other in that way. Yet, still fearing the fallen flesh, the church has always been tempted to mimic the ways and attitudes of the world, which it does when any of God's people feel superior to others.

Christians **despise** each other in many different ways. We despise one another when we flaunt our liberty before weaker believers, causing them to go against their consciences or to overreact and fall deeper into legalism. "Let not him who eats regard with contempt him who does not eat, and let not him who does not eat judge him who eats, for God has accepted him" (Rom. 14:3). To use one's liberty in Christ in such a callous way is to use it "as a covering for evil" instead of as a servant of God (1 Pet. 2:16).

Christians also **despise** one another when they show partiality. We are never to hold "faith in our glorious Lord Jesus Christ with an attitude of personal favoritism" (James 2:1). God loves and cares for His children equally. He "is not one to show partiality, but in every nation the man who fears Him and does what is right, is welcome to Him" (Acts 10:34-35). That has always been the Lord's attitude and it has always been the attitude He expects of His people. The believer who pleases the Lord and who sincerely honors Him is the one who honors all others who belong to Him (Ps. 15:1-4). He never looks down on God's other children, however insignificant they might seem to be.

By the same token, the believer who pleases the Lord does not give special honor to a fellow Christian because of wealth, high position, or influence. That, too, has always been a temptation for Christians. James warned believers in the early church:

> If a man comes into your assembly with a gold ring and dressed in fine clothes, and there also comes in a poor man in dirty clothes, and you pay special attention to the one who is wearing the fine clothes, and say, "You sit here in a good place," and you say to the poor man, "You stand over there, or sit down by my footstool," have you not made distinctions among yourselves, and become judges with evil motives? Listen, my beloved brethren: did not God choose the poor of this world to be rich in faith and heirs of the kingdom which He promised to those who love Him? But you have dishonored the poor man. Is it not the rich who oppress you and personally drag you into court? Do they not blaspheme the fair name by which you have been called? If, however, you are fulfilling the royal law, according to the Scripture, "You shall love your neighbor as yourself," you are doing well. (James 2:2-8)

A third way believers **despise** fellow believers is by withholding help from those in need. When Paul confronted that problem in the Corinthian church he rebuked them with the words, "When you meet together, it is not to eat the Lord's Supper, for in your eating each one takes his own supper first; and one is hungry and another is drunk. What! Do you not have houses in which to eat and drink? Or do you despise the church of God, and shame those who have nothing? What shall I say to you? Shall I praise you? In this I will not praise you" (1 Cor. 11:20-22). That situation would correspond to a church today having a potluck supper before a Communion service, with those who brought food eating it all and not sharing with those who had none. To do such a thing is to show contempt for God's church and for His poorer children.

The exhortations of James 2:15-16 and 1 John 3:17-18 are valuable additions to this same point, warning against withholding from fellow believers any basic necessity of life.

A fourth way believers **despise** fellow believers is by ridiculing their physical appearance. Such insensitive, heartless criticism was directed against Paul by some of the haughty, worldly members in the Corinthian church who said that "his letters are weighty and strong, but his personal presence is unimpressive, and his speech contemptible" (2 Cor. 10:10). Although they admitted his teaching was sound, they had the meanness and stupidity to despise him merely because of his physical looks.

Paul commended the Galatians for not despising or loathing his "bodily condition," perhaps a serious eye infection related to malaria, when he first preached the gospel to them (Gal. 4:14). To mock another person because of physical, mental, or cultural deficiencies not only is contemptible in men's sight but in God's.

During one of Dwight L. Moody's British campaigns he was repeatedly mocked in the press for his lack of proper English and his homey style. When asked to speak at Cambridge University, the epitome of British intellectualism and sophistication, Moody apparently decided to capitalize on that image in order to gain the attention of the audience. His comment no doubt also had the effect of pointing up the superficiality and irrelevance of the criticism of his grammar. He opened his message with the words, "Don't let nobody never tell you God don't love you, cause He do."

Believers **despise** other believers when they are indifferent to or judgmental of a fellow believer who spiritually stumbles. When a brother or sister falls into sin, especially if the sin is public and well known, there is a temptation to write them off, saying in effect, if not in words, "He knew better and he made his choice. Let him live with the consequences. Until he changes, I'll stay at arm's length." But Paul's counsel is otherwise. "Brethren," he wrote the Galatians, "even if a man is caught in any trespass, you who are spiritual, restore such a one in a spirit of gentleness; each one looking to yourself, lest you too be tempted. Bear one another's burdens, and thus fulfill the law of Christ" (Gal. 6:1-2). Christ's way for His followers is that they humbly help a sinning brother, realizing that they, too, could fall into the same or equally bad sin and that it is only by God's grace if they do not.

Believers also **despise** other believers by resenting a fellow Christian who confronts their sinfulness. Instead of facing and repenting of a sin that is brought to their attention and being grateful to the one who confronts them, the old self often makes them strike back and charge the other person with being judgmental, self-righteous, legalistic, and hypocritical. Even when church discipline is carried out in careful conformity to Scripture and is done graciously and in love, it is often resented. Paul warned the Corinthian believers not to resent and despise Timothy if he came to them (1 Cor. 16:10-11), no doubt because he would confront them about many of the sins for which Paul had often, including in that letter, confronted them. The apostle also counselled Titus not to allow those under his care to disregard him for exhorting and reproving them (Titus 2:15).

A seventh way believers **despise** other believers is by taking advantage of them for personal gain. Although Paul was referring specifically to sexual immorality, his warning to the Thessalonians applies to taking advantage of a fellow believer in any way—financially, socially, or any other. A Christian is not to "defraud his brother" in any regard, "because the Lord is the avenger in all these things" (1 Thess. 4:6).

THE REASONS

for I say to you, that their angels in heaven continually behold the face of My Father who is in heaven. [For the Son of Man has come to save that

which was lost.] What do you think? If any man has a hundred sheep, and one of them has gone astray, does he not leave the ninety-nine on the mountains and go and search for the one that is straying? And if it turns out that he finds it, truly I say to you, he rejoices over it more than over the ninety-nine which have not gone astray. Thus it is not the will of your Father who is in heaven that one of these little ones perish. (18:10b-14)

After stating the negative rule regarding care for God's children, Jesus gives three reasons for the rule: believers' relation to angels, their relation to Himself, and their relation to the Father.

BELIEVERS' RELATION TO ANGELS

for I say to you, that their angels in heaven continually behold the face of My Father who is in heaven. (18:10b)

The expression I say to you is emphatic, pointing up the importance of what the Lord is about to say. The idea is, "With all My authority I solemnly affirm to you." He then gives the first compelling reason Christians should never despise other Christians: their relation to their angels in heaven.

The writer of Hebrews explains that the holy, elect angels are "all ministering spirits, sent out to render service for the sake of those who will inherit salvation" (Heb. 1:14). Their purpose is to serve God by attending to the care of His people. These angels in heaven live in the very presence of God, where they wait attentively for His commands to serve the people of His love. "They continually behold the face of My Father who is in heaven," Jesus said. The implication is that the holy angels never take their eyes off God, lest they miss some direction from Him regarding a task they are to perform on behalf of a believer.

Neither of these texts, however—nor any other Scripture—teaches the idea of an individual guardian angel for every believer, as Jewish tradition in Jesus' day taught and as many people still believe and teach. When Peter knocked at the door of Mary's house after he was miraculously released from prison, a servant girl named Rhoda answered. Upon seeing Peter she was so overjoyed she forgot to open the gate. When she reported his presence to the believers gathered inside, it was probably the notion of individual guardian angels that was behind their insistence that she had only seen "Peter's angel" (Acts 12:12-15). But that superstitious belief is merely reflected in this text; it is neither taught nor substantiated here or anywhere else in Scripture.

In Matthew 18:10 Jesus speaks of believers and their angels in a collective sense. These angels, whether a distinct group or the whole body of holy angels, are responsible for the care of God's little ones, those who believe in His Son (v. 6). It is in part because of these angels who live in the presence of the Father who is in

heaven that believers are warned not to despise one another.

The fact that Almighty God is so concerned about the care of His beloved children that He has hosts of angels in His presence ready to be dispatched to their aid demonstrates clearly how valuable believers are and how unthinkably wicked it is to look with disdain on someone whom God so highly prizes.

As indicated by brackets in the NASB text, verse 11 (**For the Son of Man has come to save that which was lost**) is not found in the best early manuscripts of this gospel. The almost identical phrase, however, is in Luke 19:10, where "to seek and" is added before **to save**. Because there is no question about the authenticity of the Luke text, there is no question that Matthew 18:11 teaches a genuinely scriptural truth. The phrase was probably picked up from Luke by a well-meaning copyist and added to Matthew. But because it is not a part of Matthew's original gospel, it will not be discussed here.

BELIEVERS' RELATION TO CHRIST

What do you think? If any man has a hundred sheep, and one of them has gone astray, does he not leave the ninety-nine on the mountains and go and search for the one that is straying? And if it turns out that he finds it, truly I say to you, he rejoices over it more than over the ninety-nine which have not gone astray. (18:12-13)

As implied, though not stated, in this passage, a second reason believers are not to despise each other is their relation to Jesus Christ. The Lord had just said that "whoever receives one such child in My name receives Me" (v. 5). Every true believer—no matter how young, immature, unfaithful, unattractive, or deprived— is one with Jesus Christ, purchased with His own precious blood. Therefore, to look down on any Christian and consider him to be worthless and useless is to despise Christ Himself. "The one who listens to you listens to Me," Jesus told the seventy when He commissioned them, "and the one who rejects you rejects Me; and he who rejects Me rejects the One who sent Me" (Luke 10:16).

The Pharisees and scribes considered the uneducated and lower classes to be morally and religiously inferior and worth little, if any, of their attention. Jesus, on the other hand, would not break off a battered reed or put out a smoldering wick (Matt. 12:20; cf. Isa.42:3), both of those figures being pictures of treatment given to afflicted and helpless humanity. He would not further break someone who was already broken and suffering, nor would He further quench someone whose remaining life and hope were already about to be extinguished. Throughout His earthly ministry Jesus demonstrated just the opposite concern as He fed the hungry, healed the sick, encouraged the hopeless, and offered forgiveness to sinners. He did "not come to destroy men's lives, but to save them" (Luke 9:56).

It is that gracious, divine concern that Jesus illustrates here in the parable of the lost sheep. **What do you think?** was a common phrase used by teachers to get their students to ponder carefully about what was being taught.

Although none of the Twelve is identified as a shepherd by trade, every Palestinian Jew was familiar with shepherds and their ways. In this hypothetical story, Jesus told of a **man** who was a shepherd and who had **a hundred sheep,** one of which went **astray.** In the rugged terrain of Palestine there were many ravines, gullies, caves, and crevices into which a sheep could wander or fall. "When the shepherd discovers a sheep is missing," Jesus asked, **"does he not leave the ninety-nine on the mountains and go and search for the one that is straying?"**

The idea seems implied that the shepherd sensed the **straying** sheep's absence without having to check the entire flock. The shepherd knew his sheep intimately, both as a flock and individually (cf. the analogy of John 10:1-18). He therefore instinctively knew when something was wrong or when one of them was missing. He was also an expert at tracking lost sheep, and love for his defenseless and utterly dependent flock would not allow him to give up until he had found and rescued the one that was missing. The loyal shepherd would fight off wolves, bears, lions, thieves, or any other threat to the sheep. When an errant animal was found, the shepherd would pour olive oil over any wounds or scratches and he would bind up a broken leg. He would then tenderly place the sheep on his shoulders and carry it back to the fold.

From this parable we see that Christ's love, illustrated in that of the shepherd, is personal and individual. It does not matter which sheep goes astray. The Lord is equally concerned for any **one of them.** He is just as much aware and concerned when a poor believer in the slums wanders from Him as when a respected church leader stumbles into sin.

The parable also illustrates the truth that the Lord's care for His people is patient. He is infinitely patient with their self-willed, sinful foolishness and He will not give up on a single one, even though that person might be the least promising and the least faithful of all His children.

We also see here God's seeking care. He does not wait for a lost sheep to return on its own but personally goes as far into the wilderness as necessary to find and rescue it. The Savior is infinitely more anxious and determined for restoration than is even the most repentant believer.

If a human shepherd can exhibit so much concern for each sheep under his care, how much more does the Lord Jesus Christ, "the great Shepherd of the sheep through the blood of the eternal covenant" (Heb. 13:20), care when a single one of His people spiritually goes astray? And when He **finds it** and restores it to Himself, how much more heavenly rejoicing is there **over it . . . than over the ninety-nine which have not gone astray?**

On another occasion, Jesus used the same parable to teach God's concern for unbelievers. "I tell you," He explained, "that in the same way, there will be more joy in heaven over one sinner who repents, than over ninety-nine righteous persons who need no repentance" (Luke 15:3-7).

There is special joy expressed for the sheep that is found not because it is more valued or loved than the others but because its danger, hardship, and great need elicit special concern from the caring shepherd. In the same way, when one child in a family is ill, particularly if it is seriously ill, a mother will devote much more time and attention to him than to the other children, often more than to all the rest together. And when that child finally gets well, the mother does not rejoice for the children who have been healthy all along but for the one who was sick and suffering. And if the brothers and sisters are loving, they, too, will rejoice in the restoration of their sibling.

For several days in the fall of 1987, the whole world had its attention and compassion fixed on a little girl, not quite two years old, who was trapped in an abandoned well shaft in west Texas for three days. When, after much strenuous work, difficult drilling, and painstaking excavation, she was finally rescued, there was rejoicing all across the land, and she was sent thousands of cards and presents as she recuperated in the hospital. It was not that she was more precious or worthy than countless other little girls, but that her need at that time was so great.

Because the Lord Jesus has such tender compassion on all His needy little ones, so that their well-being brings Him great joy, we should find ourselves in holy fear of ever looking down on such ones.

BELIEVERS' RELATION TO THE FATHER

Thus it is not the will of your Father who is in heaven that one of these little ones perish. (18:14)

A third reason believers are not to despise each other is their relation to their **Father who is in heaven,** who joins the Son and the angels in rejoicing over a believer who is restored.

Although *apollumi* (**perish**) often carried the idea of total destruction or death, it sometimes, as here, referred to nonpermanent ruin or loss. In Romans 14:15 the word parallels *lupeō*, which means to cause pain or grief: "For if because of food your brother is hurt (*lupeō*), you are no longer walking according to love. Do not destroy (*apollumi*) with your food him for whom Christ died" (cf. 1 Cor. 8:11).

The **perish** of which Jesus here speaks relates to spiritual progress in the Christian life. God the **Father** does not want a single one of His **little ones** to be spiritually wounded or marred, even for a brief time. When His children fall into sin it destroys their usefulness to Him and to the church and it undercuts their happiness and their right relationship to Him and to one another.

Peter tells believers that they should cast all their cares on God, because He graciously cares for them (1 Pet. 5:7). Like the shepherd who searches for the lost sheep until it is found, the **Father** individually cares for each person who comes to Him through the Son and will see to it that every one of them who becomes wayward eventually will be brought back into the fellowship of His family and kingdom.

William Arnot makes the beautiful observation that, "If it did not please [God] to get me back, my pleasure would be small." It should be great comfort to stumbling believers to know that, when they repent and return, their angels, their Lord Jesus Christ, and their **Father who is in heaven** will all be overjoyed.

For one believer to wound another is to attack the will of God and set himself up as God's antagonist. The Lord seeks the spiritual well-being of all His children, and we had better not do less.

This section of Matthew speaks powerfully to the church today. The Body of Christ is filled with believers who look down on their spiritual brothers and sisters, treating them with disdain, indifference, and rudeness because they consider them unworthy of special care and ministry. It is at that very point of the church's sin that it sets itself in opposition to the holy angels, to the Son of God, and to the Almighty Himself.

The Discipline of God's Children

(18:15-20)

14

And if your brother sins, go and reprove him in private; if he listens to you, you have won your brother. But if he does not listen to you, take one or two more with you, so that by the mouth of two or three witnesses every fact may be confirmed. And if he refuses to listen to them, tell it to the church; and if he refuses to listen even to the church, let him be to you as a Gentile and a tax-gatherer. Truly I say to you, whatever you shall bind on earth shall be bound in heaven; and whatever you loose on earth shall be loosed in heaven. Again I say to you, that if two of you agree on earth about anything that they may ask, it shall be done for them by My Father who is in heaven. For where two or three have gathered together in My name, there I am in their midst. (18:15-20)

God's desire for His children here on earth is purity of life. It is impossible to study Scripture attentively and not be overwhelmingly convinced that God seeks above all else for His people to be holy and that He is grieved by sin of any kind. Directly quoting God's command to His Old Covenant people Israel, Peter wrote the same command to Christ's church: "You shall be holy, for I am holy" (1 Pet. 1:16; cf. Lev. 11:44).

Because God is so concerned for the holiness of His people, they should be equally concerned. The church cannot preach and teach a message it does not live and have any integrity before God, or even before the world. Yet in many churches where there is no tolerance for sin in principle there is much tolerance for it in practice. And when preaching becomes separated from living, it becomes separated both from integrity and from spiritual and moral effectiveness. It promotes hypocrisy instead of holiness. Divorcing biblical teaching from daily living is compromise of the worst sort. It corrupts the church, grieves the Lord, and dishonors His Word and His name.

It is not surprising, therefore, that public discipline for sin is rare in the church today. Where there is little genuine desire for purity there will also be little desire to deal with impurity. The misinterpreted and misapplied statement of Jesus that we should not judge lest we be judged (Matt. 7:1) has been used to justify the tolerance of every sort of sin and false teaching. The ideas that every person's privacy is essentially to be protected and that each is responsible only to himself have engulfed much of the church. Under the guise of false love and spurious humility that refuse to hold others to account, many Christians are as dedicated as some unbelievers to the unbiblical notion of "live and let live." The church, however, is not nearly so careful not to gossip about someone's sinning as it is not to confront it and call for it to stop.

The church has always had need for confronting the sins of its people. During its early days many foreign visitors to Palestine were converted to Christ and decided to stay in or near Jerusalem in order to enjoy the fellowship of believers there. A large number of native Jewish converts were ostracized from their families and lost their jobs because of their new-found faith. To help support those needy brothers and sisters, many of whom were virtually destitute, the believers who had property and possession sold them and gave the proceeds to the apostles, who "distributed to each, as any had need" (Acts 4:35). That practice was the spontaneous reaction of generous, Spirit-filled hearts to meet the practical needs of fellow Christians.

During that time, a couple named Ananias and Sapphira sold a piece of their property and pledged to God that they would give all the proceeds to the apostles for use in the church. Somewhere in the process, however, they decided to keep back a portion of the pledged money for themselves. In order not to appear less generous than their fellow believers, however, they falsely reported that they were giving the full amount. When the Lord revealed the duplicity to Peter, he first confronted the husband. "Ananias," he asked, "'why has Satan filled your heart to lie to the Holy Spirit, and to keep back some of the price of the land? While it remained unsold, did it not remain your own? And after it was sold, was it not under your control? Why is it that you have conceived this deed in your heart? You have not lied to men, but to God.' And as he heard these words, Ananias fell down and breathed his last." Several hours later, Sapphira came to the apostles, not knowing what had happened to her husband. When Peter asked her if the property was sold for the price claimed by her husband, she confirmed his lie and suffered his fate. Not surprisingly, "great fear came upon the whole church, and upon all who heard of these things" (Acts 5:1-11).

The selfishness of Ananias and Sapphira was deplorable, but their great sin was in lying about what they had done, not only to the church but to God. In this particular case in the early church, God took discipline directly into His own hands and demonstrated before all how sin is to be dealt with by removing the offenders from the church and from the earth! The purity of the church not only was protected by making God's people more fearful of sin but also by helping to keep out of the fellowship those who were not true believers (v. 13).

Even in apostolic times, such direct and severe divine intervention in chastening apparently was rare, although Paul reports that some of the Corinthian believers became weak, ill, and even died as the result of gross immorality and disregard for the sacredness of the Lord's Table (1 Cor. 11:30; cf. 1 John 5:16-17). God has not changed His attitude about sin or about purity. He is every bit as much concerned for the holiness of His people today as He was when the church was born. Sin has to be dealt with or it will destroy both those who practice it and those who tolerate it. God may still act in supernatural ways to purge the church, but He has primarily given that responsibility to the church itself. The church must be "self-policing" with regard to sin. The horrendous scandals that have tarnished the church recently reflect the abysmal failure of believers to confront sinning leaders and followers. The world often has had to expose what the church tried to cover up.

The Lord has always disciplined His people, and He has always instructed His people to discipline themselves. Old Testament believers were told not to "reject the discipline of the Lord, or loathe His reproof, for whom the Lord loves He reproves, even as a father, the son in whom he delights" (Prov. 3:11-12). Just as human fathers discipline their children out of love in order to make them better, so God does with His children. Human parents know that instruction to their children without enforcement is futile. Children not only must be told what is right but must be led to do what is right, by correction, rebuke, and often punishment. "He who spares his rod hates his son, but he who loves him disciplines him diligently" (Prov. 13:24). Contrary to much popular thinking, even among Christians, it is not love but indifference that causes parents to allow their children's misbehavior to go uncorrected. "Discipline your son while there is hope," the writer of Proverbs wisely advises (19:18; cf. 22:15; 23:13).

After quoting the proverb (3:11-12) mentioned above, the writer of Hebrews says,

> It is for discipline that you endure; God deals with you as with sons; for what son is there whom his father does not discipline? But if you are without discipline, of which all have become partakers, then you are illegitimate children and not sons. Furthermore, we had earthly fathers to discipline us, and we respected them; shall we not much rather be subject to the Father of Spirits, and live? For they disciplined us for a short time as seemed best to them, but He disciplines us for our good, that we may share His holiness. All discipline for the moment seems not to be joyful, but sorrowful; yet to those who have been trained by it, afterwards it yields the peaceful fruit of righteousness. (Heb. 12:7-11)

It is an illusion to think that the church can take a strong verbal stand against sin without enforcing that stand among its own members and at the same time expect them to conform to God's standards of holiness. Physical children do not respond to that approach in discipline, and neither do spiritual children. Because of the remaining sinfulness of the flesh, Christians still have a strong bent toward disobedience. Without enforcement of its standards, holiness will never flourish. That is why discipline is so essential to the spiritual well-being of a church.

The foolish, pretentious, and sometimes immoral actions of a few highly visible figures in the evangelical church today have caused evangelicalism to become a byword among many liberal Christians and in the world at large. Such lack of integrity is often rightly depicted as the epitome of religious superficiality, self-indulgence, and hypocrisy.

It is with the church's responsibility to keep itself pure that Jesus deals in Matthew 18:15-20. He is still teaching about the childlikeness of believers, illustrated by the young child He had called to Himself and set before the Twelve (v.2). He had declared that a person enters and is considered great in the kingdom by becoming like a little child (vv. 3-4) and that, once in the kingdom, believers are to be protected like little children (vv. 5-9) and cared for like little children (vv. 10-14). He now declares that they must also be disciplined like little children.

In verses 15-20 Jesus presents five elements involved in godly discipline of sinning believers: the person who receives discipline, the person who initiates it, the purpose of it, the process and place for it, and the authority for it.

THE PERSON WHO RECEIVES DISCIPLINE

And if your brother sins, (18:15a)

The person to be disciplined is a **brother** who **sins.** In this context, as in many other places in Scripture, **brother** refers to any fellow believer, whether male or female. The candidate for confrontational discipline is any Christian who **sins.** The implication is that it is a sin that continues in one's life and is unconfessed.

The general, unqualified reference to **your brother** is absolutely inclusive, allowing for no exceptions. *Every* child of God, whether young or old, man or woman, educated or uneducated, wealthy or poor, leader or follower, is to be confronted when he or she **sins.**

Sins is from *hamartanō,* which has the literal meaning of "missing the mark" and is the basic New Testament verb for sin, missing the mark of God's standards. Just as the category of the sinner is inclusive, so is the category of sin. Any sin, by any believer, requires discipline from the church. All sin is an offense against God's holiness and corrupts the holiness of His people. It mars a believer's fellowship with God and his fellowship with other believers.

As reflected in the King James Version and several other translations, some of the most reliable ancient manuscripts of Matthew's gospel add the phrase "against you" after **sins,** indicating an offense committed directly against a fellow Christian.

Peter's question in verse 21 regarding forgiveness of those who sin against us gives support to the inclusion of "against you," as does the Lord's teaching about rebuking and forgiving in Luke 17:3-4.

In either case, however, the basic responsibility is the same, because a person can be sinned against both directly and indirectly. If he is maligned, abused, deceived, cheated, or the like, the sin against him is direct and obvious. In such a case, the offending brother or sister is not only to be rebuked by the one who is offended but also forgiven if he repents. The one who is sinned against should approach the offender in a spirit of humility and meekness, and his motive for rebuke should be the restoration of the brother or sister to holiness. It should never come from a spirit of vindictiveness. He should manifest a spirit of love and forgiveness even while he is rebuking, and he should be deeply concerned about the spiritual damage being suffered by the brother who sinned and have a genuine desire for him to be restored to holiness and its consequent blessing.

Rebuke of a sinning brother should be undertaken as soon as the offense is known, in order to turn the sinning believer from his sin as soon as possible and also to help head off resentment and bitterness by the one offended. Those destructive emotions are also sins, and they tend to fester as long as a break in relationship remains unresolved. The longer sin continues, the more difficult it becomes to be forsaken by the sinner and to be forgiven by the one sinned against. God calls His children always to "be kind to one another, tender-hearted, forgiving each other, just as God in Christ also has forgiven" them (Eph. 4:32).

But in a broader sense, believers are sinned against by any sin committed by any other believer. Whenever a believer commits a sin, all other believers are indirectly sinned against. "A little leaven" does affect all (see 1 Cor. 5:6). That Jesus here included indirect offenses seems clear from the fact that He makes no mention of forgiveness. The focus is solely on repentance and restoration.

Some years ago a man in our church told me he had invited an attorney friend of his to attend the church. But when he told the friend the church's name, the friend said, "I'd never go there. That's where the most crooked attorney in Los Angeles attends." That man's sin indirectly affected everyone in our congregation and tarnished the whole cause of Christ.

Every sin by a believer stains the entire fellowship of believers. Whether it is slander, stealing, gossip, sexual immorality, dishonesty, doctrinal error, lack of submission, cruelty, blasphemy, profanity, drunkenness, or anything else, every sin not dealt with by the offending child of God must be dealt with by the church.

THE PERSON WHO INITIATES DISCIPLINE

go and reprove him in private; (18:15*b*)

The understood subjects of **go and reprove** are indicated by the plural pronouns "you" and "your" (vv. 15-16). Jesus was giving general instruction to His followers, and therefore this category is also inclusive. The person responsible for initiating discipline is any believer who is aware of another believer's sin. Discipline is not simply the responsibility of church officials but of every member.

Reprove is from *elenchō,* which has the root meaning of bringing to light or exposing. The Greek verb is in the aorist imperative, suggesting that the brother is to be shown his sin in such a way that he cannot escape recognizing it for what it is.

The first confrontation of a sinning brother must be **in private,** one on one. If the erring person confesses and repents, no further discipline is necessary and no one else need ever be brought into the matter. The more a person's sin is known and discussed by others, no matter how well-meaning they may be, the easier it is for him to become resentful and the harder it may be for repentance and restoration. When he is corrected **in private,** and in a spirit of humility and love, his change of heart is much more likely. And if he does repent, a unique and marvelous bond of intimacy is established between the two believers, indicated by the phrase **you have gained your brother.**

When Peter was intimidated by the Judaizers in Antioch and began to separate himself from Gentile believers, Paul "opposed him to his face, because he stood condemned" (Gal. 2:11). Peter admitted his sin and repented, and years later he wrote of his "beloved brother Paul" (2 Pet. 3:15). Their deepened friendship no doubt was due in no small measure to Paul's caring enough to rebuke his fellow apostle and turn him back to the purity of the gospel of grace.

A Christian who is not deeply concerned about bringing a fellow Christian back from his sin needs spiritual help himself. Smug indifference, not to mention self-righteous contempt, has no part in the life of a spiritual Christian, nor do sentimentality or cowardice that hide behind false humility. The spiritual Christian neither condemns nor justifies a sinning brother. His concern is for the holiness and blessing of the offending brother, the purity and integrity of the church, and the honor and glory of God.

At least three things are necessary for effectively undertaking the private first step of confronting a fellow Christian about sin. First is the obvious requirement of willingness **to go and reprove** the sinning brother **in private.** If he does not listen, we must then be willing to take one or two more believers with us and confront him again (v. 16). And if he still refuses to listen, we must be willing to report his impenitence to the whole church (v. 17).

God does not mock His children by demanding of them anything which, by His power, He does not enable them to do. No Christian, therefore, has an excuse for not initiating church discipline when it is necessary, because God will provide the necessary wisdom, insight, and boldness when a sincere desire is present.

Not every believer is given the gift of preaching or teaching or evangelism or helps. But every believer is given the command to **go and reprove** a brother or sister who is sinning. That is part of God's work, and it is a ministry as surely as any other. In our day it is a much-needed and much-neglected ministry. The absence of it may well be the most severe and debilitating problem in the church of this century. All believers are called in this way to be ministers of holiness, helping guard the purity and integrity of Christ's Body. When they minister discipline in a spirit of love, gentleness, and humility, they can be effective weapons in God's hands for purifying the church and restoring His fallen children.

The Lord commanded Israel, "You shall not go about as a slanderer among your people, and you are not to act against the life of your neighbor; I am the Lord. You shall not hate your fellow countryman in your heart." But, the Lord went on to say, "you may surely reprove your neighbor" (Lev. 19:16-17). Unwillingness to reprove a sinning believer is a form of hatred of him, not loving him enough to warn him of his spiritual danger. Not to reprove a sinning brother can do him more harm than slandering him. Terrible as it is, slander affects primarily the other person's reputation and his feelings. Failing to help him confront and confess his sin, however, contributes to his spiritual downfall. The person who claims to be too loving to rebuke his brother or sister in Christ is simply deceived. He is not too loving but too uncaring. The loving Christian, like the loving heavenly Father and loving earthly fathers, desires the proper discipline of those he loves (see Heb. 12:5-11).

In the eyes of much of the world and even in the eyes of many immature believers, such action is considered unloving. But discipline given in the right way expresses the deepest kind of love, love that refuses to do nothing to rescue a brother from unrepentant sin and its consequences. Love that winks at sin or that is more concerned for superficial calm in the church than for its spiritual purity is not God's kind of love. Love that tolerates sin is not love at all but worldly and selfish sentimentality.

To preach love apart from God's holiness is to teach something other than God's love. No awakening or revival of the church has ever occurred apart from strong preaching of God's holiness and the corresponding call for believers to forsake sin and return to the Lord's standards of purity and righteousness. No church that tolerates known sin in its membership will have spiritual growth or effective evangelism. In spite of that truth, however, such tolerance is standard in the church today—at all levels.

History has seen excesses in preaching what is commonly known as hell fire and damnation, but that is not the church's danger today. Beginning in the nineteenth century, there has been a drift away from forceful preaching of the holiness of God and His demand for holiness in men. Even in many evangelical churches and organizations emphasis has shifted to the almost exclusive preaching of God's love, with little, if any, reference to His wrath and judgment.

Commenting on the contemporary church, Richard Lovelace writes:

The whole church was . . . avoiding the biblical portrait of the sovereign and holy God who was angry with the wicked every day and whose anger remains upon those who will not receive His Son. Walling off this image into an unvisited corner of its consciousness, the church substituted a new god who was the projection of grandmotherly kindness mixed with the gentleness and winsomeness of a Jesus who hardly needed to die for our sins. Many American congregations were, in effect, paying their ministers to protect them from the real God. . . . It is partially responsible not only for the general spiritual collapse of the church in this century but also for a great deal of [evangelistic] weakness; for in a world in which the sovereign and holy God regularly employs plagues, famines, wars, disease, and death as instruments to punish sin and bring mankind to repentance, the idolatrous image of God as pure benevolence cannot really be believed, let alone feared and worshiped in the manner prescribed by both the Old Testament and New Testament. (*Dynamics of Spiritual Life* [Downers Grove, Ill.: InterVarsity, 1979], pp. 83-84)

Belief in a God who is all love and no wrath, all grace and no justice, all forgiveness and no condemnation is idolatry (worship of a false god invented by men), and it inevitably leads to universalism—which, of course, is what many liberal churches have been preaching for generations. Salvation becomes meaningless, because sin that God overlooks does not need to be forgiven. Christ's sacrifice on the cross becomes a travesty, because He gave His life for no redemptive purpose. Not only that, but it becomes apologetically impossible to explain the common question about why a loving God allows pain, suffering, disease, and tragedy. Removing God's holy hatred of sin emasculates the gospel and hinders rather than helps evangelism.

Profoundly aware of the danger of mistaking emotional stimulation for spiritual awakening, in his *Treatise on Religious Affections* Jonathan Edwards observed:

Fallen human nature is fertile ground for a fleshly religiosity which is impiously "spiritual" but ultimately rooted in self-love. High emotional experiences, effusive religious talk, and even praising God and experiencing love for God and man can be self-centered and self-motivated. In contrast to this, experiences of renewal which are genuinely from the Holy Spirit are God-centered in character and based on worship, an appreciation of God's worth and grandeur divorced from self-interest. Such genuine experiences create humility in the convert rather than pride and issue in a new creation and a new spirit of meekness, gentleness, forgiveness, and mercy. They leave the believer hungering and thirsting for righteousness instead of satiated with self-congratulation.

True evangelism and revival have nothing to do with building self-esteem, self-acceptance, and feeling good about oneself. They have nothing to do with gaining health, wealth, and fleshly happiness. They have much to do with acknowledging one's sinfulness, unworthiness, weakness, and helplessness and much to do with humble gratitude for God's infinite patience, mercy, and grace.

Richard Lovelace again observes that "most congregations of professing Christians today are saturated with a kind of dead goodness and ethical respectability, which has its motivational roots in the flesh rather than in the Holy Spirit. Surface righteousness does not spring from faith and the spiritual renewing action but from religious pride and conditioned conformity to tradition as a form of godliness which denies it power." He describes such religion as "counterfeit piety."

Over and over in the gospels Jesus proclaimed that He came to earth solely to do the will of His heavenly Father (see, e.g., John 5:19, 30; 6:38; 7:16). And the will of the Father can be reduced to the declaration quoted at the beginning of this chapter: "You shall be holy, for I am holy" (1 Pet. 1:16; cf. Lev. 11:44). Above all, God wants His people to be holy.

Speaking to believers, James wrote, "Cleanse your hands, you sinners; and purify your hearts, you double-minded. Be miserable and mourn and weep; let your laughter be turned into mourning and your joy to gloom. Humble yourselves in the presence of the Lord, and He will exalt you" (James 4:8-10). It is God's will that His people be holy, and the purpose of discipline is to promote holiness by purging and purifying the church. The Word, the Spirit, and God's people join in working for the purity of the church. Believers act in Christ's behalf when, with humility and according to scriptural guidelines, they discipline fellow members who persist in sin.

A second requirement for effective discipline is zeal. When Jesus came to Jerusalem for the Passover and found merchants in the Temple exploiting the people and desecrating God's house by selling animals and changing money, "He made a scourge of cords, and drove them all out of the temple, with the sheep and the oxen; and He poured out the coins of the moneychangers, and overturned their tables; and to those who were selling the doves He said, 'Take these things away; stop making My Father's house a house of merchandise'" (John 2:13-16). Jesus' holy zeal for the purity of His Father's house would not allow Him to stand by and watch it being desecrated. Willingness to confront sin in the church is manifested in righteous zeal to uphold God's name and holiness and in a corresponding unwillingness for them to be stained and dishonored.

A third requirement for effective discipline is personal purity. A believer who is not concerned about his own purity will have no obedient willingness or righteous zeal to help protect the purity of the church. Nor can he be effectively used by the Lord in helping others deal with their sin if he is unwilling to deal with his own. His concern about other Christians' sins might be strong, but it will be judgmental and censorious, not humble and loving. To such believers the Lord says, "Why do you look at the speck that is in your brother's eye, but do not notice the log that is in your own eye? Or how can you say to your brother, 'Let me take the speck out of your eye,' and behold, the log is in your own eye? You hypocrite, first take the log out of your own eye, and then you will see clearly to take the speck out of your brother's eye" (Matt. 7:3-5).

When a church sincerely and humbly moves out to enforce holiness and purity within its membership, by virtue of that very movement it is in the process of self-purification, because believers who genuinely desire the purity of the church will first confront sin in their own lives and determine for the Lord to bring purity there. Christians can become ministers of holiness only as they themselves are holy.

THE PURPOSE OF DISCIPLINE

if he listens to you, you have won your brother. (18:15c)

The purpose of discipline is the spiritual restoration of fallen members and the consequent strengthening of the church and glorifying of the Lord. When a sinning **brother** is rebuked and he turns from his sin and is forgiven, he is **won** back to fellowship with the Body and with its head, Jesus Christ.

The goal of discipline is not to throw people out of the church or to feed the self-righteous pride of those who administer the discipline. It is to bring the sinning **brother** back. "He who is wise wins souls," the writer of Proverbs declared (11:30). Paul admonishes Christians, "If a man is caught in any trespass, you who are spiritual, restore such a one in a spirit of gentleness; each one looking to yourself, lest you too be tempted" (Gal. 6:1). "My brethren, if any among you strays from the truth, and one turns him back," James says, "let him know that he who turns a sinner from the error of his way will save his soul from death, and will cover a multitude of sins" (James 5:19-20). In some cases, as in that of the James passage, you may be confronting a professing Christian who is not even saved. Enacting discipline has often, in my experience, led to the admission by the sinner that he had never been saved and then to his desire for true conversion.

Won is from *kerdainō*, which was originally a term of commerce referring to financial gain or profit. Here it refers to the gaining back of something of value that is lost, namely, an erring **brother**. As Jesus had just taught in the parable of the lost sheep, God highly values every one of His children, and when one of them goes astray He will not rest until the lost child is found and returned to the fold. It is not His will "that one of these little ones perish" (v. 14). Nor should it be the will of Christians that even one of their brothers or sisters in the faith perishes. When they are lost to the fellowship, a valuable treasure is lost, and, like our heavenly Father, we should not be content until they are restored. Every person who has become one with the great Shepherd should himself reflect that Shepherd's heart.

When a church member falls into sin, the fellowship as a whole and each of the other members individually suffers loss, because no individual believer in the Body is reproducible. Each believer is a unique individual and is uniquely gifted. People go to great lengths to regain material wealth that is lost. To how much greater lengths should Christians go to regain a spiritual treasure more valuable than any earthly possession?

Churches as well as individual Christians are tempted to say of a sinning brother, in effect if not in words, "We have no business getting involved. It's his life, his decision, and his responsibility. He's accountable to God, and what he is and does is only between him and the Lord." That attitude may sound loving and spiritual on the surface, but it does not square with Scripture. It reflects ungodly indifference, not loving concern for the brother who has fallen.

THE PROCESS AND THE PLACE FOR DISCIPLINE

But if he does not listen to you, take one or two more with you, so that by the mouth of two or three witnesses every fact may be confirmed. And if he refuses to listen to them, tell it to the church; and if he refuses to listen

even to the church, let him be to you as a Gentile and a tax-gatherer. (18:16-17)

As already noted, the process of discipline begins with an individual believer going privately to a sinning brother and rebuking him (v. 15). The three subsequent steps are mentioned in verses 16-17.

If a sinning brother **does not listen** to the one who has rebuked him privately, the next step in the discipline process is to **take one or two more** believers along, **so that by the mouth of two or three witnesses every fact may be confirmed.** This basic procedure for confirming facts in a dispute or in an allegation of wrongdoing had been set forth by Moses (Deut. 19:15) and was therefore familiar to every Jew. To guard against a person's being slanderously or spitefully accused of a sin, crime, or other offense he did not commit, the Mosaic law required that at least **two or three witnesses** must corroborate any charge brought against someone. That was an important protection against the false accusation of an innocent person.

In the context of Jesus' instruction here, however, if the testimony of the **two or three witnesses** becomes necessary, it is not only to confirm that the sin was committed but, in addition, to confirm that the sinning believer was properly rebuked and that he has or has not repented. It should be hoped that the **one or two** who are brought along to confront the sinner will not have to become public **witnesses** against him before the rest of the church but that their added rebuke will be sufficient to induce a change of heart in the offending brother that the initial rebuke did not cause.

The guards against abuse and unjust accusation in discipline are to protect church leaders as well as other believers. "Do not receive an accusation against an elder except on the basis of two or three witnesses," Paul charged Timothy. But "those who continue in sin, rebuke in the presence of all, so that the rest also may be fearful of sinning" (1 Tim. 5:19-20).

If the second stage of the discipline process fails to bring repentance, **if he does not listen** to the two or three, then they are to **tell it to the church.** The first rebuke is to be completely private and the second semi-private, but the third is to be public, before the **church.** The brother or sister is to be brought before the whole congregation to be further rebuked and encouraged to repent. The whole church is responsible to call that person back to holiness.

It has been the custom in our church, upon enacting this third step, to clearly indicate to the congregation that they are to pursue the person aggressively and plead with him to repent before the fourth step becomes necessary. That crucial and potent procedure often draws the sinner to repentance and obedience.

This great passage also indicates that the place for discipline is *within* the church. *Ekklēsia* (church) is here used in its basic, nontechnical meaning of a congregation or assembly. In secular Greek literature it was used of town meetings, local gatherings of citizens called together by their rulers to hear official announcements or witness government ceremonies. In the context of Jesus' teaching at this point in His ministry, **church** refers to any group of redeemed people who assemble in His name (v. 20).

Some commentators maintain that Jesus was referring to the Jewish synagogue, which also has the root meaning of assembly or congregation. But Jesus always used another term (*sunagōgē*) when referring to a synagogue, which, in any case, would never have gathered in His name. And although He frequently taught in synagogues and called the worshipers there to believe in Him, His purpose was not to revise or reform the synagogue but to establish His own *ekklēsia*, **the church.**

No organizational structure is mentioned or intimated here. The reference is not to a committee, board, or other group of leaders, but to the entire body. There is no higher court beyond the local congregation in which discipline is to be administered. No bishop, cardinal, synod, conference, or council has the responsibility for discipline. To delegate discipline to an individual or group beyond the local church is to go beyond the Word of God. Whether a local **church** is composed of a handful of believers or of several thousand members, whether it is a highly organized urban congregation or an informal group of five or six believers on a remote mission field, that is where, and only where, discipline is to be administered.

Even less justified is taking church discipline or grievances to a secular court for resolution. Paul strongly indicted Corinthian Christians who did that. "Does any one of you," he wrote, "when he has a case against his neighbor, dare to go to law before the unrighteous, and not before the saints? Or do you not know that the saints will judge the world? And if the world is judged by you, are you not competent to constitute the smallest law courts? Do you not know that we shall judge angels? How much more, matters of this life?" (1 Cor. 6:1-3).

The fourth and final step in church discipline is ostracism. If a sinning believer **refuses to listen even to the church,** he is to be ostracized from the fellowship. **Let him be to you,** Jesus said, **as a Gentile and a tax-gatherer.** Both were seen as despised outcasts.

A non-Jew who worshiped the true God and who became identified with Judaism was commonly called a God-fearer (cf. Acts 10:1, 22), whereas the term **Gentile** was primarily used of non-Jews who held to their traditional paganism. Such a **Gentile** had no part in the covenant, worship, or social life of Jews. Because he was a traitor to his own people, however, a **tax-gatherer** was in many ways more despised than Gentiles. He was not an outcast by birth but by choice.

Jesus was not appealing to Jewish prejudice. He came to save all men, and among His most ardent and faithful followers were former tax-gatherers such as Matthew and Zaccheus and Gentiles such as the centurion who asked Him to heal his paralyzed servant. Jesus' point was that a believer who persists in impenitence is to be put out of the church and treated as an unbelieving, unrepentant outsider.

When a man in the Corinthian church refused to forsake an incestuous relationship with his stepmother, Paul commanded that he be removed from their midst (1 Cor. 5:1-2). Tolerance of his sin had reached the point of arrogance. Although none of the other members apparently engaged in that particular immorality, their perverted sense of liberty led them to defend the man's right to continue in the sin. "In the name of our Lord Jesus," Paul went on to say, "when you are assembled, and I with you in spirit, with the power of our Lord Jesus, I have decided to deliver such a one to Satan for the destruction of his flesh, that his spirit may be saved in the day of the Lord Jesus. Your boasting is not good. Do you not know that a little leaven leavens the whole lump of dough?" (vv. 4-6). That man's evil influence, described by Paul as leaven, had corrupted the moral sensitivity of the entire church.

Persistently unrepentant believers are to be totally ostracized from the fellowship of the church. They are no longer to know the blessedness of the church's company and encouragement. Because they willingly reject the standards of the gospel, they make shipwreck of their faith. When Hymenaeus and Alexander would not forsake their profane use of the Lord's name, Paul "delivered [them] over to Satan, so that they may be taught not to blaspheme" (1 Tim. 1:20). Such people are to be given the choice of repenting and staying with God's people or of holding on to their sin and being given over to the world and the devil.

The final step in discipline is not optional. **Let him be** translates a present imperative and is therefore a command. Paul gave a similar command to the Thessalonians: "Now we command you, brethren, in the name of our Lord Jesus Christ, that you keep aloof from every brother who leads an unruly life and not according to the tradition which you received from us" (2 Thess. 3:6). A few verses later he says, "If anyone does not obey our instruction in this letter, take special note of that man and do not associate with him, so that he may be put to shame" (v. 14).

When a church has done everything it can, but without success, to bring a sinning member back to purity of life, that brother is to be left to his sin and his shame. If he is truly a Christian, God will not cast Him away, but He may have to allow him to sink still deeper before he becomes desperate enough to turn from his evil.

As Paul explained to the Corinthian church, separation from a sinning believer is to be more radical than separation from sinful unbelievers.

> I wrote you in my letter not to associate with immoral people; I did not at all mean with the immoral people of this world, or with the covetous and swindlers, or with idolaters; for then you would have to go out of the world. But actually, I wrote to you not to associate with any so-called brother if he should be an immoral person, or covetous, or an idolater, or a reviler, or a drunkard, or a swindler—not even to eat with such a one. For what have I to do with judging outsiders? Do you not judge those who are within the church? But those who are outside, God judges. Remove the wicked man from among yourselves. (1 Cor. 5:9-13)

But putting an unrepentant member out the fellowship is not the end of the discipline process. It should not end until the brother has either repented or died. As far as the welfare of the church is concerned, the purpose of putting the brother out is to protect the purity of the fellowship and to give a testimony of righteousness to the watching world. But as far as the welfare of the brother himself is concerned, the purpose of the ostracism is not to punish but to awaken, and it must therefore be done in humble love and never in a spirit of self-righteous superiority. "Do not regard him as an enemy," Paul says, "but admonish him as a brother" (2 Thess. 3:15).

Not to have fellowship or even social contact with the unrepentant brother does not exclude all contact. When there is opportunity to admonish him and try to call him back, the opportunity should be taken. In fact, such opportunities should be sought. But the contact should be for the purpose of admonishment and no other.

The fourth step in the discipline process is therefore to put out and to call back—to keep the sinning brother out of fellowship until he repents, but also to keep calling him back in the hope that he will.

Administering discipline is never the prerogative of a single person in a church, no matter what his position or qualifications. One of the early churches had such a self-appointed disciplinarian named Diotrephes, whom John described as one "who loves to be first." "For this reason, if I come," the apostle said, "I will call attention to his deeds which he does, unjustly accusing us with wicked words; and not satisfied with this, neither does he himself receive the brethren, and he forbids those who desire to do so, and puts them out of the church" (3 John 9-10). Autocratic self-righteousness has no part in Christ's plan for His church and can never be successful in purifying it. Only the local body of believers has the right to put a member out of its fellowship, and that only after the first three steps of discipline have failed.

A man was apparently put out of the church at Corinth after having caused great sorrow to Paul and the others there because of his sin. But "sufficient for such a one is this punishment which was inflicted by the majority," Paul said, "so that on the contrary you should rather forgive and comfort him, lest somehow such a one be overwhelmed by excessive sorrow. Wherefore I urge you to reaffirm your love for him" (2 Cor. 2:5-8). When a believer repents, he is to be welcomed back into the fellowship and not held at arm's length as a second-class member. He is to be forgiven and embraced, just as the Savior forgave and embraced the prodigal Peter when he returned from his disobedience (John 21:15-22).

The Authority for Discipline

Truly I say to you, whatever you shall bind on earth shall be bound in heaven; and whatever you loose on earth shall be loosed in heaven. Again I say to you, that if two of you agree on earth about anything that they may ask, it shall be done for them by My Father who is in heaven. For where two or three have gathered together in My name, there I am in their midst. (18:18-20)

To emphasize the absolute trustworthiness of what He was about to say, Jesus declared, **"Truly I say to you."** That phrase, which the Lord often used, should always be noted with special care, because it introduces a teaching of unusual importance.

The work of discipline should be undertaken with the greatest care. Done in the wrong way or in the wrong spirit it can do great damage by fostering self-righteousness and legalism, just as discipline not done at all causes great damage by allowing sin's influence to spread like leaven.

Jesus' promises in verses 18 and 19 have suffered serious misinterpretation throughout the history of the church, the most extreme being the Roman Catholic doctrine that the church has the divine authority to forgive sin. Many charismatics use these promises—along with others, such as those of Matthew 7:7 and 21:22—to claim from God every imaginable blessing and privilege just for the asking.

But in light of the context of what Jesus had just said, in the light of common rabbinical expressions of that day, and in light of the grammatical construction of the text, it is clear that He was not teaching that God's power can be bent to men's will. He was not saying that men can force heaven to do things. Quite to the contrary, His promise was that when His people bend their wills to His, He will endorse and empower their act of obedience. (See comments on Matthew 16:19, in chapter 4 of this volume.)

Jesus was here continuing His instruction about church discipline. He was not speaking about petitioning God for special blessings or privileges, and even less was He teaching that the church or any of its leaders has power to absolve the sins of its members. He was declaring that the church has a divine mandate to discipline its members when they refuse to repent.

The rabbis sometimes spoke of a principle or action as being **bound in heaven** or **loosed in heaven** to indicate, respectively, that it was forbidden or permitted in light of God's revealed Word. A Jew of that day would have understood that Jesus did not mean that men could bend heaven's will to their own but that God (here called **heaven,** a common Jewish substitute for God's covenant name, Yahweh, or Jehovah) had an expressed principle with which the church must conform.

The grammatical construction in the passage also clarifies its meaning. As in Matthew 16:19, **shall be bound** and **shall be loosed** translate future perfect passives and are more accurately rendered "will have been bound" and "will have been loosed." The idea is not that God is compelled to conform to the church's decisions but that, when the church follows Christ's pattern for discipline, it conforms its decisions to what God has already done and thereby receives heaven's approval and authority.

Perfect passives are also used in John 20:23 in regard to forgiving or retaining sins. Believers have authority to declare that sins are either forgiven or not forgiven when that declaration is based on the teaching of God's Word. If a person has received Jesus Christ as Savior and Lord, the church can tell him with perfect confidence that his sins are **loosed,** that is, forgiven, because he has met God's condition for forgiveness, namely, trust in His Son. If, on the other hand, a person refuses to receive Christ as Savior and acknowledge Him as Lord, the church can tell him with equal confidence that his sins are **bound,** that is, *not* forgiven, because he has not met God's condition for forgiveness.

Some years ago a man told me he believed he was going to heaven because he was following the religious system prescribed by a popular cult. Because the bizarre beliefs of that group were utterly contrary to the gospel, I told him that he was lost, was still in his sins, and could not possibly be destined for heaven. On the basis of his own confession matched against God's Word, the man could not have been saved. To tell him that he was still bound in his sins was not to judge his heart supernaturally nor sovereignly condemn him but simply to affirm what God's own Word clearly says about him and about every person who hopes to come to God by any other path than trust in His Son.

Obviously, this is a serious ministry in the church and one that may be approached with great reluctance. "Who are we to do such work?" we ask. "What authority do we have for such strong dealings with fellow believers? We're sinful, too." But when the church administers discipline according to the pattern of Matthew 18:15-17, it can have perfect confidence that it acts in the authority and power of heaven, as promised in verses 18-20.

The Lord gives no command without giving the necessary power and authority to obey it. In these three climaxing verses in Jesus' instruction about church discipline we learn that, when the Lord's people sincerely seek to purify His church in His way, they have the energy, approval, and authority both of the Father and of the Son.

Jesus first assures His people that the Father acts with them when they work to purify the church: **Again I say to you, that if two of you agree on earth** (referring back to the two witnesses of v. 16) **about anything that they may ask** (in seeking the purity of the church) **it shall be done for them by My Father who is in heaven.** When the church acts in God's behalf and in accordance with His Word in matters dealing with sin, He acts in their behalf by confirming and empowering their faithful decisions and actions.

Agree is from *sumphōneō,* which literally means to sound together and is the term from which we get *symphony.* If even **two** of Jesus' followers are in agreement with each other that a sinning believer has either repented or refused to repent, they can be sure they are also in agreement with the **Father who is in heaven.**

As already mentioned, to interpret this verse as promising believers a blank check for anything they might agree to ask God for not only does not fit the context of church discipline but does violence to the rest of Scripture. Such an interpretation is tantamount to magic, in which God is automatically bound to grant the most foolish or sinful request, simply because two of His children conspire to ask Him for it. The idea flies in the face of God's sovereignty and completely undercuts the countless scriptural commands for believers' obedient submission to His will.

Jesus also assures His people that He Himself acts with them when they work to purify the church: **For where two or three have gathered together in My name, there I am in their midst.** Not only does the Father confirm discipline when it is administered according to His Word, but the Son adds His own divine confirmation.

This verse is also frequently misinterpreted, though not with such serious error as in the misinterpretations of the two previous verses. To use this statement to claim the Lord's presence at a small worship service or prayer meeting does not fit the context of church discipline and is superfluous. Christ is always present with His people, even with a lone believer totally separated from fellow Christians by prison walls or by hundreds of miles.

The context demands that the **two or three** are witnesses in the process of discipline. To ask or to do anything in God's **name** is not to utter His name but to ask and to work according to His divine will and character. For the witnesses to **have gathered in** His **name** is therefore for them to have faithfully performed their work of verifying the repentance or impenitence of a sinning brother or sister on the Lord's behalf. When the church gathers in the Lord's name and for His cause and glory, it must be engaged in self-purifying ministry under His power and authority, and with His heavenly confirmation and partnership.

Dietrich Bonhoeffer, a German theologian of rather liberal persuasion who was caught in the terrors of Nazi Germany, wrote a book entitled *Life Together.* In it he gives some profound insights into the need for restoring a sinning brother to the fellowship of the church.

> Sin demands to have a man by himself. It withdraws him from the community. The more isolated a person is, the more destructive will be the power of sin over him, and the more deeply he becomes involved in it, the more disastrous is his isolation. Sin wants to remain unknown. It shuns the light. In the darkness of the unexpressed it poisons the whole being of a person. This can happen even in the midst of a pious community. In confession, the light of the gospel breaks into the darkness and seclusion of the heart. The sin must be brought into the light. The unexpressed must be openly spoken and acknowledged. All that is secret and hidden is made manifest. It is a hard struggle until the sin is openly admitted, but God breaks gates of brass and bars of iron (Ps. 107:16).
>
> Since the confession of sin is made in the presence of a Christian brother, the last stronghold of self-justification is abandoned. The sinner surrenders; he gives up all his evil. He gives his heart to God, and he finds the forgiveness of all his sin in the fellowship of Jesus Christ and his brother. The expressed, acknowledged sin has lost all its power. It has been revealed and judged as sin. It can no longer tear the fellowship asunder. Now the fellowship bears the sin of the brother. He is no longer alone with his evil for he has cast off his sin from him. Now he stands in the fellowship of sinners who live by the grace of God and the cross of Jesus Christ. . . . The sin concealed separated him from the fellowship, made all his apparent fellowship a sham; the sin confessed has helped him define true fellowship with the brethren in Jesus Christ. ([New York: Harper & Row, 1954], 112-13)

Learning to Forgive
(18:21-35)

15

Then Peter came and said to Him, "Lord, how often shall my brother sin against me and I forgive him? Up to seven times?" Jesus said to him, "I do not say to you, up to seven times, but up to seventy times seven. For this reason the kingdom of heaven may be compared to a certain king who wished to settle accounts with his slaves. And when he had begun to settle them, there was brought to him one who owed him ten thousand talents. But since he did not have the means to repay, his lord commanded him to be sold, along with his wife and children and all that he had, and repayment to be made. The slave therefore falling down, prostrated himself before him, saying, 'Have patience with me, and I will repay you everything.' And the lord of that slave felt compassion and released him and forgave him the debt. But that slave went out and found one of his fellow slaves who owed him a hundred denarii; and he seized him and began to choke him, saying, 'Pay back what you owe.' So his fellow slave fell down and began to entreat him, saying, 'Have patience with me and I will repay you.' He was unwilling however, but went and threw him in prison until he should pay back what was owed. So when his fellow slaves saw what had happened, they were deeply grieved and came and reported to their lord all that had happened. Then summoning him, his lord said to him, 'You wicked slave, I forgave you all that debt because you entreated me. Should you not also have had mercy on your fellow slave, even as I had mercy on you?' And his lord, moved with anger, handed him over to the torturers until he should repay all that was owed him. So shall My heavenly Father also do to you, if each of you does not forgive his brother from your heart." (18:21-35)

Forgiveness is not natural to man. Because it is so foreign to fleshly human nature, people find it very difficult to forgive others. King Louis XII of France articulated the feeling of many people when he said, "Nothing smells so sweet as the dead body of your enemy."

Yet nothing so characterizes the new nature of Christians as forgiveness, because nothing so characterizes the nature of their Lord. Jesus' most striking and humanly incomprehensible words from the cross were, "Father, forgive them; for they do not know what they are doing" (Luke 23:34). After being betrayed, falsely convicted, beaten, spat upon, and unjustly nailed to a cross to die an agonizing death, the Son of God harbored no hatred for His tormentors but instead offered them forgiveness. Following his Lord's example, Stephen's last words were, "Lord, do not hold this sin against them!" (Acts 7:60). He was at that moment being pummelled to death by stones for having committed no greater crime than preaching the gospel, yet his heart was not filled with bitterness but with compassion for his executioners. Forgiveness is the stuff of true godliness.

It is not difficult to forgive children, and most people, especially their parents, do it almost instinctively. We understand that children are uninformed, inexperienced, and immature. We expect them to do some things that are inconsiderate, but we tend to tolerate those things and forgive them, even when they hurt us deeply. It is hard to hold a grudge against a child. That analogy also should be true in a spiritual sense, because all believers are children, as Jesus repeatedly points out in Matthew 18.

Although Joseph had been terribly wronged by his jealous brothers when they sold him into slavery, he held no grudge. Years later, when they were in the midst of a great famine and he was the only person who could help them, he was quick to offer his forgiveness, to embrace them in love, to provide the food they needed, and even to give them the lush region of Goshen to live in. When they had begged his forgiveness and fallen down before him, he "said to them, 'Do not be afraid, for am I in God's place? And as for you, you meant evil against me, but God meant it for good in order to bring about this present result, to preserve many people alive. So therefore, do not be afraid; I will provide for you and your little ones.' So he comforted them and spoke kindly to them" (Gen. 50:19-21).

One of the reasons David was a man after God's own heart was his own forgiving and merciful heart. Although King Saul repeatedly tried to kill David with a javelin and pursued him relentlessly in the hills of Judah with his army, David not only refused to harm Saul because he was the Lord's anointed but even refused to harbor any hatred against him (see 1 Sam. 24:6, 12; 26:11). In another example, although David was at first enraged by Nabal's ungrateful refusal to give food and provisions to David's men who had helped protect Nabal, he was persuaded by Nabal's wife, Abigail, to withhold revenge. David did not punish Nabal and was grateful to Abigail for bringing him to his senses. "Blessed be the Lord God of Israel, who sent you this day to meet me," he said to her, "and blessed be your discernment, and blessed be you, who have kept me this day from bloodshed, and from avenging myself by my own hand" (1 Sam. 25:32-33). When Shimei asked David's forgiveness for having cursed and thrown stones at him, David was quick to show him mercy, despite the insistence of his officers that the man deserved to be put to death (2 Sam. 19:22-23; cf. 16:5-6).

Forgiveness reflects the highest human virtue, because it so clearly reflects the character of God. A person who forgives is a person who emulates godly character. Nothing so much demonstrates God's love as His forgiveness. A person who does not forgive is therefore a person lacking in godly character and without Christlike love, no matter how orthodox his theology or how outwardly impeccable his morals appear to be. A Christian who will not relinquish a hateful, resentful attitude toward someone who has wronged him is a person who knows neither the true glory of his redeemed humanity nor the true glory of God's gracious divinity. An unforgiving Christian is a living contradiction of His new nature in Christ. It is central to the heart of God to forgive, and only the Christian who radiates forgiveness radiates true godliness.

Considering forgiveness from another direction, Christians need to forgive because they themselves need forgiveness. They are spiritual children and, like all children, are ignorant, weak, selfish, disobedient, and regularly in need of forgiveness, both from God and from each other. Forgiving is a give-and-take issue of life.

Forgiveness is therefore the key to spiritual unity in the church, because it is the key to love and the key to all meaningful relationships. Only forgiveness can break down the barriers that sin continually and inevitably erects between people, including God's people. "A man's discretion makes him slow to anger, and it is his glory to overlook a transgression" (Prov. 19:11). Christians are at their best when they are forgiving. Because they themselves have been forgiven so much by God, they, of all people, should be most forgiving of others, especially of fellow believers. Christians are most like their Lord when they forgive "each other, just as God in Christ also has forgiven" them (Eph. 4:32). Paul declared the same truth to the Colossians, telling them to bear with one another and forgive one another, "just as the Lord forgave you" (Col. 3:13). Because they have been forgiven every sin by Christ, believers should be willing and eager to forgive each other in everything.

In this closing part of His teaching about believers as children (Matt. 18), Jesus gives a powerful and sobering declaration of the need for believers to be forgiving. Just as a person enters and is considered great in the kingdom only by becoming like a little child (vv. 3-4) and, once in the kingdom, is to be protected like a little child (vv. 5-9), cared for like a little child (vv. 10-14), and disciplined like a little child (vv. 15-20), so also, Jesus now says, must he be forgiven like a little child. In verses 21-35 we first see Peter's inquiry about forgiveness and then Jesus' teaching about the extent of God's forgiveness of believers and a negative example of their duty to forgive each other.

Then Peter came and said to Him, "Lord, how often shall my brother sin against me and I forgive him? Up to seven times?" (18:21)

Peter knew human nature and how many times people need forgiveness, often for the same offense. He understood the human tendency to commit a sin, be forgiven, and then before long commit the same sin or some other equally as bad.

In light of Jesus' teaching about discipline in the church, Peter wondered how many times Christians as a body and as individuals were obliged to forgive fellow believers who persisted in wrongdoing. How many times should they be allowed to repent and be restored to fellowship?

As pointed out in the previous chapter, Jesus' teaching about discipline includes both direct and indirect offenses. Believers are to rebuke a sinning brother or sister for *any* sin. And they are to bring the offender before the church if that becomes necessary, because every sin not only is directly against God but is also either directly or indirectly against the church and every individual believer. "Be on your guard," Jesus said on another occasion. "If your brother sins, rebuke him; and if he repents, forgive him" (Luke 17:3). The commands to rebuke and to forgive cover any sin a fellow believer may commit, not just those committed directly against us.

Commendably, **Peter** personalized Jesus' teaching, and his primary concern at this time was about his own responsibility. He therefore asked, **"Lord, how often shall my brother sin against me and I forgive him?"**

Throughout the discourse of chapter 18, Jesus was speaking about believers, whom He refers to as little ones, children, sheep, and brothers (vv. 3-6, 10, 12, 14, 15). From His reference to **my brother,** it is clear that Peter also was thinking about a believer, represented by himself, forgiving other believers.

We are greatly indebted to Peter for many things, one of which was his penchant for asking questions. He wanted to be sure he understood what Jesus' words and actions meant, and his inquisitive mind elicited much wonderful teaching from the Lord. God blesses those who ask sincere questions of Him, because He blesses those who sincerely seek to know Him and His truth. "You will seek Me and find Me," he said through Jeremiah, "when you search for Me with all your heart" (Jer. 29:13).

Peter's question was: "Does forgiveness have a limit? Granted that a person who commits an offense and repents should be forgiven and restored a few times. But what if he continually falls into sin, over and over again? **How often** must **I forgive him?"**

Perhaps to demonstrate how magnanimous he thought he was, Peter suggested a limit of **seven times,** which was more than twice that allowed by Jewish tradition. Using references in the book of Amos (see 1:3, 6, 9, 11, 13; cf. Job 33:29), the rabbis had taken a repeated statement by God against neighboring enemies of Israel and made it into a universal rule for limiting God's forgiveness and, by extension, also man's. If God forgives men only three times, they spuriously reasoned, it is unnecessary and even presumptuous for men to forgive each other more times than that. Rabbi Jose ben Hanina, for instance, said, "He who begs forgiveness from his neighbor must not do so more than three times." Rabbi Jose ben Jehuda said, "If a man commits an offense once, they forgive him; if he commits an offense a second time, they forgive him; if he commits an offense a third time, they forgive him; the fourth time they do not forgive him."

Peter therefore probably thought Jesus would be impressed with the seemingly generous suggestion of **up to seven times.** Compared to Jewish tradition, it *was* generous and no doubt was based on Peter's growing understanding of Jesus' teaching and personal example of compassion and mercy. Realizing that the Lord's graciousness was in marked contrast to the self-centered legalism of the scribes and Pharisees, Peter doubled their narrow limit for forgiveness and added one more time for good measure.

THE EXTENT OF FORGIVENESS

Jesus said to him, "I do not say to you, up to seven times, but up to seventy times seven." (18:21*b*-22)

Peter was still thinking like the scribes and Pharisees and like fallen human nature is always inclined to think. He was thinking in the measurable and limited terms of law, not the immeasurable and unlimited terms of grace. Law keeps count; grace does not. Therefore **Jesus said to him, "I do not say to you, up to seven times, but up to seventy times seven."**

The Lord was not extending the legal limit of forgiveness. He was not speaking of law or limits at all. By **seventy times seven** He did not mean 490. He simply picked up on Peter's number and multiplied it by itself and then by ten, indicating a number that, for all practical purposes, was beyond counting. Record keeping is not to be considered, and a Christian with a forgiving heart thinks nothing about it. He forgives the hundredth offense or the thousandth just as readily and graciously as the first—because that is the way he is forgiven by God.

Perhaps Jesus had in mind Lamech's arrogant boast that "if Cain is avenged sevenfold, then Lamech seventy-sevenfold" (Gen. 4:24). The inclination of sinful man is to return evil for evil without limit. God's standard is just the opposite; Jesus said to return good for evil without limit.

Even if a brother "sins against you seven times a day," the Lord said on another occasion, "and returns to you seven times, saying, 'I repent,' forgive him" (Luke 17:4). Jesus was not setting a daily limit, but rather the opposite. He was speaking of repeated, regular sinning that is committed many times a day, day after day, and of corresponding repeated forgiveness. He was saying that even if a fellow Christian sins against you every day for seven times each day, you should be ready and willing to forgive him that often. The faithful, godly Christian will never allow his own forgiveness to be surpassed by a brother's sin. Reflecting his heavenly Father's nature, where sin against him increases, so does his gracious forgiveness (cf. Rom. 5:20).

Of that paralleling extent of forgiveness, Paul declared that Christians are to be "forgiving [of] each other, just as God in Christ also has forgiven you" (Eph. 4:32). Commenting on the rarity of such grace among believers, John Wesley wrote, "If this be Christianity, where do Christians live?"

THE EXAMPLE OF FORGIVENESS

For this reason the kingdom of heaven may be compared to a certain king who wished to settle accounts with his slaves. And when he had begun to settle them, there was brought to him one who owed him ten thousand talents. But since he did not have the means to repay, his lord commanded him to be sold, along with his wife and children and all that he had, and repayment to be made. The slave therefore falling down, prostrated himself before him, saying, 'Have patience with me, and I will repay you everything.' And the lord of that slave felt compassion and released him and forgave him the debt. But that slave went out and found one of his fellow slaves who owed him a hundred denarii; and he seized him and began to choke him, saying, 'Pay back what you owe.' So his fellow slave fell down and began to entreat him, saying 'Have patience with me and I will repay you.' He was unwilling however, but went and threw him in prison until he should pay back what was owed. So when his fellow slaves saw what had happened, they were deeply grieved and came and reported to their lord all that had happened. Then summoning him, his lord said to him, 'You wicked slave, I forgave you all that debt because you entreated me. Should you not also have had mercy on your fellow slave, even as I had mercy on you?' And his lord, moved with anger, handed him over to the torturers until he should repay all that was owed him. So shall My heavenly Father also do to you, if each of you does not forgive his brother from your heart." (18:23-35)

This parable is so severe that many people conclude that the principle Jesus teaches through it could not possibly apply to believers. But just as it is sometimes necessary for a parent to deal harshly with a persistently disobedient child, it is also sometimes necessary for the Lord to deal harshly with His disobedient family. The writer of Hebrews reminded his readers of what the Lord had taught His people almost a thousand years earlier: "Those whom the Lord loves He disciplines, and He scourges every son whom He receives" (Heb. 12:6; cf. Prov. 3:12). Some of the

Corinthian believers had become so immoral and impenitent that God put them on sickbeds and even caused some to die (1 Cor. 11:30). He struck Ananias and Sapphira dead for lying to the Holy Spirit (Acts 5:1-10). The Lord is sometimes stringent with His errant children because that is sometimes the only way He can correct their disobedience and protect the purity and holiness of His church.

Jesus introduces the parable by specifically stating that it is about **the kingdom of heaven,** whose true citizenship includes only believers. Not only that, but He tells the parable **for this reason,** that is, as a direct response to Peter's question about forgiving a brother (v. 21), which in turn was a response to His teaching about discipline within the church (vv. 15-20). Peter himself obviously was a believer, and his reference to "brother" indicates a fellow believer, especially in light of the fact that chapter 18 focuses on believers, the Lord's "little ones who believe in [Him]" (v. 6; cf. v. 10). Jesus is illustrating the need for believers to forgive each other.

As already seen in Matthew 13, much of the Lord's teaching about **the kingdom of heaven** was given in the form of parables. In the present parable Jesus presents the attitude of God, the **certain king,** concerning forgiveness of and by His subjects, the **slaves.** The citizens of God's kingdom are also children in His heavenly family, and the parable speaks of Him both as Lord, represented by the **king,** and as heavenly Father (v. 35).

Slaves is here used in the broadest sense of those in submission to a sovereign, as all subjects of ancient monarchies were, regardless of their rank or wealth. All citizens of an ancient kingdom were slaves in the sense that they owed total allegiance to the **king,** who typically had life and death power over them. In that sense, noblemen were as much the king's **slaves** as were the most menial servants. Those extremes are suggested in the parable, indicating that its truth applies to every believer, every citizen of **the kingdom of heaven.** The first slave was obviously of high rank and probably possessed considerable personal wealth, whereas the fellow slave whom he refused to forgive the debt was perhaps relatively poor.

A **king** usually appointed governors, or satraps, over the various provinces of his kingdom, and their primary responsibility was to collect taxes on his behalf. It was probably in regard to such taxes that the **king . . . wished to settle accounts,** and the man **who owed** the king **ten thousand talents** was probably such a tax-collecting official. In any case, he was a person with great responsibility who **owed** a great amount of money to the king.

The occasion was perhaps the regular, periodic time that the **king** had established **to settle accounts** with His governors. The idea of an ultimate end-of-life accounting, representing God's final judgment, does not correspond to the way a ruler normally collected taxes from his officials. Nor does it fit the fact that the forgiven man went on with normal relationships with other men. The accounting could not represent God's final judgment, because, after he was judged, the man would have had no more opportunity either to forgive or to be forgiven.

Just as "seventy times seven" (v. 22) represents a limitless number of times,

ten thousand talents represents a limitless amount of money. Because monetary values change so widely from one point in history to another, it is never possible to calculate accurately how much a given coin of an ancient society would be worth in modern currency. And that is not necessary to make the point. But historical records give considerable light on the immense value that **ten thousand talents** would have had in Jesus' day.

From historical documents of the time it has been determined that the total annual revenue collected by the Roman government from Idumea, Judea, Samaria, and Galilee was about 900 talents. Based on those figures, **ten thousand talents** amounted to more than eleven years of taxes from those four provinces. From the Old Testament we learn that the total amount of gold given for use in the Temple was just over 8,000 talents (1 Chron. 29:4, 7) and that "the weight of gold which came in to Solomon in one year was 666 talents of gold" (1 Kings 10:14).

Although *murias* literally means **ten thousand**, because it was the largest numerical term in the Greek language it was also used figuratively to represent a vast, uncountable number. In that sense it has the same connotation as the English *myriad,* which is derived from it. *Murias* is therefore sometimes translated "countless" (1 Cor. 4:15) or "myriads" (Rev. 5:11). Jesus' point in this parable, therefore, was that the man who owed the king **ten thousand talents** owed an incalculable and unpayable debt.

That incalculable, unpayable debt represents the debt for sin that every man owes God. When the Holy Spirit convicts a person of his sin (John 16:8), that person is faced with the fact that the extent of his sin is beyond comprehension and humanly unpayable. Like Paul when he saw his sin in the clear light of God's law, every convicted sinner has a glimpse of the utter sinfulness of sin (Rom. 7:13). It is such a glimpse that Job had of himself and that caused him to "repent in dust and ashes" (Job 42:6), and it is such a glimpse that Ezra had of himself and his fellow Israelites that caused him to pray, "O my God, I am ashamed and embarrassed to lift up my face to Thee, my God, for our iniquities have risen above our heads, and our guilt has grown even to the heavens" (Ezra 9:6).

Life is a stewardship from God to be used for His glory. Unbelievers take life from God, and, rather than returning it to Him wisely invested for His glory and making the most of what used to be called "gospel privilege," they squander it on themselves. They are like the prodigal son and the slave who buried his talent in the ground, both of whom Jesus used to illustrate wasted "gospel privilege."

Regardless of how much harm a sin does to other people, it is first of all an offense against God. In his great penitential psalm David declared, "Against Thee, Thee only, I have sinned, and done what is evil in Thy sight" (Ps. 51:4). Every sin ever committed is committed against God. And every sin is committed in His sight, just as surely as if it were committed, were that possible, before His very throne in heaven.

The **slave**, then, represents the unbeliever who has been given the knowledge of God (Rom. 1:18ff.), life from God (Acts 17:25), and the opportunity to give God what is due Him (cf. Rom. 11:36; Col. 1:16) but squanders God's property in sin.

Because the man in Jesus' parable **did not have the means to repay, his lord commanded him to be sold, along with his wife and children and all that he had, and repayment to be made.** The man not only embezzled what belonged to the king but consumed it on himself until nothing was left. That is the state of the bankrupt sinner! The **payment to be made** from the proceeds of selling his family into servitude and redeeming all his personal possessions would not have paid a fraction of the debt, but it was exacted as a punishment and so the king could get at least a portion of what he was due.

Just as the unpayable amount of money in the parable is a picture of man's unpayable debt for sin, the punishment mentioned here makes one think of hell, where condemned men will spend eternity paying for the unpayable. The glory stolen from God by man cannot be repaid by man, and therefore, even after spending an eon in hell, a person would be no nearer paying his debt and being fit for heaven than when he entered. The utter spiritual bankruptcy of every child of Adam makes it impossible for him to pay the limitless debt he has incurred because of his sin.

By the standards of that day the king in the parable had been gracious just by his not demanding an accounting earlier. In an infinitely greater way God is gracious to the most hardened sinner just in allowing him to go on living. Life itself is a great gift of divine mercy.

But there will be a day, and often many days, when every man faces the King to give account for what he is doing with his life. This is not a picture of a final judgment day but of a time of conviction when men are made to face their sin and the need for salvation. It depicts the times when the gospel is preached or the Scripture is read or a personal witness is given to them. They are faced with the reality that they have to give God an accounting for their sinful life.

Realizing his inexcusable guilt and sensing the king's goodness, **the slave therefore falling down, prostrated himself before him.** His falling down and prostrating himself was more than the usual homage given a king. It was an act of total submission, of throwing himself completely on the monarch's mercy. The man was guilty, condemned, devastated, and genuinely penitent. He had no defense and offered none.

In the same way, the sinner confronted by the Holy Spirit with the gospel and the conviction of his sin should acknowledge that he stands guilty and condemned before God. And in the same way his only hope is to humble himself, confess his sin, and cast himself upon God's mercy in Jesus Christ. Every sinner should be overwhelmed by his sin as that man was overwhelmed by his debt. He should have the attitude of the tax collector who "was even unwilling to lift up his eyes to heaven, but was beating his breast, saying, 'God, be merciful to me, the sinner!'" (Luke 18:13). The Beatitudes (Matt. 5:3-12) express the contrite attitude of this repentant sinner, who in spiritual bankruptcy mourns over his sin and cries out for the righteousness of salvation.

As the man lay broken at the feet of the king, he did not realize that he could never have repaid the debt no matter how long and hard he worked. But his terrible plight prompted the desperate plea, **"Have patience with me,"** and then the unrealistic promise, **"I will repay you everything."** Impossible as the prospect was, he nevertheless begged for a chance to make good on his debt. His understanding was faulty, but his attitude was right.

When first convicted of their sin, people are often inclined to make promises to God similar to the one the man gave to the king. A person under conviction will sometimes say, "I've got to shape up my life and be a better person. I must turn over a new leaf, make some resolutions, and reform myself." He acknowledges his sin and sincerely wants to make amends, not yet realizing that he cannot.

Commenting on the servant in this parable, Martin Luther wrote,

> Before the king drew him to account, he had no conscience, does not feel the debt, and would have gone right along, made more debt, and cared nothing about it. But now that the king reckons with him, he begins to feel the debt. So it is with us. The greater part does not concern itself about sin, goes on securely, fears not the wrath of God. Such people cannot come to the forgiveness of sin, for they do not come to realize that they have sins. They say, indeed, with the mouth that they have sin; but if they were serious about it they would speak far otherwise. This servant, too, says, before the king reckons with him, so much I owe to my lord, namely ten thousand talents; . . . But now that the reckoning is held, and his lord orders him, his wife, his children, and everything to be sold, now he feels it. So, too, we feel in earnest when our sins are revealed in the heart, when the record of our debts is held before us. . . . Then we exclaim: I am the most miserable man, there is none as unfortunate as I on the earth! Such knowledge makes a real humble man, works contrition, so that one can come to the forgiveness of sins.

The king well knew that, despite his good intentions, the servant could never do what he promised; but he did not chide the man for his foolish and worthless offer. Rather, **the lord of that slave felt compassion and released him and forgave him the debt.**

Here is an extraordinary picture of God's compassionate love for the genuinely repentant sinner who throws himself on His mercy. The man only asked for patience so that he might try to repay the king, but instead the king **released him and forgave him the debt.** That is what God does with the sin debt of those who come to Him in humble and sincere penitence.

It must be noted that this parable is not intended to present every aspect of salvation. Obviously the Person and work of Christ and the essence of saving faith in that work are not portrayed. The purpose of our Lord here was to illustrate the matter of forgiveness between believers, and the story is limited to that idea. It simply depicts a man with an unpayable debt, who sought mercy and was given it abundantly.

Daneion (**debt**) literally means "loan," implying that in his graciousness the king considered the embezzled fortune a loan and then **forgave** it. Even more graciously does God forgive the sinner who confesses his sin and trusts in Jesus Christ. The moment a person acknowledges the sinfulness of his sin and turns to the only Savior from sin, his mountain of debt to God is paid in full forever.

It was not until the prodigal son reached the absolute bottom of life that he faced up to his wicked foolishness. He had forsaken his father and his family and lived an utterly selfish and debauched life in a foreign and pagan land. And when his money was gone, so were his high living and his supposed friends. The only work he could find was the most demeaning conceivable for a Jew, slopping pigs. While in the pigpen he "came to his senses" and said to himself, "How many of my father's hired men have more than enough bread, but I am dying here with hunger! I will get up and go to my father, and will say to him, 'Father, I have sinned against heaven, and in your sight; I am no longer worthy to be called your son; make me as one of your hired men.'" But even before the son spoke those words to his father, "while he was still a long way off, his father saw him, and felt compassion for him, and ran and embraced him, and kissed him." The father did not chide or rebuke him, nor did he accept the son's offer to be only a hired hand. Rather he commanded "his slaves, 'Quickly bring out the best robe and put it on him, and put a ring on his hand and sandals on his feet; and bring the fattened calf, kill it, and let us eat and be merry; for this son of mine was dead, and has come to life again; he was lost, and has been found'" (Luke 15:11-24).

One commentator suggests that when the father ran out to meet his son he must have had to gather up his long robe under his arms and thereby expose his undergarments, a great shame for an older, dignified man of that day. But the father had no concern but to be reunited with his beloved son whom he had given up for dead.

In an infinitely greater way, God allowed Himself to be humiliated as He came to earth, emptying "Himself, taking the form of a bond-servant" (Phil. 2:7). To redeem fallen men back to Himself, He willingly and lovingly "endured the cross, despising the shame" (Heb. 12:2).

What happens next in the parable seems inconceivable—until we realize that each one of us is guilty, in various ways, of doing what that forgiven slave did. He **went out and found one of his fellow slaves who owed him a hundred denarii; and he seized him and began to choke him, saying, "Pay back what you owe."**

The implication is that the first thing the forgiven slave did after he left the king's presence was to search out a **fellow** slave who owed him some money and violently demand repayment of a mere pittance compared to the vast amount he himself had just been forgiven.

The second man's being described as **one of his fellow slaves** suggests that he represents a fellow believer and that the principle Jesus teaches here primarily relates to believers' treatment of each other. Although Christians should be forgiving of everyone, they should be especially forgiving of one another, because they are **fellow slaves** who serve the same King.

A hundred denarii represented a hundred days' wages for a common laborer in New Testament times, an infinitesimal sum compared to ten thousand talents, which, as already noted, amounted to some eleven years of Roman taxes from the provinces of Idumea, Judea, Samaria, and Galilee combined.

Although the second debt was extremely small by comparison to the first, it was nevertheless a real debt and represents a real offense committed by one believer against another. If the offense were not real, it would need no forgiveness. Jesus was not teaching that sins against fellow believers or against anyone else are insignificant but that they are minute compared to the offenses every one of us has committed against God and for which He has freely and completely forgiven us.

The power of the sinful flesh that remains in a transformed believer is seen in the first servant's hardheartedness against his fellow servant, who perhaps was a low echelon official responsible for collecting taxes from a small village within the province governed by the first servant. Even so, the first man was much further removed from the king in status than he was from the other servant, and the amount of debt he had been forgiven by the king was immeasurably greater than the amount he refused to forgive his fellow servant. Those two facts should have made the man not only especially grateful but especially merciful. His inclination should have been to search out his fellow slave to forgive him rather than condemn him. There is no indication, however, that his own experience of mercy made him grateful, and it clearly did not make him merciful. Instead, he became proud, presumptuous, and hardhearted.

Unfortunately, as Christians we sometimes reflect a similar arrogance and insensitivity. Although we have been totally and forever forgiven of all offenses before God, on the basis of His grace, we often act as if we were forgiven on the basis of our own merit. We may even look down on our brothers and sisters in Christ with disdain and a sense of superiority.

Instead of reflecting the king's compassion, the first servant became angry at the thought that he himself was still owed some money. When he found his debtor, **he seized him and began to choke him, saying, "Pay me back what you owe."** According to ancient Roman writers, it was not uncommon for a creditor to actually wrench a debtor's neck until blood ran from his nose.

This kind of behavior seems unthinkable, even bizarre, and it is hard to believe someone could act in such a way. And that is exactly the Lord's point to Peter and the other disciples. For Christians to be unwilling to forgive one another is unthinkable and bizarre.

The self-deceptive nature of the flesh is such that sometimes anger and vengeance override even greed, and self-will overshadows even self-interest. A person who is severely strangled or beaten, not to mention imprisoned, is put in a poor position to earn money to repay a debt. Even from a purely practical standpoint, such debt-collecting practices are foolish and counterproductive, but they have persisted throughout history and even into modern times.

The subordinate official made his plea with exactly the same words his creditor had used before the king: **"Have patience with me and I will repay you"** (cf. v. 26). That should have shocked the forgiven slave's memory into a right response, but those familiar words evoked no sympathetic reaction in him, even though the debt he had been forgiven would have been unrepayable in a lifetime, whereas the debt owed to him was payable by a few months' work.

With unimaginable callousness, the forgiven slave **was unwilling however, but went and threw** his subordinate **in prison until he should pay back what was owed.** Even to ask for repayment after he himself had been forgiven so much was grossly insensitive; to abuse and imprison his debtor for failure to repay so little was, in the words of one commentator, a "moral monstrosity," to say nothing of foolishness, because in prison the man could not earn money to pay his debt. Such unforgiveness not only is morally unthinkable and bizarre but irrational.

Yet as both Scripture and personal experience make clear, that is the way Christians sometimes treat each other. The parable is an unflattering picture of the sinful flesh that still resides in every believer and that has caused great conflict and damage within the church since its birth.

The church at Corinth was not typical of early congregations, but it shows clearly the extremes to which the flesh can lead those who belong to Christ and who possess His own nature and Spirit. The wealthier members there had no sensitivity for their poorer brethren, eating their own food at the Lord's Supper and leaving nothing for and embarrassing those who had nothing (1 Cor. 11:22). And rather than resolving their differences among themselves, they brought each other before pagan courts (6:1).

Paul instructed Titus to remind the believers under his care "to malign no one, to be uncontentious, gentle, showing every consideration for all men." He then gives the reason God commands those virtues of His children:

> For we also once were foolish ourselves, disobedient, deceived, enslaved to various lusts and pleasures, spending our life in malice and envy, hateful, hating one another. But when the kindness of God our Savior and His love for mankind appeared, He saved us, not on the basis of deeds which we have done in righteousness, but according to His mercy, by the washing of regeneration and renewing by the Holy Spirit, whom He poured out upon us richly through Jesus Christ our Savior, that being justified by His grace we might be made heirs according to the hope of eternal life. (Titus 3:2-7)

Jesus' point in the parable is the same as Paul's here: Those who have been graciously, totally, and permanently forgiven by God for their immeasurable sins against Him are to act like the divine children and heirs they have become by reflecting the love and compassion of their heavenly Father. They are to "be kind to one another, tender-hearted, forgiving each other, just as God in Christ also has forgiven [them]" (Eph.4:32).

Believers still have the capacity to give way to the sinful, spiteful ways of their unredeemed humanness, but "even so," Paul says, "consider yourselves to be dead to sin, but alive to God in Christ Jesus. Therefore do not let sin reign in your mortal body that you should obey its lusts" (Rom. 6:11-12).

Knowing of the great debt the first slave had been forgiven by the king and his subsequent treatment of his indebted slave, the **fellow slaves** were understandably indignant that this man would, in effect, place himself above the king by acting as if he had a right to be less gracious and merciful than his sovereign. Therefore, when they **saw what had happened, they were deeply grieved and came and reported to their lord all that had happened.**

Christians should be **deeply grieved** when a fellow believer is unforgiving, because his hardness of heart not only tends to drive the offender deeper into sin but also causes dissention and division within the church, tarnishes its testimony before the world, and deeply grieves the Lord Himself.

The other slaves went to the king with the awful story, expecting that proper action would be taken against the unforgiving creditor. This feature of the parable forms an interesting insight into the believer's responsibility not only to go through the steps of disciplining a sinning brother but to petition the Lord Himself to act in chastening and purging the ungracious sinning child of God.

As would be expected, the king was incensed when he heard the news, and **summoning him, his lord said to him, "You wicked slave, I forgave you all that debt because you entreated me. Should you not also have had mercy on your fellow slave, even as I had mercy on you?"**

When a Christian allows remaining sin to control an attitude or action, he is being **wicked**, because sin is always sin, whether committed by a believer or unbeliever. The sin of unforgiveness is in some ways even more **wicked** in a believer, because he has infinitely greater motivation and power to be forgiving than does a person who has never experienced God's redeeming grace. How can a person accept God's mercy for all his sin, an unpayable debt, and then not forgive some small offense committed against himself?

It is not that the king expected the first slave to give his subordinate a chance to repay the debt but that he expected him to **have had mercy on** his **fellow slave** and to forgive his debt entirely, **even as** the king had **had mercy on** the forgiven slave and had forgiven his debt entirely. Again, the principle of Ephesians 4:32 is directly parallel.

And his lord, moved with anger, handed him over to the torturers until he should repay all that was owed him. On the earlier occasion, the first slave's plea for patience had moved the king to compassion and forgiveness. Now the man's refusal to forgive his fellow servant **moved** the king to **anger.**

Because He is holy and just, God is always **moved with anger** at sin, including the sin of His children. Paul expressed something of this kind of righteous anger toward unrepentant church members at Corinth when he asked them if they were going to continue in sin and make him come to them with a rod (1 Cor. 4:21).

God has holy indignation whenever a Christian sins (cf. Ps. 6; Acts 5:1-10). As chastening for his sin, the unforgiving slave was **handed over to the torturers** (not executioners) **until he should repay all that was owed him,** that is, until he had a change of heart and forgave his offending brother, which is what the king wanted him to **repay**. Lord Herbert once said, "He who cannot forgive others breaks the bridge over which he himself must pass."

Some commentators contend that the first slave was reencumbered with the debt he had been forgiven and became obligated to pay it all back. But that interpretation hopelessly convolutes the parable by making either the salvation temporary or the forgiveness conditional on one's subsequent behavior. Both views are undesirable. Furthermore, the original debt was said to be unpayable and the man was still without resources, so it would make no sense to reassign him the debt with the provision that it must be paid in full. It is much better to see the repayment simply as the proper duty a believer owes the Lord. In this case, it would mean forgiving your brother any offense.

God does not chasten His children out of hatred but out of love. "Those whom the Lord loves He disciplines, and He scourges every son whom He receives" (Heb. 12:6). He does not chasten them to drive them away but to bring them back to Himself and to His righteousness. "He disciplines us for our good, that we may share His holiness" (v. 10). Every Christian feels the Lord's scourging at some time or another, because every Christian deserves His discipline occasionally. It is natural that God's "discipline for the moment seems not to be joyful, but sorrowful; yet to those who have been trained by it, afterwards it yields the peaceful fruit of righteousness" (v. 11).

When believers forget their own divine forgiveness by God and refuse to extend human forgiveness to fellow believers, the Lord puts them under such **torturers** (the word can refer to inquisitors) as stress, hardship, pressure, or other difficulties until the sin is confessed and forgiveness is granted. As James tells us, "Judgment will be merciless to one who has shown no mercy" (James 2:13).

That is what Jesus unmistakably declared to be the parable's point: **So shall My heavenly Father also do to you, if each of you does not forgive his brother from your heart.** The unforgiving believer (**you**) will satisfy God only by offering his own forgiveness to those who sin against him, most especially **his brother** in Christ.

Jesus is not speaking here of the forgiveness that brings salvation, saying that God only saves those who are forgiving. That would be works righteousness. He is speaking of people forgiving each other after they have experienced His free grace. Those who are saved, transformed, given a new nature in Christ, and have the indwelling Holy Spirit generally will manifest that changed life by having a forgiving attitude (see Matt. 6:14-15). But there will be times when we fall into the sin of unforgiveness, and this instruction is for those times.

As mentioned earlier, if the first man does not represent a Christian, a person who has been forgiven by God for his immeasurable debt of sin, the instruction in the context of the parable completely breaks down. Jesus was speaking to the Twelve, who not only were believers but apostles. All believers, no matter what their position or accomplishments in the church might be, are held accountable to forgive every offense against them committed by fellow believers, for the very reason that they themselves have already been forgiven an incalculable debt by God. They are expected to *reflect* God's forgiveness because they have *experienced* God's forgiveness.

Believers experience two kinds of forgiveness by God. The first is once and for all and is permanent. When a person trusts in Jesus Christ as Savior and Lord, all of his sins—past, present, and future—are judicially forgiven, totally and eternally. But because believers are still subject to the temptations and weaknesses of the flesh, they fall into sin even after they are saved. For that sin they need God's daily forgiveness and cleansing, not to preserve their salvation but to restore the broken relationship with the Lord that the sin causes. Jesus had these two aspects of forgiveness in mind when He said, "He who has bathed needs only to wash his feet, but is completely clean; and you are clean" (John 13:10).

Believers' forgiveness of each other has no power to absolve or cleanse sin as God's forgiveness has absolved and continues to cleanse theirs. Nevertheless their forgiveness of each other should reflect the two kinds of forgiveness they receive from God. They are to have in their hearts an internal, general spirit of forgiveness that is ready to forgive even before they know of a sin committed against them and whether or not the person has asked or ever asks for forgiveness. That forgiveness should be constant and unchanging, reflecting a divinely empowered love that Peter says "covers a multitude of sins" (1 Pet. 4:8). If and when the offending person repents, then relational forgiveness is readily given and the broken relationship is fully restored.

Christians are to be marked as forgiving people, because they have been forgiven as no others on earth. When they are not forgiving, they are living in opposition to their new nature in Christ. When they refuse to forgive fellow Christians they cut themselves off from God's relational forgiveness that cleanses them of the sins they continue to commit. They also forfeit the inner peace, power, and depth of spiritual life that only close communion with the Lord can produce. When a believer falls into a time of spiritual shallowness and indifference, the cause is often a heart that is unforgiving because it has allowed the flesh to vault itself into prominence.

An anonymous saint of long ago wrote,

> Revenge, indeed, seems often sweet to men; but, oh, it is only sugared poison, only sweetened gall, and its aftertaste is bitter as hell. Forgiving, enduring love alone is sweet and blissful; it enjoys peace and the consciousness of God's favour. By forgiving, it gives away and annihilates the injury. It treats the injurer as if he had not injured, and therefore feels no more the smart and sting that he had inflicted. Forgiveness is a shield from which all the fiery darts of the wicked one harmless rebound. Forgiveness brings heaven to earth, and heaven's peace into the sinful heart. Forgiveness is the image of God, the forgiving Father, and an advancement of Christ's kingdom in the world.

"Blessed are the merciful," Jesus said, "for they shall receive mercy" (Matt. 5:7). If we want mercy and cleansing from the Lord for our repeated sins against

Him, we must be willing, **from** our **heart,** to offer mercy to fellow Christians even for repeated offenses against us. Then we can pray with confidence, "Forgive us our debts, as we also have forgiven our debtors" (Matt. 6:12).

Genuine forgiveness that is **from your heart** is trusting forgiveness, forgiveness that sees the offending brother just as he was before he sinned. If we truly forgive a person, we trust him just as we trusted him before. We do not hold the offense over his head or even in our minds, thinking that he will likely sin again.

Although sin against God, the church, and a fellow brother in Christ can bring long-lasting pain and suffering, and sometimes even permanent loss of a once-cherished intimacy, the road to full restoration can be paved with generosity and trust. For example, to entrust a forgiven person with something that is dear and important to you is perhaps the surest evidence that the forgiveness is genuinely **from** the **heart.** If the offense was stealing, the offender can again be entrusted with something precious. If the offense was shirking responsibility, he can be given other important work to do. Even if the offense was slander, he again can be trusted with your reputation and become a friend who is fully loved and fully trusted.

To forgive is not necessarily to forget. Although the truly forgiving person will refuse to dwell on an offense, there are sometimes continual reminders of it that we cannot control. Nor does forgiveness involve excusing a sinful offense. Sin is always sin, and true love and mercy never try to make sin anything but what it is. But forgiveness does involve ending the bitterness, anger, and resentment that not only do not remove a sin but rather add to it.

Heart forgiveness is not possible for the believer in his own power. Genuine forgiveness is not natural but supernatural and is possible only as the indwelling Holy Spirit empowers. Only as we "walk by the Spirit" are we able not to "carry out the desire of the flesh," which, among other things, is to hold a grudge rather than forgive. "For the flesh sets its desire against the Spirit, and the Spirit against the flesh; for these are in opposition to one another, so that you may not do the things that you please" (Gal. 5:16-17).

The great commentator William Arnot told the following account to illustrate how believers are enabled to obey the command to forgive each other. After fording a river, a traveler in Burma discovered that his body was covered with small leeches, busily sucking his blood. His first impulse was to pull them off, but his servant warned him against it, explaining that to do that would leave part of the leeches buried in the skin and cause serious infection. The native prepared a warm bath for the man and added certain herbs to the water that irritated but did not kill the leeches. One by one they voluntarily dropped off. "Each unforgiven injury rankling in the heart is like a leech sucking the life-blood," Arnot goes on to explain. "Mere human determination to have done with it will not cast the evil thing away. You must bathe your whole being in God's pardoning mercy; and those venomous creatures will instantly let go their hold."

When someone says or does something against us that seems unforgivable, it is helpful to offer a prayer such as this: "O God, put in me the heart of forgiveness, so that I may commune with You in the fullness of fellowship and joy and not experience the chastening that comes when You don't forgive me because I won't forgive a brother or sister in Christ. May I remember that for everyone who sins against me I have multiplied times sinned against You, and You have always forgiven me. At no time has any of my sin caused me to forfeit my eternal life; therefore, no one else's sin should cause them to forfeit my love and my mercy toward them."

Jesus' Teaching on Divorce

(19:1-12)

16

And it came about that when Jesus had finished these words, He departed from Galilee, and came into the region of Judea beyond the Jordan; and great multitudes followed Him, and He healed them there.

And some Pharisees came to Him, testing Him, and saying, "Is it lawful for a man to divorce his wife for any cause at all?" And He answered and said, "Have you not read, that He who created them from the beginning made them male and female, and said, 'For this cause a man shall leave his father and mother, and shall cleave to his wife; and the two shall become one flesh'? Consequently they are no longer two, but one flesh. What therefore God has joined together, let no man separate." They said to Him, "Why then did Moses command to give her a certificate and divorce her?" He said to them, "Because of your hardness of heart, Moses permitted you to divorce your wives; but from the beginning it has not been this way. And I say to you, whoever divorces his wife, except for immorality, and marries another woman commits adultery." The disciples said to Him, "If the relationship of the man with his wife is like this, it is better not to marry." But He said to them, "Not all men can accept this statement, but only those to whom it has been given. For there are eunuchs who were born that way from their mother's womb; and there are eunuchs who were made eunuchs

**by men; and there are also eunuchs who made themselves eunuchs for the
sake of the kingdom of heaven. He who is able to accept this, let him accept
it."** (19:1-12)

Some years ago a journalist for a national news magazine asked rhetorically,
"Are there any persons left in the land who have not heard a friend or a child or a
parent describe the agony of divorce?" Divorce has become pandemic, to the point
that hardly a person can be found who has not been affected by it either directly or
indirectly. Many marriages, including a tragic number of Christian marriages, seem
to be little more than a socially recognized battleground where warfare between the
spouses is the rule and harmony the exception.

Each year in the United States there are well over one million divorces, and
beneath the rubble of those numbing statistics lie the crushed lives of men, women,
and children. For every million divorces, there are two million adults and several
more million children who are directly involved. None of them escapes suffering
and damage, no matter how amicable the divorce may be. Nearly every state has
enacted "no fault" divorce laws, making divorce almost as easy as marriage. It is not
surprising that the largest caseloads in civil courts today relate to family disputes.

In past years in this nation the vast majority of marriages held together, and
divorce was difficult and rare. The reasons for that stability are not hard to find.
First was the family moral force. Not only the immediate family but the extended
family of grandparents, aunts and uncles, and cousins was the center of personal
loyalty and activity and usually had a tradition of moral and religious convictions. It
was these intimate loved ones that all family members, adults as well as children,
knew they could depend on for help, comfort, encouragement, and security. But as
moral permissiveness, feminism, humanism, easier mobility, and the disruptive and
worldly influences of television, movies, and other media began to undermine the
family, divorce rapidly increased. The number of single adults living apart from any
close family relationship has also increased dramatically, adding to the decrease of
family support, encouragement, and influence.

The second reason for family stability in the past was community expectation.
Society in general, and the legal system in particular, recognized and strongly
supported and protected the primacy of the family as well as a biblically-based
morality. Strict laws made divorce difficult, and community ethics and peer pressure
made the stigma of it severe.

The third and strongest of forces that helped maintain family stability was
the teaching of the church. Until modern times, every branch of Christendom—
Catholic, Orthodox, and Protestant—strongly supported family life and just as
strongly opposed divorce. But as their constituencies pled for more concessions to
worldly standards and practices, church bodies acquiesced, and the family has
suffered the bitter consequences of those compromises.

In the name of Christian love, some individuals and groups not only condone
divorce but insist that it is sometimes God's will. A well-known entertainer claimed

that her divorce was justified because her husband was a detriment to her career. She claimed that she did not believe her divorce related to her religious beliefs in any significant way and that, even if the divorce were wrong, God loved her in spite of it. In other words, it made no real difference to God. The final evidence given to justify the divorce was the fact that she and her husband would be happier as divorced friends than as married enemies.

Even when Christians go to Scripture for guidance concerning divorce and remarriage, they often do so with preconceptions and predispositions that make responsible interpretation impossible. Some people consult Scripture solely to find justification for views they already hold. Others fall into the trap either of adding to or taking from what it teaches. To justify divorce, some people lower the biblical standard in the name of love. To try to stem the tide of divorce and promote spirituality, others raise the standard higher than the Bible teaches. But that which is contrary to Scripture can never be either loving or spiritual. A human standard may be more lenient or more restrictive than Scripture, but it can never be better. When God's Word is ignored or perverted in any area, tragedy is always the consequence. The matter of marriage and divorce standards is no exception.

The first sin of mankind was not marital, but it was committed within the framework of marriage. God created man and woman equal in many ways, but He gave them clearly different roles. Man was to be the provider and leader and woman his helper in a perfect, balanced, and majestic coregency over all the earth (Gen. 1:27-28). The man's headship and the woman's submission were blended in a loving interdependence that allowed them to multiply and fill the earth together, subdue the earth together, and rule the earth together. But because Eve did not consult Adam, her head and protector, when temptation came she easily succumbed to Satan's wiles. And when Adam forfeited his role of headship and willingly followed her lead, he also succumbed to sin.

As a consequence of that sin, God cursed Eve and all other women to pain in childbirth and cursed Adam and all other men to the hardship of laboring for their food and sustenance (Gen. 3:16-19). In addition to that, because the God-given harmony between man and woman had been broken, God also placed a curse upon their relationship to each other. Because they reversed their roles, with Eve usurping the place of leadership and Adam submitting to the place of follower, God destined them to continual conflict.

God declared to Eve, "Your desire shall be for your husband, and he shall rule over you" (Gen. 3:16b). The desire spoken of here does not refer to her original God-given desire for loving submission and companionship, which she already had before the Fall. Her desire would no longer be to submit to his rule but to usurp it. The use of the Hebrew word translated "desire" in this text relates to seeking control and dominance. It is the same term used in the next chapter in the same way to describe sin's personified desire to corrupt and gain control over Cain (4:7).

Just as the fallen woman's role of submission was subverted, so was the fallen man's role of headship. His rule over her would no longer be benevolent and selfless but overbearing and selfish. It was at the Fall that both feminism and male chauvinism were born, when women began to seek supremacy and men began to be suppressive.

Because men are naturally stronger, male chauvinism has been the dominant of those two perversions throughout history. In many ancient cultures, including Jewish, women were frequently treated more like animals than human beings, and wives were treated more like possessions to be bought and traded than partners to be loved and cherished.

But God did not change His standard because men changed theirs. "I, the Lord, do not change," He declared (Mal. 3:6). Just prior to that declaration God had given a stinging rebuke to Jewish men who "dealt treacherously" with their wives. He Himself was witness between husband and wife when they made their marital covenant, as the One who ordains all marriage and every marriage. Therefore "'I hate divorce,' says the Lord, the God of Israel, 'and him who covers his garment with wrong'" (Mal. 2:14-16).

The prophet Hosea pictured the epitome of God-ordained and God-empowered marital love. He was a living illustration of God's undying love for His people Israel. The prophet married a woman named Gomer, who became an adulterous prostitute. He had children by her and continued to love, care for, and protect her despite her persistent unfaithfulness. He even bought her back from the slave market after she had sunk to the pits of immorality. His life with Gomer was surely not without times of anger and resentment, but he forgave her and did whatever was necessary to bring her back to himself. His love for Gomer and his commitment to her as his wife, like God's love for and covenant with His people Israel, was exceedingly gracious and forgiving.

By the power of the indwelling Holy Spirit, God expects His redeemed people in Christ to exemplify the original beauty and mutuality of the marriage relationship as well as the grace of forgiveness. "Wives, be subject to your own husbands, as to the Lord," Paul declares. "For the husband is the head of the wife, as Christ also is the head of the church, He Himself being the Savior of the body. But as the church is subject to Christ, so also the wives ought to be to their husbands in everything." The divinely ordained and exemplified responsibility of the husband is just as clear: "Husbands, love your wives, just as Christ also loved the church and gave Himself up for her" (Eph. 5:18, 22-25).

The two key attitudes in a successful marriage are self-denial and self-giving, both of which are contrary to human nature but made possible to Christians through the Holy Spirit. The husband and wife who are walking in the Spirit will be walking in unselfish humility and forgiving, restoring love that always puts the other first.

In Matthew 19:1-12 Jesus gives a clear discourse on God's revelation about marriage and divorce.

THE BACKGROUND AND SETTING

And it came about that when Jesus had finished these words, He departed from Galilee, and came into the region of Judea beyond the Jordan; and great multitudes followed Him, and He healed them there. (19:1-2)

These two verses mark an especially significant transition in Jesus' ministry. For about two years He had been preaching, teaching, and healing in Galilee in northern Palestine. For the last two months He had concentrated almost entirely on private instruction to the Twelve.

To mark the end of each of Jesus' major discourses Matthew used a phrase such as **when Jesus had finished these words** (cf. 7:28; 11:1; 13:53; 26:1). In the present passage, the phrase **these words** refers to the Lord's discourse on childlikeness recorded in chapter 18 and given to the disciples just before He left Capernaum. At the end of that discourse, **He departed from Galilee.**

As Jesus had already announced to the Twelve, it was necessary that He "go to Jerusalem, and suffer many things from the elders and chief priests and scribes, and be killed, and be raised up on the third day" (16:21). He would not, however, go directly south to Jerusalem but rather east and then south by way of **the region of Judea beyond the Jordan** and Jericho (20:29).

This **region** later came to be called Perea, a name taken from the Greek *peran*, which means **beyond.** Lying to the east of **the Jordan** River, this territory which had long been sparsely populated was now well settled. Because the Passover time was nearing, Jesus would be able to minister not only to the residents of Perea but also to the many Jews traveling through there as they also made their annual Passover pilgrimage to Jerusalem.

As Jesus preached and taught in Perea (see Mark 10:1), **great multitudes followed Him, and He healed them there.** His ministry in that region is recorded in Matthew 19-20, and as always, by demonstrating His power and His compassion, Jesus' healing miracles attested to His divine, messianic credentials.

THE ATTACK

And some Pharisees came to Him, testing Him, and saying, "Is it lawful for a man to divorce his wife for any cause at all?" (19:3)

Almost from the beginning of His ministry (see Matt. 9:11), Jesus had been criticized by the **Pharisees,** who even before this time had become His arch-enemies and planned to kill Him (12:14). They were the largest and most influential party in the Jewish religious establishment, whose unbiblical traditions and hypocritical life-styles were the antithesis of true righteousness (5:20). They despised Jesus because He undermined their false teaching and exposed their deceitful living.

Therefore when they **came to Him,** this group of religious leaders obviously was asking questions **testing Him** in the hope that He would fail publicly. They wanted to discredit Him in the eyes of the people so that He would lose His popularity and be easier for them to destroy. This time their test question was well thought out, carefully calculated to place Him at odds with Moses, the great giver of God's law.

For many centuries divorce had been a volatile issue for debate among the

Jews. As women came to be treated almost like merchandise to be bought, sold, or traded, divorce inevitably became common. Because of their spurious, self-serving interpretations of the Mosaic law to justify their lusts for other women, the **Pharisees** had become the leading exponents of easy divorce. They were known for frequently divorcing their wives **for any cause at all** to marry another woman and for teaching that the practice not only was permissible but sometimes mandatory.

At the other extreme was an opposing and much less influential faction of rabbis, represented by a certain Shammai, who maintained that divorce was never permissible. That narrow-minded, hard-line view not only was unpopular but, like the liberal position of the Pharisees, was also unscriptural.

Representing the liberal Pharisaic view was rabbi Hillel, who had died only about twenty years before Jesus began His ministry. He taught that a man could divorce his wife for the most trivial of reasons, for such things as taking her hair down in public or talking to other men and even for burning the bread or putting too much salt in the food. For her to speak ill of her mother-in-law or to be infertile were more than sufficient grounds for divorce.

From His previous teaching, the Pharisees knew Jesus did not hold to such a liberalized view of divorce. They had heard Him say that "everyone who divorces his wife, except for the cause of unchastity, makes her commit adultery; and whoever marries a divorced woman commits adultery" (Matt. 5:32). They now expected Him to take the same stand and thereby alienate and intimidate the many other Jews besides themselves who accepted the idea of divorce **for any cause at all.** They hoped to discredit Him by identifying Him in the minds of the people with the narrow and intolerant view of the Shammai school.

Ultimately, of course, they wanted to destroy Him. The clever Pharisees were well aware that Perea, where Jesus now ministered, was under the rule of Herod Antipas. He was the tetrarch who had John the Baptist imprisoned and eventually beheaded for condemning his unlawful marriage to Herodias, whom he had seduced away from his brother Philip (see Matt. 14:3-12). No doubt the Pharisees hoped that, by denouncing divorce **for any cause at all,** Jesus would thereby publicly condemn Herod's adulterous relationship just as John had done—and suffer John's fate.

The Answer

And He answered and said, "Have you not read, that He who created them from the beginning made them male and female, and said, 'For this cause a man shall leave his father and mother, and shall cleave to his wife; and the two shall become one flesh'? Consequently they are no longer two, but one flesh. What therefore God has joined together, let no man separate." (19:4-6)

Instead of giving a direct yes or no, Jesus went back beyond rabbinical tradition, and even further back than the law of Moses, all the way to God's creation of man.

Jesus' opening words had nothing directly to do with the question of divorce but were a sarcastic and biting rebuke to the learned Pharisees, who prided themselves on their great knowledge of Scripture. Responding to their question with a question of His own, Jesus was in effect asking, "**Have you not read** the book of Genesis? Are you not aware of what God Himself declared at the very creation? Don't you know the very first thing God said about marriage? Don't you recall **that He who created them from the beginning made them male and female, and said, 'For this cause a man shall leave his father and mother, and shall cleave to his wife; and the two shall become one flesh?'**" By quoting from Genesis 1:27 and 2:24, Jesus was saying, "Your argument is not with Me, but with God." His words must have stung the proud, self-righteous Pharisees, who considered themselves to be the supreme authorities on Scripture.

From those two verses, taken from the first two chapters of Scripture, the Lord presented four reasons why divorce was never in God's plan. First, He said, God **created them from the beginning . . . male and female.** In the Hebrew text of Genesis 1:27, both **male** and **female** are in the emphatic position, giving the sense of "the one male and the one female." In other words, God did not create a group of males and females who could pick and choose mates as it suited them. There were no spares or options. There was no provision, or even possibility, for multiple or alternate spouses. There were only one man and one woman in the beginning, and for that very obvious reason, divorce and remarriage was not an option.

Second, Jesus said, "**For this cause a man shall leave his father and mother, and shall cleave to his wife.**" Since Adam and Eve had no parents to leave, the leaving of **father and mother** was a principle to be projected into and applied to all future generations.

The Hebrew word (*dābaq*) behind **cleave** refers to a strong bonding together of objects and often was used to represent gluing or cementing. Job used the word when he spoke of his bones clinging to his skin and flesh (Job 19:20; cf. Ps. 102:5). It could also have the connotation of following closely. The two ideas were, in fact, sometimes carried together, as in Ruth's clinging to Naomi (Ruth (1:14) and the men of Judah remaining steadfast to David (2 Sam. 20:2). Several times the term is used of the Israelites' holding to the Lord in love and obedience (Deut. 10:20; 11:22; 13:4; Josh. 22:5; 23:8).

The idea of close bonding and interrelationship is seen in the modern Hebrew word for marriage, *kiddushin,* a word closely related to the terms for holy and sanctified, which have the basic meaning of being set apart and consecrated. This meaningful word for marriage beautifully expresses the consecration of husband and wife to each other as well as to God. Marriage as God has always intended it to be involves the total commitment and consecration of husbands and wives to each other and to Him as the divine author of their union and witness to their covenant.

The third reason Jesus gives for divorce not being in God's plan is that, in marriage, **the two . . . become one flesh.** As Paul declares in 1 Corinthians 7:4, spouses belong to each other in the physical relationship of marriage: "The wife does not have authority over her own body, but the husband does; and likewise also the husband does not have authority over his own body, but the wife does."

"Consequently," Jesus said, "when a man and woman are joined in marriage **they are no longer two, but one flesh.**" They are therefore indivisible and inseparable, except through death. In God's eyes they become the total possession of each other, one in mind and spirit, in goals and direction, in emotion and will. When they have a child it becomes the perfect emblem and demonstration of their oneness, because that child is a unique product of the fusion of two people into **one flesh** and carries the combined traits of both parents.

But it is not, as some foolishly argue, that becoming **one flesh** in the sex act is what constitutes marriage. If that were true, there would be no such thing as fornication, because as soon as an unmarried man and woman engaged in the sex act they would be automatically married, rather than guilty of wickedness. Under the Mosaic law, the act of fornication obligated the man to marry the woman or pay compensation to her father (Ex. 22:16-17), further indicating that the sexual act itself is not the equivalent of marriage.

On the other hand, the act of adultery, shattering as it is to the marriage relationship, does not in itself dissolve a marriage. Marriage is a mutual covenant, a God-ordained obligation between a man and a woman to lifelong companionship. When rebuking the Israelites for their adultery and frequent divorces, the Lord declared that by divorcing his wife a man "dealt treacherously" with her, "though she is your companion and your wife by covenant" (Mal. 2:14-16). In God's eyes, *every* wife is a "wife by covenant," never merely a wife by fornication, convenience, or whim.

The fourth reason Jesus gives for divorce not being in God's perfect design is that, in the creative sense, every marriage is made in heaven. From the very first marriage of Adam and Eve, **God has joined together** every husband and wife. Marriage is first of all God's institution and God's doing, regardless of how men may corrupt it and deny or disregard His part in it. Whether it is between faithful believers or between rank pagans or atheists, or whether it was arranged by the parents or by the mutual desire and consent of the bride and groom, marriage as a general social relationship is above all the plan and work of God for the procreation, pleasure, and preservation of the race. Whether it is entered into wisely or foolishly, sincerely or insincerely, selfishly or unselfishly, with great or little commitment, God's design for every marriage is that it be permanent until the death of one of the spouses.

God engineered man and woman to complement, support, and give joy to each other through the mutual commitment of the marriage bond. It is by His divine hand that they are created to fulfill each other, encourage each other, strengthen each other, and produce children as fruit of their love for each other. Whether they recognize it or not, every couple who has enjoyed the companionship, happiness, and fulfillment of marriage has experienced the miraculous blessing of God. There is no good thing in marriage that is not derived from Him.

No child can be conceived by the procreative act of a man and woman who is not first conceived by the creative act of God. Every marriage and every child is a creation of God, and therefore divorce and abortion share this tragically evil common denominator: they kill a creation of God.

To destroy a marriage is to destroy a creation of Almighty God. **"What therefore God has joined together,"** Jesus warned, **"let no man separate."** The word **separate** is from *chōrizō,* which in the context of marriage always carried the idea of divorce, not simply temporary separation. It is translated "leave" in 1 Corinthians 7:10, where Paul is clearly speaking of divorce.

Jesus' point is that marriage is always the work of **God,** whereas divorce is always the work of **man,** and that no **man**—whoever he is or wherever he is or for whatever reason he may have—has the right to **separate** what **God has joined together.** A pagan husband and wife who divorce break God's law just as surely as believers who divorce. In the ultimate sense, every marriage is ordained of God and every divorce is not. At best, divorce and remarriage is only permitted by the Lord, never commended and certainly never commanded, as some of Jesus' contemporary rabbis taught. Jesus said that God permits it only on the basis of sexual immorality and even then as a gracious concession to man's sinfulness (vv. 8-9). To claim, as some professing Christians do, that the Lord led them out of a marriage is to lie and to make God a liar.

Although Jesus here mentions only Genesis 1:27 and 2:24, the Old Testament is replete with other teachings about the divine sanctity and permanence of marriage. Two of the Ten Commandments—the one against the physical act of adultery (Ex. 20:14) and the one against coveting a neighbor's wife (v. 17), which is the mental act of adultery (Matt. 5:28)—specifically protect the sanctity of marriage. Adultery was such a heinous sin that its punishment was death (Lev. 20:10; Deut. 22:22-24). God made no legal provision for divorce. Adultery could bring the end of a marriage, but by execution, not divorce.

THE ARGUMENT

They said to Him, "Why then did Moses command to give her a certificate and divorce her?" (19:7)

No doubt anticipating Jesus' appeal to Scripture, the Pharisees were prepared with what they considered to be a scriptural rebuttal. They were so intent on defending their own fleshly standards and on trying to discredit and destroy Jesus that they totally disregarded what He had just said. They were not interested in the divine standard for marriage God had established at creation but in defending their own low, self-centered standards. They were classic examples of the natural man looking for moral and spiritual loopholes to accommodate his sin.

To give the appearance of divine support for their liberal divorce customs, they appealed to **Moses,** seeking to pit Jesus against God's great law giver. Because it is the only passage in the five books of **Moses** that mentions any grounds for divorce, the passage to which the Pharisees referred had to be Deuteronomy 24:1-4. But that passage clearly does not **command** divorce, as the Pharisees claimed. And all the other Pentateuch passages that mention divorce simply acknowledge its existence (see Lev. 21:7, 14; Deut. 22:19, 29).

A careful reading of the Deuteronomy 24 text shows that, far from commanding divorce, the passage does not teach about divorce at all. **Moses** was giving a command with regard to a particular case of remarriage. That passage neither commends nor condemns the reason and procedure for the divorce mentioned there. It states that the reason was "indecency," without detailing what that might involve, and it then mentions the giving of a certificate of divorce, without commenting on the propriety of that procedure. The only **command** in the passage relates to the issue of remarriage, not divorce. The **command** is simply that, if a divorced woman remarries and that husband divorces her or dies, her first "former husband who sent her away is not allowed to take her again to be his wife, since she has been defiled" (v. 4). It is to that commandment regarding remarriage, not a commandment to divorce, as some have supposed, that Jesus refers here and in Mark 10:5.

Because the penalty for adultery was death, the indecency mentioned here obviously referred to some kind of sexual looseness or lewdness that came short of adultery. And it was because such indecency, vile as it might have been, was *not* sufficient grounds for divorce that the divorced wife was defiled by remarriage and could not be taken back by her first husband. Because her divorce to her first husband had no sufficient grounds and thus was invalid, she became an adulteress, and therefore defiled, when she married again. That is why John the Baptist declared that Herod and Herodias were living in adultery. In God's sight, she was still "the wife of his brother Philip" (Matt. 14:3-4). For the first husband to take back a defiled woman would be unholy.

THE AFFIRMATION

He said to them, "Because of your hardness of heart, Moses permitted you to divorce your wives; but from the beginning it has not been this way. And I say to you, whoever divorces his wife, except for immorality, and marries another woman commits adultery." (19:8-9)

After clarifying that the Mosaic law did not commend, much less command, divorce, Jesus affirmed that it **permitted** divorce under certain conditions. Speaking to them as representatives of their fleshly forefathers, Jesus told the Pharisees that it was only because of **your hardness of heart** that **Moses permitted you to divorce your wives.**

As noted above, even the scriptural permission for divorce is implied rather than explicitly taught. In no Old Testament passage, including the Deuteronomy 24:1-4 text to which the Pharisees no doubt were referring, is specific permission for divorce given. One reason is not hard to surmise. If the Israelites so abused implied permission for divorce, how much more would they have abused explicit permission?

Because of His loving grace God did not always exact the death penalty for adultery under the Mosaic covenant. Israel's later history is replete with instances of adultery that did not lead to execution. David was strongly rebuked and severely punished for his adultery with Bathsheba, but he was not put to death. Because of his hundreds of wives and concubines, Solomon lived in virtual unremitting adultery on the basis of the one-man, one-woman standard of Genesis 1-2. Yet, like his father David, he did not suffer the death penalty.

When the Jewish exiles returned from the seventy years of captivity in Babylon and were seeking to restore the Temple and to begin living according to God's Word, they were brought face to face with the problem of their many intermarriages with pagan women. Consequently, under Ezra they decided they would put away their unbelieving wives and the children born of those marriages, based on "the commandment of our God" and "according to the law" (Ezra 10:3).

There is no record that this action was specifically approved by God, but lack of any condemnation implies that the resulting divorces were **permitted** by Him. And the historical context supports the idea that those divorces were on the grounds of adultery. Not only were all pagans of that day idolatrous, which Scripture repeatedly refers to as spiritual adultery (see, e.g., Jer. 3:8; 13:27; Ezek. 16:32), but most pagan religious systems involved gross immorality as an integral part of their rites and ceremonies. It is therefore likely that most, if not all, of the foreign wives the Israelite men had married were both physical and spiritual adulterers, thereby giving their husbands legitimate grounds for divorce.

God had taken Israel as a wife, and like Hosea's Gomer, she too was unfaithful. Through Isaiah the Lord rebuked Israel for her spiritual adultery in worshiping pagan deities. "Where is the certificate of divorce," He asks them rhetorically, "by which I have sent your mother away?" (Isa. 50:1). The answer, of course, was that God had not given such a certificate, because, just as Hosea with Gomer, God was not ready to put Israel away, despite her constant spiritual adultery committed against Him. She had no freedom from her relationship to God that would allow her to consummate relations with other gods.

Finally, however, by the time of Jeremiah, after pleading with His people for some 700 years to forsake idolatry and return to Him, God did something startling. "Have you seen what faithless Israel did?" He asked the prophet. "She went up on every high hill and under every green tree, and she was a harlot there. And I thought, 'After she has done all these things, she will return to Me'; but she did not return." Because of her unrelenting hardness of heart in persisting with her unfaithfulness, "I had sent her away," the Lord said, "and given her a writ of divorce" (Jer. 3:6-8). It was on the basis of her spiritual adultery that God, as it were, finally gave Israel a certificate of divorce.

It is remarkable that, since the Exile and even to our present day, no significant number of Jews has been involved in idolatry. Because His people have not "married" the false gods with whom they commit spiritual adultery, just as Gomer had not married any of her lovers, God predicts that one day He will take Israel back to Himself:

> "Behold, days are coming," declares the Lord, "when I will make a new covenant with the house of Israel and with the house of Judah, not like the covenant which I made with their fathers in the day I took them by the hand to bring them out of the land of Egypt, My covenant which they broke, although I was a husband to them," declares the Lord. "But this is the covenant which I will make with the house of Israel after those days," declares the Lord, "I will put My law within them, and on their heart I will write it; and I will be their God, and they shall be My people." (Jer. 31:31-33)

In light of God's spiritual divorce and eventual remarriage to Israel, it is surely not possible to claim that Scripture recognizes no grounds at all for divorce and remarriage, as some ancient rabbis claimed and as some Christians still claim today. God does not give us illustrations of His own righteous behavior that we cannot follow. If He finally divorced idolatrous and unrepentant Israel, after long years of forgiveness and mercy, it cannot be wrong for a man or woman to divorce a continually adulterous and unrepentant partner after long years of tolerance.

Before Joseph realized that Mary "was with child by the Holy Spirit, . . . being a righteous man, and not wanting to disgrace her, [he] desired to put her away secretly" (Matt. 1:18-19). Had his assumption about her been correct, that is, that she was pregnant by another man and therefore an adulteress, Joseph, who was only engaged to her, knew he had legitimate grounds for divorce. The engagement was by a legal and binding contract, though the union was not yet physically consum-mated. The context suggests that, because he was "a righteous man," he felt he was obligated to divorce her. To protect her reputation, however, not to mention her life, he planned to do it privately.

Hardness of heart suggests the condition where adultery was prolonged and the sinning spouse was unrepentant, making reconciliation and a normal marriage relationship impossible. When an adulterous husband or wife became totally insensitive to marital fidelity, God through **Moses** indirectly and reluctantly **permitted . . . divorce.**

Reminding His adversaries again of the Genesis teaching about God's plan for marriage, Jesus then declared that **from the beginning it has not been this way.** Divorce was never in God's original, ideal design for mankind and will never be.

When a man obtains a divorce for any reason **except immorality, and marries another woman,** he **commits adultery.** When giving the same basic teaching in the Sermon on the Mount, Jesus emphasized that the divorced wife and her new husband would be led to commit adultery. The man "who divorces his wife, except for the cause of unchastity," He said, "makes her commit adultery; and whoever marries a divorced woman commits adultery" (Matt. 5:32). In other words, the message Jesus wanted to get across to those exponents of easy divorce and remarriage is that illegitimate divorce followed by remarriage makes adulterers of everyone involved.

Porneia, here translated **immorality,** is a broad term that encompasses all illicit sexual activity. In the context of marriage it always constituted **adultery,** which, by definition, is illicit sex by a married person. The verb form of the term is used by Paul to describe the immorality for which 23,000 (of the total of 24,000) Israelites were killed by a plague in one day (1 Cor. 10:8; cf. Num. 25:9). Because the majority, if not all, of those slain were probably married, *porneia* clearly includes **adultery.**

Although in this passage and in Matthew 5:32 Jesus spoke only of a man who divorces his wife, the same principle applies to a woman who divorces her husband. That situation is not mentioned by the Lord because it was virtually unheard of. Although a Jewish man could divorce his wife on the most trivial grounds, "for any cause at all" (Matt. 19:3), a Jewish woman could rarely divorce her husband even on the most serious grounds.

A divorce on any other grounds than **immorality,** that is, adultery by one of the spouses, is always illegitimate, regardless of which one initiates the divorce. Jesus here uses **immorality** and **adultery** synonymously. He was saying that divorce that does not result *from* adultery results *in* **adultery** if there is remarriage.

If God is gracious to the sinning spouse by tolerating divorce instead of requiring execution, He would surely also be gracious to the innocent spouse by permitting remarriage, which was permissible when a spouse died (cf. Rom. 7:2-3). The purpose of permitting divorce is to show mercy to the sinning spouse, not to condemn the innocent one to a lifetime of singleness and loneliness that would not be required if the Lord had the sinning partner executed. Should His grace to the sinner penalize the innocent? The Lord allows divorce in order that the adulterer might have opportunity to repent rather than be put to death. And both here and in Matthew 5:32 Jesus specifically allows remarriage by the innocent spouse in order that he or she might have opportunity to enjoy again the blessings of marriage that were destroyed by the other partner's adultery. The qualification **except for immorality** clearly permits the innocent party who **marries another** to do so *without* committing **adultery.**

Jesus' declaration here not only reinforced His previous teaching about divorce and remarriage but was a devastating indictment of the Pharisees who were then trying to devastate Him. During the Sermon on the Mount, and in the context of contrasting God's true righteousness with the false and hypocritical righteousness typified by the scribes and Pharisees (Matt. 5:20), Jesus had declared that even looking on a woman lustfully constituted adultery (v. 28). Very shortly after that statement, as in the present text, Jesus then declared that divorce on any grounds but **immorality** also resulted in **adultery** when there was remarriage, as was almost always the case. The strong implication of that statement, which the self-righteous Pharisees could not have missed, was that they themselves were guilty of proliferating **adultery.**

It should be noted that the Holy Spirit adds one other gracious concession by also allowing divorce and remarriage as an option for a believer who is deserted by an unbeliever. (For a full treatment of this issue, see the author's *1 Corinthians* [Chicago: Moody, 1984], pp. 153-86.)

THE APPROPRIATION

The disciples said to Him, "If the relationship of the man with his wife is like this, it is better not to marry." But He said to them, "Not all men can accept this statement, but only those to whom it has been given. For there are eunuchs who were born that way from their mother's womb; and there are eunuchs who were made eunuchs by men; and there are also eunuchs who made themselves eunuchs for the sake of the kingdom of heaven. He who is able to accept this, let him accept it." (19:10-12)

By this time the Pharisees had disappeared. They doubtlessly were thoroughly enraged, both because they had not succeeded in making Jesus contradict Moses and because, on the contrary, Jesus had succeeded in showing that they themselves were condemned by Moses in their illegitimate divorces and consequent adulteries.

Jesus was now alone in a house with **the disciples** (Mark 10:10), where they felt free to comment on what He had just been saying. They may have discussed divorce and remarriage with the Lord at some length before finally saying **to Him, "If the relationship of the man with his wife is like this, it is better not to marry."**

Because they had grown up in a culture where divorce was rampant, largely due to that rabbinical teaching which not only permitted but even required divorce for virtually any reason, the Twelve were more than a little perplexed by what Jesus taught. Many Jews considered divorce a virtue almost on a par with marriage itself. Among the Talmudic writings of the rabbis is the statement, "A bad wife is like leprosy to her husband. What is the remedy? Let him divorce her and be cured of his leprosy." Another rabbi wrote, "If a man has a bad wife, it is a religious duty to divorce her."

The difference between what the disciples had been taught all their lives and what Jesus was teaching was so radical that they were completely nonplussed. It is probable that they had looked on marriage like most of their Jewish male counterparts—and like many people today—believing that if things did not work out, there was always divorce as an out. But if adultery is the only justification for divorce, they concluded, **it is better not to marry.**

Although their response was not well thought out, it shows that they rightly understood what Jesus was saying. They realized that the Lord was declaring that marriage is a lifetime commitment that can legitimately be broken only by death or adultery, and that even adultery does not *require* divorce. The idea of "for better or worse" was more than they could accept. **Better,** they thought, **not to marry** at all.

They had difficulty accepting the idea of lifelong marital commitment because of the existing shallow and unbiblical view of marriage. Had they paid more attention to God's Word than to the traditions of the rabbinical elders (cf. Matt. 15:6), they would have realized that God instituted marriage as the epitome of pleasant, joyful, and fulfilling human relationships. "Let your fountain be blessed," the writer of Proverbs said, "and rejoice in the wife of your youth, as a loving hind and a graceful doe" (Prov. 5:18-19). In the same book they could read, "He who finds a wife finds a good thing, and obtains favor from the Lord" (18:22) and "House and wealth are an inheritance from fathers, but a prudent wife is from the Lord" (19:14).

Like most people of both sexes today, many Jewish men in New Testament times looked on marriage only as a means of gratifying their own lusts and of fulfilling their own purposes. Marriage was the accepted means of sexual indulgence and of procreating children, and it also provided a convenient cook and housekeeper. Unlike modern people, however, most Jewish men appear to have been little concerned about romance.

Romance can be a beautiful part of marriage that lasts even through old age. But romantic feelings cannot be the basis for a sound and enduring marriage, because they are largely composed of pleasant sensations toward the other person that are easily subject to change. A sound marriage is based on permanent, unconditional commitment to one's spouse, even if romantic feelings flicker or are extinguished altogether. If romantic feelings are the basis of a marriage, when a spouse begins to lose attractiveness, the other's attention is turned to someone else who seems more promising and exciting. When one romantic fling after another is pursued, emotional burnout is inevitable. Such a superficial relationship cannot last long and never achieves the expected fulfillment. Each successive failure brings less satisfaction and more disappointment, disillusionment, and emptiness. The collective result, as seen so dramatically and tragically in modern society, is a generation of disoriented, lonely, isolated, untrustworthy, untrusting, and emotionally bankrupt misfits looking for the next arousing sensation.

Some years ago I heard the story of an elderly minister who had been married for fifty years. One morning at breakfast his wife slumped over the table, unconscious. By the time her husband got her to the hospital she was dead. After the funeral he said to his sons, "This is a good day, a wonderful day." When they asked what he meant, he explained, "Well, I know she is with the Lord now. And I am glad she went first. That's the way I wanted it to be, because I didn't want her to have the grief of burying me and of having to live alone."

Some years later that minister was asked to speak at a feminist meeting on the subject of marriage. He recounted his wife's death and his gratitude that she had died first. "Listen," he told them, "anybody who knows the meaning of true love always wants the other person to go first, because they don't want them to endure the pain and the sorrow and the anxiety and loneliness of burying the one they've loved. I daresay that the modern romantic relationships that try to pass for love are a far cry from that kind of feeling and that kind of reality." He was right.

Most people, including many Christians, know little of the self-giving, self-committing, and self-sacrificing love that knits two souls together for a lifetime of sharing and happiness. Instead of the rich, deepening, meaningful, and thrilling friendship that only such love can bring, they settle for a cheap, shallow substitute that fluctuates with every mood and that is doomed from the beginning to be disappointing and short-lived. A relationship that is built only on pleasant emotions and good feelings will soon die, because those emotions and feelings are built on circumstances and on superficial and selfish expectations. But amazingly, a relationship that is built on loving commitment and self-giving concern for the other person will produce emotions and feelings that not only do not die but grow richer and more satisfying with every year. Feelings are a poor foundation for marriage, but they can be a wonderful, glorious by-product.

The committed marriage is the only happy and enduring marriage. When two Christians love each other for the other's sake rather than their own and live their lives in humble submission to God's Word and to each other, a bond is formed that can withstand every temptation, disappointment, and failure that Satan and the world can hurl against them. They become lovers and friends in a way that the unbeliever and the disobedient Christian can never know. In sharing everything together, they forge a friendship that knows no limitations, no bounds, no secrets, and no conditions.

Like the disciples, some Christians today seem afraid that lifelong, unconditional commitment would destine them to a life of boredom and frustrating restrictions. They conclude with the Twelve that it is therefore simply **better not to marry.** But God planned and designed marital commitment to bring just the opposite. No marriage can be happy and satisfying, much less enduring, without it. God blesses a committed union in ways that a single person, or an uncommitted husband and wife, can never experience and hardly imagine. Far from being a reason to avoid marriage, lifelong and loving commitment is the very thing that makes it most fulfilling and desirable.

Obviously a Christian's marriage partner should be chosen carefully and with much prayer. Marriage commitment should only be given to a person who shares one's spiritual values and commitments. But there is no human joy or fulfillment that can measure up to that which is experienced by a husband and wife who love Jesus Christ and each other and who live together in obedience to His Word and in the power of His Spirit.

There was a certain truth to what the disciples had just said about it being better not to marry, but the context suggests that it was not that truth they had in mind. Their view of marriage, like that of their fellow Jews, focused primarily on selfish, shallow satisfaction and fulfillment. From a purely practical standpoint they therefore concluded that lonely singleness is preferable to risky marriage. (For a detailed discussion of Paul's statement about the benefits of singleness, see the author's *1 Corinthians,* pp. 153-86.)

Jesus reminded them that **not all men can accept this statement, but only those to whom it has been given.** Singleness has its own problems and temptations, and not every Christian is capable of living a godly single life. Paul said that it is good to remain single for spiritual purposes, but that it was "better to marry than to burn" with lust (1 Cor. 7:8-9).

Accept is from *chōreō*, which has the basic idea of making room or space for something. Metaphorically it means to completely embrace an idea or principle with the heart and mind so that it becomes part of one's very nature. Singleness cannot be wholeheartedly accepted simply by human willpower or sincerity. Nor can it be successfully lived out simply by applying the right biblical principles. Celibate singleness is a kind of spiritual gift (1 Cor. 7:7), and **only those to whom it has been given** can hope to spiritually survive in it, much less find happiness and be effective in the Lord's service.

Many single Christians endure continual frustration, temptations, and unnecessary loneliness because, for one reason or another, they intentionally avoid marriage. Some perhaps are more concerned about a mate's looks than character. Some do not want anyone around who may invade and disrupt their selfish world. Others may be looking for the perfect mate, someone who measures up in every detail to their vision of the perfect husband or wife. Others, like certain religious orders, have the mistaken belief that there is spiritual merit in celibacy and choose singleness as a means of gaining God's favor through self-sacrifice. But singleness based on any such reasons dooms one to a life of disappointment and unfulfillment.

Jesus proceeds to mention the only three categories where there can be successful singleness. First **are eunuchs who were born that way from their mother's womb.** These are people who are born with congenital deformities that involve undeveloped sexual capacity. Second **are eunuchs who were made eunuchs by men,** such as were male harem guards of that day. In some ancient religions, castration was considered a way of pleasing and serving a pagan deity, and parents sometimes even had their infant sons castrated for that purpose. Obviously, castrated men do not have normal desires for a woman.

Third are **eunuchs who made themselves eunuchs for the sake of the kingdom of heaven.** Unlike the other two forms, this one is not physical. Mutilation of the flesh in order to please God is a purely pagan idea. Jesus is speaking of the voluntary celibacy of those to whom that gift has been granted by God (v. 11). In that case, celibacy can indeed be **for the sake of the kingdom of God** and be pleasing to Him and used by Him.

Paul had the gift of celibacy and strongly exhorted others who had the gift to be content with it and to use its obvious advantages for God's glory. "One who is unmarried is concerned about the things of the Lord, how he may please the Lord," he said; "but one who is married is concerned about the things of the world, how he may please his wife, and his interests are divided. And the woman who is unmarried, and the virgin, is concerned about the things of the Lord, that she may be holy both in body and spirit; but one who is married is concerned about the things of the world, how she may please her husband" (1 Cor. 7:32-34).

He who is able to accept this, let him accept it, Jesus said. In the narrowest and most specific sense the Lord was saying that those who by God's gift are **able to accept** a life of celibate singleness should **accept it** as God's will for them. But He seems also to have been speaking more broadly about the disciples' accepting everything He had just taught about marriage, divorce, remarriage, and singleness. They were to put aside the false ideas and practices they had inherited from the humanly-devised and unscriptural rabbinical traditions. In other words, **accept** what I have been teaching as God's Word and live accordingly.

The unsaved person cannot **accept** Jesus' standards for marriage and divorce, and would not have the resources to live up to those standards if he did accept them. The idea of self-giving, unconditional, and lifelong commitment in any area of life, including marriage, runs completely against the grain of fallen human nature. God's truth has no authority in an unredeemed life because God Himself has no place in that life.

Even the worldly believer has great difficulty accepting the idea of total, unconditional commitment, because he has lost his first love and has turned his interests back on himself. Only those who truly honor Jesus as Lord and Savior can truly **accept** His teachings. Even then His teachings become fully acceptable only in the life walked in the Spirit, who alone can keep believers from carrying out the natural "desire of the flesh" (Gal. 5:16), which is committed to self rather than to God, one's life partner, or others.

For further study of what God's Word says about divorce and remarriage, see the author's *The Family* (Chicago: Moody, 1982).

Jesus Loves the Little Children

(19:13-15)

17

Then some children were brought to Him so that He might lay His hands on them and pray; and the disciples rebuked them. But Jesus said, "Let the children alone, and do not hinder them from coming to Me; for the kingdom of heaven belongs to such as these." And after laying His hands on them, He departed from there. (19:13-15)

All children raised in a Christian home or who have attended Sunday school when they were young, long remember singing such songs as "Jesus Loves Me" and "Jesus Loves the Little Children." Those lovely sentiments are based on clear biblical truth. Jesus *does* love little children, as this text from Matthew attests. The parents of these children wanted Jesus to touch them and bless them, and He was more than willing to accommodate that desire.

Some years ago, a family in our church experienced a great tragedy. The mother and the two daughters were planning to fly the next day to New Zealand to join the husband and father, who was on a preaching mission there. As the wife was learning some new crotchet stitches to use on the long flight, the girls went outside to play. A few moments later the mother heard the screeching of automobile tires, but since there was no sound of a crash she thought little of it—until her older daughter came running into the house crying that her sister, Tanya, had been hit by a car.

The girl was unconscious but showed no sign of serious injury. While the mother bent over her, Tanya breathed a heavy sigh and turned her head to the side. At the hospital the neurosurgeon told the mother that the girl had suffered massive brain damage and had little chance of surviving. Relatives and friends prayed fervently and the mother kept a vigil with her precious daughter throughout the night, praying with great intensity that God would spare and restore her daughter. But she also prayed that, above all, God's will be done, even if it meant taking Tanya to be with Himself.

A relative who was a doctor explained that Tanya's breathing and heartbeat were functioning at the hospital solely by artificial means. "Her body is being kept working," he said, "but Tanya isn't there anymore. She is with the Lord." With a radiant face her mother said to the Lord, "Have thy will, not mine." To her friends and loved ones she explained, "I shall not forsake my Lord; because if I did, I would be saying Tanya is gone forever. I [will] do as King David in the Old Testament had done when his child was taken. He washed his face, changed his clothes, and went about his business, satisfied that God knew best."

At that moment she determined there would be no more begging God to bring her little girl back. Tanya was in the Lord's care, and her mother believed she had entered His presence when, lying unconscious on the street, she sighed and turned her head. The mother testifies that she was filled with an inner strength that was foreign to her. She recalled that for several months previously Tanya had prayed, "Lord, I want to go and be with You while I'm young." When her mother asked why she made that request, Tanya smiled and replied, "Because I want to sit on Jesus' lap when I get there; and I don't want to be too big." On remembering those words, said the mother, "New assurance and peace surged through my sorrowful soul. I was refreshed with a joy that we were all in good hands and that God hadn't forsaken us for an instant."

That mother and the rest of the family could rejoice even in the death of that beloved little girl because they knew where she had gone. Because she had been led to the Savior, she was now gathered into His arms, where she had longed to be.

Every Christian parent should take deeply to heart Paul's admonition to bring up their children "in the discipline and instruction of the Lord" (Eph. 6:4). If the children die, parents know where they are. If the children live, parents know to Whom they belong and for Whom they live.

Perhaps only a short while after Jesus had finished teaching the Twelve about marriage, divorce, remarriage, and singleness (Matt. 19:3-12), another group of people **then** came seeking His ministry. At that time **some children were brought to Him,** doubtlessly by their parents. Both Mark and Luke use the imperfect tense ("they were bringing"), indicating a continuing process and likely an extended period of time (Mark 10:13; Luke 18:15). When word spread that Jesus was in the area, parents were drawn to this Teacher whose love of **children** had become known throughout Palestine (cf. 17:18; 18:2-3; John 4:50).

The Greek word used here for **children** was *paidia,* a term referring to young children from infancy through perhaps toddler age. In his parallel passage, Luke tells us "they were bringing even their babies" (18:15).

But **the disciples** resented the intrusion into their private time with Jesus, and they **rebuked** the parents. The Greek verb behind **rebuked** could carry the idea of threatening, and its being in the imperfect suggests that the rebuke was as continuous as the bringing. As more and more parents brought their children to Jesus, **the disciples** continued to try to repulse them. Obviously the Twelve, who had spent the better part of two years living with Jesus and hearing every word He spoke and observing everything He did, did not yet fully share His mind and heartbeat.

Only a few days earlier Jesus had taken a young child in His arms in the disciples' presence. Specifically for the sake of the disciples, who were in the midst of a dispute about who was the greatest in the kingdom, He had declared, "Whoever then humbles himself as this child, he is the greatest in the kingdom of heaven" (Matt. 18:1-4). No doubt at countless other times the Twelve had witnessed similar expressions of Jesus' tenderness and gentleness and His great patience with those who came to Him for help. They had seen His compassion pour out in an endless flow of healing, encouragement, and comfort.

They also knew that the Talmud taught Jewish parents to bring their children to respected rabbis for blessings and prayer. A father would customarily bring his infant child to the synagogue and pray for the child himself. He would then hand it to the elders, who would each hold it and pray for God's blessing on the young life. Many churches today follow a somewhat similar pattern in prayerfully dedicating small children to the Lord.

Following in that tradition, those Jewish parents in Perea, "the region of Judea beyond the Jordan" (v. 1), brought their children to Jesus to be blessed. He not only was a popular, if controversial, rabbi known for His miracle working power but was also known for His compassion and His willingness to meet the needs of even the lowliest and most helpless people of society. If He were indeed the Messiah, as He claimed to be, those parents saw a marvelous opportunity to have their children blessed by the Lord's own Anointed One, the Deliverer of Israel.

Because Jesus did not rebuke the parents or resist blessing their children, it is obvious that their motives were pure. They did not comprehend Jesus' true greatness, and probably few, if any, of them had put their trust in Him as Lord and Savior. But they recognized Him as a genuine teacher from God who loved them and who cared for their precious little ones. They therefore sought His intercession with God on their children's behalf, in the hope that they might grow up as the Talmud admonished: strong in the law, faithful in marriage, and known by good works.

Jesus was not naively sentimental about children. Having created them, He well knew they are born with a sinful nature. Children have a certain innocence, but they are not sinless. He knew that they did not have to be taught to do wrong, that their little hearts were naturally bent toward evil. But He loved them with a special compassion and, because of their natural openness and trustfulness, He held them up as examples of the attitude required for kingdom citizenship (Matt. 18:3-5).

Those who share the mind of Christ share His concern and love for children. No church or Christian movement has prospered spiritually that has disregarded or neglected the care and training of its children. The heart that is warm toward the Lord will inevitably be warm toward children.

One writer has made this beautiful observation:

> As the flower in the garden stretches toward the light of the sun, so there is in the child a mysterious inclination toward the eternal light. Have you ever noticed this mysterious thing that, when you tell the smallest child about God, it never asks with strangeness and wonder, "What or who is God? I have never seen Him"—but listens with shining face to the words as though they were soft loving sounds from the land of home? Or when you teach a child to fold its little hands in prayer, it does this as though it were a matter of course, as though there were opening for it that world of which it had been dreaming with longing and anticipation. Or tell them, these little ones, the stories of the Savior, show them the pictures with scenes and personages of the Bible [and] see how their pure eyes shine, how their little hearts beat. (R. C. H. Lenski, *The Interpretation of St. Matthew's Gospel* [Minneapolis: Augsburg, 1943], p. 743)

Jesus therefore **said** to the Twelve, and still says to His disciples today: **"Let the children alone, and do not hinder them from coming to Me.** The Greek verb behind **let . . . alone** is in the aorist tense, whereas the verb behind **do not hinder** is in the present tense with a negative, indicating a call to stop something. The Lord was therefore saying, **"Let the children alone**, beginning immediately, **and** stop hindering **them from coming to Me."**

From Mark we learn that Jesus was greatly indignant with the disciples (10:14). They frequently frustrated and disappointed the Lord by their insensitivity and selfishness, but this is one of only two or three occasions on which He actually became angry with them.

It is likely there were a number of reasons He was angry with them. He was angry because He loved little children with great affection, and He no doubt felt special compassion for them because of the sinful, painful, corrupt world into which they had been born and whose evils they would progressively have to face as they grew up. He was angry because He also loved parents and understood the special longings and anxieties they have for their children. He realized that loving little children was a way to their parents' hearts. He was angry because no one, not even the tiniest infant, is outside the care and love of God. He was angry because of the disciples' persistent spiritual dullness and hardness. And He doubtlessly was angry because the disciples presumed to determine who could and could not approach Him, the Christ and Son of God. It was neither within their prerogative nor their competency to make such choices. It was rank presumption for them **to hinder** the parents and their children **from coming** to Jesus. Specifically, He was angry because **the kingdom of heaven belongs to,** that is, it encompasses and is characterized by, children **such as these.**

There is nothing in the text to indicate that, as some claim, Jesus was isolating **these** supposedly elect children from others who were nonelect. Furthermore, He makes no mention of baptism, parental covenant, parental faith, or ecclesiastical rite. Nor does He mention personal faith on the part of the children, who were probably too young to have exercised such belief. The Lord was simply saying that those children, representative of all children, were a picture of the humility, dependency, and trust of those of any age who enter His **kingdom.**

The kingdom of heaven is the sphere of God's rule in Christ through gracious salvation. For those who have reached the age when personal saving faith can be exercised, the kingdom is entered only by a divinely illuminated understanding of what it means to trust in Jesus Christ as Lord and Savior. The implication of **such as these** is that for those who, because of young age or mental deficiency, are incapable of exercising saving faith, God grants them, in the event of death, entrance into **the kingdom** by the sovereign operation of His grace. When children die before they reach the age of decision, they go into the presence of Jesus Christ, because they are under the special protection of the sovereign King.

It was that glorious and comforting truth that David expressed when he lost his infant son born to Bathsheba. "I shall go to him," David said, "but he will not return to me" (2 Sam. 12:23). While that statement may indicate little more than a resignation to their both entering the realm of the dead, the personal pronouns *I* and *him,* as well as David's confident belief in the life to come (see Acts 2:25-28; Ps. 16:8-11), lend credence to the idea that he was confident of personal consciousness and identity in the life to come. David knew that he himself belonged to God and would one day enter His presence, and he had equal confidence that, when he entered the Lord's presence he would meet the little son who had preceded him there.

It is not that small children are regenerate and then lose their salvation if they do not later receive Christ as Lord and Savior. It is rather that His atoning death is applied on their behalf if they die before they are able to choose on their own. It may be that the infant mortality rate is so high in many countries where the gospel has not yet penetrated because the Lord is taking those little ones to Himself before they can grow up in a culture where it is so difficult to encounter the gospel and believe.

But what an awesome responsibility faces Christian parents to make sure that their children are taught about Christ and are led to receive Him as Savior when they are able to exercise saving faith.

Just as the children's parents requested, Jesus laid **His hands on them** and blessed them. In Mark's account of this incident (10:16), the Greek form behind "blessing" is intensive, indicating a passionate fervency. Jesus must have smiled with infinite kindness as He looked into the faces of those tiny children. We do not know the specific nature of His blessing, but we can surmise that He promised the provision of God on their behalf and the care of God over each one of them.

Luke reports that Jesus then declared, as He had a short while earlier, "Truly I say to you, whoever does not receive the kingdom of God like a child shall not enter it at all" (Luke 18:17; cf. Matt. 18:3). In other words, the kingdom is populated by only two kinds of subjects, those who die while little children and those who come in the trusting and humble attitude of little children. Only those enter God's kingdom who come to Him in the simplicity, openness, dependency, lack of pretension, and lack of hypocrisy of little children. As John Calvin commented, "The passage broadens to give kingdom citizenship to both children and those who are like them."

Some years ago a young Hindu man from southern India named Paul Pillai was converted to Christ and received a call to reach the northern part of his country for Christ. After attending seminary in the United States, he returned to India and founded Grace Bible College, dedicated solely to training young men called to the ministry.

After graduation, students are helped by the school for a period of some six months in establishing a local church in a village or city. One of their most effective means of winning converts, however, is a children's home. Orphaned and abandoned children are taken to the home, where they are fed, clothed, and sheltered. They attend public schools in order to keep identity with their own culture, but they are also given concentrated study in God's Word. Although adult Hindus and Muslims are extremely difficult to evangelize, those young children are open to the gospel, and many of them confess Christ as Lord and Savior. A large percentage of the boys from that home go on to attend the Bible college and become effective evangelists and pastors. Because they were reached with the gospel at an early age, they were open and responsive to the claims of Christ.

Five key words can prove helpful in giving guidance to parents and Christian workers in leading children to Christ. The first word is *remember*. We should remember that every child is created by God and, in that sense, already belongs to Him. "Thou didst form my inward parts," the psalmist declared, "Thou didst weave me in my mother's womb. . . . I am fearfully and wonderfully made" (Ps. 139:13-14). All "children are a gift of the Lord; the fruit of the womb is a reward," given to parents as gracious blessings (Ps. 127:3). It is God's plan and desire that every child be returned to Him for His use. "Train up a child in the way he should go," we are told in Proverbs, and "even when he is old he will not depart from it" (Prov. 22:6).

A second key word is *teach*. Christian parents have the high calling of bringing up their children "in the discipline and instruction of the Lord" (Eph. 6:4). Timothy became especially useful to the Lord and to the apostle Paul in part because from childhood his mother, Eunice, and his grandmother, Lois, had taught him "the sacred writings which are able to give . . . the wisdom that leads to salvation through faith which is in Christ Jesus" (2 Tim. 3:15; cf. 1:5).

That pattern for godly instruction was set forth early in Israel's history. Through Moses, God commanded His people to believe in and worship in the right way: "Hear, O Israel! The Lord is our God, the Lord is one!" (Deut. 6:4). He also commanded them to personally and sincerely accept that truth with uncompromising conviction and devotion: "And you shall love the Lord Your God with all your heart and with all your soul and with all your might. And these words, which I am commanding you today, shall be on your heart" (vv. 5-6). More than that, they were commanded to teach godly truth and obedience to their children, talking about those things at home and in the community, from the time they arose until the time they went to bed (v. 7). God's Word was to be taught to their children and exemplified before them.

As important as special times of family Bible study and prayer are, only consistent godly living by parents will clarify and cement God's Word in their children's minds, hearts, and lives. Parents should also provide visual reminders of God's Word. Just as Israelites were to bind God's Word on their hands and foreheads and write it on the their doorposts and gates (Deut. 6:8-9), so Christian parents can have Bible verses and plaques throughout the house to reinforce scriptural truths. When Bible stories and truths are sung, further reinforcement is given.

In that Deuteronomy passage God gave ancient Israel a final warning not to forget Him and His Word after they had come into the Promised Land and were surfeited with material blessings, "lest you forget the Lord who brought you from the land of Egypt, out of the house of slavery" and "follow other gods, any of the gods of the people who surround you" (6:12, 14). Like their parents, children need to beware of the many false idols by which the world lures them away from the Lord.

A third key word is *model*. Children not only need godly precepts put godly patterns. Eli the priest was a negative example to his two sons. Following the ungodly model of their father's life, they went even to further extremes of immorality and sacrilege. When Eli rebuked them they paid no attention, partly because his rebuke was halfhearted and far too mild and partly because they had no respect for him due to his own compromised living (1 Sam. 2:12-25).

In a similar way, even the great David failed to be a godly example to his sons. His son Absalom was so wicked and rebellious that he sought to kill his father and usurp his throne. His son Solomon took hundreds of wives and concubines, including many foreigners whose pagan ways turned him from loyalty to the Lord. Not only was Solomon's family shattered but also the kingdom. King Hezekiah disobeyed God's instruction by showing the royal jewels to the king of Babylon, and his son Manasseh surpassed his father's compromise and totally abandoned God's law.

Writing in *Eternity* magazine (May 1979, p. 35), Tom Cowan observed,

> Parents must be aware of the personal value of truth for their own sakes and not just for the sakes of their children. We cannot simply make a child believe in a truth because it's good for them. Their perceptive spirits will sense when we are doing something to engineer or manipulate a certain response. Instead it is the authenticity of parental commitment to truth

apart from the lives of children that brings the freedom to share and to pass on that truth to them. In other words, a mature motive for passing on truth is that as a parent I hold that truth to have value for my life, independent of my children and their response to it.

A fourth key word is *love,* so obviously imperative that little needs to be said about it. Only parents who lovingly weep with their children, rejoice with them, hurt with them, unselfishly serve them, show them genuine affection, and sacrifice for them will effectively influence them in the things of the Lord.

A final key word is *trust.* After parents have done everything humanly possible to raise their children in the way of the Lord, they must ultimately trust Him to make those efforts fruitful. Only the Holy Spirit can reach into the human heart, including the heart of a child, and only His power can give spiritual life and empower spiritual faithfulness.

How to Obtain Eternal Life

(19:16-22)

18

And behold, one came to Him and said, "Teacher, what good thing shall I do that I may obtain eternal life?" And He said to him, "Why are you asking Me about what is good? There is only One who is good; but if you wish to enter into life, keep the commandments." He said to Him, "Which ones?" And Jesus said, "You shall not commit murder; You shall not commit adultery; You shall not steal; You shall not bear false witness; Honor your father and mother; and You shall love your neighbor as yourself." The young man said to Him, "All these things I have kept; what am I still lacking?" Jesus said to him, "If you wish to be complete, go and sell your possessions and give to the poor, and you shall have treasure in heaven; and come, follow Me." But when the young man heard this statement, he went away grieved; for he was one who owned much property. (19:16-22)

At first one might wonder what kind of message Jesus was trying to give this man who came to Him. The truth is summarized in Jesus' statement on another occasion: "So therefore, no one of you can be My disciple who does not give up all his own possessions" (Luke 14:33).

Some years ago the young man in the seat next to me on an airplane asked, "Sir, you wouldn't know how I could have a personal relationship with Jesus Christ, would you?" Taken somewhat by surprise by his openness and seeming readiness for salvation, I told him that he needed to receive Jesus Christ as his Lord and Savior. He said, "I'd like to do that," and we prayed together and rejoiced in his decision. He was on his way to a new job near our church, so he was baptized and began attending services. But some months later I was extremely disappointed to discover that he had developed no interest at all in the things of the Lord and was living in such a way that it was apparent he had not been transformed. He soon disappeared from the church and has never returned.

Anyone who has done much personal witnessing has encountered persons who make a profession of faith in Christ but whose subsequent lives show no change in attitudes or behavior. And when they indicate no love for God and Christ, no interest in the Bible, in prayer, or in the fellowship of God's people, there is no good reason to believe they were ever saved.

Our Lord gave this young man a test. He had to make a choice between Christ and his possessions and sin, and he failed the test. No matter what he may have believed, because he was unwilling to forsake all, he could not be a disciple of Christ. Salvation is for those who are willing to forsake everything.

The incident recorded in Matthew 19:16-22 gives insight into how some people who show great interest in the gospel never come to a saving relationship with Jesus Christ. This young man went away from Christ not because he heard the wrong message or because he did not believe but because he was unwilling to admit his sin, forsake all that he had, and obey Christ as Lord.

THE REQUEST TO JESUS

And behold, one came to Him and said, "Teacher, what good thing shall I do that I may obtain eternal life?" (19:16)

From verse 20 we learn that the **one** who **came to Him** was a young man, and from verse 22 that he was wealthy. Luke informs us that he was also a ruler (18:18), probably a ruler in the synagogue, an especially honored position for a young man. He was a religious leader—devout, honest, wealthy, prominent, and influential. He had it all. **Behold** suggests how unusual and unexpected it was that he would admit he lacked eternal life and come to Jesus to find it.

Several factors are clear as we analyze this unique encounter. First, He came genuinely seeking **eternal life**, motivated by his sense of need for a true spiritual hope. The term *eternal life* is used some 50 times in Scripture, and always refers primarily to quality rather than quantity. Although **eternal life** obviously carries the idea of being an everlasting reality, it does not refer simply to unending existence. Even ancient pagans knew that mere unending existence would not necessarily be desirable. According to Greek mythology, Aurora, goddess of the dawn, fell in love with a young mortal named Tithonus. When Zeus offered to provide anything she wished for her human lover, she asked that he might never die. The wish was granted, but because she had not asked that Tithonus remain forever young, he continued to grow older and more decrepit. Instead of being blessed, he was cursed to perpetual degeneration.

If, as William Hendriksen insightfully observes, " 'life' means active response to one's environment," then **eternal life** must mean active response to that which is eternal, namely God's heavenly realm. Just as physical life is the ability to live and move and respond in the physical world, **eternal life** is the ability to live and move and respond in the heavenly world.

Eternal life is first of all a quality of existence, the divinely-endowed ability to be alive to God and the things of God. The Jews saw it as that which fills the heart with hope of life after death. The unsaved person is spiritually alive only to sin. But when he receives Christ as Lord and Savior, he becomes alive to God and to righteousness (Rom. 6:1-13). That is the essence of **eternal life,** the **life** of God's own Son dwelling within.

The young ruler could not have understood the full meaning of what he asked for, but he realized there was an important dimension to his present life, religious and prestigious as it was, that was missing. Despite his high standing in men's eyes, he knew he did not have the God-given peace, rest, hope, assurance, and joy of which the psalmists and the prophets spoke. He may have sensed that he needed a closer relationship to God than he had. Simply by asking that question of Jesus he showed himself to be beyond the hypocritical religiosity of the scribes and Pharisees. He recognized a deep spiritual need that, for all his religious efforts, was unfulfilled. He knew he did not possess the life of God that satisfies here and now and gives hope for the life to come.

The fact that he came to Jesus publicly and asked such a personal and revealing question shows the man's sincerity. He was not haughty or presumptuous, but was humbly determined to find satisfaction for the overwhelming need he felt in his life, and he was oblivious to what people around him may have thought.

The young ruler not only knew his need but deeply felt that need, and he was desperate. Many people who admit they do not have **eternal life** nevertheless feel no need for it. They know they are not alive to God and do not care. They know there is no divine dimension to their lives but consider that fact irrelevant and unimportant. They have no hope for the life to come but are perfectly content to remain as they are.

The young ruler felt his need so keenly that, when he heard Jesus was in the vicinity, he "ran up to Him and knelt before Him" (Mark 10:17). He could not wait to ask this great Teacher how to find the answer to his deep longing. He was not embarrassed by the fact that he was known and respected by most of the people who crowded around Jesus. He did not mind the risk of losing face with those who probably considered him already to be religiously fulfilled and specially favored by God.

Although he was probably in the midst of the multitude of parents who had brought their young children to be blessed, this man was not ashamed to request a blessing for himself. He was saying to Jesus, in effect, "I need your help just as much as these little children." Just as the children submitted to Jesus by being taken in His arms, the rich young ruler submitted by kneeling down before Him. He prostrated himself before the Lord in a position of humility. He appeared serious, sincere, highly motivated, and anxious.

This young ruler came seeking for the right thing—eternal life—and he came to the only One who could give it. **Him,** of course, refers to Jesus, who not only is the way to **eternal life** but is Himself that life. "God has given us eternal life," John declares, "and this life is in His Son," who "is the true God and eternal life" (1 John 5:11, 20). There was nothing wrong with his motivation, because it certainly is good to desire eternal life.

By addressing Jesus as **Teacher** (*didaskalos*), the young man acknowledged Him to be a respected rabbi, an authority on the Old Testament, a teacher of divine truth. Although the two other synoptic gospels report that the man also called Jesus "good" (Mark 10:17; Luke 18:18), there is no reason to believe he considered **Him** to be the promised Messiah and Son of God. But he obviously considered Jesus to have a stature of righteous character above the typical rabbi. The authority of Jesus' teaching and the power of His miracles surely qualified Him as someone who knew the way to **eternal life.** Even though he did not acknowledge that Jesus was Messiah and God in the flesh, he had come to the right person (cf. Acts 4:12).

Not only did the young man come to the right source but he asked the right question: **"What good thing shall I do that I may obtain eternal life?"** Many interpreters have criticized the man for asking about what he must **do,** suggesting that his question was works oriented. Doubtlessly he was steeped in the Pharisaic legal system that had come to dominate Judaism and was trained to think that doing religious things was the way to gain divine favor. But taken at face value, his question was legitimate. There *is* something one must do in order to come to God. When the multitude near Capernaum asked Jesus, "What shall we do, that we may work the works of God?" He replied, "This is the work of God, that you believe in Him whom He has sent" (John 6:28-29).

The main point of the question was to discover how to **obtain eternal life,** and that is the most crucial question a person can ask. The entire purpose of evangelism is to bring lost people to Jesus Christ in order that they may **obtain eternal life.** The very purpose and meaning of salvation is to bring **eternal life** to those who, because of sin, face eternal death (Rom. 6:23).

The issue on this occasion was the man's salvation, not some higher level of discipleship subsequent to salvation. Most of the work of evangelism is to bring people to the point where they sense their need for salvation, but this young man was already there. He was ready to sign the card, raise his hand, walk the aisle, or whatever. He was ripe and eager—what many modern evangelists would consider a "hot prospect."

THE RESPONSE BY JESUS

And He said to him, "Why are you asking Me about what is good? There is only One who is good; but if you wish to enter into life, keep the

**commandments." He said to Him, "Which ones?" And Jesus said, "You shall
not commit murder; You shall not commit adultery; You shall not steal; You
shall not bear false witness; Honor your father and mother; and You shall
love your neighbor as yourself." (19:17-19)**

Jesus' response is even more amazing than the young man's request. **He said
to him, "Why are you asking Me about what is good? There is only One
who is good; but if you wish to enter into life, keep the commandments."**
Instead of taking the young man at face value and asking him to "make a
decision for Christ," Jesus went much deeper in searching out the state of his heart
and tested his true purpose and motivation. Instead of rejoicing that the man was
apparently willing to receive eternal life and encouraging him to simply pray a
prayer or affirm his faith, Jesus asked him a question in return that was immensely
disconcerting.

The Lord's abrupt and seemingly evasive words, **"Why are you asking Me
about what is good?"** reveal that He could read the man's heart. He had asked
about eternal life verbally, and his heart was longing to know what good work could
bring him that life. Jesus' comment that **"there is only One who is good"** was
perhaps a means of prying out of the man just who he thought Jesus was. Did he
realize that the One whom he was asking **about what is good** was Himself **the
One who is good**, namely, God? Had he come to Jesus for divine help because he
believed Jesus Himself to be divine? Because the man made no response concerning
the **only One who is good**, it seems certain that he viewed Jesus as no more than
an especially gifted human teacher. He had indeed come to the right source for the
answer to his question and the fulfillment of his need, but he did not recognize that
Source for who He really was.

Jesus did not respond by immediately showing the way of salvation because
the man was missing an essential quality. He lacked the sense of his own sinfulness,
and Jesus had to point that out.

Jesus' next comment, **"If you wish to enter into life, keep the commandments,"** was more than familiar to the man. Jews were taught all their lives that the
way **into life** was through obedience to God's **commandments.** Leviticus 18:5
clearly refers to such a truth: "So you shall keep My statutes and My judgments, by
which a man may live if he does them; I am the Lord" (cf. Ezek. 20:11). Perhaps
Jesus was simply saying to the man, "You know what to do. Why are you asking
Me? I haven't taught anything that is not already written in the Scriptures. You are a
learned and devoted Jew and you know what God's law requires. Go do it."

Judged by the principles and strategy of much contemporary evangelism,
Jesus seems to have made a serious and insensitive mistake. He not only did not
take advantage of the man's obvious readiness to make a decision but He even
seemed to be teaching righteousness by works.

But Jesus knew this man's heart was not ready to believe in Him, just as the
hearts of many people who express great interest in Him are not ready to believe.
The man had a deep longing for something important in his life that he knew was

missing. He doubtlessly had anxiety and frustration and longed for peace, joy, hope, and assurance. He wanted all the inner blessings the Old Testament associated with spiritual life. He longed for God's blessings, but he did not long for God. He wanted to know what **good** things he should do, but he did not want to know **the only One who is good.**

Throughout history, and certainly in our own day, the church has witnessed many questionable principles and methods of evangelism, often exercised with sincerity and good intent. Undue emphasis on such external acts as raised hands, cards signed, and verbal decisions can lead many people—Christian workers and professed converts alike—into believing salvation has occurred when it has not. A premature and incomplete decision is not a decision Christ recognizes as valid.

The gospel is not a means of adding something better to what one already has, a means of supplementing human effort by divine. Nor is it simply a means of fulfilling psychological needs, no matter how real and significant they may be. Jesus did not die simply to make people feel better by relieving their frustrations and anxieties. And relief from such feelings is no certain evidence of salvation.

Many people are simply looking for solutions to their felt needs, but that is not enough to bring them to legitimate salvation. Jesus therefore did not offer any relief for the young man's felt needs. Instead, He gave an answer designed to confront him with the fact that he was a living offense to Holy God. Proper evangelism must lead a sinner to measure himself against the perfect law of God so he can see his deficiency. Salvation is for those who hate their sin.

The young ruler must have sounded more than a little perplexed as he asked, almost rhetorically, **"Which ones?"** The implication seems to be, "I have read the commandments many times. I memorized them when I was a small boy, and I have carefully kept them ever since. How could I have missed any? **Which ones** could you possibly have in mind?"

Jesus responded by quoting five of the Ten Commandments: to **not commit murder,** to **not commit adultery,** to **not steal,** to **not bear false witness,** and to **honor your father and mother** (see Ex. 20:12-16). He then added the second greatest commandment: **You shall love your neighbor as yourself** (Lev. 19:18; cf. Matt. 22:39).

No words of Scripture would have been more familiar to the young ruler than those. But again he missed Jesus' point. Just as he failed to recognize that the One to whom he spoke was Himself God and the source of eternal life, he also failed to see that those well-known commandments, and all the other commandments, could not provide the life to which they pointed. If a person were able to perfectly keep all the commandments throughout his entire life, he would indeed have life, just as Jesus had said (v. 17). What He was trying to show the man, however, is that no one is able to keep all the commandments perfectly, not even one of them.

The Lord did not mention the first four of the Ten Commandments, which center on man's attitude toward God (Ex. 20:3-11), or the first and greatest commandment, "You shall love the Lord your God with all your heart and with all your soul and with all your might" (Deut. 6:5; cf. Matt. 22:38). Those commandments are even more impossible to keep than the ones Jesus quoted. The Lord therefore challenged the young ruler against the least impossible of the commandments, as it were.

THE RESPONSE TO JESUS

The young man said to Him, "All these things I have kept; what am I still lacking?" Jesus said to him, "If you wish to be complete, go and sell your possessions and give to the poor, and you shall have treasure in heaven; and come, follow Me." But when the young man heard this statement, he went away grieved; for he was one who owned much property. (19:20-22)

The man's response—**"All these things I have kept; what am I still lacking?"**—was probably sincere but it was far from true. Like most of the scribes and Pharisees, he was convinced in his own mind that he had **kept** all of God's law. He told Jesus, "Teacher, I have kept all these things from my youth up" (Mark 10:20). Because the commandments concerning attitudes toward God were just as familiar to the man as the one's Jesus quoted, he obviously thought he had fulfilled those as well. His view of the law was completely superficial, external, and man-oriented. Because he had not committed physical adultery or murder, because he was not a liar or a thief, and because he did not blaspheme the Lord's name or worship idols, he looked on himself as being virtually perfect in God's eyes.

By asking, **"What am I still lacking?"** he implied that there either must have been a commandment of which he had never heard or that something in addition to keeping the law was required to obtain eternal life. It simply did not occur to him that he fell short in obedience to any part of God's known law. Because his outward, humanly observed life was upright and religious, he never suspected that his inner, divinely observed life was "full of dead men's bones and all uncleanness" (Matt. 23:27). He would not admit to himself that lust is a form of adultery, that hate is a form of murder, or that swearing by anything in heaven or on earth is a form of taking the Lord's name in vain (Matt. 5:22, 28, 34-35). And it certainly never occurred to him that "whoever keeps the whole law and yet stumbles in one point, . . . has become guilty of all" (James 2:10).

Like most of his Jewish contemporaries, he totally failed to see that the Mosaic commands were not given as means for humanly achieving God's standard of righteousness but were given as pictures of His righteousness. The law was also given to show men how impossible it is for them to live up to His standards of righteousness in their own power. Obedience to the law is always imperfect because the human heart is imperfect.

One of sin's greatest curses is the spiritual and moral blindness it produces. It would not seem to require special revelation from God for men to realize that even the commandments concerning their relationship to other men are impossible to keep perfectly. What truly honest person would claim he has never told a single falsehood of any sort, never coveted anything that belongs to someone else, and always treated his parents with respect and honor—much less that he had always loved his neighbors as much as he loved himself? But one of Satan's chief strategies is to blind sinners to their sin; and because pride is at the heart of all sin, there is a natural inclination toward self-deceit. And nothing is more effective in producing self-deceit than works righteousness, which is the basis of every man-made religion, including the God-given but humanly corrupted religion of first-century Judaism.

The young ruler was aware of what he *did not have* and needed to receive, namely eternal life. But he was not willing to admit what he *did have* and needed to be rid of, namely sin. He had too much spiritual pride to acknowledge that he was sinful by nature and that his whole life fell short of God's holiness and was an offense to Him. His desire for eternal life was centered entirely in his own felt needs and longings.

He had no hatred for sins that needed forgiving and no admission of a heart that needed cleansing. He was therefore not looking for what God needed to do for him but for what he still needed to do for God. Like most Jews of his day, and like most people in all times and cultures, he believed his destiny was in his own hands and that if his lot were to improve it would have to be by his own efforts. All he wanted from Jesus was another commandment, another formula, another rite or ceremony by which he could complete his religious obligations and make himself acceptable to God.

But salvation is for people who despair of their own efforts, who realize that, in themselves and by themselves, they are hopelessly sinful and incapable of improving. Salvation is for those who see themselves as living violations of His holiness and who confess and turn from their sin and throw themselves on God's mercy. It is for those who recognize they have absolutely nothing good to give God, that anything good they receive or accomplish can be only by His sovereign, gracious provision in Jesus Christ.

Paul spends three full chapters of Romans declaring the sinfulness of man before he ever discusses the way of salvation. John 1:17 declares, "The Law was given through Moses; grace and truth were realized through Jesus Christ." Law always precedes grace; it is the tutor that leads to Christ (Gal. 3:24).

Jesus took the focus off the young man's felt religious and psychological needs and placed it on God. He tried to show the man that the real problem in his life was not his feeling of emptiness and incompleteness, legitimate and important as those feelings were. His great problem, from which those felt needs arose, was his separation from God and his total inability to reconcile himself with God. Scripture says, "God is angry with the wicked every day" (Ps. 7:11 KJV). In himself this man not only fell far short of God's righteous standards but was, in fact, an enemy of God and under His wrath (Rom. 5:10; Eph. 2:3). And God will not save those who try to come to Him harboring sin.

Evangelism or personal witnessing that does not confront people with their utter sinfulness and helplessness is not faithful to the gospel of Jesus Christ, no matter how much His name and His Word may be invoked. A profession of Christ that does not include confession and repentance of sin does not bring salvation, no matter how much pleasant emotion may result. To tell an unbeliever that God has a wonderful plan for his life can be seriously misleading. If the unbeliever turns to Christ and is saved, God does indeed have a wonderful plan for him. But if he does not turn to Christ, God's only plan for him is damnation. In the same way it is misleading and dangerous to tell an unbeliever only that God loves him, without telling him that, in spite of that love, he is under God's wrath and sentenced to hell.

God's grace cannot be faithfully preached to unbelievers until His law is preached and man's corrupt nature is exposed. It is impossible for a person to fully realize his need for God's grace until he sees how terribly he has failed the standards of God's law. It is impossible for him to realize his need for mercy until he realizes the magnitude of his guilt. As Samuel Bolton wisely commented, "When you see that men have been wounded by the law, then it is time to pour in the gospel oil."

Instead of being wounded by the law, however, the rich young ruler was self-satisfied in regard to the law. He diligently sought eternal life, but he sought it on his own terms and in his own power. He would not confess his sin and admit his spiritual poverty. Confession of sin and repentance from sin are utterly essential to salvation. John the Baptist began his ministry preaching repentance (Matt. 3:2), Jesus began His ministry preaching repentance (4:17), and both Peter and Paul began their ministries preaching repentance (Acts 2:38; 26:20). Peter even used repentance as a synonym for salvation when he wrote that "the Lord . . . is patient toward you, not wishing for any to perish but for all to come to repentance" (2 Pet. 3:9).

True conviction, confession, and repentance of sin are as much a work of the Holy Spirit as any other part of salvation (John 6:44; 16:8-9). They are divine works of grace, not pre-salvation works of human effort. But just as receiving Christ as Lord and Savior demands the action of the believer's will, so do confession and repentance. It is not that an unbeliever must understand everything about confession, repentance, or any other aspect of salvation. A person can genuinely receive Christ as Lord and Savior with very little knowledge about Him and the gospel. But genuine belief is characterized by willingness to do whatever the Lord requires, just as unbelief is characterized by unwillingness to do whatever He requires.

In another attempt to make the self-satisfied young ruler face his true spiritual condition, **Jesus said to him, "If you wish to be complete, go and sell your possessions and give to the poor, and you shall have treasure in heaven; and come, follow Me."** In this context, **complete** is used as a synonym for salvation, as it frequently is in the book of Hebrews, where the same basic Greek word is translated "perfect" (see 7:19; 10:1, 14; 12:23). Jesus was saying, "If you truly desire eternal life, prove your sincerity by selling **your possessions and** giving what you have **to the poor.**" If he truly lived up to the Mosaic command to love his neighbor as himself, he would be willing to do what Jesus now commanded. His willingness to obey that command would not merit salvation but it would be evidence that he desired salvation above everything else, as a priceless treasure or a pearl of great value for which no sacrifice could be too great (see Matt. 13:44-46).

The ultimate test was whether or not the man was willing to obey the Lord.

The real issue Jesus presented was, "Will you do what I ask, no matter what? Who will be Lord in your life, you or Me?" That hit a sensitive nerve. Jesus demands to be Lord, sovereign over all. There was no better way to find out if the man was ready to accept Christ's sovereignty than to ask him to give up his riches. The Lord challenged his wealth to force him to admit what was most valuable to him—Jesus Christ and eternal life or his money and possessions. The latter was clearly the man's priority, and therefore for him salvation was forfeited.

The first part of Jesus' command was quite capable of being obeyed in the man's own power. But he refused to comply with it, not because he *could not* but because he *would not.* He not only failed to keep God's impossible commands but failed to keep this one that was easily possible, proving conclusively that he really did not want to do God's perfect will and be spiritually **complete.**

Mark tells us that as He gave the man that command, "Jesus felt a love for him" (10:21). The Lord must have felt for him as He did for Jerusalem as He looked out over that great city and cried, "O Jerusalem, Jerusalem, the city that kills the prophets and stones those sent to her! How often I wanted to gather your children together, just as a hen gathers her brood under her wings, and you would not have it" (Luke 13:34). Jesus was approaching the time when He would shed His own blood for the sins of the rich young ruler, and for the sins of Jerusalem and of the whole world. But as much as He loved the man and desired for him not to perish, He could not save him while he refused to admit he was lost. The Lord can do nothing with a life that is not surrendered to Him, except to condemn it.

It is possible the man did not even hear Jesus say, **"Come, follow Me."** He was so dismayed by the command to sell his possessions and give to the poor that Jesus' call to discipleship did not register on his conscious mind. His call to discipleship always falls on deaf ears when there is unwillingness to give up everything for Him (see Matt. 8:19-22).

The young man did not want Jesus either as Savior or as Lord. He was not willing to give Him his sins to be forgiven or his life to be ruled. Therefore when he heard Jesus' **statement, he went away grieved; for he was one who owned much property.** Contrary to his own self-assessment, he did not live up to any of God's law, but he was especially guilty in the area of materialism. The **property** he thought he **owned** really owned him, and he would rather be its servant than Jesus'.

He went away grieved because, although he came to Jesus for eternal life, he left without it. He did not desire it above the possessions of his present life. He wanted to gain salvation, but not as much as he wanted to keep his **property.**

Zaccheus was also a wealthy man. But when Jesus called him, "he hurried and came down, and received Him gladly." Spontaneously he volunteered to do essentially what Jesus commanded the rich young ruler to do. "Half of my possessions I will give to the poor," Zaccheus said, "and if I have defrauded anyone of anything, I will give back four times as much." Jesus then told him, "Today salvation has come to this house" (Luke 19:5-9). Zaccheus was not saved because of his new-found generosity. Rather his new-found generosity was evidence that he was truly saved.

As implied in the next verse, Zaccheus was saved because he confessed he was lost (v. 10).

Although every sin must be forsaken for Christ's sake, there is often a certain sin or group of sins that a person finds particularly difficult to give up. For that **young man** it was love of his wealth and the prestige associated with it. Willingness to give up his **property** would not have saved him, but it would have revealed a heart that under the convicting work of the Holy Spirit was ready for salvation.

When Jesus declared, "No one of you can be My disciple who does not give up all his own possessions" (Luke 14:33), He was not referring only to material possessions. For some people the supreme obstacle to salvation might be a career, an unsaved boyfriend or girlfriend, or some cherished sin. Many people who are materially destitute are just as far from the kingdom as the rich young ruler. Yet they must be willing to give up whatever they do possess, even if all they have left is pride, if they would be saved.

Salvation involves a commitment to forsake sin and to follow Jesus Christ at all costs. He will take disciples on no other terms. A person who does not "confess with [his] mouth Jesus as Lord, and believe in [his] heart that God raised Him from the dead," cannot be saved, "for with the heart man believes, resulting in righteousness, and with the mouth he confesses, resulting in salvation" (Rom. 10:9-10).

The Poverty of Riches and the Riches of Poverty

(19:23-29)

19

And Jesus said to His disciples, "Truly I say to you, it is hard for a rich man to enter the kingdom of heaven. And again I say to you, it is easier for a camel to go through the eye of a needle, than for a rich man to enter the kingdom of God." And when the disciples heard this, they were very astonished and said, "Then who can be saved?" And looking upon them Jesus said to them, "With men this is impossible, but with God all things are possible." Then Peter answered and said to Him, "Behold, we have left everything and followed You; what then will there be for us?" And Jesus said to them, "Truly I say to you, that you who have followed Me, in the regeneration when the Son of Man will sit on His glorious throne, you also shall sit upon twelve thrones, judging the twelve tribes of Israel. And everyone who has left houses or brothers or sisters or father or mother or children or farms for My name's sake, shall receive many times as much, and shall inherit eternal life." (19:23-29)

The rich young ruler came to Jesus seeking eternal life, but the barriers of his self-centeredness and self-righteousness stood in the way of his receiving it (19:16-22). He would not recognize his need for repentance and Christ's forgiveness nor would he submit to Christ's lordship. He sincerely wanted eternal life, but he wanted his riches and his self-righteousness even more. Whoever wants anything more than Christ will forfeit Christ.

In this present passage the Lord elaborates on the spiritual danger of trusting in material riches and the spiritual blessings of forsaking them for His sake. He first focuses on what might be called the poverty of riches (vv. 23-26) and then on the riches of poverty (vv. 27-29).

THE POVERTY OF RICHES

And Jesus said to His disciples, "Truly I say to you, it is hard for a rich man to enter the kingdom of heaven. And again I say to you, it is easier for a camel to go through the eye of a needle, than for a rich man to enter the kingdom of God." And when the disciples heard this, they were very astonished and said, "Then who can be saved?" And looking upon them Jesus said to them, "With men this is impossible, but with God all things are possible." (19:23-26)

The expression **Truly I say to you** was a common Jewish figure of speech used to introduce a teaching of great importance. It carried the idea of, "Pay special attention to what I am about to say." The important truth Jesus wanted to convey to **His disciples** at this time was that, as they had just seen tragically illustrated by the rich young ruler, **it is hard for a rich man to enter the kingdom of heaven.**

The kingdom of heaven refers to the sphere of God's gracious rule and, as is clear from the fact that Jesus uses both in the same statement, is synonymous with **the kingdom of God.** By intertestamental times, **heaven** had become a common Jewish substitute term for the covenant name of God (Yahweh, Jehovah), which they preferred not to speak. In this context the terms are also synonymous with eternal life, which the rich young ruler was seeking (v. 16), and therefore with salvation. Following up on the incident of that young man, whose wealth was for him an impenetrable barrier to receiving Christ as Lord and Savior, Jesus explained to the Twelve the eternal danger of trusting in material possessions.

The Lord repeatedly emphasized that following Him required willingness to sacrifice everything a person had, economic, personal, social, and all else. "He who loves father or mother more than Me is not worthy of Me," He said; "and he who loves son or daughter more than Me is not worthy of Me. And he who does not take his cross and follow after Me is not worthy of Me. He who has found his life shall lose it" (Matt. 10:37-39). A person must desire salvation more than anything else, so that no sacrifice is too great to make for Christ's sake. That is why "the gate is small, and the way is narrow that leads to life, and few are those who find it" (Matt. 7:14).

Duskolōs (**hard**) is used in the New Testament only here and in the parallel synoptic accounts (Mark 10:23; Luke 18:24). Jesus went on to explain that, as far as **a rich man** entering **the kingdom of heaven** is concerned, **hard** is equivalent to impossible: "**Again I say to you, it is easier for a camel to go through the**

eye of a needle, than for a rich man to enter the kingdom of God."

The expression **easier for a camel to go through the eye of a needle** was a Jewish colloquialism for the impossible. It was probably a modified form of a Persian expression for impossibility, "easier for an elephant to go through the eye of a needle," that is quoted in the Talmud. Being the largest animal known in Palestine, the camel was substituted for the elephant.

Some have been confused by this text, thinking it appears to say that the rich have no hope of salvation. So in order to make the expression signify something difficult but not impossible, interpreters have suggested numerous explanations, many of them farfetched. Some propose that there was a very small gate in the ancient wall of Jerusalem called the Needle's Eye. In order for a camel to go through it, they surmised, the animal would have to be completely unloaded and then crawl through on its knees. But neither the Persian nor the Jewish saying used the term *gate,* and no Jerusalem gate by that name is mentioned in any extant historical or archeological record. In any case, no sensible person would go to such trouble when he could take his camel a few hundred yards down the wall and go through a larger gate.

Other scholars have suggested that scribal error changed the Greek word *kamilos* (a large rope or cable) into *kamēlos* (a camel). But a large rope would also be impossible to thread through the eye of a needle. More than that, it is hard to conceive that the scribes who made copies from the original manuscript all made the same mistake and made it in all three gospel accounts!

Even if an ancient manuscript were found with the word for camel changed to *rope,* it would be rejected for the reason that it would indicate a scribe had changed it to make it more acceptable. Because no scribe would turn *rope* into *camel,* the latter would be considered the original reading. The expression clearly refers to an impossibility. It is impossible for a rich man such as the one just encountered to enter the kingdom of heaven.

Before considering what Jesus meant by saying it is impossible, let us consider some reasons why it is difficult. For one thing, the rich tend to have false security in their riches. Because wealth can provide for all physical needs and a great many things beyond needs, the wealthy are inclined to rely on their money to buy whatever they want, so they see little reason to depend on God. That is one reason there are "not many wise, . . . mighty, . . . noble; but God has chosen the foolish, . . . weak, . . . base, . . . despised" (1 Cor. 1:26-28). The poor, on the other hand, became the special objects of and responders to our Lord's teaching (Luke 4:18).

An attitude of self-sufficiency plagued the church at Laodicea. Because they said, "I am rich, and have become wealthy, and have need of nothing," they did not realize that spiritually they were "wretched and miserable and poor and blind and naked" (Rev. 3:17). In A.D. 60 Laodicea had a devastating earthquake that virtually levelled the city. Although the Roman government offered to rebuild the city for them, the proud inhabitants insisted on doing it themselves. They succeeded in raising the entire city out of the ashes, as it were, without any outside help. That proud, self-sufficient attitude obviously had spilled over into the church, whose members came to think of themselves as able to do without the help even of God.

Those who have great material resources tend to imagine they do not require divine resources. Paul therefore told Timothy to "instruct those who are rich in this present world not to be conceited or to fix their hope on the uncertainty of riches, but on God, who richly supplies us with all things to enjoy" (1 Tim. 6:17). More than that, the apostle goes on to say, "Instruct them to do good, to be rich in good works, to be generous and ready to share, storing up for themselves the treasure of a good foundation for the future, so that they may take hold of that which is life indeed" (vv. 18-19).

Paul's advice to Timothy was that he confront prospective converts who were rich in the same way Jesus confronted the rich young ruler. If a person prefers his earthly fortune to the lordship of Jesus Christ, his heart is not prepared for salvation. Willingness to give up everything for the Lord will not in itself save him, but it demonstrates that he is desperate for salvation and has found the "pearl of great price" for which he will sell all he has if need be.

Only godliness brings gain that has lasting value and satisfaction, Paul assures us. "But those who want to get rich fall into temptation and a snare and many foolish and harmful desires which plunge men into ruin and destruction. For the love of money is a root of all sorts of evil, and some by longing for it have wandered away from the faith, and pierced themselves with many a pang" (vv. 6, 9-10).

It is especially difficult for rich people not to be closely tied to this world, to their bank accounts, investments, and possessions. A person's heart is where his treasure is (Matt. 6:21), and the wealthy usually find it hard, and seemingly unnecessary, to treasure the things of God. When they hear the gospel, its divine seed frequently falls on thorny hearts that may have an initial response but are full of "the worries of the world, and the deceitfulness of riches, and the desires for other things" that choke the Word and make it unfruitful (Mark 4:18-19).

The successful farmer who tore down his old barns and built bigger ones to hold all his grain was oblivious to the welfare of his soul. Completely content in his riches, he said to himself, "Soul, you have many goods laid up for many years to come; take your ease, eat, drink and be merry." And because he refused to recognize God as the source of his many goods or to allow Him to have any place in his life, his life was forfeited. "God said to him, 'You fool! This very night your soul is required of you; and now who will own what you have prepared?' So is the man," Jesus explained, "who lays up treasure for himself, and is not rich toward God" (Luke 12:18-21).

Every possession a person has is by the provision of God and ought to be used to His glory. Even Christians run the danger of being sidetracked and trapped by their possessions, giving to God only what remains after they have accumulated what they want and fulfilled their own plans.

All that may explain why it is so hard for the rich to enter God's kingdom, but why it is impossible is a completely different issue—and is the whole point here.

The young ruler was not a denouncer of Christ but a seeker who wanted eternal life, who wanted kingdom citizenship. But the flaw was that he thought he himself had the resources to procure it. That is the point here.

In Mark's parallel account, Jesus makes clear that the impossibility of entering **the kingdom** by any humanly devised or empowered means extends to everyone, not just the rich. We learn from Mark that after the disciples expressed amazement about His statement concerning the wealthy, Jesus said, "Children, how hard it is to enter the kingdom of God!" (Mark 10:24). The rich young ruler's problem was not his wealth itself but his trust in his wealth and in his own ability to meet God's standards for acceptance. He wanted to enter the kingdom and receive eternal life on his own terms, through his own money, and by his own efforts. But, Jesus said, it is so **hard** for anyone to get saved on his own terms and by his own efforts that it is absolutely impossible. The poorest of the poor have no better chance to gain eternal life by their own efforts at righteousness.

Jesus is not here teaching how hard it is for rich people to get unhooked from their riches and bow their knees to Him in humble faith. He is saying how impossible it is for them or for anyone else to be saved by self-effort of any kind. In effect, He was saying the same thing God said through the Mosaic law. It was humanly impossible to live up to a single one of the Ten Commandments or to the two great commandments (Lev. 19:18; Deut. 6:5; Matt. 22:37-39), and those laws were intended to show God's people the impossibility of meeting His perfect, holy standards in their own power. Salvation has always been impossible by human effort.

Paul expressed the same truth when he wrote: "Now we know that whatever the Law says, it speaks to those who are under the Law, that every mouth may be closed, and all the world may become accountable to God; because by the works of the Law no flesh will be justified in His sight; for through the Law comes the knowledge of sin" (Rom. 3:19-20).

Jesus declared that all works-righteousness, which is the basis of every man-made religion, is worthless, affirming what Jeremiah had written hundreds of years earlier: "Can the Ethiopian change his skin or the leopard his spots? Then you also can do good who are accustomed to do evil" (Jer. 13:23). Every human being since the Fall is by nature "accustomed to do evil" and is therefore unable to do good in any way that is acceptable to God. No one can save himself any more than he can change the color of his skin or than a leopard can change his spots.

Jesus was not separating out the rich as being more inherently far from **the kingdom** than other people but was pointing out that their riches on the one hand were a formidable barrier and on the other hand that their money gave them no advantage at all, though they might be able to buy more sacrifices, give more alms, and make more offerings at the Temple.

The wealthy are also inclined to be selfish and self-centered. Their time and interests are often devoted to enlarging, protecting, and enjoying what they have, and consequently they have little time or concern for the interests or welfare of others. I once talked with a man who had worked for several multimillionaires. He said that they had three things in common: they not only were rich but were capable of getting even richer, they were eccentric, and they were extremely selfish and self-centered. Although there are exceptions, those characteristics are generally universal. Like the self-indulgent rich man who was oblivious to the diseased and destitute Lazarus who laid outside his gate hoping to have a few table crumbs (Luke 16:20-31), the wealthy are inclined to be interested only in themselves.

Jesus' teaching about the impossibility of the rich entering the kingdom by their own efforts was a shocking idea to Jews. Therefore, **when the disciples heard this, they were very astonished and said, "Then who can be saved?"** For many centuries the rabbis had taught that accumulation of wealth was a virtue and that it was not only unwise but sinful for a person to give away more than one fifth of what he owned. They had designed a religious law to protect their selfishness and greed. Envisioning the Lord in their own materialistic image, they reasoned that God was pleased with a gift in direct proportion to its size. Therefore, the more one gave out of the permissible one fifth limit, the more favor he found with God.

Such ideas were so strongly entrenched that in much Jewish thinking alms giving was virtually a means of buying salvation. Much like the indulgences of the Middle Ages, alms giving was considered a means of literally purchasing a more favored place in the kingdom. For Jesus to teach that wealth was actually a serious *barrier* to the kingdom was diametrically contrary to everything most Jews had been taught. The rich could afford the largest and choicest of the sacrificial animals. They could give large amounts to the Temple and their local synagogues. They never lacked for money to drop into the thirteen trumpet-shaped receptacles in the court of the women that were conspicuously located so that their generous giving to the Lord's work could be observed by fellow worshipers.

But if even the rich cannot enter the kingdom by their own efforts and generosity, the disciples wondered, what could the poor hope for? In total bewilderment they therefore asked Jesus, **"Then who can be saved?"**

And looking upon them Jesus said to them explicitly what the Mosaic law said implicitly: **"With men this is impossible."** Just as it is not merely difficult but impossible for a camel to go through the eye of a needle, it is not merely difficult but **impossible** for **men** to please the Lord and come into His kingdom on their own terms and by their own efforts. In one simple declaration, Jesus utterly destroyed the current perspective in the religion of Israel and, at the same time, all hope in works-righteousness. Whatever his material possessions and earthly accomplishments, every person stands totally helpless and powerless before God. He stands condemned before a righteous God, and in his depraved nature he can do nothing to make himself holy and worthy of God's forgiveness and acceptance. With that statement Jesus swept all religions of human achievement and works-righteousness into hell. Left to any work of man, salvation is impossible.

"But with God all things are possible," Jesus went on to say. Because **God** is able to change sinful hearts, it is **possible** for Him to save helpless men. God can do what men cannot do. The rich young ruler went away without eternal life because he sought it on the impossible basis of his own human resources and goodness. Salvation is entirely a gracious and sovereign work of God, and the work of His human witnesses is simply to proclaim the full truth of the gospel as clearly and lovingly as possible and to rely on God to apply that truth to an unbeliever's heart and bring him to recognize his spiritual bankruptcy and come to repentance and obedient faith. Although repentance and faith require an act of human will, they are prompted by the power of God.

"No one can come to Me, unless the Father who sent Me draws him," Jesus said (John 6:44). That is why Paul admonished that "the Lord's bondservant must not be quarrelsome, but be kind to all, able to teach, patient when wronged, with gentleness correcting those who are in opposition, if perhaps God may grant them repentance leading to the knowledge of the truth, and they may come to their senses and escape from the snare of the devil, having been held captive by him to do his will" (2 Tim. 2:24-26).

THE RICHES OF POVERTY

Then Peter answered and said to Him, "Behold, we have left everything and followed You; what then will there be for us?" And Jesus said to them, "Truly I say to you, that you who have followed Me, in the regeneration when the Son of Man will sit on His glorious throne, you also shall sit upon twelve thrones, judging the twelve tribes of Israel. And everyone who has left houses or brothers or sisters or father or mother or children or farms for My name's sake, shall receive many times as much, and shall inherit eternal life." (19:27-29)

With hope perhaps tinged with uncertainty, **Peter** ventured to ask Jesus, **"Behold, we have left everything and followed You; what then will there be for us?"** "We came on Your terms, didn't we?" he said in effect. "Do we thereby qualify for eternal life? The rich young ruler refused to surrender his possessions and his life to You, and he forfeited the kingdom. But we forsook our jobs, our families, our friends, and everything else we had in order to be Your disciples. We have repented of our sins and surrendered to Your lordship. Just as You commanded, we have denied ourselves and taken up our crosses for your sake. Doesn't that qualify us for a place in Your kingdom?"

Peter was speaking for all of the Twelve, because he had no suspicion of Judas's betrayal. As that false disciple would soon make evident, he had *not* forsaken everything for Christ but was instead seeking to use Him for his own ends. He expected Jesus to overthrow Rome and set up His own earthly kingdom, with the disciples given the highest places of honor and power. Judas was much further from the kingdom than the rich young ruler, who at least knew he needed eternal life and had a certain desire for it. Judas, on the other hand, was totally concerned with his present, earthly life.

But the rest of the Twelve, despite their small faith and slowness to understand Jesus' teaching, had truly given themselves to Him. They shared with Judas many of the common Jewish misconceptions about the Messiah and His kingdom. They may still have been expecting Him to establish the kingdom during their lifetimes and therefore could not bring themselves to accept the idea of His suffering and death. But they nevertheless continued to follow and obey Him. As Peter had declared in behalf of the Twelve, "You have words of eternal life. And we have believed and have come to know that You are the Holy One of God" (John 6:68-69).

Although Peter and the others were still confused about much of Jesus' message and mission, they knew they truly belonged to Him and that He truly loved them and would not forsake them. They were certain He had something divinely good in store for them, even if they had a distorted idea of what it was. Peter therefore asked to hear from Jesus' own lips concerning **what then will there be for us?** "What are the benefits of Your kingdom for us?" they wanted to know. "What do we have to look forward to as Your disciples?"

Some have criticized Peter for his expectation of blessing and reward. But Jesus gave no hint of dissatisfaction with the question. Instead, He acknowledged that they were indeed His true and sincere disciples, referring to them as **you who have followed Me.** The Greek aorist participle characterizes them as His followers.

Next, He gave them the marvelous and unique promise that **in the regeneration when the Son of Man will sit on His glorious throne, you also shall sit upon twelve thrones, judging the twelve tribes of Israel.**

The term *palingenesia* (**regeneration**) literally means new birth. It was used by Josephus for the new birth of the Jewish nation after the Babylonian Captivity and by Philo of the new birth of the earth after the Flood and after its destruction by fire. It is used only twice in the New Testament, here and in Titus 3:5, where Paul uses it to refer to the personal new birth of believers. In the present passage, however, Jesus uses it to represent the rebirth of the earth under His sovereign dominion at the time of His second coming. It will be paradise regained and a global parallel to the individual rebirth of Christians.

The earth and the world of men will be given a new nature, described in great detail by the Old Testament prophets and by John in Revelation 20:1-15. Just as they have been given spiritual life and a new nature in Jesus Christ but are not yet perfected, so there will be a rebirth of the earth that is divinely recreated. Although it will not yet be a totally new earth (Rev. 21:1), it will nevertheless be wonderfully superior to the present fallen and unredeemed earth. It was the belief of the Jews that Messiah would renew the earth and heavens, based on the prophecy of Isaiah 65:17 and 66:22. Peter called it "the period of restoration of all things about which God spoke by the mouth of His holy prophets from ancient times" (Acts 3:21).

All believers will sit on the throne of Christ (Rev. 3:21), exercising authority over the people of the earth (Rev. 2:26), while the apostles are uniquely ruling restored Israel. This cannot be the eternal state described in Revelation 21:12-14, where twelve gates in the New Jerusalem are inscribed with the names of the twelve tribes and twelve foundations are inscribed with the names of the twelve apostles.

At the time of the restoration of the earth, righteousness will flourish, peace will abound, Jerusalem will again be exalted, health and healing will prevail, the earth will produce food as never before, the lion will lay down in peace with the lamb, the deserts will blossom, and life will be long. The age-old curse that began with the Fall will then be *limited,* in anticipation of its being *eliminated* completely in the eternal state to follow (Rev. 22:3).

As God had long before predicted, the Messiah, the Lord's Anointed, will then receive all the nations as His inheritance and have the very ends of the earth as His possessions. "Thou shalt break them with a rod of iron," the psalmist declared; "Thou shalt shatter them like earthenware" (Ps. 2:2, 8-9). Then **the Son of Man will sit on His glorious throne,** as King of kings and Lord of lords (Rev. 19:16). This is a reference to the prophecy of Daniel 7:13-14, where God, "the Ancient of Days," gives the kingdom to the Son of Man. Jesus is affirming the reality that He will rule in the coming kingdom.

At that time the redeemed of all the ages will also reign with Him. "Then the sovereignty, the dominion, and the greatness of all the kingdoms under the whole heaven will be given to the people of the saints of the Highest One; His kingdom will be an everlasting kingdom, and all the dominions will serve and obey Him" (Dan. 7:27; cf. 1 Cor. 6:2; Rev. 20:4). The nation of Israel will be restored, and sharing Christ's rule over her will be the Twelve apostles, who **also shall sit upon twelve thrones, judging the twelve tribes of Israel.** Matthias, who took Judas's place among the apostles shortly before Pentecost (Acts 1:26), will join the other eleven on the **twelve thrones** (cf. Dan. 7:22 and Isa. 1:26).

Because amillennial interpreters do not believe in a literal thousand-year kingdom on earth or in Israel's national restoration, they take the **twelve thrones** and **the twelve tribes** as being purely figurative. One such writer made no attempt to discern Jesus' meaning but simply commented, "Now we have to wonder what our Lord meant by the twelve tribes of Israel."

If Jesus was referring to a real reigning on His part when He spoke of His throne, He must be referring to literal **thrones** that the apostles would **sit upon** while literally **judging the twelve tribes of Israel.** And as already noted, this millennial truth is also revealed elsewhere in Scripture.

The Word makes clear that in the reign of Christ over the world, He will be sovereign and rule over Jews and Gentiles with righteousness, peace, and immediate justice. He will be worshiped as supreme Lord, and His kingdom will bring prosperity, healing, health, and blessedness.

Not only that, Jesus continued, but **"everyone who has left houses or brothers or sisters or father or mother or children or farms for My name's sake, shall receive as much, and shall inherit eternal life."** Those who renounce their possessions and become poor for Christ's **name's sake** are going to share with the apostles in His triumph and reign. Mark reports that Jesus said the person who gives up those things for His sake and the gospel's "shall receive a hundred times as much now in the present age" (Mark 10:30).

When a person comes to Jesus Christ he must often have to turn his back on certain relationships, even with those who are very dear to him. Many times his conversion turns his own family and closest friends against him, in some cases even to the point of seeking his disinheritance or even his life. But the one who gives up everything for Christ's sake, not only will **inherit eternal life** but also the family of God in this present life. He will have a host of new fathers and mothers, brothers and sisters with whom he will forever be united in God's divine family. Wherever he goes, he meets spiritual loved ones, many of whom he has never seen or heard of before. Throughout the world he finds those who will share his sorrows, encourage his spirit, and help meet his needs, material as well as spiritual.

The believer in Jesus Christ will have blessings now, blessings in the millennial kingdom, and blessings throughout all eternity. To be poor for the sake of Christ is to be rich indeed. Jim Elliot, a young missionary martyred by the Auca Indians of Ecuador whom he was seeking to reach for Christ, wrote shortly before his death, "He is no fool who gives what he cannot keep to gain what he cannot lose."

Equality in the Kingdom
(19:30–20:16)

20

But many who are first will be last; and the last, first.

For the kingdom of heaven is like a landowner who went out early in the morning to hire laborers for his vineyard. And when he had agreed with the laborers for a denarius for the day, he sent them into his vineyard. And he went out about the third hour and saw others standing idle in the market place; and to those he said, "You too go into the vineyard, and whatever is right I will give you." And so they went. Again he went out about the sixth and the ninth hour, and did the same thing. And about the eleventh hour he went out, and found others standing; and he said to them "Why have you been standing here idle all day long?" They said to him, "Because no one hired us." He said to them, "You too go into the vineyard." And when evening had come, the owner of the vineyard said to his foreman, "Call the laborers and pay them their wages, beginning with the last group to the first." And when those hired about the eleventh hour came, each one received a denarius. And when those hired first came, they thought that they would receive more; and they also received each one a denarius. And when they received it, they grumbled at the landowner, saying, "These last men have worked only one hour, and you have made them equal to us who have borne the burden and the scorching heat of the day." But he answered and said to one of them, "Friend, I am doing you no wrong; did you not agree with me for a denarius? Take what is yours and go your way, but I wish to give to this last man the same as to you. Is it not lawful for me to do what I wish with what is my own? Or is your eye envious because I am generous?" Thus the last shall be first, and the first last. (19:30—20:16)

The prophet Ezekiel ministered to the children of Israel during the Babylonian Captivity. Like the other true prophets of God, he repeatedly had to remind them of and warn them about their sins, especially those for which they were exiled in the first place. One of those sins was that of accusing God of being unfair and unjust.

They liked to use the proverb, "The fathers eat the sour grapes, but the children's teeth are set on edge," which brought into question God's justice. "'As I live,' declares the Lord God, 'you are surely not going to use this proverb in Israel anymore. Behold all souls are Mine; the soul of the father as well as the soul of the son is Mine. The soul who sins will die'" (Ezek. 18:2-4). Twice in that chapter the Lord declares, "Yet you say, 'The way of the Lord is not right.' Hear now, O house of Israel! Is My way not right? Is it not your ways that are not right?" (v. 25; cf. v. 29).

When men doubt the justice and fairness of God, it is always because of their own perverted views of justice and of Him. God Himself is the standard for righteousness, and it is as impossible for Him to be unjust as to lie. Confronting the same false principle reflected in the ancient Israelite proverb, Paul declared, "There will be tribulation and distress for every soul of man who does evil, of the Jew first and also of the Greek, but glory and honor and peace to every man who does good, to the Jew first and also to the Greek. For there is no partiality with God" (Rom. 2:9-11). To the Colossians he wrote, "From the Lord you will receive the reward of the inheritance. It is the Lord Christ whom you serve. For he who does wrong will receive the consequences of the wrong which he has done, and that without partiality" (Col. 3:24-25). God punishes those who do wrong and blesses those who do right, with utter impartiality.

In no area is God's impartiality more significant and wonderful than in regard to salvation. No matter what men's circumstances might be when they come to Christ, and no matter how well or poorly they may serve Him after coming, they receive the same glorious salvation. That is the great truth Jesus teaches in Matthew 19:30—20:16.

The Participants in Kingdom Equality

But many who are first will be last; and the last, first.

For the kingdom of heaven is like a landowner who went out early in the morning to hire laborers for his vineyard. And when he had agreed with the laborers for a denarius for the day, he sent them into his vineyard. And he went out about the third hour and saw others standing idle in the market place; and to those he said, "You too go into the vineyard, and whatever is right I will give you." And so they went. Again he went out

about the sixth and the ninth hour, and did the same thing. And about the eleventh hour he went out, and found others standing; and he said to them "Why have you been standing here idle all day long?" They said to him, "Because no one hired us." He said to them, "You too go into the vineyard." (19:30—20:7)

Jesus' words, **"Many who are first shall be last; and the last, first,"** may have been a common proverb. But since He used it on several occasions and it is not found in other literature, it seems more likely that He originated the expression Himself.

In the parable that follows, Jesus illustrated His intended application of the proverb. He states plainly that the theme of the parable is **the kingdom of heaven,** the subject He had been dealing with since the rich young ruler approached Him. That man wanted to know how to receive eternal life (19:16), which every Jew knew was equivalent to the hope of salvation and heavenly citizenship. Following up on that incident, Jesus warned His disciples about the great barrier that riches can be to entering **the kingdom,** and then declared the impossibility of entering by man's own resources and efforts and the possibility of entering only by God's gracious power (vv. 23-29).

This parable teaches a magnificent and blessed truth about **the kingdom of heaven,** which, Jesus said, **is like a landowner who went out early in the morning to hire laborers for his vineyard.** He is giving an illustration of the spiritual realm where God sovereignly reigns in righteousness and grace, and in particular, an illustration of the equal and just basis on which it is entered through His grace. As He often did, He used a common earthly story to illustrate a heavenly truth.

The estate of **the landowner** included a large **vineyard,** for which he needed **to hire laborers.** It is not stated whether he was preparing a new vineyard, pruning the vines of an existing one, or getting ready to harvest the grapes. But all of those tasks required considerable hard labor. Vineyards generally were planted on terraced hillsides, most of which were stony. Preparing the terraces involved digging out the tiers and using the stones to build small retaining walls on the outside edges. Then the terraced areas had to be filled with good soil, most of which often had to be carried a considerable distance up the slopes from more fertile ground below.

Every summer, both new and old vines had to be pruned back to improve production, and that, too, was demanding work. The final major operation was, of course, the harvesting, done in late September. The weather was still hot then (see v. 12), and it was necessary to gather the grapes before the fall rainy season began. If for some reason the grapes were slow in ripening, the time for harvesting could be significantly shortened. Consequently, the grape harvest was a hectic and demanding time.

Because most owners did not have enough household servants or regular workers to do those jobs, temporary day **laborers** were hired from nearby towns and villages. These **laborers** were usually unskilled at a trade and were near the bottom of the social-economic scale, many of them not far above beggars. They worked from job to job, many of which lasted no more than a day, and often less. They had no guarantee of work beyond what they might be doing at the time. They would gather in the market place before dawn to be available for hiring, and that is where the landowner found these particular men **early in the morning**.

Because they were unskilled, desperate for work, and therefore vulnerable, they were often underpaid and otherwise disadvantaged. Because of His great compassion for the poor and downtrodden, God commanded His people, "You shall not oppress your neighbor, nor rob him. The wages of a hired man are not to remain with you all night until morning" (Lev. 19:13). In other words, they were to pay hired workers decent wages and pay them at the end of every day, because that was often all a man would have with which to feed his family the following day. As Moses explains elsewhere, "You shall give him his wages on his day before the sun sets, for he is poor and sets his heart on it; so that he may not cry against you to the Lord and it become sin in you" (Deut. 24:15). Because they worked only from day to day, they were to be paid day to day.

After he found them in the market place, the landowner **agreed with the laborers for a denarius for the day**, and he then **sent them into his vineyard** to begin work. **A denarius for the day**, the wage of a Roman soldier, was good pay for such workers. It is likely they were usually paid less, and they readily agreed to this man's equitable offer.

The Jewish workday began at 6:00 a.m., which was called the first hour. When it was **about the third hour**, that is, nine o'clock, the owner went into town again and **saw others standing idle in the market place**. These **others** may have been latecomers who had to travel a greater distance or perhaps were less able-bodied than the others and moved more slowly. Or they may have had only a few hours' work to do at the beginning of the day and were now back in the employment line. In light of the owner's generosity, it may have been that he had seen those men earlier in the morning but did not need them. Perhaps he now came back out of compassion and hired them because of their need rather than his own. For whatever reasons, an additional group of laborers had gathered.

Standing idle does not signify laziness or indolence but merely points up the fact that they were unemployed at the time. They were entirely dependent on someone's hiring them, and the fact that they were **in the market place** shows they were looking for work.

The owner did not offer a particular wage to these men but simply told them, **"You too go into the vineyard, and whatever is right I will give you."** As in all rural communities, everyone knew everyone else, and these workers no doubt trusted the owner as a man of his word. In any case, they were doubtlessly extremely glad to have work to do at any wage, **and so they went**.

At **about the sixth hour** (noon) **and the ninth hour** (3:00 p.m.) the landowner went back into the village **and did the same thing**. At each of those times he found more men hoping for work and hired them.

Then, near the very end of the day, at **about the eleventh hour** (5:00 p.m.), he went back still again **and found others standing; and he said to them, "Why have you been standing here idle all day long?"** No explanation is given as to why these men had **been standing . . . idle all day long** and yet not been hired. Perhaps they were in another section of the market or had somehow been overlooked. Or perhaps they were the oldest, weakest, and least productive workers, whom no one else wanted to hire. But those particulars are irrelevant to the parable. The point is that, even at that late hour, there were men still looking for work, **because,** as they explained, **no one hired us.**

This last group had worked only one hour (v. 12) **when evening had come,** which was the twelfth hour, or six o'clock. Following the Mosaic requirement to pay such workers at the end of each day, **the owner of the vineyard said to his foreman, "Call the laborers and pay them their wages."** That is what every conscientious Jewish employer did in obedience to Old Testament law.

Jesus' next instruction, however, was quite unusual. The men were to be paid **beginning with the last group to the first.** Here is where Jesus was able to demonstrate men's self-serving ideas of fairness, and where the parable begins to intersect with the proverb "Many who are first will be last; and the last, first" (19:30; cf. 20:16).

The primary idea of the parable, and of Jesus' application of the proverb, is not a simple reversal of payment order. Although that procedure was certainly not customary, it would not in itself have caused much concern. The radical action of the landowner, which reflects the parable's main point, is that **those hired about the eleventh hour . . . each . . . received a denarius,** a whole day's wage, as their pay.

THE OBJECTION TO KINGDOM EQUALITY

And when those hired about the eleventh hour came, each one received a denarius. And when those hired first came, they thought that they would receive more; and they also received each one a denarius. And when they received it, they grumbled at the landowner, saying, "These last men have worked only one hour, and you have made them equal to us who have borne the burden and the scorching heat of the day." (20:9-12)

The account does not mention the fact, but it is obvious from the eleventh-hour workers' wages that the men hired at the third, sixth, and ninth hours were also paid **a denarius.** It is therefore understandable that **when those hired first came, they thought that they would receive more.** At this point they had no problem with what the owner had done but, in fact, were elated. Because he had paid the other men a full day's wage for a partial day's work, they assumed that **they would receive more** than a day's wage. At the rate the eleventh-hour group was paid, they would have received 12 day's pay for one day's work! They were more than willing to be paid last if that meant being paid so handsomely.

But their hopes were soon dashed when **they also received each one a denarius,** and they reacted exactly as we would expect. **They grumbled at the landowner, saying, "These last men have worked only one hour, and you have made them equal to us who have borne the burden and the scorching heat of the day."** Their normal, very human reaction was, "That's not fair! Those men only worked an hour at the end of the day. We worked hard all day long, including during **scorching heat.** Why should they get paid as much as we did?" They may have been overdramatizing their case, but their basic description of the situation was correct. In any case, they were exceedingly disgruntled at this perceived injustice and were determined not to leave until they had satisfaction from **the landowner,** who was standing near his foreman when the wages were handed out.

THE VINDICATION OF KINGDOM EQUALITY

But he answered and said to one of them, "Friend, I am doing you no wrong; did you not agree with me for a denarius? Take what is yours and go your way, but I wish to give to this last man the same as to you. Is it not lawful for me to do what I wish with what is my own? Or is your eye envious because I am generous?" Thus the last shall be first, and the first last. (20:13-16)

To their charges, the owner **answered and said to one of them,** probably the spokesman for the group, **"Friend, I am doing you no wrong; did you not agree with me for a denarius?"** *Hetairos* (**friend**) is not the term for a close friend but rather a casual companion. The owner let them know firmly but courteously that they were out of line. He was **doing** them **no wrong,** because they had a clear agreement early in the morning at the market place (v. 2) that they would be paid **a denarius** apiece, a fair wage. "You worked the twelve hours you agreed to work," he said, "and I paid you the **denarius** I agreed to pay you. We both lived up to our sides of the bargain, and therefore you have no legitimate complaint. **Take what is yours and go your way.** It should not be your concern, if **I wish to give to this last man the same as to you."**

More than that, he asked rhetorically, **"Is it not lawful for me to do what I wish with what is my own?"** What he paid the late-coming workers, or any others, was strictly his own business, and he was perfectly within his **lawful** rights. He could do whatever he might **wish with what** were his **own** assets.

The problem was not injustice on the part of the landowner and foreman but jealousy on the part of the workers. **"Is your eye envious because I am generous?"** the owner asked the angry spokesman. As he had just reminded the group, he completely lived up to their mutual agreement, and that should have been their only concern. But jealousy and envy are not based on reason but on selfishness. The charge of unfairness was not grounded in a love for justice but in the selfish assumption that the extra pay they *wanted* was pay they *deserved*. In reality, of course, what the latter-day workers were paid had absolutely no bearing on what the all-day workers were paid. They had, as it were, entirely separate contracts with the owner.

But selfishness sees what it wants to see, and all those envious men could see was that they did not receive the grand bonus they expected and thought they deserved. It was not that they did not get the wage that they earned and had agreed upon but that they could not stand seeing someone who was hired at the last minute get paid the same as they did. Instead of rejoicing at the good fortune of their co-workers, they envied them and were bitter. It is possible that the eleventh-hour workers were less capable and more needy than the all-day men, who probably were hired first because they were the best workers. The other men had a hard time finding work at all, and when they did it may have been menial, demanding, and low-paying. But regardless of the differences between the men's situations, capabilities, accomplishments, or needs, none of them was wrongly paid. In fact, all of them were well paid by a man who was not obligated to hire them in the first place.

Although the parable includes clear warnings about impugning the fairness of someone and about the ugly sin of envy, its primary point is that of the owner's right to pay all the workers the same wage. Jesus, of course, was not teaching economic or business principles but rather using such principles to teach an infinitely more wonderful spiritual truth.

To understand the parable's spiritual meaning it is necessary to understand who and what are represented in it. Jesus explicitly said the parable is about "the kingdom of heaven" (v. 1). The vineyard is therefore the kingdom itself, the landowner is God the Father, and the foreman is the Son, Jesus Christ. The laborers are believers, and the denarius is eternal life, which all received equally for trusting in Christ. The work day is the believer's lifetime of service to his Lord and the evening is eternity.

God's sovereign principle for salvation is that every person who comes in faith to His Son, Jesus Christ, receives the same gracious salvation prepared by the Father and given by the Son. There are no exceptions or variations. Whether a person comes to God as a small child and lives a long life of faithful, obedient service, or whether he comes to Him on his deathbed, all come into the kingdom on the same basis and receive the same glorious, eternal blessings. The penitent thief who turned to Jesus on the cross with his last breath received the same salvation and heavenly glory as the apostles. He died justly as a criminal, whereas most of them died unjustly because of their faithfulness to Christ. He did not have even one hour to serve Christ, whereas some of them served Him far into old age. He knew just enough about Christ to be saved, and his service was limited to a brief time of praise and thankfulness, whereas the disciples were privileged to live intimately with Him for three years and were given unique divine revelation from and about Him. Yet all of them were received equally by their divine Savior and King and stand equally before Him in heaven.

The Lord will indeed *reward* His saints at His coming (cf. 1 Cor. 4:5; Rev.

22:12) according to their faithfulness. As Jesus had taught earlier, "The Son of Man is going to come in the glory of His Father with His angels; and will then recompense every man according to his deeds" (Matt. 16:27; cf. 5:12; 6:4; 10:42). "Each man's work will become evident," Paul declared, "for the day will show it, because it is to be revealed with fire; and the fire itself will test the quality of each man's work. If any man's work which he has built upon it remains, he shall receive a reward. If any man's work is burned up, he shall suffer loss; but he himself shall be saved, yet so as through fire" (1 Cor. 3:13-15). But individual rewards are another matter completely and relate to the specific nature of our faithfulness and diligence in serving Christ on earth. The subject of the parable of the landowner is not personal rewards that will determine the nature and scope of our ruling and serving in eternity but rather the common blessedness of eternity that will belong to all believers.

Here the Lord is not teaching about the differences of rewards but the equality of salvation. He is saying that Christians who have spent a life of ease and spiritual indolence have the same eternal salvation as those who suffer a martyr's death. The immature, weak, and disobedient Christian has the same prospect of inheriting the kingdom as one who is mature, self-giving, and spiritual. All believers will receive "the crown of life" (James 1:12; Rev. 2:10), "the crown of righteousness" (2 Tim. 4:8), and the "crown of glory" (1 Pet. 5:4). The Greek genitives of apposition behind each of those three phrases refer to the future blessing of *all* believers— eternal life, eternal righteousness, and eternal glory!

From a human perspective, that seems inequitable; but from the divine perspective, it is totally just. Because no person is worthy of salvation, eternal life is a gracious gift for which only Jesus Christ could have paid the cost. Differences among human beings are infinitely smaller than the difference between even the most righteous human being and God. Before receiving Christ as Lord and Savior all men are equally lost, and after they receive Him they are equally saved. Relative merit is irrelevant, because all that even the greatest human righteousness can merit is damnation. "All our righteous deeds are like a filthy garment," Isaiah declared (Isa. 64:6). By God's perfect standard of righteousness, no person comes to Christ with more or less merit, and no one is received by Him with more or less grace.

How wonderful that truth is. The Christian who is envious of other Christians, for whatever reason, not only is unspiritual but foolish. If God really did give him what he deserved, he would be destined for hell rather than for heaven. The spiritual believer rejoices in the salvation of others, no matter what the circumstances of their conversion. If he sees someone come to Christ on a deathbed, after a life of profligacy and infidelity, he rejoices with the angels in heaven that one more sinner has repented (Luke 15:10) and that God has again been glorified through His marvelous grace.

A pastor friend told me that his father not only had been an unbeliever all his life but was a vocal Christ rejecter, openly criticizing the things of God and wanting no part of the gospel. When his father was hospitalized with a severe stroke and no longer able to communicate, the son again presented the gospel to him as he had many times before. "I witnessed to him with all my heart," he said. "I told him how he could embrace Christ even at this point in his life, even though he had so strongly rejected Him. I don't know whether he did or not, because he had no way of letting me know. But I know that if he did believe he will inherit the same eternal life that I have. And how I hope that he did."

Jesus told the parable of the landowner in response to Peter's query in behalf of the apostles about what was in store for them, which, in turn, was in response to Jesus' teaching about the impossibility of entering the kingdom by human means or effort. The apostles represented the all-day workers who began at 6:00 a.m. and stayed on the job until 6:00 p.m. They had forsaken everything to follow Christ and had been with Him for nearly three years. Although they had suffered nothing like they would suffer a few years later, they nonetheless had endured considerable hardship and ridicule for the Lord's sake. Their faith was genuine and they truly loved Christ.

But as events would soon prove, they were still terribly self-centered. Only a day or so later, the mother of James and John, no doubt with their approval and perhaps even at their request, asked Jesus to promise that in His kingdom "these two sons of mine may sit, one on Your right and one on Your left" (Matt. 20:20-21). Jesus had just spoken again of His imminent suffering and death, yet the minds of these two disciples were on their own personal aggrandizement. They were playing one-upmanship while their master was at that very time on His way to Jerusalem to be crucified (v. 18-19). When the other disciples heard what had happened, they "became indignant with the two brothers" (v. 24). But their indignation was far from righteous. As they would soon demonstrate, they were just as ambitious as James and John. Not many weeks later, in the Upper Room a few hours before Jesus' arrest, the disciples were still arguing among themselves "as to which one of them was regarded to be greatest" (Luke 22:24).

After Jesus had arisen and appeared to the disciples and they had gotten over the shock of His crucifixion, their minds returned again to their own selfish, worldly ambitions. In light of everything they had said and done before, their question, "Lord, is it at this time You are restoring the kingdom to Israel?" (Acts 1:6) was no doubt centered more on the prospects for their own glory than on Christ's.

In the parable of the gracious landowner Jesus was dealing with the selfish, indulgent, envious, and ambitious orientation of the disciples. He wanted them to see, and He wants all His followers to see, that salvation is not in any way deserved or earned. It is the free gift of God, dispensed sovereignly and impartially to whomever believes in His Son.

Believing tax collectors, prostitutes, criminals, and social outcasts will have the same heavenly residence as Paul, Augustine, Luther, and Wesley. There are no servant quarters or lower-class neighborhoods in heaven. Everyone will have a room in the Father's house specially prepared for him by the Son (John 14:2). Every believer is a part of the church, which is the bride of Christ (Rev. 21:2, 9), every believer is a child of God and a fellow heir with Christ (Rom. 8:16-17), and every believer is blessed "with every spiritual blessing in the heavenly places in Christ" (Eph. 1:3). It is not that every believer receives an equal *part* but that every believer receives equally *the whole* of God's grace and blessing. Just as hell is the total absence of God, heaven is the total presence of God. And every one of His children will enjoy equally the fullness of His presence there. Everyone who belongs to God has all of God. That great reality is summed up in the truth of John's marvelous declaration, "We shall be like Him, because we shall see Him just as He is" (1 John 3:2).

From this parable flow many spiritual principles that are closely related to the central truth that the gift of eternal life is equal for all believers. First is the principle that God sovereignly initiates and accomplishes salvation. The landowner went out looking for workers, and it was he who asked them to labor in his vineyard. And because God does the seeking and the saving in His own initiative and power, we have no demands on His special favor or privilege. Every person who believes has first been sought out by the Father and given to the Son (John 6:39). And whether He sought us early in our lives or late, and whether we answered His call early or late, all merit and glory belongs to Him.

A second principle is that God alone establishes the terms of salvation. Because the laborers in the vineyard came at different times, they worked a different number of hours, and we can assume they worked with many different degrees of productivity. But they did not receive different pay. The measure of God's gift of salvation is not man's merit or accomplishments but His own grace, which does not vary.

A third principle is that God continues to call men into His kingdom. He keeps going back and going back into the market places of the world calling men to Himself. And He will continue to call until the last hour of this age. The night of judgment is coming when no man can work, but while it is day, the Father will continue to draw men to Himself. "My Father is working until now, and I Myself am working," Jesus said (John 5:17), because the Lord does not wish "for any to perish but for all to come to repentance" (2 Pet. 3:9).

A fourth principle is that God redeems everyone who is willing. "The one who comes to Me I will certainly not cast out," Jesus said (John 6:37, 39). All the laborers who went to the vineyard recognized they were needy. They had no hope of work except what the landowner would give them, and they received it gladly and thankfully. They had given up dependence on their own resources and looked only to him.

A fifth principle is that God is compassionate to those who have no resources and acknowledge their hopelessness. He reaches out to those in need who know they are in need. When the men in the last group told the landowner they were standing idle because no one would hire them, he hired them. And when anyone comes to God knowing he has no other prospect for life but Him, the Lord will always lovingly and mercifully accept that person for His own.

A sixth principle is that all who come into the vineyard worked. They may have come at the last hour, but they worked. Even the penitent thief on the cross, who died within hours if not moments after confessing his faith in Christ, still testifies today to the saving grace of God. The history of the church is replete with stories of those whose deathbed conversions were used by God to lead others to Himself.

A seventh principle is that God has the divine authority and ability to keep His promises. At every hour of the day that the landowner went to the market place, he hired all who wanted to work, and at the end of the day there was no shortage of funds to pay each one the full amount. Christ's sacrifice on the cross was sufficient to pay for the sins of the whole world, from the Fall of Adam until the day of judgment. If any person is not saved it is because he will not be saved. Man's sin can never outstrip God's grace, because where sin increases, grace increases all the more (Rom. 5:20).

An eighth principle is that, just as God always gives what He has promised, He also always gives more than is deserved. The 6:00 a.m. workers were envious of those who came at 5:00 p.m. because, in their selfish view, they deserved to be paid more. But the landowner was no more obligated to hire the first workers than the others. He would have been entirely justified to have passed them all by, and all of them were paid more than they were worth. In an infinitely greater way, no believer is qualified to receive God's least favor, much less salvation, and even the best person by human standards is blessed immeasurably beyond what he could possibly deserve.

A ninth principle, which is a corollary of the previous one, is that humility and a genuine sense of unworthiness is the only right attitude in which a person may come to the Lord. Like the elder brother who was resentful when the prodigal son returned home and was royally received by their father, the early workers lost some of their humility at the end of the day because of their jealousy. But they had come to the vineyard in the same attitude of submissiveness in which the others came.

A tenth and final principle is that of God's sovereign, overarching grace. From beginning to end, the parable pictures God's divine, boundless grace. The men's work had absolutely no relationship to what they were paid. Even less do men's works of supposed righteousness have any relationship to what they receive through faith in Jesus Christ. Just as sin is the great equalizer that causes every man to "fall short of the glory of God" (Rom. 3:23), God's grace is the great equalizer that removes sin and makes every believer equally acceptable to Him in Christ.

The Sufferings of Christ
(20:17-19)

And as Jesus was about to go up to Jerusalem, He took the twelve disciples aside by themselves, and on the way He said to them. "Behold, we are going up to Jerusalem; and the Son of Man will be delivered to the chief priests and scribes, and they will condemn Him to death, and will deliver Him to the Gentiles to mock and scourge and crucify Him, and on the third day He will be raised up." (20:17-19)

In this passage Jesus gives the third (see 16:21; 17:22-23) and last prediction of His impending suffering, death, and resurrection. Both His words and the truths they convey are simple, clear, and explicit. He was not speaking in a parable or in figures of speech but in very ordinary, unambiguous terms. He was not revealing a mystery or explaining deep theological truths. He was simply stating what would soon become historical facts.

The death and resurrection of Jesus Christ form the central events of biblical revelation in both the Old and New Testaments. It is those two historical events, and certain others surrounding them, that Jesus now again predicts to the Twelve as being imminent.

Throughout history, some people have portrayed Jesus as a well-meaning, loving, gentle, peaceful, but naive visionary who somehow got caught in a hostile world and accidentally wound up being crucified. Others have less generously pictured Him as a self-styled, would-be conqueror who tried to pull off a coup of sorts and became a victim of His own ambition.

But such views do not reflect at all the biblical record. The suffering and death of Christ were no miscalculation or accident. They were not the least surprising to Jesus. On the contrary, He knew about them even before His murderers had thought of their evil plans. The Messiah's suffering and death were planned by our holy God ages before they were plotted in the minds of evil men. Jesus' first recorded words were, "I must be about My Father's business" (Luke 2:49, KJV), and among His last words before His death were, "It is finished!" (John 19:30). Jesus knew why He was on earth, including every detail of His life and ministry. And because He had that divine foreknowledge, He must have endured many sufferings a thousand times in His mind before they transpired in His life.

Clearly the Lord wanted the disciples to understand what He would soon face, as well as prepare them for what would also be a time of severe suffering and danger for them. More than that, He wanted them to understand that these things, evil as they were, were nevertheless a part of God's great redemptive plan and were the very reason He had come to earth.

Jesus knew how difficult it was for the disciples to comprehend what He was trying to tell them. They were so attuned to the popular Jewish concepts of the glorious, conquering, reigning Messiah that anything He taught to the contrary seemed to go by them. To most Jews of that day, just as to most Jews of our own time, the idea of a suffering and dying Messiah was unthinkable, an absolute self-contradiction. Like their fellow Jews, the disciples were looking for a lion, not a lamb.

So for the third time it is recorded that the Lord calls them aside and seeks to impress on them the reality of what is about to happen to Him. First He assures them that these events are a part of God's revealed plan. Then He gives detailed predictions of the particular events, and finally an idea of the proportion and power of the sufferings He would endure.

THE PLAN OF HIS SUFFERING

And as Jesus was about to go up to Jerusalem, He took the twelve disciples aside by themselves, and on the way He said to them. "Behold, we are going up to Jerusalem; (20:17-18a)

Jesus had finished His Galilean ministry and had crossed into Perea, on the other side of the Jordan River (19:1). As Jewish travelers from Galilee often did in order to avoid going through Samaria, Jesus traveled down the east side of the Jordan and crossed over to Jericho (20:29). From there He would **go up to Jerusalem.**

Jericho is near the northern end of the Dead Sea, which is over 1,000 feet below sea level. Although **Jerusalem** is only 14 miles due west of the Dead Sea, it is at an elevation of 2,500 feet above sea level, making the trip **up** from Jericho quite steep.

The fact that Jesus **took the twelve disciples aside by themselves** indicates they were traveling in the company of others, probably a large crowd. Some of the group doubtlessly had been following Jesus for some time (cf. v. 29), and others were part of the thousands of Jews making the yearly Passover pilgrimage to Jerusalem who found themselves in the company of this astounding Teacher and Healer. But His public ministry was nearing an end, and He devoted the great majority of His time to private instruction of the **disciples.**

Behold was a common exclamation, a means of calling special attention to something of importance. In this context it also carried the idea of resolution and conviction. Even more than on the earlier occasion that Luke describes, Jesus now "resolutely set His face to go to Jerusalem" (Luke 9:51). He did not plan to go alone, but told the Twelve, **"We are going up to Jerusalem."**

As already noted, they still had great difficulty accepting the idea of a suffering and dying Messiah, and it was common knowledge that the Jewish leaders in **Jerusalem** sought to kill Him. Therefore the disciples "were amazed, and those who followed were fearful" (Mark 10:32). They thought it not only unnecessary but foolhardy for Jesus even to think of going to Jerusalem.

The Greek word behind *amazed* is *thambeō,* which refers to great astonishment or bewilderment, and sometimes even carried the idea of immobility because of fright. It denoted complete inability to correctly comprehend and react to an idea or event. The disciples had witnessed nearly three years of Jesus' divine, miraculous power and of hearing His authoritative teaching. They had left everything for Him and had put themselves completely into His care. Now everything seemed hopeless and pointless, and they could make no sense at all of what was happening.

The disciples were so disbelieving and confused that they had perhaps given up, emotionally if not intellectually, on the idea of an immediate inauguration of the kingdom. Yet they could not imagine what the alternative might be. Jesus was doing nothing to establish a political following and certainly was not raising up an army. If He was powerless against the Jewish establishment, He was totally insignificant as far as the Roman government was concerned. To go to Jerusalem was certain death, and "Thomas therefore, who is called Didymus, said to his fellow disciples, 'Let us also go, that we may die with Him'" (John 11:16). The most positive attitude they could muster was a heroic but hopeless resignation to go and die with their Master.

Mark reports that Jesus was walking ahead of the disciples and the crowd (Mark 10:32). It was as if He were a military commander going into battle at the head of his troops, bravely putting himself in the most dangerous and vulnerable position. But Jesus had no troops and no weapons, only a small band of confused, helpless disciples and a thrill-seeking multitude that would flee at the first sign of danger.

Yet it was the divine plan that Jesus go **to Jerusalem** in order that "all things which are written through the prophets about the Son of Man will be accomplished" (Luke 18:31). Going to Jerusalem was no accident, no quirk of fate. Jesus would not be caught off guard and unexpectedly trapped there by His enemies. The Lord not only knew of but foretold those events through His prophets. Now He moved resolutely toward their fulfillment. They were, indeed, the very culmination of the redemptive plan of God.

Through Moses, God had predicted that none of the Messiah's bones would be broken (Ex. 12:46). Through the psalmists, He predicted that, on the cross, the Messiah would be pierced (22:16), that lots would be cast for His garments (22:18), that He would be given vinegar to drink (69:21), that He would cry out in pain (22:1), that He would rise from the dead (16:10), and that He would ascend into heaven (110:1). Zechariah predicted the Messiah's entering Jerusalem on a colt (Zech. 9:9), His betrayal for 30 pieces of silver (11:12), His desertion by His friends (13:7), and His being pierced (12:10).

The whole sweep and flow of the Old Testament in its types and symbols demanded that the Messiah, the Lord's Anointed, die for the sins of a world that could never itself atone for those sins. The death of Christ has been called the scarlet thread of Scripture, the supreme truth around which all others are woven.

When Adam and Eve sinned, they immediately became aware of their nakedness, and to provide them clothing of skins, animals had to be killed. From the beginning, guilt and shame had to be covered by sacrifice. That was the first great principle of redemption taught in Scripture. But those skins, like all the countless sacrifices thereafter, were only symbolic. They could cover man's nakedness but not his sin.

The second great principle of redemption that God revealed is that He Himself will provide the necessary sacrifice for man. God commanded Abraham to sacrifice Isaac, his only son through whom the divine promise could be fulfilled. Abraham was able to raise the knife and be willing to plunge it into Isaac's heart because of his sure belief that God could raise his son from the dead (Heb. 11:19). When the Lord stayed Abraham's hand and provided a ram to take Isaac's place on the altar, Abraham named that place of sacrifice, "The Lord Will Provide" (Gen. 22:14).

The third great principle of redemption God revealed was that acceptable sacrifice had to be unblemished. When the death angel was about to pass over Egypt, striking dead all the first-born, God provided for the Israelites to be protected by smearing the blood of an unblemished lamb on their doorposts and lintels (Ex. 12:5-7).

During the wilderness wanderings, God revealed to Moses the fourth great principle of sacrifice: that it is the central act of acceptable worship. In the details of the intricate sacrificial system, God showed Israel that sacrifice would be inherent in every act of true worship, because it opened the way to God.

But in the requirements and rituals of the Old Testament, those principles were only pictured. No sacrifice offered by man could cover sin, provide a substitute for himself, be morally and spiritually unblemished, or become an acceptable act of worship to God. Only God Himself could present such a sacrifice, and it is that divine sacrifice to whom all the other sacrifices pointed. And when that perfect sacrifice was made, the others no longer had significance. When Jesus died on the cross, the veil of the Temple was torn in two and the validity of the sacrificial system ended. Less than forty years later, with the total destruction of the Temple in A.D. 70, even the possibility of other Old Testament sacrifices ended.

The disciples knew they were going to Jerusalem to celebrate the Passover with Jesus, but they did not know that Jesus was Himself God's ultimate and only true Passover Lamb. They were still thinking lion, but He was thinking Lamb. They were thinking kingdom, but He was thinking sacrifice. They were thinking glory, but He was thinking suffering and death.

The disciples did not fully understand what the Old Testament taught about the Messiah, and they did not understand what Jesus Himself repeatedly told them about Himself. Even after the resurrection He rebuked two of the disciples for their lack of comprehension of what Scripture had long before revealed. "O foolish men and slow of heart to believe in all that the prophets have spoken! Was it not necessary for the Christ to suffer these things and to enter into His glory?" (Luke 24:25-26). A short while later He told the eleven and some other believers gathered with them in Jerusalem, "Thus it is written, that the Christ should suffer and rise again from the dead the third day" (v. 46).

Paul had to remind the Corinthian Christians of the central truth he had taught them many times before: that "Christ died for our sins according to the Scriptures, and that He was buried, and that He was raised on the third day according to the Scriptures" (1 Cor. 15:3-4). Many years later, Peter reminded the believers to whom he wrote that "As to this salvation, the prophets who prophesied of the grace that would come to you made careful search and inquiry, seeking to know what person or time the Spirit of Christ within them was indicating as He predicted the sufferings of Christ and the glories to follow" (1 Pet. 1:10-11).

Jesus' suffering and death were always in God's plan. When Jesus was only a few weeks old and was brought by His parents to the Temple to be presented to the Lord, the godly Simeon told Mary, "Behold, this Child is appointed for the fall and rise of many in Israel, and for a sign to be opposed—and a sword will pierce even your own soul" (Luke 2:34-35). John the Baptist announced Jesus' ministry by declaring, "Behold, the Lamb of God who takes away the sin of the world!" (John 1:29), and every Jew who heard that message knew John was speaking of a sacrificed lamb. In his great vision on the Island of Patmos, the apostle John saw "a Lamb standing, as if slain," and heard a great host of angels "saying with a loud voice, 'Worthy is the Lamb that was slain'" (Rev. 5:6, 12).

Jesus was going to Jerusalem because that is where He was to sacrifice Himself for the sins of the world, in perfect accordance with God's revealed plan.

THE PREDICTIONS OF HIS SUFFERING

and the Son of Man will be delivered to the chief priests and scribes, and they will condemn Him to death, and will deliver Him to the Gentiles (20:18b-19a)

By His own divine omniscience, Jesus knew how many husbands the woman at Sychar had, although He had never met or heard of her before (John 4:16-18). He told the disciples exactly what they would find when He sent them into Jerusalem to find a colt (Matt. 21:2). He forecast the destruction of Jerusalem nearly forty years before it would occur (Matt. 24:1-2). Now Jesus omnisciently adds additional details of His suffering and death to the many prophecies of the Old Testament.

Jesus referred to Himself or was referred to by the gospel writers some eighty times as **the Son of Man,** an Old Testament title that connoted the Messiah's divinity but emphasized His incarnation and humiliation. As the divine/human **Son of Man,** Jesus declared that He would **be delivered to the chief priests and scribes.**

The Lord made no mention of the one by whom He would **be delivered,** although He knew it would be Judas. That is why some translators have chosen to render the verb as "betrayed," instead of the more literal **delivered** or "handed over."

The Jewish priesthood was composed of several ranks and levels. The Levites were the lowest level and numbered in the many thousands. They did not perform priestly functions as such but were responsible for serving the priests. The ordinary priests served in various capacities in the Tabernacle and later the Temple. By New Testament times a group had developed called **the chief priests,** who were the hereditary aristocracy of the priesthood. The highest position within that group was that of the high priest, an office handed down from father to son.

Next in importance among the Jewish religious leaders were the **scribes,** who gained their positions not by heredity but by learning. They were authorities on the Old Testament, especially the Mosaic law, as well as on the thousands of rabbinical traditions they had developed over the past several hundred years since the return from Babylon. **Scribes** were often called lawyers, rabbis, or doctors and, as is abundantly evident from the gospels, were closely associated with the Pharisees.

The chief priests and scribes therefore respectively comprised the hereditary and the intellectual aristocracy of Judaism. That elite group of religious leaders came to vehemently hate and oppose Jesus because He threatened their hypocritical and ungodly system of power. And as the executive body of the high Jewish council, the Sanhedrin, they would soon **condemn Him to death.**

Because Rome did not allow subject nations to impose the death penalty, the Jewish religious leaders could **condemn** Jesus **to death** but could not execute **Him** without Roman approval. It was therefore necessary for them to **deliver Him to the** pagan Roman **Gentiles** in order to carry out their murderous scheme. And because they could not convince Pilate, the Roman governor, that Jesus' religious offenses deserved the death penalty, they resorted to blackmail. "If you release this Man," they told the governor, "you are no friend of Caesar; everyone who makes himself out to be a king opposes Caesar" (John 19:12).

THE PROPORTION AND POWER OF HIS SUFFERING

to mock and scourge and crucify Him, and on the third day He will be raised up. (20:19b)

The first phrase describes what might be called the proportion of Jesus' suffering, the degree of agony to which He was unjustly but willingly condemned.

While Jesus was being held by the Gentile Roman authorities, they proceeded to **mock and scourge** Him, as the custom was with prisoners who were not Roman citizens, even if they had not been convicted of a crime. First Pilate had Jesus scourged with leather whips in which sharp pieces of bone and metal were embedded. Then his soldiers "took Jesus into the Praetorium and gathered the whole Roman cohort around Him. And they stripped Him, and put a scarlet robe on Him. And after weaving a crown of thorns, they put it on His head, and a reed in His right hand; and they kneeled down before Him and mocked Him, saying, 'Hail, King of the Jews!' And they spat on Him, and took the reed and began to beat Him on the head" (Matt. 27:26-30). Only after that painful humiliation did they take Him away **and crucify Him.**

It is significant that, when referring to Christ's sufferings before and during His crucifixion, the New Testament always uses the plural (see 2 Cor. 1:5; Phil. 3:10; Heb. 2:10; 1 Pet. 1:11; 4:13). His pain was not one dimensional, but involved sufferings of many sorts.

The physical pain of crucifixion was excruciating, which was the reason why it was Rome's preferred means of execution for enemies of the state. But by itself it was not always fatal, and there are numerous historical records of men surviving it. When they wanted death to be certain, the victim was scourged beforehand. The great loss of blood, as well as frequent exposure of internal organs, not only greatly increased suffering but assured death.

Jesus' physical sufferings cannot be minimized. He felt every sting of the reed and every cut of the lash. He felt the agony of His bruised and lacerated muscles trying to carry the heavy cross out of the city and up to Golgotha. He felt the surges of pain as the nails were driven through His hands and feet and He was hoisted to an upright position so that the entire weight of his body rested on those nails. He suffered great thirst, which was yet exceeded by the suffocating pull of His body against His lungs.

But the greatest sufferings He endured were not physical but emotional and spiritual, just as Isaiah had vividly predicted.

> He has no stately form or majesty that we should look upon Him, nor appearance that we should be attracted to Him. He was despised and forsaken of men, a man of sorrows, and acquainted with grief; and like one from whom men hide their face, He was despised, and we did not esteem Him. Surely our griefs He Himself bore, and our sorrows He carried; yet we ourselves esteemed Him stricken, smitten of God, and afflicted. But He was pierced through for our transgressions, He was crushed for our iniquities; the chastening for our well-being fell upon Him, and by His scourging we are healed. . . . The Lord has caused the iniquity of us all to fall on Him. He was oppressed and He was afflicted, yet He did not open His mouth. . . . He was cut off out of the land of the living, for the transgression of my people to whom the stroke was due. (Isa. 53:2-8)

As the prophet makes clear, Jesus' sufferings went much deeper than the physical. The Messiah would endure inner sufferings far more devastating than the pain in His body. He had to suffer as a sinless Man for the offenses of sinful men who despised and rejected Him. He was, indeed, stricken even by His own heavenly Father in order that He could bear the penalty that fallen man deserved but could not survive. "The Lord was pleased to crush Him, putting Him to grief; if He would render Himself as a guilt offering. . . . He poured out Himself to death, and was numbered with the transgressors; yet He Himself bore the sin of many, and interceded for the transgressors" (Isa. 53:10, 12).

Jesus suffered the pain of disloyalty. It was one of His own disciples, one of the specially chosen Twelve, who betrayed Him to the chief priests. He could declare with the psalmist, "Even my close friend, in whom I trusted, who ate my bread, has lifted up his heel against me" (Ps. 41:9). One whom He had called, taught, and loved had turned against Him and delivered Him into the hands of His enemies. The anguish of betrayal must have cut deeply into Jesus' heart many times before the night when the wicked deed was actually committed. He not only was betrayed by a friend but with a kiss. There can be little human suffering more overwhelming than that caused by someone close and dear who violates the intimacy and trust of friendship even to the point of treachery.

Jesus also suffered the pain of rejection. He was turned over to the chief priests and scribes, who, in the name of all Israel, God's own chosen people, rejected His messiahship and treated Him instead as a criminal worthy of death. He was the Stone the builders rejected. The Redeemer of Israel "came to His own, and those who were His own did not receive Him" (John 1:11). His disciples fled from Him, ashamed even to be called His friends, much less His servants. He had to endure the rejection even of His own Father, who could not look upon the sin borne in the body of the Son.

Jesus suffered the pain of humiliation. He was mocked by the leaders of His own people and then mocked by the Gentiles to whom they sent Him. Those pagans humiliated Him with a mock crown, a mock scepter, a mock robe of royalty, and mock obeisance. They scorned Him, spat on His face, and nailed Him naked to a cross for the world to behold.

Jesus suffered the pain of unjust guilt. The guilt He took upon Himself and for which He suffered and died was not His own. It was for the sins of others that He paid the penalty. All the guilt of all the people who had ever lived and who would ever live was placed on Him. It was perhaps the prospect of bearing that guilt and shame that caused the sin-despising Christ to sweat great drops of blood as He prayed that last night in Gethsemane.

Jesus suffered the pain of injury. As already noted, Roman scourging was done with a whip tipped with sharp bits of bone and metal that tore deep gashes into the flesh and even into the organs and bones of the victim. The customary ordeal consisted of forty lashes, administered with such intensity that it often required a second man to finish the beating. Because of the extreme shock and profuse bleeding, victims frequently died before the full number of lashes could be applied.

Finally, Jesus suffered the pain of death itself. Physiologically, it may have been from suffocation that He died. But the most painful suffering that killed Him was the cumulative grief He had to endure as penalty for the sins of mankind. To save the lost whom He loved with infinite love, He had to become for them the sin He hated with infinite hatred. God "made Him who knew no sin to be sin on our behalf, that we might become the righteousness of God in Him" (2 Cor. 5:21).

But contrary to what both His friends and His enemies thought, Jesus' death was not the end. The Father would never allow His "Holy One to undergo decay" (Ps. 16:10). Therefore, **on the third day** Jesus would **be raised up,** never to face suffering or death again. He died to conquer sin and its penalty, which is death. He died that those who believe in Him would never have to die.

How to Be Great in the Kingdom

(20:20-28)

22

Then the mother of the sons of Zebedee came to Him with her sons, bowing down, and making a request of Him. And He said to her, "What do you wish?" She said to Him, "Command that in Your kingdom these two sons of mine may sit, one on Your right and one on Your left." But Jesus answered and said, "You do not know what you are asking for. Are you able to drink the cup that I am about to drink?" They said to Him, "We are able." He said to them, "My cup you shall drink; but to sit on My right and on My left, this is not Mine to give, but it is for those for whom it has been prepared by My Father." And hearing this, the ten became indignant with the two brothers. But Jesus called them to Himself, and said, "You know that the rulers of the Gentiles lord it over them, and their great men exercise authority over them. It is not so among you, but whoever wishes to become great among you shall be your servant, and whoever wishes to be first among you shall be your slave; just as the Son of Man did not come to be served, but to serve, and to give His life a ransom for many." (20:20-28)

We live in a proud and egotistical generation. People push and promote themselves in ways that would have been abhorrent and totally unacceptable only a generation ago. Yet in a great part of modern culture, pride and high self-esteem have come to be redefined not only as virtues but as the supreme virtues.

Our day is reminiscent of the time in history when at the height of the ancient Greek and Roman empires pride was exalted and humility belittled. This tragic development will surely contribute to the demise of modern society as it did to the demise of Greece and Rome. No society can survive the self-destructiveness of pride run rampant, because every society depends for its preservation and success on the mutually supportive and harmonious relationships among its people. When a significant number of them become committed only to themselves and to their own interests, with little regard for their families, friends, neighbors, and fellow citizens, society disintegrates. As self becomes stronger, relationships become weaker. As self-rights become supreme, the interpersonal bonds that hold society together are severed.

The promotion of self-esteem, self-fulfillment, and self-glory has become a major industry that ranges from exercise programs to motivation for executive success. Tragically, the cult of selfism has found its way into evangelical Christianity. Books, seminars, conferences, magazines, and organizations that promote self under the guise of personal spiritual development abound. The movement has found little resistance in the church, which often seems determined to beat the world at its own fleshly game. From countless sources, claims are heard that God's great design for His people is health, prosperity, success, happiness, and self-fulfillment. The Bible's teaching of suffering and cross-bearing for Christ's sake are either ignored altogether or foolishly explained away. A weak gospel, easy believism, and nonsacrificial Christian living are the reflections of this new "evangelical" selfism.

Whenever the church has been spiritually strong it has distrusted its own wisdom and strength and looked to the Lord's, it has shunned its own glory and sought only His, and it has condemned pride and exalted humility. Times of spiritual awakening are inevitably characterized by a sincere sense of brokenness, contrition, and unworthiness. There is always reverential fear of the Word of God, which, working through genuine meekness, gives the church great power. Like Paul, the church becomes strong when it knows it is weak (2 Cor. 12:10).

But a great part of the western church has become self-indulgent, self-satisfied, and self-reliant, claiming numerical and financial growth as evidence of spiritual blessing. It has replaced sacrifice with success, suffering with self-satisfaction, and godly obedience with fleshly indulgence.

Yet the Bible's testimony is clear and consistent. It was out of pride that Adam and Eve doubted God, believed Satan, and relied on their own judgment, and since that time pride has continued to be the chief characteristic of fallen, sinful mankind. The book of Proverbs warns that "a proud heart, the lamp of the wicked, is sin" (Prov. 21:4), that "everyone who is proud in heart is an abomination to the Lord" (16:5), and that "the fear of the Lord is to hate evil . . . pride, arrogance, and the evil way" (8:13). Insolence, arrogance, and boasting have always been marks of a depraved, reprobate mind (Rom. 1:30). Conceit is a favorite trap of Satan, even for believers, and has always been a trait of false teachers (1 Tim. 3:6; 6:4). "The boastful pride of life is not from the Father, but is from the world," John declared (1 John 2:16).

Since the first rebellion in the Garden, God has sternly resisted the proud (James 4:6; Ps. 138:6), brought them into contempt (Isa. 23:9), abased them (Ps. 18:27), judged them (Ps. 31:23), humbled them (Dan. 4:37), scattered them (Luke 1:51), and punished them (Mal. 4:1). By the same token, God has always honored humility and meekness. "He regards the lowly" (Ps. 138:6), hears "the desire of the humble" (Ps. 10:17), and values humility even above honor (Prov. 15:33). The Lord intends humility to be part of His children's daily clothing (Col. 3:12; 1 Pet. 5:5) and daily living (Eph. 4:1-2). He seeks to bless that one "who is humble and contrite of spirit, and who trembles at [His] word" (Isa. 66:2).

Abraham, that special servant and friend of God, humbly said, "Now behold, I have ventured to speak to the Lord, although I am but dust and ashes" (Gen. 18:27). His son Isaac was selflessly willing to die as a sacrifice to God (Gen. 22:7-9). Isaac's son Jacob cried out to God, "I am unworthy of all the lovingkindness and of all the faithfulness which Thou has shown to Thy servant" (Gen. 32:10). Jacob's son Joseph, dishonored and sold into slavery by his wicked brothers, forgave them without a trace of bitterness or revenge. When they begged him for forgiveness, he lovingly told them, "'Do not be afraid, for am I in God's place? And as for you, you meant evil against me, but God meant it for good. . . . So therefore, do not be afraid; I will provide for you and your little ones.' So he comforted them and spoke kindly to them" (Gen. 50:19-21).

Moses, the meekest man on the earth, humbly pleaded before the Lord, "Who am I, that I should go to Pharaoh, and that I should bring the sons of Israel out of Egypt?" (Ex. 3:11). After Israel's defeat at Ai because of the sin of Achan, Joshua, in humiliation in behalf of his people, "tore his clothes and fell to the earth on his face before the ark of the Lord until evening" (Josh. 7:6). David, a man after God's own heart, humbly prayed, "Thine, O Lord, is the greatness and the power and the glory and the victory and the majesty, indeed everything that is in the heavens and the earth; Thine is the dominion, O Lord, and Thou dost exalt Thyself as head over all. Both riches and honor come from Thee, and Thou dost rule over all, and in Thy hand is power and might; and it lies in Thy hand to make great, and to strengthen everyone" (1 Chron. 29:11-12).

There were also Hezekiah, king of Judah, who "humbled the pride of his heart" (2 Chron. 32:26); Manasseh, another king of Judah, who "humbled himself greatly before the God of his fathers" (2 Chron. 33:12); Josiah, king of Judah, to whom the Lord said, "Because your heart was tender and you humbled yourself before God, . . . I truly have heard you" (2 Chron. 34:27); Isaiah, who confessed, "I am a man of unclean lips" (Isa. 6:5); and many others who were great in God's sight because of their humility and their self-sacrifice for His sake.

The humility that accompanies true spiritual greatness is also illustrated throughout the New Testament. Although he was Jesus' first cousin and had been called to the exalted task of announcing and preparing the way for the Messiah,

John the Baptist humbly said, "He who is coming after me is mightier than I, and I am not fit to remove His sandals" (Matt. 3:11). It was because of such self-effacing and genuine humility that Jesus declared, "Truly I say to you, among those born of women there has not arisen anyone greater than John the Baptist" (Matt. 11:11).

Peter's first hint of greatness was expressed in his saying to Jesus, "Depart from me, for I am a sinful man, O Lord!" (Luke 5:8). And at the end of his life, when "the laying aside of [his] earthly dwelling [was] imminent," he could say of Christ with perfect sincerity, "To Him be the glory, both now and to the day of eternity" (2 Pet. 1:14; 3:18). Paul's greatness is seen in his declaring to the Ephesian elders that he had served "the Lord with all humility" (Acts 20:19).

Each of those heroes of Scripture characterized the person who is great in God's sight, because they refused to seek personal prominence but gave all prominence to the Lord. It is only the humble heart, the servant heart, that enjoys greatness in the kingdom of God.

While they were with Jesus during His earthly ministry, the twelve disciples desperately needed to learn humility. Not only did they need it for its own sake but also to enable them to understand clearly many other things their Master taught. It was not so much limited intelligence but excessive pride that prevented them from understanding and accepting Jesus' teaching about such things as servanthood, self-sacrifice, humility, persecution, and His clear and repeated predictions about His own forthcoming sufferings and death. They were too encumbered with self-promotion, self-service, self-esteem, and self-glory for those truths to penetrate their minds or hearts. They sought the high places of power and honor for themselves, with little regard for the welfare of their fellow disciples or even for their Lord.

The disciples had, indeed, left everything to follow Jesus. They had genuinely confessed Him as the Messiah and as their Lord and Savior. But, like many Christians in every age since that time, they often focused on what they would gain, revealing that they had not completely let go of pride, selfishness, and worldly standards. No doubt the greatest hindrance to their accepting the idea of a suffering, dying Messiah was that they did not *want* to believe in such a Messiah. If Jesus were to suffer and die, they feared that they would suffer the same fate. At best, they would be disgraced outcasts rather than honored rulers. They much preferred focusing on such promises as that of their one day sitting "upon twelve thrones, judging the twelve tribes of Israel" and of their receiving back many times what they had given up for Christ (Matt. 19:28-29).

Not only had Jesus told them on at least three occasions that He would be arrested and would suffer and die, but He had also told them explicitly that they should themselves expect and be willing to endure the same things. They had heard Jesus tell a certain would-be follower, "The foxes have holes, and the birds of the air have nests; but the Son of Man has nowhere to lay His head" (Matt. 8:20). He had warned the disciples, "Behold, I send you out as sheep in the midst of wolves. . . . But beware of men; for they will deliver you up to the courts, and scourge you in their synagogues; and you shall even be brought before governors and kings for My sake. . . . And you will be hated by all on account of My name" (10:16-18, 22). He had called for self-sacrifice when He told them, "He who loves father or mother more than Me is not worthy of Me; and he who loves son or daughter more than Me is not worthy of Me. And he who does not take his cross and follow after Me is not worthy of Me" (10:37-38; cf. 16:24). He had pointed them to humility when He told them, "Unless you are converted and become like children, you shall not enter the kingdom of heaven" and that "whoever then humbles himself as this child, he is the greatest in the kingdom of heaven" (18:3-4).

But the disciples persisted in bickering among themselves, in refusing to take Jesus' words at face value, and in continuing to exalt and promote their own selfish interests. Their primary concern was expressed in Peter's question to Jesus, "What then will there be for us?" (19:27).

Nineteen hundred years later, many Christians are still echoing Peter's question: "What's in it for me?" Many Christians look at grace as a free lunch, a divine open door to health, prosperity, and self-fulfillment, a celestial storehouse of good things they can order on demand from God.

John Stott has observed that "A chorus of many voices is chanting in unison today that I must at all costs love myself." In his book *The Danger of Self-Love,* Paul Brownback writes along the same line, saying, "This sudden escalation of teaching on self-love . . . was the spontaneous response of those who were firmly convinced of the solid biblical basis of self-love. And . . . almost immediately the Christian public felt warmly at home with its newfound friend; self-love has been easily incorporated into the mind-set of evangelical Christians" ([Chicago: Moody, 1982], p. 13).

Also commenting on the current cult of self-love, John Piper writes,

> Today the first and greatest commandment is, "Thou shalt love thyself." And the explanation for almost every interpersonal problem is thought to lie in someone's low self-esteem. Sermons, articles, and books have pushed this idea into the Christian mind. It is a rare congregation, for example, that does not stumble over the "vermicular theology" of Isaac Watts's "Alas! And Did My Saviour Bleed": "Would He devote that sacred head/For such a worm as I?" ("Is Self-Love Biblical?" *Christianity Today,* August 12, 1977, p. 6)

Referring to that last phrase from Watts's hymn, critics often accuse evangelicals of being victims of "worm theology," because they preach and teach the total depravity of man.

Embracing self-love is not a new danger in the church. It was clearly a threat to the unity, faithfulness, and purity of the Corinthian church and doubtlessly to many others of that day as well. Several hundred years later, Augustine wrote in his classic *The City of God:* "Two cities have been formed by two loves: the earthly by the love of self, even to the contempt of God; the heavenly by the love of God, even to the contempt of self. The former, in a word, glories in itself. The latter in the Lord."

About a thousand years later, John Calvin said, "For so blindly do we all rush in the direction of self-love that everyone thinks he has a good reason for exalting himself and despising all others in comparison." He then comments that "there is no other remedy than to pluck up by the roots those most noxious pests, self-love and love of victory. This the doctrine of Scripture does. For it teaches us to remember that the endowments which God has bestowed upon us are not our own, but His free gifts, and that those who plume themselves upon them betray their ingratitude."

Someone has wisely written,

> The cross of popular evangelicalism is not the cross of the New Testament. It is, rather, a bright ornament upon the bosom of the self-assured and carnal Christian whose hands are indeed the hands of Abel, but whose voice is the voice of Cain. The old cross slew men; the new cross entertains them. The old cross condemns; the new cross assures. The old cross destroyed confidence in the flesh; the new cross encourages it. The old cross brought tears and blood; the new cross brings laughter. The flesh, smiling and confident, preaches and sings about the cross, and before that cross it bows and toward that cross it points with carefully staged histrionics, but upon that cross it will not die and the reproach of that cross it stubbornly refuses to bear.

It is to the cross of suffering and death that Jesus calls His disciples, and to the obedience and self-giving that lead to that cross. But the believer's cross is small and his suffering insignificant compared to what his Lord's suffering and death purchased for him. "For if we died with Him," Paul assured Timothy, "we shall also live with Him; if we endure, we shall also reign with Him" (2 Tim. 2:11-12). To the Roman church he testified, "For I consider that the sufferings of this present time are not worthy to be compared with the glory that is to be revealed to us" (Rom. 8:18). And at the end of his life Peter had long since stopped asking, "What's in it for me?" Instead, he confidently counselled fellow believers: "After you have suffered for a little while, the God of all grace, who called you to His eternal glory in Christ, will Himself perfect, confirm, strengthen and establish you" (1 Pet. 5:10).

But while Jesus ministered on earth, the Twelve were far from such self-giving, self-effacing discipleship. Consequently, Jesus' third and most detailed prediction of His passion and death fell on deaf ears. No sooner had He again finished mentioning His death and resurrection than two of the disciples tried to secure from Him a place of honor and greatness for themselves in the anticipated kingdom. In that event and in Jesus' response to it we can see four wrong, worldly ways by which men pursue greatness. Following that, the Lord gave an exhortation and example of what constitutes the true greatness that God honors.

How Not to Be Great

Then the mother of the sons of Zebedee came to Him with her sons, bowing down, and making a request of Him. And He said to her, "What do you wish?" She said to Him, "Command that in Your kingdom these two

sons of mine may sit, one on Your right and one on Your left." But Jesus answered and said, "You do not know what you are asking for. Are you able to drink the cup that I am about to drink?" They said to Him, "We are able." He said to them, "My cup you shall drink; but to sit on My right and on My left, this is not Mine to give, but it is for those for whom it has been prepared by My Father." And hearing this, the ten became indignant with the two brothers. But Jesus called them to Himself, and said, "You know that the rulers of the Gentiles lord it over them, and their great men exercise authority over them. (20:20-25)

It is impossible for the principles of the world to be effective in or adaptable to God's kingdom. By their very nature they are contrary to His way and destructive of His work. They not only never produce greatness but always produce disharmony, pettiness, and spiritual weakness in the Body. In this passage four of those worldly principles are clearly seen.

POLITICAL POWER PLAY

Then the mother of the sons of Zebedee came to Him with her sons, bowing down, and making a request of Him. And He said to her, "What do you wish?" She said to Him, "Command that in Your kingdom these two sons of mine may sit, one on Your right and one on Your left." (20:20-21)

The first worldly principle for greatness might be called political power play and is reflected in the attempt of **the mother of the sons of Zebedee** to persuade Jesus to give those two **sons**, James and John, the highest places of honor in His kingdom.

Throughout history, one of the most common tactics for getting ahead has been using the influence of family and friends to one's own advantage. These people are manipulated to gain political office, a promotion in business, a lucrative contract, or whatever else is craved. As the saying goes, "It's who you know that counts." Some years ago a pastor frankly admitted that for his denomination's annual convention he always reserved a hotel room next to the leaders in order to cultivate their friendships and thereby help secure future pastorates in larger churches.

It seems incredible that James, John, and their **mother** could ask Jesus such a crass, self-serving favor immediately after His prediction of the persecution and death He would soon face in Jerusalem. There is no indication, either in this text or in Mark's parallel account (see 10:35), that any of the disciples made a response to what Jesus had just said about His own imminent death. They may simply have discounted His prediction as being merely figurative and symbolic, or they may have been so preoccupied with their own interests and plans that His words went by them. In any case, they did not pursue the subject. They did, however, continue to pursue their own interests.

From the Mark passage it is clear that **the mother** was speaking at the behest of her **two sons.** In fact, Mark makes no mention of her at all. The three obviously came with a common purpose and plan they had discussed among themselves beforehand. The mother probably spoke first, and then James and John spoke for themselves.

It is implied in Matthew but explicit in Mark that the first request was intentionally general and indefinite: "Teacher, we want You to do for us whatever we ask of You" (Mark 10:35). Their approach was like a child trying to get a parent to promise something before saying what it is for fear that a specific request for it might be denied.

The three of them may have been trying to capitalize on their family relationship to Jesus. By comparing the gospel accounts of the women who stood vigil near the cross, it becomes evident that the mother of James and John was named Salome and was a sister of Mary, the Mother of Jesus (see Matt. 27:56; Mark 15:40; John 19:25), making her Jesus' aunt and James and John His first cousins. In addition to relying on their relationship as Jesus' cousins, the brothers perhaps also thought to play on Jesus' affection for his mother by having her sister approach Him for the favor.

Bowing down was a common act of obeisance given to ancient monarchs, and the mother may have been trying to flatter Jesus by appealing to His sense of power and royalty. By treating **Him** like a king, she hoped to manipulate Him into making a gesture of magnanimity. Near Eastern kings liked to pride themselves in having the resources to grant any favor or request. It was such pride that induced Herod Antipas to swear to the daughter of Herodias, "Whatever you ask of me, I will give it to you; up to half of my kingdom" (Mark 6:23).

The fact that James, John, and their mother made **a request of** Christ for a blank check strongly suggests that they knew the request was not legitimate. The **request** was purely self-seeking, for her as well as for them. As their mother, she could bask vicariously in their exalted positions, and her own prestige would be greatly enhanced. In marked contrast to what they would become after Pentecost, James and John were not noted for their shyness or reticence, and Jesus had nicknamed them "Sons of Thunder" (Mark 3:17). Their request of Jesus not only was bold but brash. In effect, they were claiming that, of all the great people of God who had ever lived, they deserved to have the two highest places of honor beside the King of heaven.

Like the scribes and Pharisees who loved "the place of honor at banquets, and the chief seats in the synagogues" (Matt. 23:6), James and John longed for prestige and preeminence and to be exalted over the other apostles. Like the self-seeking Diotrephes (3 John 9), they loved to be first. But that is not the way to greatness in the kingdom of God.

SELF-SERVING AMBITION

But Jesus answered and said, "You do not know what you are asking for. Are you able to drink the cup that I am about to drink?" They said to Him,

"We are able." He said to them, "My cup you shall drink; but to sit on My right and on My left, this is not Mine to give, but it is for those for whom it has been prepared by My Father." And hearing this, the ten became indignant with the two brothers. (20:22-24)

These verses reflect a second wrong way to spiritual greatness, that of self-serving ambition. The request of James, John, and their mother not only was brash but foolish. Bypassing the mother, Jesus **answered** the two brothers directly **and said, "You do not know what you are asking for. Are you able to drink the cup that I am about to drink?"** The three had no idea of the full implications of their request.

The cup that Jesus was **about to drink** was the cup of suffering and death, which He had just finished describing to them (vv. 18-19). Jesus was saying, "Don't you realize by now that the way to eternal glory is not through worldly success and honor but through suffering? Haven't you heard what I've been teaching about the persecuted being blessed and about taking up your own crosses and following Me?"

The apostle Paul learned that the way to great glory is through great affliction for Christ's sake. Although he suffered extreme hardship, persecution, and suffering, he considered those things to be insignificant compared to what awaited him in heaven. He told the self-serving, pleasure-loving Corinthians, "For momentary, light affliction is producing for us an eternal weight of glory far beyond all comparison" (2 Cor. 4:17). It is those who are persecuted "on account of Me" who Jesus said will have great reward in heaven (Matt. 5:11-12).

Suffering from physical afflictions such as disease, deformity, and accident or from the emotional distresses of a lost job or the death of a loved one can be used by the Lord to strengthen believers spiritually. He can help them grow even through problems and hardships they bring on themselves because of foolishness or sin. But the affliction that brings eternal glory is that which is brought about and is willingly endured because of faithfulness to the Lord. It is suffering because of the gospel, being "persecuted for the sake of righteousness" (Matt. 5:10). The one who has the greatest glory beside Christ in heaven will be the one who has faithfully endured the greatest suffering for Him on earth.

To drink the cup meant to drink the full measure, leaving nothing. It was a common expression that meant to stay with something to the end, to endure to the limits, whatever the cost. **The cup** that Jesus was **about to drink** was immeasurably worse than the physical agony of the cross or the emotional anguish of being forsaken by His friends, painful as those were. The full measure of His **cup** was taking the world's sin upon Himself, an agony so horrible that He prayed, "My Father, if it is possible, let this cup pass from Me; yet not as I will, but as Thou wilt" (Matt. 26:39).

Either because they completely misunderstood what Jesus meant or because, like Peter promising never to forsake Christ, they self-confidently thought they could endure anything required of them, James and John foolishly declared, **"We are able."** And just as Peter denied the Lord three times before the cock crowed, those two brothers, along with all the other disciples, fled for their lives when Jesus was arrested (Matt. 26:56).

No doubt with great tenderness and compassion, the Lord then assured the brothers, **"My cup you shall drink."** But it would not be in their own power but in the power of the Holy Spirit that they would suffer greatly for their Master's sake. James was the first apostle to be martyred (Acts 12:2), and John ended his long life as a condemned exile on the island of Patmos (Rev. 1:9). They did indeed share in the "fellowship of His sufferings" (Phil. 3:10).

Nevertheless, He continued, **"to sit on My right and on My left, this is not Mine to give."** Not only were James and John presumptuous in asking **to sit on** Jesus' **right and . . . left,** but it was not, in any case, His prerogative to grant such a request. Rather, Jesus said, **"It is for those for whom it has been prepared by My Father."** It would not be on the basis of favoritism or ambition that those honors would be bestowed, but on the basis of the Father's sovereign choice. Personal ambition is not a factor in the eternal, sovereign plan of God. It is therefore not only sinful but a foolish and useless waste of effort.

The response of **the ten** other disciples seems righteous on the surface. But they **became indignant with the two brothers** not because of their own righteousness but because of their envious resentment. They had in the past expressed the same proud and selfish sentiments, and they would express those sentiments again. On the way from Caesarea Philippi to Capernaum "they had discussed with one another which of them was the greatest" but were ashamed to admit it to Jesus (Mark 9:33-34). Even at the Last Supper "there arose also a dispute among them as to which one of them was regarded to be greatest" (Luke 22:24). They were all guilty of the same self-serving ambition that had just been demonstrated by **the two brothers.**

DOMINANT DICTATORSHIP

But Jesus called them to Himself, and said, "You know that the rulers of the Gentiles lord it over them, (20:25a)

The other ten disciples had been standing near **Jesus** and overheard what He had been discussing with James, John, and their mother. Now the Lord **called them to Himself** and reminded them of another wrong way of achieving spiritual greatness besides the two they had just demonstrated. It could be called the way of the dominant dictator. *Katakurieuō* (**lord it over**) is a strong term carrying the idea of ruling *down* on people, the prepositional prefix *kata* intensifying the verb.

"The rulers of the Gentiles lord it over their subjects," Jesus said. Virtually every government of that day was a form of dictatorship, often of a tyrannical sort. The world seeks greatness through power, epitomized by despotic **rulers of the Gentiles** such as the pharaohs, Antiochus Epiphanes, the caesars, the Herods, and Pilate—under all of whom the Jews had suffered greatly.

One of the reasons many countries in the third world today are susceptible to the deceitful attractions of Communism is that they have lived so long under oppressive dictatorship. Centuries of abuse by vain, cruel, exploitive rulers has made them ripe for revolution.

Though not in as absolute or destructive form as those, the same philosophy of dominance is found in modern businesses and even in some Christian organizations. Many people in high positions cannot resist the temptation to use their power to **lord it over** those under them. Some are radical egomaniacs, whereas others are respectable and orthodox. But they share a common worldly desire to control others. Peter therefore warned Christian leaders against "lording it over those allotted to [their] charge" (1 Pet. 5:3).

CHARISMATIC CONTROL

and their great men exercise authority over them. (20:25b)

A fourth wrong way to achieve spiritual greatness is that of charismatic, manipulative control. The expression **great men** (*megaloi*) carries the idea of distinguished, eminent, illustrious, or noble. It represents those who have high personal appeal and have achieved high stature in the eyes of the world and who seek to control others by personal influence. They can be seen as different in style from those in verse 25a. Whereas the dominant dictator uses the sheer power of his position and is often hated, the charismatic leader uses the powers of popularity and personality. By flattery, charm, and attractiveness, he manipulates others to serve his own ends.

Exercise authority over also translates a strong and intensified Greek verb, combining *kata* (down) and *exousiazō* (to have authority), and could be rendered "to play the tyrant."

The church has never been without self-seeking leaders who capture the fascination of the people who willingly follow them while they make merchandise of the gospel in order to feather their nests and build up their reputations. By telling people what they like to hear (2 Tim. 4:3), they skillfully take advantage of selfish, gullible believers.

HOW TO BE GREAT

It is not so among you, but whoever wishes to become great among you shall be your servant, and whoever wishes to be first among you shall be your slave; just as the Son of Man did not come to be served, but to serve, and to give His life a ransom for many." (20:26-28)

This simple, clear passage is one of the most beautiful in the gospels. The principle it teaches needs little explanation, but it is in great need of emulation by those who call Jesus Lord.

First Jesus presents the precept and then the pattern.

It is not so among you, but whoever wishes to become great among you shall be your servant, and whoever wishes to be first among you shall be your slave; (20:26-27)

Jesus turned the world's greatness upside down. The self-serving, self-promoting, self-glorying ways of the world are the antithesis of spiritual greatness. They have no place in God's kingdom and are **not** to be **so among you,** Jesus told the Twelve. In many different ways He had taught them what He told Pilate: "My kingdom is not of this world" (John 18:36).

The world's way of greatness is like a pyramid. The prestige and power of the great person is built on the many subordinate persons beneath him. But in the kingdom, the pyramid is inverted. As the great commentator R. C. H. Lenski has observed, God's "great men are not sitting on top of lesser men, but bearing lesser men on their backs."

Unfortunately, however, there are still many people in the church who, like James and John, continually seek recognition, prestige, and power by manipulating and controlling others to their own selfish advantage. A tragic number of Christian leaders and celebrities have gained great followings by appealing to people's emotions and worldly appetites. But that **is not** to be **so among** Christ's disciples today any more than among the Twelve.

Jesus went on to explain that it is not wrong to desire great usefulness to God, only wrong to seek the world's kind of greatness. Paul assures us that "it is a trustworthy statement: if any man aspires to the office of overseer, it is a fine work he desires to do" (1 Tim. 3:1). As the apostle goes on to point out (vv. 2-7), the standards for an overseer in Christ's church are high. But the man who is willing to meet those standards for the Lord's sake and in the Lord's power will have the Lord's blessing.

Therefore, Jesus said, **"Whoever wishes to become great among you,** that is, great by God's standards rather than men's, **shall be your servant."** He was not, as some have suggested, contradicting what He had just taught. He was speaking of an entirely different kind of greatness than the sort James and John were seeking and that the world promotes. This kind of greatness is pleasing to God, because it is humble and self-giving rather than proud and self-serving. The way to the world's greatness is through pleasing and being served by men; the way to God's greatness is through pleasing Him and serving others in His name. In God's eyes, the one who is great is the one who is a willing **servant.**

It is not only not wrong but very much right to seek eternal glory, because that glory is God-given. Paul declared, "Nor did we seek glory from men, either from you or from others, even though as apostles of Christ we might have asserted our authority" (1 Thess. 2:6). But he also declared to those same believers in

Thessalonica that "it was for this He called you through our gospel, that you may gain the glory of our Lord Jesus Christ" (2 Thess. 2:14). The way to that divine and eternal glory, which comes from God, is the way of renouncing the worldly and temporal glory that comes from men. The way to God's glory is the way of the **servant**. Man's focus must be on rendering spiritual service with consummate excellence and leaving the success of that service to the Lord.

Jesus was speaking of being a true servant, not a sham. He did not have in mind the "public servant" who uses his office for personal gain and power. Godly greatness comes from genuine humility. Only God knows a person's heart, and Paul assures us that the Lord "will both bring to light the things hidden in the darkness and disclose the motives of men's hearts; and then each man's praise will come to him from God" (1 Cor. 4:5).

Servant is from *diakonos,* from which the term *deacon* is derived. The original Greek word was purely secular, referring to a person who did menial labor, such as house cleaning or serving tables. It was not necessarily a term of dishonor but simply described the lowest level of hired help, who needed little training or skill.

But Christ elevated *diakonos* to a place of great significance, using it to describe His most faithful and favored disciples. He could have chosen any number of more noble words to characterize obedient discipleship, but He chose this one because it best reflects the selfless, humble life that He honors. It is also the life that He Himself exemplified, as He would go on to say (v. 28).

The surest mark of the true **servant** is willing sacrifice for the sake of others in the name of Christ. The sham servant avoids suffering, while the true servant accepts it.

Paul had the pure, genuine heart of a servant. He readily acknowledged his apostleship and the divine authority that came with that unique, high office. But he even more readily acknowledged that his office and authority belonged to God and were only entrusted to him as a steward (1 Cor. 4:1). To the proud, self-centered, factious, and worldly Corinthians he said, "What then is Apollos? And what is Paul? Servants through whom you believed, even as the Lord gave opportunity to each one" (1 Cor. 3:5). Later in that letter he says sarcastically,

> You are already filled, you have already become rich, you have become kings without us. . . . For, I think, God has exhibited us apostles last of all, as men condemned to death; because we have become a spectacle to the world, both to angels and to men. We are fools for Christ's sake, but you are prudent in Christ; we are weak, but you are strong; you are distinguished, but we are without honor. To this present hour we are both hungry and thirsty, and are poorly clothed, and are roughly treated, and are homeless; and we toil, working with our own hands; when we are reviled, we bless; when we are persecuted, we endure; when we are slandered, we try to conciliate; we have become as the scum of the world, the dregs of all things, even until now." (4:8-13)

In his book *A Serious Call to a Devout and Holy Life,* William Law writes,

Let every day be a day of humility; condescend to all the weaknesses and infirmities of your fellow-creatures, cover their frailties, love their excellencies, encourage their virtues, relieve their wants, rejoice in their prosperities, compassionate their distress, receive their friendship, overlook their unkindness, forgive their malice, be a servant of servants, and condescend to do the lowliest offices of the lowest of mankind.

Another great saint of past years, Samuel Brengle, wrote,

If I appear great in their eyes, the Lord is most graciously helping me to see how absolutely nothing I am without Him, and helping me to keep little in my own eyes. He does use me. But I am so concerned that He uses me and that it is not of me the work is done. The axe cannot boast of the trees it has cut down. It could do nothing but for the woodsman. He made it, he sharpened it, and he used it. The moment he throws it aside, it becomes only old iron. O That I may never lose sight of this. (Quoted in Oswald Sanders, *Spiritual Leadership* [Chicago: Moody, 1967], p. 58.)

Jesus reiterated and intensified His description of God's way to greatness: **"Whoever wishes to be first among you shall be your slave."** The position and work of a **slave** were much lower and demeaning even than those of a servant. A servant was to some degree his own person. He often owned little more than the clothes on his back, but he was free to go where he wanted and to work or not work as he pleased. But a **slave** (*doulos*) did not belong to himself but to his master and could go only where the master wanted him to go and do only what the master wanted him to do. He did not belong to himself but was the personal property of someone else.

In several of his letters Paul identified himself as Christ's slave (*doulos*) even before identifying himself as His apostle. He greeted the Romans with the words, "Paul, a bond-servant of Christ Jesus, called as an apostle" (Rom. 1:1; cf. Phil. 1:1; Titus 1:1). That is why he could say, "If we live, we live for the Lord, or if we die, we die for the Lord; therefore whether we live or die, we are the Lord's" (Rom. 14:8). Slaves were the property of their owners and could therefore be bought and sold. Like such a **slave**, Christians "have been bought with a price" (1 Cor. 6:20; cf. 7:23) and are the property of the Lord who bought them with His own precious blood (1 Pet. 1:18-19).

Paul greatly desired to be exalted and to receive glory, but the exaltation and glory he sought were God's and he sought them in God's way, through the suffering of servanthood and the bondage of slavery. It was said of one leader in the early church that "He belonged to that class of early martyrs whose passionate soul made an early holocaust of the physical man."

In one of her most beautiful poems Amy Carmichael wrote,

> Hast thou no scar?
> No hidden scar on foot, or side, or hand?
> I hear thee sung as mighty in the land,
> I hear them hail thy bright ascendant star;
> Hast thou no scar?
>
> Hast thou no wound?
> Yet, I was wounded by the archers, spent.
> Leaned me against the tree to die, and rent
> By ravening beasts that compassed me, I
> swooned:
> Hast thou no wound?
>
> No wound? No scar?
> Yes, as the master shall the servant be,
> And pierced are the feet that follow Me;
> But thine are whole. Can he have followed far
> Who has no wound? No scar?

The cost of true greatness is humble, selfless, sacrificial service. The Christian who desires to be **great** and **first** in the kingdom is the one who is willing to serve in the hard place, the uncomfortable place, the lonely place, the demanding place, the place where he is not appreciated and may even be persecuted. Knowing that time is short and eternity long, he is willing to spend and be spent. He is willing to work for excellence without becoming proud, to withstand criticism without becoming bitter, to be misjudged without becoming defensive, and to withstand suffering without succumbing to self-pity.

When faithful believers have done everything they can for the Lord to the limit of their abilities and energy, they say to Him, "We are unworthy slaves; we have done only that which we ought to have done" (Luke 17:10). It is to such disciples that the Lord will say in return, "Well done, good and faithful slave; . . . enter into the joy of your master" (Matt. 25:21).

William Barclay has succinctly commented, "The world may assess a man's greatness by the number of people whom he controls and who are at his beck and call; or by his intellectual standing and his academic eminence; or by the number of committees of which he is a member; or by the size of his bank balance and the material possessions which he has amassed; but in the assessment of Jesus Christ these things are irrelevant."

THE PATTERN FOR TRUE GREATNESS

just as the Son of Man did not come to be served, but to serve, and to give His life a ransom for many." (20:28)

The emphasis of this verse is in the words **just as the Son of Man.** What Jesus says about Himself should also characterize His followers. "I am your perfect Pattern," He was saying, "your supreme Example. My attitude should be Your attitude, and My kind of living should be your kind of living. If you want to be great as God wants you to be great, be like Me."

To discover what it means to become a godly servant and slave, the disciples had only to look at **the Son of Man** Himself. Many years after John presumptuously asked to be seated at Jesus' side in the kingdom, the now humble apostle wrote, "The one who says he abides in Him ought himself to walk in the same manner as He walked" (1 John 2:6). As once his life had centered in himself and his great desire had been to lord it over others, now it was centered in Jesus Christ and was abandoned to the selfless service of others in His name. He no longer sought to manipulate Jesus but only to emulate Him.

In His incarnate role as **the Son of Man,** Jesus **did not come to be served, but to serve.** "Although He existed in the form of God, [He] did not regard equality with God a thing to be grasped, but emptied Himself, taking the form of a bond-servant, and being made in the likeness of men. And being found in appearance as a man, He humbled Himself by becoming obedient to the point of death, even death on a cross. Therefore also God highly exalted Him, and bestowed on Him the name which is above every name" (Phil. 2:6-9).

Jesus is the supreme example of humility and servanthood, because, as the sovereign of the universe and of all eternity, He subjected Himself to humiliation and even to death. He is the most exalted because He faithfully endured the most humiliation. Although He was the King of kings and had the right **to be served** by others, He ministered as a Servant of servants and gave His life **to serve** others.

During the Last Supper, after the disciples had again been arguing about which of them was the greatest, Jesus asked, "Who is greater, the one who reclines at the table, or the one who serves? Is it not the one who reclines at the table? But I am among you as the one who serves" (Luke 22:27). It was probably at this time that Jesus gave them the beautiful object lesson of servanthood recorded by John.

> [Jesus] laid aside His garments; and taking a towel, He girded Himself about. Then He poured water into the basin, and began to wash the disciples' feet, and to wipe them with the towel with which He was girded. . . . And so when He had washed their feet, and taken His garments, and reclined at the table again, He said to them, "Do you know what I have done to you? You call Me Teacher and Lord; and you are right, for so I am. If I then, the Lord and the Teacher, washed your feet, you also ought to wash one another's feet. For I gave you an example that you also should do as I did to you. Truly, truly, I say to you, a slave is not greater than his master; neither is one who is sent greater than the one who sent him. If you know these things, you are blessed if you do them." (John 13:4-5, 12-17)

Jesus' ultimate act of servanthood, however, was **to give His life.** "Greater love has no one than this," He said, "that one lay down his life for his friends" (John 15:13).

Some years ago, Joe Delaney, a star football player for the Kansas City Chiefs, saw three young boys out in a lake, crying out for help and struggling to stay above the water. Although he was himself a poor swimmer, Joe dived into the water and tried to save them. One of the boys was rescued, but Joe and the other two boys drowned. He willingly laid down his life in an effort to save those boys, making the ultimate sacrifice in their behalf.

Although such heroes are lauded, the world understands little of that kind of selflessness, which runs counter to man's natural inclination to self-preservation. But self-giving is to be the normal pattern for Christians, just as it was the normal pattern for Christ.

In His next statement, Jesus presents the first explicit New Testament teaching about the redemptive work of the Messiah. He would vicariously suffer for the sins of mankind as **a ransom** for those who trust in Him. He did not simply **give His life** an example for others. He was no mere martyr for a godly cause, as some claim. Nor was He merely an example of life-giving selflessness, although He was indeed the supreme example of that. Jesus not only lived and died for others but died as **a ransom** for others.

In that redemptive aspect, of course, His followers cannot follow His example. Nothing that a believer can do will have any direct spiritual benefit for himself or others. If he could not merit his own salvation, he surely cannot merit the salvation of someone else.

Lutron (**ransom**) was the term commonly used for the redemption price of a slave, the amount required to buy his freedom. It is used only twice in the New Testament (see also Mark 10:45), both times in reference to Christ's giving of Himself to redeem others. Here it is followed by the preposition *anti* ("instead of"), expressing an exchange. In 1 Timothy 2:6, the word used for "ransom" is *antilutron*, which simply combines the two words used here. In both cases the idea is that of a price paid for a life.

The unbeliever is a slave to sin, the flesh, Satan, and death, and it was to redeem men from those slaveries that Jesus gave **His life a ransom** in exchange for sinners. "There is therefore now no condemnation for those who are in Christ Jesus," Paul explained to believers in Rome. "For the law of the Spirit of life in Christ Jesus has set you free from the law of sin and of death. For what the Law could not do, weak as it was through the flesh, God did: sending His own Son in the likeness of sinful flesh and as an offering for sin, He condemned sin in the flesh" (Rom. 8:1-3). "Having been freed from sin," the apostle had told them earlier, "you became slaves of righteousness" (6:18). Christ's sacrifice bought us back from the slavery of sin.

And although the noun *lutron* is used only twice in the New Testament, other forms of the root word are used frequently, as are numerous synonyms. "For you have been bought with a price," Paul reminded the worldly Corinthian believers; "therefore glorify God in your body" (1 Cor. 6:20). To the Galatians he wrote, "Christ redeemed us from the curse of the Law, having become a curse for us" (Gal. 3:13; cf.

4:5); to the Ephesians he wrote, "In Him we have redemption through His blood, the forgiveness of our trespasses, according to the riches of His grace" (Eph. 1:7; cf. v. 14; 4:30); and to Titus he wrote, "[Christ] gave Himself for us, that He might redeem us from every lawless deed and purify for Himself a people for His own possession, zealous for good deeds" (Titus 2:14). Peter reminds believers that they "were not redeemed with perishable things like silver or gold, . . . but with precious blood, as of a lamb unblemished and spotless, the blood of Christ" (1 Pet. 1:18-19). In John's magnificent vision on Patmos he heard the four living creatures and the twenty-four elders proclaim of Christ, "Worthy art Thou to take the book, and to break its seals; for Thou wast slain, and didst purchase for God with Thy blood men from every tribe and tongue and people and nation" (Rev. 5:9).

Jesus' **ransom** was paid to God to satisfy His holy justice, and it was more than sufficient to cover the sins of everyone who has ever lived and ever will live. His death was sufficient for "the whole world," says John (1 John 2:2). It is not the Lord's will "for any to perish but for all to come to repentance" (2 Pet. 3:9). And because He "desires all men to be saved and to come to the knowledge of the truth" (1 Tim. 2:4), He has therefore provided atonement for every person. "For this is the will of My Father," Jesus said, "that everyone who beholds the Son and believes in Him, may have eternal life; and I Myself will raise him up on the last day" (John 6:40).

Although His **ransom** is sufficient for every person, it is valid only for those who believe in Him. It is in that sense that His redemption is **for many**, rather than for all. The Lord was not teaching limited atonement, the idea that He died only for the sins of a select few. Paul makes it clear that Christ died for the whole world: "The man Christ Jesus . . . gave Himself as a ransom for all" (1 Tim. 2:5-6).

The basic idea behind *anti* (**for**) is that of being set over against something else, and the word was often used to denote an exchange or substitution. In becoming **a ransom for many,** Jesus exchanged His life for the lives of the **many** who would believe in Him. It became His death for the deaths of those **many,** His undeserved punishment for the punishment they deserved. As Isaiah had predicted 700 years earlier, "Surely our griefs He Himself bore, and our sorrows He carried; . . . He was pierced through for our transgressions, He was crushed for our iniquities; the chastening for our well-being fell upon Him, and by His scourging we are healed" (Isa. 53:4-5).

Christ, then, is the pattern for all to follow in being servant leaders. By giving His life He gained the eternal glory and esteem of God and men. That is the path to greatness.

The Blind Who Saw

(20:29-34)

23

And as they were going out from Jericho, a great multitude followed Him. And behold, two blind men sitting by the road, hearing that Jesus was passing by, cried out, saying, "Lord, have mercy on us, Son of David!" And the multitude sternly told them to be quiet; but they cried out all the more, saying, "Lord, have mercy on us, Son of David!" And Jesus stopped and called them, and said, "What do you want Me to do for you?" They said to Him, "Lord, we want our eyes to be opened." And moved with compassion, Jesus touched their eyes; and immediately they regained their sight and followed Him. (20:29-34)

Jesus was now on His way to Jerusalem to celebrate the Passover with His disciples. Infinitely more important than that, however, He was going there to suffer and die (20:18-19). He would be celebrating the Passover for the last time and then giving Himself as the one, final, perfect Passover Lamb, sacrificed for the sins of the whole world (Heb. 7:27).

His arrest, trial, and crucifixion were but a few weeks away. Why, we may wonder, did He take time to minister to two blind beggars? In light of the disciples' slowness to learn and believe, why did He not spend the last few days alone with them, drilling into them what He so much wanted them to understand?

The reason was His compassion (v. 34). When better could Jesus have demonstrated the depth and breadth of divine compassion than while He was on the way to His crucifixion? The Twelve would one day look back on the healing in Jericho and on all His other acts of mercy and realize that their Lord was never too preoccupied to be compassionate, never in too much of a hurry to heal the afflicted, never in too much agony Himself to be insensitive to the agony of others. That realization itself would be one of the most important lessons they would learn from their Master. In these few verses is found one of the most beautiful portrayals of the loving, compassionate heart of God.

THEIR PERSISTENT PLEA

And as they were going out from Jericho, a great multitude followed Him. And behold, two blind men sitting by the road, hearing that Jesus was passing by, cried out, saying, "Lord, have mercy on us, Son of David!" And the multitude sternly told them to be quiet; but they cried out all the more, saying, "Lord, have mercy on us, Son of David!" (20:29-31)

As Jesus and the disciples **were going out from Jericho, a great multitude followed Him.** The Lord had finished His ministry in Galilee, ministered on the east side of the Jordan in Perea, and had now recrossed the Jordan back into Judah, just above the Dead Sea near **Jericho.**

The city of **Jericho** was a jewel in the barren wilderness that surrounded the Dead Sea, an oasis of fresh water, beautiful trees, and productive crops of figs, citrus, and other fruit. Among other things, it was known as the city of the palms. Herod built a fort and winter palace there, and Josephus reports that, when there was snow in Jerusalem, only fifteen miles away, Jericho was warm and pleasant.

Jericho doubtlessly brought many memories to Jesus' mind. It was there that Rahab the harlot lived, a very special woman in Israel's history and in Jesus' own ancestry. Though a prostitute and a pagan Gentile, she trusted in the God of Israel and, with her family, was spared when the Lord destroyed the ancient city. Along with Ruth, another Gentile, Rahab is one of only two women named in the genealogy of Jesus (Matt. 1:5). And it was in the wilderness hills to the west of **Jericho,** clearly visible from the city, that Jesus was tempted for forty days by Satan.

Whereas Matthew's account has Jesus **going out from Jericho,** Mark reports that He was coming "to Jericho" (10:46) and Luke that "He was approaching Jericho" (18:35). The difficulty can be explained by the idea that Matthew was referring to the old Jericho, some of the ruins of which are still evident today, and that the other two writers were referring to the contemporary city. In that case, Jesus would have been moving out of the ruins of the old city and into the new. Or it may have been that Jesus had gone through the city to the outskirts and was now leaving. When He responded to the cries of the two blind men whom He had passed, He may have turned and gone back toward the city. After that He decided to go into the city again, where He later encountered Zaccheus (Luke 19:1-2). In any case, **a great multitude followed Him** now, as they often did.

Behold was used to call special attention to something or someone, in this case **two blind men** who ordinarily would have gone unnoticed. Blind people were extremely common in the Near East, especially in the cities. Because none of them could work and few had families who could or would support them, the majority of blind people were beggars, as were these two (see Mark 10:46). Like most other beggars, they congregated outside the city gates to take advantage of travelers, who were more likely to be carrying money than the average person on the street.

A special balsam bush grew in Jericho from which a medicine was made to treat blindness. Consequently, that city had an unusually large number of blind people who came there in hope of a cure. The two blind men who cried out to Jesus were but two among perhaps hundreds in the vicinity.

Blindness was common in ancient times, as it still is today in underdeveloped areas of the world. Many people were blinded by such things as accidents or battle wounds. But many others became blind shortly after birth from gonorrheal infection of the eyes, contracted from the mother during birth. Many women carried the bacterium, although most of them were not affected by it themselves. Other infants were blinded by trachoma, a virulent form of conjunctivitis. Although it usually took several days or weeks for such diseases to cause total blindness, for all practical purposes infected babies were blind from birth. Birth eye infection is still a great danger, even in modern societies, and doctors therefore routinely place antiseptic drops in the eyes of newborns.

Mark and Luke mention only one man, whom Mark identifies as "Bartimaeus, the son of Timaeus," and who apparently was spokesman for the two of them (see Mark 10:46; Luke 18:35). Mark touches a distinctly human chord by naming this man and even his father. Although Bartimaeus was doubtlessly unknown while he was a blind beggar, it is possible that he later became highly respected in the early church and well known to Mark and those to whom he wrote. Mark would have been saying to his readers, in effect, "And do you know who one of those blind men was? Bartimaeus, our dear friend and brother in Christ!"

Hearing that Jesus was passing by, Bartimaeus and his friend **cried out, saying, "Lord, have mercy on us, Son of David!"** *Krazō,* from which **cried out** is taken, is an onomatopoeic word that was used for any sort of screaming or anguished shout. It was used of the rantings of insane people and of a woman's cries at childbirth. It was used of the Canaanite woman near Tyre and Sidon who cried out for Jesus to heal her daughter (Matt. 15:22), of the crowd's shouting for Jesus' crucifixion (Mark 15:13-14), and even of Jesus' crying out from the cross (Matt. 27:50).

These two blind men were absolutely desperate, realizing that the last possible hope of their seeing would soon depart. They could hardly have known of Jesus' impending crucifixion, but they seemed to sense that they would never encounter Him again and that this was their last chance. They were therefore shouting at the top of their voices, not caring who else heard them as long as Jesus did.

The amazing thing about these two men was not their physical blindness, which was common in their day, but their spiritual sight, which is uncommon in any day. Physically they could see nothing, but spiritually they saw a great deal.

In itself, their addressing Jesus as **Lord** does not indicate that they considered Him to be the Messiah. **Lord** was a common term of honor used to address not only dignitaries but anyone due special respect. But their asking Him for **mercy**, and most certainly their calling Him by the messianic title **Son of David**, clearly shows their recognition of who He was. In announcing Jesus' birth to Mary, the angel declared that her Son would be given "the throne of His father David" (Luke 1:32). When a few days after this incident in Jericho Jesus came into Jerusalem on Palm Sunday, He was greeted by the crowds shouting, "Hosanna to the Son of David; Blessed is He who comes in the name of the Lord; Hosanna in the highest!" (Matt. 21:9). It was common knowledge among all Jews that "the Scripture said that the Christ [Messiah] comes from the offspring of David" (John 7:42).

But the blind men's knowledge of Christ and their great determination were tempered by humility. In asking for healing they acknowledged their unworthiness of help and threw themselves entirely on Jesus' **mercy**. Their actions were necessarily loud and obtrusive, because that was the only way they could have been heard over the din of the multitude. But their hearts were right, because despite their great need, they knew they deserved nothing from the Son of David and that only His grace could help them. One cannot be dogmatic about the extent of their faith at this point, but they clearly recognized Jesus' messiahship and His supernatural power to heal.

When a person steps out to God on all the faith he has, even if it is incomplete and weak, the Lord will meet him at that point and lead him to redemption. As He declared through Jeremiah, "You will seek Me and find Me, when you search for Me with all your heart" (Jer. 29:13). Speaking of the two blind men of Jericho, Alfred Edersheim beautifully observed that "the faith of the blind rose to the full height of divine possibility."

Resenting the intrusion of the two men, **the multitude sternly told them to be quiet.** The world, and many Christians, can often be callous and cruel. Everyone in the **multitude** was doubtlessly better off physically, economically, and socially than the two blind men, but they thought only of their own selfish concerns, in light of which these needy men were but an annoyance.

But as F. F. Bruce has expressed it, the two blind men "refused to be bludgeoned into silence by the indifferent crowd," and **they cried out all the more, saying** again, **"Lord, have mercy on us, Son of David!"**

THEIR SUPERNATURAL PRIVILEGE

And Jesus stopped and called them, and said, "What do you want Me to do for you?" They said to Him, "Lord, we want our eyes to be opened." And moved with compassion, Jesus touched their eyes; and immediately they regained their sight and followed Him. (20:32-34)

Jesus doubtlessly heard them the first time, but for His own reasons He waited until they cried out again before responding. He **stopped and called them, and said, "What do you want Me to do for you?"** Mark says that Jesus had first sent someone else to tell them, saying, "Take courage, arise! He is calling for you." Bartimaeus was so elated at hearing those words that he cast "aside his cloak, . . . jumped up, and came to Jesus" (Mark 10:49-50). He apparently was so certain of being healed that he figured he could come back later and find his cloak by himself.

The men answered Jesus, **"Lord, we want our eyes to be opened."** After years of blindness their one compelling desire was to see. **And moved with compassion, Jesus touched their eyes; and immediately they regained their sight.** As the Creator of the universe reached out to those men, He suspended the natural laws which He Himself had made. **Moved with** infinite divine **compassion,** the Son of Man, who was also the Son of God, bestowed the mercy on the physical needs for which they pleaded.

The fact that Matthew says **they regained their sight,** using the same verb Bartimaeus had used in his request (Mark 10:51), suggests that these men had once been able to see. If so, they were more keenly aware of what they were missing than if they never had sight.

Jesus used many different ways to perform His healing miracles. Sometimes the afflicted person was asked to do something himself. Sometimes the Lord simply spoke a word, and sometimes He performed some action, such as putting His fingers in deaf ears or making salve from mud and anointing blind eyes. In this case **Jesus touched their eyes.** His miracles were always complete, and usually, as here, they were instantaneous, defying natural explanation.

It is significant that among the many self-acclaimed faith healers of history, including those in our own day, there is a marked absence of restoring sight and raising the dead. Many other afflictions can be faked or can be given temporary improvement by the power of suggestion working in a desperate mind. But where are the miracles of vision given to the blind? Where is the person whose eyes are permanently damaged or completely missing who has regained his sight by the laying on of a healer's hands? And where is the person who was dead and has been restored to life?

Even more common and tragic than physical blindness is the spiritual blindness the two men must have felt as they encountered the Son of God. And the context strongly suggests that they also sought deliverance from that kind of blindness.

Jesus was born into a world of people who, with few exceptions, were totally blind spiritually. He "was the true light which, coming into the world, enlightens every man. He was in the world, and the world was made through Him, and the world did not know Him. He came to His own, and those who were His own did not receive Him" (John 1:9-11; cf. 8:12). Men were spiritually blind then, and are spiritually blind today, because they do not *want* to see God's truth. As Jesus explained to Nicodemus, "This is the judgment, that the light is come into the world, and men loved the darkness rather than the light; for their deeds were evil. For everyone who does evil hates the light, and does not come to the light, lest his deeds should be exposed" (John 3:19-20).

"The lamp of the body is the eye," Jesus said in the Sermon on the Mount; "if therefore your eye is clear, your whole body will be full of light. But if your eye is bad, your whole body will be full of darkness. If therefore the light that is in you is darkness, how great is the darkness!" (Matt. 6:22-23). To man's natural spiritual blindness, Satan adds his own. "The god of this world has blinded the minds of the unbelieving," Paul declares, "that they might not see the light of the gospel of the glory of Christ, who is the image of God" (2 Cor. 4:4). And to that double blindness, God may add still more. When men persistently refuse to hear His Word and believe in Him, God may choose to judicially reinforce their willing hardness of heart. To Isaiah, the Lord gave the unenviable task of telling his fellow Israelites, "Keep on listening, but do not perceive; keep on looking, but do not understand." He was, in fact, told to "render the hearts of this people insensitive, their ears dull, and their eyes dim, lest they see with their eyes, hear with their ears, understand with their hearts, and return and be healed" (Isa. 6:9-10).

The minds of unbelieving Jews were blinded to the full meaning of God's Word because "their minds were hardened; for until this very day," Paul said, "at the reading of the old covenant the same veil remains unlifted, because it is removed in Christ" (2 Cor. 3:14; cf. Rom. 11:25). The epitome of the spiritually blind were the hypocritical, unbelieving scribes and Pharisees, the leading religionists of Israel whom Jesus called "blind guides" (Matt. 23:16, 24).

Further evidence of the former blind men's desire for spiritual as well as physical sight is the fact that, after Jesus restored their sight, they **followed Him.** It is true that many, and probably most, of the multitude who were following Him (v. 29) were not true disciples. But the fact that Luke says Bartimaeus, and presumably his friend, not only followed Jesus but were "glorifying God" (18:43) gives good reason to believe the men were restored spiritually as well as physically.

In addition to that, Mark reports that Jesus said to them, "Go your way; your faith has made you well" (Mark 10:52). "Made . . . well" is from *sōzō*, which referred to any kind of rescue or deliverance, including deliverance from physical affliction or peril (see Matt. 8:25; Mark 13:20; Luke 23:35). But it is also the most common New Testament term for salvation, the deliverance from sin through Christ, and that would seem to be its meaning in Jesus' final words to these men.

Faith was not a requirement for Jesus' healings. He healed many people at the request of someone else, as in the case of the centurion who pleaded for the healing of his paralyzed servant (Matt. 8:5-13). The infants He healed and those He raised from the dead obviously were not able to exercise any sort of faith. Whereas the New Testament tells of countless people who were healed without faith, it reports none who were saved without faith, because it is only by God's grace working through faith that a person can be saved (Eph. 2:8). It therefore seems that inherent in Jesus' declaration "your faith has made you well" was His assurance of the men's salvation. He spoke exactly the same words to the single leper who glorified God for his healing and came back to give Jesus thanks (Luke 17:12-19). All ten lepers had been healed physically, but only this man was "made . . . well" because of his faith, strongly suggesting that, whereas his cleansing (v. 14) was physical, his being made well (v. 19) was spiritual.

Three features of Jesus' healing of physical afflictions become clear in this story. First, this powerful, dramatic demonstration of God's compassion for men was a proof of Jesus' messiahship. Second, it was a preview of the millennial kingdom, when there will be a thousand-year age of freedom from sickness, disease, and other physical affliction. Third, His healings were symbolic. His healing of blindness was a picture of His immeasurably more wonderful healing of spiritual blindness. What He did for blind eyes was a vivid portrayal of what He desires to do for blind souls.

The Humble Coronation of Christ

(21:1-11)

And when they had approached Jerusalem and had come to Bethphage, to the Mount of Olives, then Jesus sent two disciples, saying to them, "Go into the village opposite you, and immediately you will find a donkey tied there and a colt with her; untie them, and bring them to Me. And if anyone says something to you, you shall say, 'The Lord has need of them,' and immediately he will send them." Now this took place that what was spoken through the prophet might be fulfilled, saying, "Say to the daughter of Zion, 'Behold your King is coming to you, gentle, and mounted on a donkey, even on a colt, the foal of a beast of burden.'" And the disciples went and did just as Jesus had directed them, and brought the donkey and the colt, and laid on them their garments, on which He sat. And most of the multitude spread their garments in the road, and others were cutting branches from the trees, and spreading them in the road. And the multitudes going before Him, and those who followed after were crying out, saying, "Hosanna to the Son of David; blessed is He who comes in the name of the Lord; hosanna in the highest!" And when He had entered Jerusalem, all the city was stirred, saying, "Who is this?" And the multitudes were saying, "This is the prophet Jesus, from Nazareth in Galilee." (21:1-11)

Most people today have little first-hand knowledge of a genuine monarchy.

Those who hold the title of king or queen in modern societies are often rulers in name only, having little if any governmental power or responsibility. An elaborate coronation is often the only notice they will ever have of any consequence. But until modern times the coronation of a monarch involved the display of great splendor and pageantry. The king would be dressed in the most expensive robes and jewels and would be driven through his capital city in an ornate carriage drawn by stately horses. Accompanying him would be his courtiers and foreign dignitaries, and following that would be a large retinue of the nation's finest soldiers. In many countries high-ranking religious leaders would also participate.

At the climax of the events, the king would be presented with a scepter or would stand on a sacred stone or participate in some other ritual signifying the transfer of power and authority into his hands. Musicians would play and sing, and the crowds would break into spontaneous choruses of praise to their sovereign. Every part of the ceremony was designed to highlight the majesty, glory, power, and dignity of the king.

At her coronation in 1838, Queen Victoria of England wore a crown encrusted with giant rubies and sapphires surrounding a 309-carat diamond. Her scepter was capped with an even larger diamond, cut from the Star of Africa and weighing 516 1/2 carats.

Matthew 21:1-11 portrays the most significant coronation the world has yet seen, but it was a coronation in marked contrast to the kind just described. It was a true coronation of a true King. He was affirmed as King and was, in a sense, inaugurated into His kingship. But there was no pomp, no splendor, and a nondescript sort of pageantry.

Traditionally, this coronation has been called Jesus' triumphal entry. It was his last major public appearance before His crucifixion and was an extremely important event in His divine ministry on earth, an event that is frequently dramatized but seldom studied carefully or understood for its true significance.

THE END OF THE PILGRIMAGE

And when they had approached Jerusalem and had come to Bethphage, to the Mount of Olives, (21:1a)

After healing the two blind men in Jericho and leading Zaccheus to Himself, the Lord made His final journey to **Jerusalem.** As He **approached Jerusalem,** He also approached the end of His three years of ministry, which had been preceded by thirty years of obscurity. He was about to reach the final goal set before Him by His heavenly Father. As the multitudes followed along with Him to celebrate the Passover, little did they know they were accompanying the Passover Lamb Himself.

During a census taken about ten years after this time, the number of sacrificial lambs slaughtered at the Passover was determined to be some 260,000. Because one lamb was allowed to be offered for up to ten people, the worshipers in Jerusalem that week could have numbered over 2,000,000. It is not likely that the number then would have been much higher than during this last Passover that Jesus celebrated, indicating that the city was teeming with people.

But before He and the Twelve entered Jerusalem they stopped at the little hamlet of **Bethphage**. Except for its being closely associated with **the Mount of Olives** and Bethany (see Mark 11:1; Luke 19:29), nothing else is known of the town, there being no other biblical, historical, or archaeological evidence of its existence.

John tells us that Jesus visited Mary, Martha, and Lazarus in Bethany "six days before the Passover" (John 12:1-3), making it probably Saturday, the Jewish Sabbath. As He faced the coming week of pain and death, He sought out the comfort and companionship of those three beloved friends.

But even in that brief time of respite, the stabs of hell continued to afflict Him. While Mary anointed His feet with costly perfume and wiped them with her hair, the traitor Judas, who was also a thief, made a hypocritical objection to that beautiful act by feigning concern for the poor. No doubt with deep anguish of heart for Judas's hardened unbelief, Jesus rebuked him, saying, "Let her alone, in order that she may keep it for the day of My burial. For the poor you always have with you, but you do not always have Me" (John 12:3-8).

Probably on the next day, which would have been the first day of the week, or Sunday, a great number of Jews came to Bethany to see Jesus and also to "see Lazarus, whom He raised from the dead" (John 12:9). And because Lazarus was a living testimony of Jesus' supernatural power, and therefore a dramatic witness against their rejection of Jesus' messiahship and a threat to their authority, "the chief priests took counsel that they might put Lazarus to death also" (v. 10).

It was therefore probably on Monday, the next day after the crowd visited Him in Bethany (John 12:12), that Jesus came to Bethphage and prepared to enter Jerusalem through the East Gate of the city. According to this chronology, the triumphal entry was on Monday rather than "Palm Sunday," as Christian tradition has long maintained.

This chronology also eliminates the problem of what is often referred to as "silent Wednesday," so called because the gospel accounts would have no record of Jesus' activities on Wednesday if the triumphal entry had been on Sunday. In what was by far the most momentous week of Jesus' ministry, such a gap is difficult to explain.

Additional support for a Monday triumphal entry is found in the Mosaic requirement that sacrificial lambs for Passover were to be selected on the tenth day of the first month (originally called Abib but after the Exile called Nisan) and kept in the household until sacrificed on the fourteenth (Ex. 12:2-6).

In the year Jesus was crucified (whether taken as A.D. 30 or 33), the tenth of Nisan was the Monday of Passover week. If Jesus entered Jerusalem triumphally on Monday, He was received into the hearts of the Jewish people as a nation much as a family received the sacrificial lamb into the home. In so doing our Lord would have fulfilled the Passover symbolism even in that small detail, being received by His people on the tenth of Nisan. Continuing that perfect fulfillment, He was then crucified on Friday the fourteenth of Nisan, as the true Passover Lamb sacrificed for the sins of the world.

THE EXACTNESS OF PROPHECY

then Jesus sent two disciples, saying to them, "Go into the village opposite you, and immediately you will find a donkey tied there and a colt with her; untie them, and bring them to Me. And if anyone says something to you, you shall say, 'The Lord has need of them,' and immediately he will send them." Now this took place that what was spoken through the prophet might be fulfilled, saying, "Say to the daughter of Zion, 'Behold your King is coming to you, gentle, and mounted on a donkey, even on a colt, the foal of a beast of burden.'" And the disciples went and did just as Jesus had directed them, and brought the donkey and the colt, and laid on them their garments, on which He sat. (21:1b-7)

From this text and many others it is clear that Jesus was always in control of the events that affected His life. He initiated His own coronation when He **sent two disciples** to procure the mount on which He would ride into Jerusalem. He thereby set into motion a series of climactic events that culminated in the voluntary, gracious sacrifice of Himself on the cross that had been divinely planned from eternity past. From beginning to end the gospels completely belie the contention of many liberal interpreters that Jesus was carried away by the enthusiasm of the mob and became caught up in a tragic web of religious and political intrigue that caught Him by surprise. He was not a well-meaning moral teacher who went too far in rankling the Jewish leaders and was helplessly swept away to an untimely execution.

The **two disciples** were told to **go into the village opposite** them, where they would **immediately . . . find a donkey tied . . . and a colt with her.** Although the **village** was nearby, the two animals obviously were out of sight, or Jesus would simply have pointed to them. The mother **donkey** was brought along no doubt in order to induce her offspring to cooperate. The young **colt** would not easily have left its mother and would have been even more difficult to handle than donkeys normally are.

Only in His omniscience could Jesus have known that the **donkey** and her **colt** would at that moment have been where they were, waiting to be found by the two disciples. Jesus also knew the disciples would be questioned about taking the animals. He therefore further instructed them, **"If anyone says something to you, you shall say, 'The Lord has need of them,' and immediately he will send them."**

Mark reports that "some of the bystanders," who Luke says were the owners, did indeed ask, "'What are you doing, untying the colt?' And they spoke to them just as Jesus had told them, and they gave them permission" (Mark 11:5-6; Luke 19:33). Because the owners readily gave permission for use of the animals when told the Lord had **need of them,** it seems likely they were believers in Jesus. We also learn from those other two gospels that the colt had never been ridden (Mark 11:2; Luke 19:30). It was a gesture of respect and honor to offer such an animal to someone, as if to say, "This animal has been reserved especially for you."

Now this took place that what was spoken through the prophet might be fulfilled, Matthew explains. Jesus' entire life and ministry were marked by two overriding purposes, to do His heavenly Father's will (Matt. 26:39, 42; John 4:34; 5:30) and to fulfill the Old Testament prophecies of the Messiah's first coming (Matt. 5:17; Luke 13:33; 24:25-27; Acts 3:21).

The daughter of Zion refers to the inhabitants of Jerusalem, which was sometimes referred to as **Zion,** because Mount Zion is the city's highest and most prominent hill. The prophecy quoted in verse 5 is from **the prophet** Zechariah, who 500 years earlier had predicted that the people of Jerusalem would hail the Messiah as their **King** as He was **coming** into the city and that He would be **gentle,** or humble, **and mounted on a donkey, even on a colt, the foal of a beast of burden** (see Zech. 9:9).

It seems incongruous and totally inappropriate that any king, much less the **King** of kings, should make His triumphal entry **mounted on a donkey** rather than a beautiful white stallion or in a regal chariot. But that is what God's prophet predicted and that is what God's Son did, because that was the divine plan. He was not at that time intended to come in earthly splendor or to reign in earthly power. He did not come in wealth but in poverty; He did not come in grandeur but in meekness; and He did not come to slay Israel's enemies but to save all mankind. The incarnation was the time of His humiliation, not the time of His glorification.

Because He was a **King** like no other king, His coronation was like no other coronation. By the standards and purposes of the earth's kings, Jesus' entry into Jerusalem was anything but triumphant; but by the standards and purposes of God, it was exactly as it was meant to be. Jesus' entry **on a donkey, even on a colt, the foal of a beast of burden** was not a put down by His rejecters. It was the sovereign choice of God the Father and of God the Son, who Himself willingly came to earth as the Servant Savior, to take upon Himself the sin of the world. Nothing could have been more appropriate than that the Bearer of the world's sin burden would enter God's holy city of **Zion** riding on a lowly **beast of burden.**

Although Matthew was speaking specifically of Zechariah's prophecy concerning Jesus' entry into Jerusalem, it is significant that the triumphal entry also fulfilled another prophecy. Through Daniel, the Lord predicted that the time from Artaxerxes's decree ordering the rebuilding of the Temple until the coming of the Messiah would be "seven weeks and sixty-two weeks" (Dan. 9:25; cf. Neh. 2:6), that is, 69 weeks total. The literal translation is "seven sevens and sixty-two sevens," seven being a common designation for a week. In the context of the passage, the idea is 69 weeks of years, or 69 times 7 years, which comes to 483. Two different systems of reckoning have endeavored to determine the chronology of the 483 years after Artaxerxes's decree. They are Sir Robert Anderson's *The Coming Prince* and Harold Hoehner's *Chronological Aspects of the Life of Christ.*

None of the **disciples,** including the two sent for the donkey, understood the Lord's purpose in this or in the other great events of the coming week. "These things His disciples did not understand at the first," John said; "but when Jesus was glorified, then they remembered that these things were written of Him, and that they had done these things to Him" (John 12:16). But the two obediently **went and did just as Jesus had directed them, and brought the donkey and the colt.** Because they had no blankets to pad the animals' backs and were not sure which one He would ride, they **laid on** both of **them their garments, on which He sat.** Jesus chose **the colt,** the smallest and lowliest of the two, and mounted it with the help of the disciples (Luke 19:35).

The Epitome of Praise

And most of the multitude spread their garments in the road, and others were cutting branches from the trees, and spreading them in the road. And the multitudes going before Him, and those who followed after were crying out, saying, "Hosanna to the Son of David; blessed is He who comes in the name of the Lord; hosanna in the highest!" (21:8-9)

As Jesus began to ride into the city on Monday, **most of the multitude spread their garments in the road.** It was an ancient custom (see 2 Kings 9:13) for citizens to throw **their garments in the road** for their monarch to ride over, symbolizing their respect for him and their submission to his authority. It was as if to say, "We place ourselves at your feet, even to walk over if necessary."

While those people were putting their clothes in Jesus' path, **others were cutting branches from the trees, and spreading them in the road.** From John 12:13 we learn that the **branches** were from palm **trees,** symbolic of salvation and joy and picturing the magnificent tribute that the "great multitude, which no one could count, from every nation and all tribes and peoples and tongues" one day will present "before the throne and before the Lamb, clothed in white robes, and palm branches . . . in their hands" (Rev. 7:9). There was great excitement and ecstasy as the multitude proclaimed praise to the Messiah, to the Rabbi from Galilee who taught with such authority and who had healed their diseases and even raised the dead.

The Lord was now completely surrounded by a mass of humanity, perhaps several hundred thousand people, some of whom were **going before Him and** some **who followed after** Him. Fickle as they would prove to be, the people now disregarded the warning of "the chief priests and Pharisees [who] had given orders that if anyone knew where [Jesus] was, he should report it, that they might seize Him" (John 11:57). The expectations that the Messiah would bring deliverance were so great that the crowd became totally caught up in what, from a human perspective, was a frenzy of mob hysteria. Yet completely in accord with God's plan, they unwittingly fulfilled prophecy, just as Caiaphas unwittingly fulfilled prophecy when, a few days earlier, he had arrogantly declared to fellow members of the Sanhedrin: "You know nothing at all, nor do you take into account that it is expedient for you that one man should die for the people, and that the whole nation should not perish." As John went on to explain, Caiaphas did not say that "on his own initiative; but being high priest that year, he prophesied that Jesus was going to die for the nation" (John 11:49-51).

Seemingly with one voice, the whole multitude was **crying out, saying, "Hosanna to the Son of David; blessed is He who comes in the name of the Lord, Hosanna in the highest!"** The Hebrew word **hosanna** is an exclamatory plea meaning "save now." But the crowd on that day was not interested in Jesus' saving their souls but only in His saving their nation. Like the Twelve, they had long wondered why, if Jesus were truly the Messiah, He had not used His supernatural powers against the Romans. Now at last, they thought, He will manifest Himself as Conqueror. They were about to celebrate Passover, which commemorated the Lord's miraculous deliverance of Israel from Egyptian bondage. What better occasion could there be for the Lord's Anointed, the Messiah, to make the ultimate and final deliverance of His people from tyranny?

The people wanted a conquering, reigning Messiah who would come in great military power to throw off the brutal yoke of Rome and establish a kingdom of justice and righteousness where God's chosen people would have special favor. But Jesus did not come to conquer Rome but to conquer sin and death. He did not come to make war with Rome but to make peace with God for men.

Although the shouts of the multitude were entirely appropriate and were, in fact, fulfillment of prophecy, the people had no idea of the true significance of what they were doing, much less of what Jesus would soon do on the cross in their behalf. They neither understood the Lord nor themselves. He intentionally did not enter Jerusalem with a powerful retinue of soldiers who would fight for Him to the death. He entered instead with a ragtag multitude of ordinary people, most of whom, despite their loud proclamation of His greatness, would soon turn against Him, and none of whom would stand by Him.

The multitude acknowledged Jesus as **the Son of David,** which was the most common messianic title. They were crying out for Messiah's deliverance, pleading, in effect, "Save us now, great Messiah! Save us now!" They were quoting from a popular praise psalm from the Hallel (Psalms 113-118), in particular Psalm 118, which was also a psalm of deliverance, sometimes called the conqueror's psalm. More than a hundred years earlier, the Jews had hailed Jonathan Maccabeus with the same psalm after he delivered the Acra from Syrian domination.

The multitude knew who Jesus was, but they did not understand or truly believe what they knew. They were right in their belief that He was the Messiah, **the Son of David,** and that He had come **in the name of the Lord.** But they were wrong in their belief about the sort of Deliverer He was. They knew He was a king, but they did not understand the nature of His kingship or His kingdom. They did not realize any more than Pilate that the kingdom He came then to bring was not of this world (John 18:36). That is why, when it dawned on them a few days later that

Jesus had not come to deliver them from the Romans, they turned against Him. When they clamored before Pilate for the release of Barabbas instead of Jesus (John 18:40), they shouted, in effect, the words Jesus had predicted in the parable of the nobleman: "We do not want this man to reign over us" (Luke 19:14).

The people wanted Jesus on their own terms, and they would not bow to a King who was not of their liking, even though He were the Son of God. They wanted Jesus to destroy Rome but not their cherished sins or their hypocritical, superficial religion. But He would not deliver them on their terms, and they would not be delivered on His. He was not a Messiah who came to offer a panacea of external peace in the world but to offer the infinitely greater blessing of internal peace with God.

Many people today are open to a Jesus who they think will give them wealth, health, success, happiness, and the other worldly things they want. Like the multitude at the triumphal entry, they will loudly acclaim Jesus as long as they believe He will satisfy their selfish desires. But like the same multitude a few days later, they will reject and denounce Him when He does not deliver as expected. When His Word confronts them with their sin and their need of a Savior, they curse Him and turn away.

The Romans were godless and cruel oppressors, and the Lord would not allow them to survive indefinitely. But they were not His people's greatest enemy. Their greatest enemy was sin, and from that they refused to be delivered. God would allow the holy Temple of His chosen people to be destroyed long before He allowed their pagan oppressors to be destroyed. He would, in fact, allow those very pagans to destroy the holy Temple.

On the day after His triumphal entry into Jerusalem Jesus "entered the temple and cast out all those who were buying and selling in the temple, and overturned the tables of the moneychangers and the seats of those who were selling doves. And He said to them, 'It is written, "My house shall be called a house of prayer;" but you are making it a robbers' den'" (Matt. 21:12-13). That cleansing of the Temple was purely symbolic and had little lasting effect. The mercenary moneychangers and sacrifice sellers were doubtlessly back in business the next day. But less than forty years later, in A.D. 70, the Romans would utterly destroy the Temple, after which, just as Jesus foretold, not one stone of it was left upon another that was not torn down (Matt. 24:2). Not until modern times, nearly two thousand years later, could even its ruins be identified.

As far as the true intent of the people was concerned, Jesus' coronation was a hollow, empty pretense. The words of the multitude were right, but their hearts were not. In any case, He had not come at that time to be crowned but to be crucified.

He will be crowned one day in a way that is perfectly befitting. The times of rejection will be over, and at His name "every knee [will] bow, of those who are in heaven, and on earth, and under the earth, and . . . every tongue [will] confess that Jesus Christ is Lord, to the glory of God the Father" (Phil. 2:10-11). The first time

He came, He came to provide men's salvation. But when He comes again, He will come to display His sovereignty. His great and ultimate coronation in that day is described by John:

> And when He had taken the book, the four living creatures and the twenty-four elders fell down before the Lamb, having each one a harp, and golden bowls full of incense, which are the prayers of the saints. And they sang a new song, saying, "Worthy art Thou to take the book, and to break its seals; for Thou wast slain, and didst purchase for God with Thy blood men from every tribe and tongue and people and nation. And Thou hast made them to be a kingdom and priests to our God; and they will reign upon the earth." And I looked, and I heard the voice of many angels around the throne and the living creatures and the elders; and the number of them was myriads of myriads, and thousands of thousands, saying with a loud voice, "Worthy is the Lamb that was slain to receive power and riches and wisdom and might and honor and glory and blessing." And every created thing which is in heaven and on the earth and under the earth and on the sea, and all things in them, I heard saying, "To Him who sits on the throne, and to the Lamb, be blessing and honor and glory and dominion forever and ever." And the four living creatures kept saying, "Amen." And the elders fell down and worshiped. (Rev. 5:8-14)

THE ELEMENT OF PERPLEXITY

And when He had entered Jerusalem, all the city was stirred, saying, "Who is this?" And the multitudes were saying, "This is the prophet Jesus, from Nazareth in Galilee." (21:10-11)

Matthew's account of Jesus' entry closes with an element of perplexity. After the great shouts of acclamation had somewhat subsided and Jesus **had entered Jerusalem**, the residents of the city began asking, **"Who is this?"** The best response **the multitude** of celebrants could give was, **"This is the prophet Jesus, from Nazareth in Galilee."** Obviously most of them had paid little attention to what they had been shouting so vociferously. They had barely finished proclaiming Jesus as the Messiah, the Son of David, who came in the name of the Lord. But they did not comprehend what they said, and when the mass emotions subsided, they were hard put to say who **Jesus** really was, other than a **prophet** who came **from Nazareth in Galilee.** They no longer called Him the Son of David or praised Him as the great Deliverer. He was now no more than a **prophet.**

The people knew but they would not believe, and because they would not believe they ceased to know. Like their forefathers to whom Isaiah preached, they heard but did not perceive and saw but did not understand, because their hearts were insensitive (Isa. 6:9-10). They heard Jesus' message, they attested to His miracles, and they even acknowledged His divinity, but they rejected His saviorhood and His lordship. They were totally earthbound, materialistic, and self-satisfied. They were interested only in the kingdoms of this world, not the kingdom of heaven. They would have accepted Jesus as an earthly king, but they would not have Him as their heavenly King.

Purging the Perverted Temple

(21:12-17)

And Jesus entered the temple and cast out all those who were buying and selling in the temple, and overturned the tables of the moneychangers and the seats of those who were selling doves. And He said to them, "It is written, 'My house shall be called a house of prayer'; but you are making it a robbers' den." And the blind and the lame came to Him in the temple, and He healed them. But when the chief priests and the scribes saw the wonderful things that He had done, and the children who were crying out in the temple and saying, "Hosanna to the Son of David," they became indignant, and said to Him, "Do You hear what these are saying?" And Jesus said to them, "Yes; have you never read, 'Out of the mouth of infants and nursing babes Thou hast prepared praise for Thyself'?" And He left them and went out of the city to Bethany, and lodged there. (21:12-17)

The triumphal entry on Monday had begun outside Jerusalem's East Gate, where a multitude followed Jesus into the city and another large group came out of the city to meet Him and then led the way before Him, spreading clothes and palm branches in the road as they went (vv. 8-9; cf. John 12:12-13). "He entered Jerusalem and came into the temple," Mark tells us; "and after looking all around, He departed for Bethany with the twelve, since it was already late" (Mark 11:11). On Tuesday morning, after spending Monday night in Bethany, He went back into Jerusalem.

As mentioned in the previous chapter, at Passover time the city of Jerusalem swelled to perhaps four or five times its normal size because of the Jewish pilgrims who came from all over the known world to celebrate this great feast. Tradition had long dictated that Passover could be celebrated properly only in Jerusalem. But because the city could not accommodate the increased multitudes that came for that occasion, the religious leaders declared a special edict each year that temporarily extended the city boundaries to include a sizable area outside the walls, including several small villages such as Bethphage and Bethany. Like many other visitors, Jesus and His disciples spent the day within the walled city proper but spent the night in a nearby community. Those who could not find rental lodging and who had no friends living in the area often camped in the open air.

While they were in Jerusalem, many Jews went to the Temple to pray, to offer sacrifices, to perform rites of ritual cleansing and purification, and to present offerings in the large trumpet-shaped receptacles located in the Court of the Women.

But as Jesus came into the Temple on this Tuesday of Passover week, He came for a unique purpose: to give further demonstration of His messianic credentials. To the thousands of celebrants, to the religious leaders, and most specifically to the chief priests and scribes (see Matt. 20:18; 21:15), He again offered clear testimony to the nature of His kingliness and of His kingdom.

From the first dramatic demonstrations of His miracle-working power, the crowds had wanted to take Him by force and make Him king (John 6:15). Their intent, of course, was for Him to be a king of their own liking who would fulfill their aspirations of deliverance from the yoke of Rome. But the Lord consistently refused to be that kind of king and perform that kind of deliverance. His coronation processional into Jerusalem the day before was marked by simplicity rather than pomp and by humility rather than splendor. He was not accompanied by influential dignitaries and a powerful army but by unarmed, powerless nobodies. And as He had predicted (20:18-19) and would soon demonstrate, He had come not to reign but to die, not to be crowned but to be crucified, and not for the purpose of delivering Israel from the power of Rome but of delivering all men from the power of sin.

But Jesus now gave a demonstration of kingliness that was in marked contrast to His humble inauguration the previous day.

He Showed He Was on a Divine Mission

And Jesus entered the temple (21:12a)

Some ancient manuscripts of Matthew contain the words "of God" after **the temple,** and that reading would seem to be authentic. As R. C. H. Lenski has commented, "The temple of God is never used in the New Testament as a phrase anywhere but here, so it seems unlikely that some scribe would put it in. But if you understand what Jesus is about to do, it makes all the sense in the world that [Matthew] would have affirmed that this was the temple of God when he is about to describe the utter ungodliness of its activities." Still, the phrase "of God" adds nothing to the basic teaching of the passage, because **the temple** in Jerusalem obviously belonged to the God of the Jews. But those two words do serve to sharpen the focus and intensify the emphasis, by highlighting the fact that Jesus was dealing with the holy earthly symbol of the presence of His heavenly Father.

If Jesus had been the military Messiah the people wanted, He would have brought an army into Jerusalem and attacked the main Roman garrison at Fort Antonius. Instead, alone and weaponless, He attacked a group of His fellow countrymen who were profaning **the temple.** The supreme issue for Jesus was not Rome's army but God's Temple. The Messiah did not come as a military, economic, political, or social savior from injustice and oppression but as a spiritual Savior from sin and death. At His second coming He will indeed make right the injustices and inequities that plague mankind. But before He comes again as King of kings and Lord of lords to establish His glorious millennial kingdom and to resolve all the conflicts of fallen mankind, He first had to come as Savior to establish His spiritual kingdom within those who trust in Him.

Jesus began His ministry at a Passover just as He now ended it at a Passover. Just as at the present time, "He found in the temple those who were selling oxen and sheep and doves, and the moneychangers seated." And just as He was about to do again, He had done before, when He "drove them all out of the temple, with the sheep and the oxen; and He poured out the coins of the moneychangers, and overturned their tables; and to those who were selling the doves He said, 'Take these things away; stop making My Father's house a house of merchandise'" (John 2:14-16).

During the hidden years of His adolescence and young adulthood, and certainly during His ministry, Jesus had seen much social injustice, much economic inequity, much deprivation and poverty, and much oppression and cruelty by the Romans. But His mission never focused on those things, because they are not man's greatest problems. It was the far more severe problem of sin that Jesus had come to conquer. Men's problem with God is infinitely greater than their problems with other men. They cannot, in fact, solve their problems with each other until their problem with Him is solved through faith and obedience.

It was in the Temple erected in His own name and by the people He had chosen for Himself that the Lord was most offended and denied. It was therefore in His own house that cleansing began. As long as things were wrong with Israel's worship, things could not be right in the nation. Worship is always the focal point. The great problem with society is not injustice, inequity, crime, or even immorality —pervasive and destructive as those evils might be. Society's evil of evils has always been its abandonment of God. And it is as true today as it was in ancient Israel that the people of God must themselves be revived and renewed before they can be His instruments for changing the world around them.

Jesus had cleansed the Temple three years earlier, yet it was now probably more profane and corrupted than ever. Why, then, would He again bother to make this seemingly futile gesture? He knew that His act of cleansing would be temporary and would not change the hearts of the religious leaders. But He was compelled to make that clear testimony to God's holiness and to God's judgment against desecration and false religion.

God had repeatedly sent prophets to warn His people of their idolatry and other sins and to call them back to Himself. Sometimes there would be reform, but the reform almost invariably would degenerate into even worse idolatry than before. Yet He sent His prophets again and again to declare His truth, His holiness, and His judgment. The Lord never stops declaring His will to His people, no matter how often or how wickedly they reject it. Revealed truth that does not result in repentance becomes the source of greater condemnation.

As Jesus entered **the temple,** it was doubtlessly filled with thousands of Jewish worshipers, milling about the outer Court of the Gentiles, where everyone was allowed to enter. Perhaps the Jewish leaders reasoned that if Gentiles could be there so could anything else. Within the past several decades the area had come to be used as a religious marketplace, operated under the auspices of the high priest, Annas. He was a corrupt and vile man, who saw the Temple and his exalted position only as means to personal power and wealth. The business enterprises in the Court of the Gentiles came to be known as the "Bazaar of Annas," whose chief priests and other associates oversaw the Temple franchises. Merchants would buy rights to a concession for selling sacrificial animals, wine, oil, or salt, or for exchanging money into the proper currency and denominations used in Temple offerings. In addition to the franchise fees the operators would often be required to pay a certain percentage of their profits to Annas.

According to levitical law, any animal approved by the priests could be offered in the Temple. But the chief priests made certain that animals not bought in one of their franchises would be judged unacceptable, giving their concessionaires the de facto right to provide all the animals. According to the Jewish-Christian historian Alfred Edersheim, a person would often have to pay as much as ten times what an animal normally cost. As if that extortion were not enough, those who needed to have foreign currency exchanged or who had to have their money converted into the exact amount for an offering were charged a twenty-five percent fee. Jesus was therefore speaking quite literally when He called the Temple marketplace "a robbers' den" (v. 13).

When He was compelled to cleanse His Father's house of sacrilege, Christ demonstrated He was on a divine mission for His heavenly Father.

HE DEMONSTRATED DIVINE AUTHORITY

and cast out all those who were buying and selling in the temple, and overturned the tables of the moneychangers and the seats of those who were selling doves. (21:12b)

The temple was the supreme place of Jewish worship, and the high priest and chief priests were therefore the most powerful religious leaders in Israel. Within the confines of the Temple, the guards of the high priest had extraordinary power. Because Jewish law required death for any non-Jew who went further into the Temple than the Court of the Gentiles, the Romans had given approval for the Temple guards to slay an offender on the spot.

Yet Jesus confronted the high priest, the chief priests, the Temple guards, and the Temple merchants with impunity. They were about to meet someone over whom they had absolutely no power. Although many of those men would later be instrumental in Jesus' arrest, trial, and crucifixion, they were able to exert that power only by the Father's allowance. Like Pilate, they had no authority over Jesus that had not "been given . . . from above" (John 19:11). As Jesus had declared to the unbelieving Pharisees on an earlier occasion in Jerusalem, He alone had power over His life. "For this reason the Father loves Me," He said, "because I lay down My life that I may take it again. No one has taken it away from Me, but I lay it down on My own initiative. I have authority to lay it down, and I have authority to take it up again" (John 10:17-18).

In a few days Jesus would submit Himself into the hands of the Jewish religious leaders for them to do with as they pleased. But on this occasion they were powerless to prevent Him from making a final demonstration of His divine authority. Without warning and without resistance, Jesus **cast out** both the merchants and their customers **and overturned the tables of the moneychangers.** Before the thousands of worshipers, the bewildered merchants, and the priests who happened to be present, Jesus made a shambles of the bazaar and declared the shame of those who profited from it. The whole arena was in confusion and disarray, with animals running loose, **doves** flying around, and money of all kinds rolling across the courtyard. But at that time the merchants, **moneychangers,** and priests did not and could not raise a hand or even a voice against Him, anymore than the lions could bite the prophet Daniel.

There were also human reasons why Jesus was not resisted. The priests and other religious leaders were fearful of the Jewish populace, many of whom had just proclaimed Jesus as the Messiah (see Luke 19:48). The merchants were also afraid of the people, whom they had cheated and extorted for so many years. Historical records reveal that several decades later the people did indeed riot against their mercenary Temple exploiters. But those reasons fall short of fully explaining what happened to those who were desecrating the Temple. They were not merely intimidated but were powerless and speechless before the authority of this Galilean Teacher whom they despised and refused to recognize as the Messiah.

Mark reports that Jesus was in such powerful control that He would not even "permit anyone to carry goods through the temple" (Mark 11:16). Because the Temple was near the East Gate, the Court of the Gentiles was often used as a thoroughfare by those travelling to or from the southwest side of the city. Jesus also put an immediate halt to that contempt for the sanctity of God's house. The implication seems to be that He made the people drop what they were carrying and leave empty-handed. Here, too, we see no hint of resistance or opposition. Jesus' commanding presence was such that it instilled fear and submission in every person there, regardless of what they thought of Him or of what He was doing.

Jesus came to earth in humiliation as the incarnate Son of God, but on this occasion, as on several others, He forcefully manifested divine hatred against sin, especially sin that profanes God's name and sullies His holiness. By this mighty, unresistable display of power He made the Temple symbolically clean. With the great clutter of animals, tables, chairs, money, and frightened people, it was far from tidy; but it was for a brief time cleansed of overt moral defilement.

It was in part out of Martin Luther's great hatred of indulgences, the supposed buying of God's grace for money, that the Protestant Reformation was born. Believers today should cry out as Luther did for Christ to cleanse the church of its many modern defilements, including making merchandise of the gospel. Judgment still must "begin with the household of God" (1 Pet. 4:17).

He Revealed Commitment to Divine Scripture

And He said to them, "It is written, 'My house shall be called a house of prayer'; but you are making it a robbers' den." (21:13)

As He often did, Jesus vindicated what He was doing by appealing to the Old Testament, here quoting from Isaiah 56:7, **"My house shall be called a house of prayer."** Following the full Isaiah text, Mark's quotation includes the phrase "for all the nations" (Mark 11:17). Matthew omits those words probably because he was writing primarily to Jews. But the major point in both accounts is that Jesus' cleansing of the Temple was consistent with the Word of God.

The Temple was to be a place of worship, quiet meditation, contemplation, praise, and devotion, a place where God's people could draw close to Him in worship, sacrifice, and offerings and could seek His will and blessing. It was not meant to be a combination marketplace, stockyard, and bank, where hucksters and charlatans carried on their greedy enterprises under the guise of serving and worshiping the Lord.

At the dedication of the Temple, Solomon prayed, "O Lord my God, . . . listen to the cry and to the prayer which Thy servant prays before Thee today; that Thine eyes may be open toward this house night and day, toward the place of which Thou hast said, 'My name shall be there,' to listen to the prayer which Thy servant shall pray toward this place. And listen to the supplication of Thy servant and of Thy people Israel, when they pray toward this place; hear Thou in heaven Thy dwelling place; hear and forgive" (1 Kings 8:28-30).

It was to the Tabernacle, which preceded the Temple as Israel's central place of worship, that Hannah went when she was grieving bitterly over her childlessness. In that holy place the Lord graciously granted her request for a son, whose name was Samuel and who became one of God's choice servants (1 Sam. 1:9-20). David declared, "One thing I have asked from the Lord, that I shall seek: that I may dwell in the house of the Lord all the days of my life, to behold the beauty of the Lord, and to meditate in His temple" (Ps. 27:4).

In charging that the chief priests and their cohorts had made the Temple into **a robbers' den,** Jesus again quoted from Scripture, this time from Jeremiah 7:11. Instead of being a place where God's faithful people could come and worship unmolested and protected, the Temple had become a place where they were extorted and their extortioners were protected. Those religiously-connected thieves found refuge in the Temple as highwaymen found refuge in **a robbers' den.** But unlike normal thieves, their robbery was public, and they stole and took refuge in the same place. The sanctuary of God had become a sanctuary for robbers.

He Manifested Divine Compassion and Power

And the blind and the lame came to Him in the temple, and He healed them. (21:14)

Fearful of Jesus, and unable to resist Him, the priests, merchants, money-changers, sacrifice-buyers, and travelers using the Court of the Gentiles as a short cut through the city apparently had all dispersed. But **the blind and the lame,** though surely awed by Jesus, were not afraid of Him. Even immediately after His dramatic display of divine indignation, those needy souls correctly sensed that the Lord's fury was in no way directed at them. Just as the wicked and unrepentant can expect God's anger, those who humbly seek for His truth and His help can expect His compassion.

The diseased and the crippled, most of whom were necessarily beggars, continually gathered at the Temple, hoping at the least for the gift of a few denarii and at the most for a miracle of healing. They were despised and ignored by most of their countrymen, in great part because they were considered to be suffering as the direct result of sins either they or their parents had committed (see John 9:2). The selfish leaders of the Temple had little compassion for them (see Matt. 23:4).

Had it not been for the countless thousands of sick, diseased, blind, deaf, and other suffering people in Palestine, both Jesus' great compassion and His great power of healing would be unknown to us. Compared with the length of eternity, all earthly afflictions are temporary. But in this life they are very real and very trying, and the Lord does not minimize them. It was to alleviate suffering as well as to demonstrate His divine power and authority that Jesus compassionately healed those who came to Him and never turned them away or chided them.

Jesus' compassion was a supreme credential of His divine kingship, not only because of the power it demonstrated but because of the gracious love it demonstrated that is so characteristic of God but so uncharacteristic of fallen man. When John the Baptist was in prison and had doubts about Jesus' messiahship, Jesus told John's disciples, "Go and report to John what you hear and see: the blind receive sight and the lame walk, the lepers are cleansed and the deaf hear, and the dead are raised up, and the poor have the gospel preached to them" (Matt. 11:4-5).

Believers know that Jesus Christ some day is going to come to this world in devastating judgment, that all judgment has been given to Him by the Father, and that He alone holds the keys to death and hell. They know He controls the destiny of every soul, and that He has the sovereign and just right to send unbelieving men and women to hell forever. But, like **the blind and the lame** who came to Jesus in the Temple, Christians come to the Lord with awe but also with perfect confidence, knowing that He will not turn them away or condemn them. They know He loves His children and will never do them harm but always do them good, even when they experience that good through His hand of discipline (Heb. 12:6).

Jesus' majestic display of divine compassion was accompanied by a mighty expression of divine power. No sooner had the blind and the lame approached Him for help than **He healed them.** Only God can restore sight to eyes totally destroyed by disease, as many blind eyes were in that day. And only God can replace limbs that are shattered or diseased beyond repair or are even missing.

He Accepted Divine Worship and Human Rejection

But when the chief priests and the scribes saw the wonderful things that He had done, and the children who were crying out in the temple and saying, "Hosanna to the Son of David," they became indignant, and said to Him, "Do You hear what these are saying?" And Jesus said to them, "Yes; have you never read, 'Out of the mouth of infants and nursing babes Thou hast prepared praise for Thyself'?" And He left them and went out of the city to Bethany, and lodged there. (21:15-17)

Along with everyone else present on that occasion, the ungodly **chief priests and scribes saw the wonderful things that** Jesus **had done.** They heard **the children who were crying out in the temple saying, "Hosanna to the Son of David,"** just as their parents had done the day before (v. 9). They well knew that **Son of David** was a messianic title and that the Messiah would perform such miracles and wonders as Jesus had been performing. But their reaction was far different from that of the **children** and adults who praised and glorified Jesus.

Children is literally "boys" and probably refers to the many young teenaged boys who had passed their bar mitzvahs and had come to Jerusalem to celebrate their first Passover as a man, just as Jesus Himself had done many years earlier (Luke 2:41-42).

But instead of joining in the worship of the Messiah, the Temple leaders **became indignant.** The term behind **indignant** carries the idea of fury and wrath. To those men, Jesus' healing of the blind and lame, though incontestably amazing, was repugnant. The Pharisees had charged Jesus with casting out demons by the power of "Beelzebul the ruler of the demons" (Matt. 12:24). **The chief priests and the scribes** now perhaps thought the same thing about His healing. Not only did He oppose them as the rulers of the Temple, but in their eyes He actually worked against God by arbitrarily healing those they thought were being divinely punished for their sins.

Like the Pharisees, **the chief priests and the scribes** felt so self-righteously superior to the common man, especially to the afflicted and poor who were thought to deserve their fate, that witnessing no amount of suffering could elicit compassion in them. And they were so adamant in their rejection of Jesus as the Messiah that no amount of evidence could elicit belief in them.

Instead of recognizing their authority, Jesus condemned their self-righteousness. Instead of praising their holiness, He condemned their hypocrisy. Instead of acknowledging their religious works as pleasing to God, He condemned them as offensive to God and worthless. Consequently, those men refused to recognize Jesus even as a legitimate rabbi, much less as the promised Son of David. What was perfectly clear to most of the common Jewish people in Jerusalem was perfect nonsense to the erudite and self-satisfied Temple elite.

They therefore **said to Him, "Do You hear what these are saying?"** They said, in effect, "Don't You realize that these children, like the rabble yesterday, are calling You the Messiah? Why don't You stop them? How can You stand there accepting acclaim that belongs only to God? How can You tolerate such blasphemy?" The true problem, of course, was that they could not tolerate Jesus' compassionate godliness, because it was a scathing indictment of their hardened ungodliness.

Letting His accusers know that He was not oblivious to what was going on, Jesus first replied simply **Yes.** He was fully aware of what was being said, and He was fully aware of its meaning and significance. "But," He went on to ask the learned men, **"have you never read, 'Out of the mouth of infants and nursing babes Thou hast prepared praise for Thyself'?"** As He did on numerous occasions, Jesus nettled the Jewish leaders by quoting the Old Testament against them, the accepted experts in Scripture.

Jesus was quoting from Psalm 8:2, and the two Hebrew words for **infants** and **nursing babes** refer to children under three years, the age at which Jewish children were normally weaned. As already noted, the children who hailed Jesus in the Temple were far past the age for weaning. Jesus' point was that if even tiny **infants and nursing babes** would be prepared by the Lord to give **praise** to Himself, how much more could older children be expected to praise Him? Christ will be praised, and if men will not praise Him, He had declared to the Pharisees a few days earlier, "the stones will cry out" (Luke 19:40).

Even Jesus' rejection by the chief priests and scribes and His willing acceptance of that rejection demonstrated His divine kingship. God knew that wicked mankind would reject His Son, and it was integral to the divine plan that the Messiah would be "despised and forsaken of men" (Isa. 53:3). At any time Christ could have thwarted the evil men who sought to kill Him. When He was being arrested in the Garden a few nights later, He explained to Peter, "Do you think that I cannot appeal to My

Father, and He will at once put at My disposal more than twelve legions of angels?" (Matt. 26:53).

In the simple but haunting words **He left them** there is a volume of truth. Jesus left the unbelieving priests and scribes because they would not come to Him. They challenged Him again the next day, asking, "By what authority are You doing these things, and who gave You this authority?" He responded by asking them, "'The baptism of John was from what source, from heaven or from men?' And they began reasoning among themselves, saying, 'If we say, "From heaven," He will say to us, "Then why did you not believe him?" But if we say, "From men," we fear the multitude; for they all hold John to be a prophet.' And answering Jesus, they said, 'We do not know.' He also said to them, 'Neither will I tell you by what authority I do these things'" (Matt. 21:23-27).

Instead of attacking Rome, Jesus attacked Judaism. Instead of being a conqueror, He was a confronter. Instead of promoting revolution, He preached righteousness. And instead of clearing out the enemy without, He cleaned out the enemy within.

This was not the kind of Messiah Judaism was looking for then or is looking for today. The majority of Jews, religious or irreligious, have no interest in the Son of righteousness. Those who look for a Messiah at all are looking for the same kind their forefathers looked for in Jesus' day. They are still looking for a military, political, and economic savior who will change the world in their behalf but who will not change them.

Jesus will not remain where He is unwanted. Although every man is accountable to God, He forces Himself on no one. And although salvation is first of all by God's sovereign initiative and power, no person is saved unwillingly. Because the unbelieving chief priests and scribes would not receive Him, **He left them and went out of the city to Bethany, and lodged there,** to be with His dear friends Mary, Martha, and Lazarus, and the other faithful disciples who trusted in and loved Him.

The Way of the Fig Tree

(21:18-22)

26

Now in the morning, when He returned to the city, He became hungry. And seeing a lone fig tree by the road, He came to it, and found nothing on it except leaves only; and He said to it, "No longer shall there ever be any fruit from you." And at once the fig tree withered. And seeing this, the disciples marveled, saying, "How did the fig tree wither at once?" And Jesus answered and said to them, "Truly I say to you, if you have faith, and do not doubt, you shall not only do what was done to the fig tree, but even if you say to this mountain, 'Be taken up and cast into the sea,' it shall happen. And all things you ask in prayer, believing, you shall receive." (21:18-22)

On Monday morning of Passover week Jesus rode into the city on a donkey colt to a Messiah's welcome and was acclaimed the Son of David, as the people shouted hosannas and placed clothes and palm branches on the road before Him (Matt. 21:1-11). On Tuesday He came into the city again and cleansed the Temple of the sacrifice merchants and moneychangers (vv. 12-17). Now, on Wednesday, He entered Jerusalem for the third time since coming up from Jericho.

From Mark we learn that the encounter with the fig tree involved two successive days. Jesus cursed the fig tree on the morning He entered Jerusalem to cleanse the Temple, and it was on the following day, Wednesday, that the disciples noticed that the tree was "withered from the roots up" (Mark 11:14, 20). Matthew condenses the two events into one account, which He mentions only in regard to Wednesday.

In light of Jesus' just having been hailed by the populace as Israel's great Messiah and King, His cleansing the Temple and cursing the fig tree were of special and monumental significance. The cleansing of the Temple was a denunciation of Israel's worship, and the cursing of the fig tree was a denunciation of Israel as a nation. Instead of overthrowing His nation's enemies as the people anticipated He might, the newly-acclaimed King denounced His own people.

It was inconceivable to Jews that their Messiah would condemn them instead of deliver them, that He would attack Israel instead of Rome. That is why the accolades of the triumphal entry were so short-lived, turning in a few days to cries for Jesus' death. He had conclusively demonstrated what both His words and His actions had testified all along—that He had not come as a political-military Messiah to free Israel from Rome and set up an earthly kingdom. When that truth finally dawned on them, whatever else Jesus did became irrelevant to most Jews. They had no use for such a Messiah and certainly no use for such a King. By joining their leaders in calling for Jesus' death, the people would declare in essence what Jesus had predicted in the parable of the nobleman: "We do not want this man to reign over us" (Luke 19:14).

Jesus' cursing of the fig tree was not nearly so powerfully dramatic as the cleansing of the Temple, but it was equally significant.

THE PREDICAMENT

Now in the morning, when He returned to the city, He became hungry. And seeing a lone fig tree by the road, He came to it, and found nothing on it except leaves only; (21:18-19*a*)

As noted above, **the morning** refers to Wednesday, the day after the cleansing of the Temple and two days after the triumphal entry. Jesus **returned to the city** of Jerusalem after spending the night in Bethany as He had been doing, doubtlessly with Mary, Martha, and Lazarus (see Mark 11:11).

It seems certain that Jesus' hosts would have prepared breakfast for Him had He wanted it, but He may have gone out very early to pray on the nearby Mount of Olives, which He often did, and had no time to return to Bethany to eat. Or it may have been that He had eaten breakfast many hours earlier and that His intense prayer and His climbing the Mount of Olives rekindled His hunger. In any case, **He became hungry.** Although He was the Son of God, in His incarnation Jesus had all the normal physical needs characteristic of human beings. Therefore, when He saw **a lone fig tree by the road, He** hoped to find fruit on it to eat.

Fig trees were common in Palestine and much prized. It was not uncommon for them to grow to a height of twenty feet and equally as wide, making them an excellent shade tree. When Jesus called him to discipleship, Nathanael was sitting under a fig tree, probably in his own yard (John 1:48). Before the Jews had entered the Promised Land, the Lord described it to them as "a land of wheat and barley, of vines and fig trees and pomegranates, a land of olive oil and honey" (Deut. 8:8). Through Zechariah the Lord promised His people that at Messiah's second coming, He would "remove the iniquity of that land in one day" and "every one of you will invite his neighbor to sit under his vine and under his fig tree" (Zech. 3:9-10). A favorite place for people to gather was under a fig tree.

Just as the presence of the fig tree was a symbol of blessing and prosperity for the nation, its absence would become a symbol of judgment and deprivation. Largely because of the many conquests of Palestine after the rejection of Christ, the land became greatly denuded and barren. Some invaders used the trees to build their war machines and others simply to fuel their fires. When lumber trees were gone, fruit and shade trees were cut down. During one occupation the rulers began taxing according to the number of trees on a piece of property, with the predictable result that many landowners cut down some of their remaining trees in order to lower their taxes.

Normally, a **fig tree** produced fruit before it sprouted leaves. Therefore when Jesus **found nothing on it except leaves**, He was disappointed, because a tree with **leaves** should already have had fruit. Fig trees bore fruit twice a year, the first time in early summer. In the much lower elevation and much hotter climate of Jericho, some plants and trees were productive almost year round. But in April, a fig tree at the altitude of Jerusalem would not usually have either fruit or leaves, because, as Mark observes, "it was not the season for figs" (Mark 11:13).

Nevertheless, if the tree produced leaves early it should have produced fruit early. Whether because of too much or too little water, the wrong kind of soil, disease, or other reason, it was not functioning as it was supposed to.

Jesus used many subjects from nature—birds, water, animals, weather, trees, flowers, and others—to illustrate His teaching. On this occasion He used a barren fig tree to illustrate a spiritually barren nation. The illustration was a visual parable designed to portray the spiritually degenerated nation of Israel.

THE PARABLE

and He said to it, "No longer shall there ever be any fruit from you." And at once the fig tree withered. (21:19b)

Because the fig tree was barren when it should have had fruit, Jesus **said to it, "No longer shall there ever be any fruit from you."** With those words He pronounced the tree's doom. It was under a divine curse (see Mark 11:21) and would be perpetually unproductive. In Matthew's account it appears that **the fig tree withered** instantly. But as already noted, although the tree may have died at

once, the withering was not evident until the next morning when Jesus and the disciples passed by it again and saw it "withered from the roots up" (Mark 11:20).

The fig tree represented spiritually dead Israel, its leaves represented Israel's outward religiousness, and its lack of fruit represented Israel's spiritual barrenness. As Paul later described his fellow Jews, they had "a zeal for God, but not in accordance with knowledge" (Rom. 10:2), a form of godliness but no godly power (cf. 2 Tim. 3:5).

Fruit is always an indication of salvation, of a transformed life in which operates the power of God. People's right relation to God is evidenced by the fruit they bear. "A good tree cannot produce bad fruit, nor can a bad tree produce good fruit," Jesus said (Matt. 7:18). In the parable of the soils, the good soil is proven by the fact that it yields a crop—sometimes a hundredfold, sometimes sixty, and sometimes thirty, but always a crop (Matt. 13:8). The good soil, Jesus went on to explain, is the person in whom the seed of God's Word takes root and grows. It "is the man who hears the word and understands it; who indeed bears fruit" (v. 23). Using another figure involving fruit, Jesus said, "I am the vine, you are the branches; he who abides in Me, and I in him, he bears much fruit" (John 15:5). Fruit is always the manifestation of true salvation.

Jesus' point regarding the fig tree was that Israel as a nation had an impressive pretense of religion, represented by the leaves. But the fact that the nation bore no spiritual fruit was positive proof she was unredeemed and cut off from the life and power of God. Just as fruitfulness is always evidence of salvation and godliness, barrenness is always evidence of lostness and ungodliness.

Empty religion almost invariably has many outward trappings in the form of clerical garments and vestments, ornate vessels, involved rituals, and other such physical accoutrements. It is also typically characterized by repetitious prayers, cited by rote and offered at prescribed times, or else by spontaneous prayers that are wordy, ostentatious, and self-glorifying. Such were the meaningless repetitions of the pagans (Matt. 6:7) and the self-righteous prayer of the Pharisee who Jesus said was actually praying to himself (Luke 18:11).

This incident was not the first time Jesus had used an illustration of a barren fig tree. On an earlier occasion He said that for three years the owner of a certain fig tree had failed to find fruit on it and therefore instructed his vineyard-keeper to cut it down. But the keeper pleaded with the owner, "Let it alone, sir, for this year too, until I dig around it and put in fertilizer; and if it bears fruit next year, fine; but if not, cut it down" (Luke 13:6-9). Presumably the request was granted. Here, too, the fig tree depicts Israel's barrenness, and the owner's willingness to wait for the tree to bear fruit represents God's patience before bringing judgment. Our Lord makes no specific comparison of that three years to the three years of His ministry, but it was three years after Jesus first presented Himself to Israel as her Messiah that the people declared their final rejection of Him by putting Him to death.

Some forty years later the curse on the nation of Israel, illustrated by Jesus' curse on the fig tree, was fulfilled. At that time, God allowed the Romans to sack Jerusalem and raze the Temple, destroying both the nation and its religion, because

Israel had not borne any fruit, as it has not to this day.

In cleansing the Temple, the King's message was that Israel's worship was unacceptable, and in cursing the fig tree it was that Israel as a nation was condemned for its sinfulness and spiritual fruitlessness. Those messages of doom the people would not tolerate. They had not accepted John the Baptist's call to repentance in preparation for the coming of the kingdom or his declaration that the Messiah was coming with "His winnowing fork . . . in His hand [to] thoroughly clear His threshing floor; and [to] gather His wheat into the barn [and to] burn up the chaff with unquenchable fire" (Matt. 3:1-12). Nor had they accepted Jesus' same call to repentance or His command to come to God in humble contrition and a genuine hunger and thirst for righteousness (4:17; 5:3-12). They were now even more ill-disposed to accept His word of judgment.

When the Lord delivered Israel out of Egypt He declared,

> Now it shall be, if you will diligently obey the Lord your God, being careful to do all His commandments which I command you today, the Lord your God will set you high above all the nations of the earth. And all these blessings shall come upon you and overtake you, if you will obey the Lord your God. Blessed shall you be in the city, and blessed shall you be in the country. Blessed shall be the offspring of your body and the produce of your ground and the offspring of your beasts, the increase of your herd and the young of your flock. Blessed shall be your basket and your kneading bowl. Blessed shall you be when you come in, and blessed shall you be when you go out. (Deut. 28:1-6)

But the Lord also declared,

> It shall come about, if you will not obey the Lord your God, to observe to do all His commandments and His statutes with which I charge you today, that all these curses shall come upon you and overtake you. Cursed shall you be in the city, and cursed shall you be in the country. Cursed shall be your basket and your kneading bowl. Cursed shall be the offspring of your body and the produce of your ground, the increase of your herd and the young of your flock. Cursed shall you be when you come in, and cursed shall you be when you go out. (vv. 15-19)

Through Isaiah, the Lord reminded Israel that He had nurtured and cared for her like a man who plants a vineyard in the best of soil and gives it the best of care and protection. But the vineyard produced nothing but worthless fruit, and the man declared that he would remove its protective hedges and walls, let it be laid waste and become choked out by briars and thorns. He would not even allow it to receive rain. "The vineyard of the Lord of hosts is the house of Israel," the prophet explains. "And the men of Judah His delightful plant. Thus He looked for justice, but behold, bloodshed; for righteousness, but behold, a cry of distress" (Isa. 5:1-7). Then follows a long series of woes, or curses, describing the calamities God's people would suffer because of their unfaithfulness and spiritual barrenness (vv. 8-30).

The people of Israel today are still under God's curse, preserved but unblessed. They are preserved because God will yet redeem them in the final days because of His promise, but they are unblessed because they continue to reject their Messiah. "He came to His own, and those who were His own did not receive Him" (John 1:11). They would not have Him as Savior to deliver them from sin or as Lord to rule them in righteousness.

In modern times, some of the world's Jews have regathered themselves to the land of Palestine and established the state of Israel. But they have not yet been regathered redemptively, because that will be the doing of the Messiah when He comes to them again to set up His kingdom. They are back in the Promised Land, but they have yet to inherit God's promised blessings. They live in continual turmoil, instability, and danger. They are far from the peaceable kingdom the Messiah will bring but are instead an armed camp, constantly under the threat of attack and invasion. Life there has been reduced virtually to the basics of survival and defense.

Israel will not be destroyed, because God protects her. But neither is she being blessed, because she will not have Him as her God. No one comes to God the Father who does not come through God the Son (John 14:6), and because Israel will not claim the Son, she has no claim on the Father.

THE PRINCIPLE

And seeing this, the disciples marveled, saying, "How did the fig tree wither at once?" And Jesus answered and said to them, "Truly I say to you, if you have faith, and do not doubt, you shall not only do what was done to the fig tree, but even if you say to this mountain, 'Be taken up and cast into the sea,' it shall happen. And all things you ask in prayer, believing, you shall receive." (21:20-22)

When **the disciples** passed the cursed fig tree the next morning and saw that it was "withered from the roots up" (Mark 11:20), they **marveled, saying, "How did the fig tree wither at once?"** A diseased tree might take many weeks or months to die, and even one that had been salted, either by accident or from maliciousness, would take several days to die. For **the fig tree** to **wither** overnight was to do so virtually **at once.**

At that point the Lord moved from the visual parable of the fig tree to another truth He wanted to teach the disciples. The principle taught in the parable was that religious profession without spiritual reality is an abomination to God and is cursed. The principle Jesus was now about to teach related to the disciples' marveling about how quickly the fig tree withered. They knew *why* it withered, because they heard Jesus curse it; they just could not understand how it could wither so fast. The Lord took the opportunity to teach them about the power of faith joined to the purpose and will of God, which can do far more than instantly wither a fig tree.

In response to their bewilderment, **Jesus answered and said to them, "Truly I say to you, if you have faith, and do not doubt, you shall not only do what was done to the fig tree, but even if you say to this mountain, 'Be taken up and cast into the sea,' it shall happen."**

Jesus obviously was speaking figuratively. He never used His own power, nor did the apostles ever use the miraculous powers He gave them, to perform spectacular but useless supernatural feats. It was precisely that sort of grandiose demonstration that He refused to give to the unbelieving scribes and Pharisees who wanted to see a sign from Him (Matt. 12:38). Jesus had already performed countless miracles of healing, many of which they probably had witnessed. And He performed many more such miracles that they could easily have witnessed. But the sign they wanted was on a grand scale, one in which fire would come down from heaven or the sun would stand still as it had for Joshua. The literal casting of a **mountain . . . into the sea** would have been just the sort of sign the scribes and Pharisees wanted to see but were never shown.

The phrase "rooter up of mountains" was a metaphor commonly used in Jewish literature of a great teacher or spiritual leader. In the Babylonian Talmud, for example, the great rabbis are called "rooters up of mountains." Such people could solve great problems and seemingly do the impossible.

That is the idea Jesus had in mind. He was saying, "I want you to know that you have unimaginable power available to you through your faith in Me. If you sincerely believe, without doubting, **it shall happen,** and you will see great powers of God at work." At the Last Supper Jesus told the Twelve, "Whatever you ask in My name, that will I do, that the Father may be glorified in the Son. If you ask Me anything in My name, I will do it" (John 14:13-14). The requirement for receiving is to ask in Jesus' name, that is, according to His purpose and will.

Jesus was not speaking about faith in faith or faith in oneself, both of which foolish and unscriptural ideas are popular today. He was speaking about faith in the true God and in God alone, not faith in one's dreams, aspirations, or ideas of what he thinks ought to be. "You ask and do not receive," James warns, "because you ask with wrong motives, so that you may spend it on your pleasures" (James 4:3). "This is the confidence which we have before Him," John says, "that, if we ask anything according to His will, He hears us" (1 John 5:14). Mountain-moving faith is unselfish, undoubting, and unqualified confidence in God. It is believing in God's truth and God's power while seeking to do God's will. The measure of such faith is the sincere and single desire that, as Jesus said, "the Father may be glorified in the Son."

True faith is trusting in the revelation of God. When a believer seeks something that is consistent with God's Word and trusts in God's power to provide it, Jesus assures him that his request will be honored, because it honors Him and His Father. When God's commands are obeyed He will honor that obedience, and when any request is asked in faith according to His will He will provide what is sought. To do what God says is to do what God wants and to receive what God promises.

When the disciples asked Jesus why they were unable to cast out the demon from a young boy, "He said to them, 'Because of the littleness of your faith; for truly I say to you, if you have faith as a mustard seed, you shall say to this mountain, "Move from here to there," and it shall move; and nothing shall be impossible to you'" (Matt. 17:20). Jesus was not commending small faith. It was the littleness of the disciples' faith that prevented their success in casting out the demon. He rebuked them for having small faith that stayed small, but exhorted them to have faith that, though it begins small, continues to grow. The point of the mustard seed illustration is not in its smallness but in its growing from smallness to greatness. In the same way, the virtue of mountain-moving faith is its growth from smallness to greatness as God blesses and provides.

Mountain-moving faith is activated by sincere petition to God. **"All things you ask in prayer, believing, you shall receive,"** Jesus explained. The parables of the friend who asked his neighbor for a favor at midnight and of the widow who petitioned the unrighteous judge (Luke 11:5-8; 18:1-8) both teach the importance of persistent **prayer**. Persistent prayer is the prayer that moves mountains, because it is truly **believing** prayer.

Whatever our finite minds may lead us to think, there is no inconsistency between God's sovereignty and man's faith, because God's Word clearly teaches both. It is not the believer's responsibility to fathom God's inscrutable ways but to obediently follow His clear teaching. Persistent **prayer** that is **believing** God's Word cannot be inconsistent with the operation of God's own sovereign will, because in His sovereign wisdom and grace He commands such prayer and obligates Himself to honor it.

The believer who wants what God wants can ask from God and **receive** it. The Christian young person who truly wants what God wants for his life will have it. The woman who truly wants what God wants for her family will have it. The pastor who truly wants what God wants for his ministry will have it.

God's will for His children does not, of course, always involve things that are pleasant to the flesh or the things one might naturally prefer. His will for His children includes their willingness to sacrifice, suffer, and die for Him if necessary. For the believer who seeks God's will, it is never a matter of succeeding or failing, of prosperity or poverty, of living or dying, but simply of being faithful (see 1 Cor. 4:2). Therefore Paul declares, "If we live, we live for the Lord, or if we die, we die for the Lord; therefore whether we live or die, we are the Lord's" (Rom. 14:8).

When the church is impotent, as so much of it is today, it is because so many Christians are impotent. And Christians are impotent because they are not persistent in praying for what God wants, believing He will provide it. God desires His children to ask and keep asking, to seek and keep seeking, to knock and keep knocking, and it is through that persistence that He promises to bless. He guarantees that they will always receive, always find, and always have the door opened to them (Matt. 7:7).

God does not build His church or build up His people by better ideas, better programs, or better methods, although such things can have a place in His work. God promises to truly reveal His power only through faithful believers who, in persistent prayer, seek only His will.

The Authority of Jesus

27

(21:23-32)

And when He had come into the temple, the chief priests and the elders of the people came to Him as He was teaching, and said, "By what authority are You doing these things, and who gave You this authority?" And Jesus answered and said to them, "I will ask you one thing too, which if you tell Me, I will also tell you by what authority I do these things. The baptism of John was from what source, from heaven or from men?" And they began reasoning among themselves, saying, "If we say, 'From heaven,' He will say to us, 'Then why did you not believe him?' But if we say, 'From men,' we fear the multitude; for they all hold John to be a prophet." And answering Jesus, they said, "We do not know." He also said to them, "Neither will I tell you by what authority I do these things. But what do you think? A man had two sons, and he came to the first and said, 'Son, go work today in the vineyard.' And he answered and said, 'I will, sir'; and he did not go. And he came to the second and said the same thing. But he answered and said, 'I will not'; yet he afterward regretted it and went. Which of the two did the will of his father?" They said, "The latter." Jesus said to them, "Truly I say to you that the tax-gatherers and harlots will get into the kingdom of God before you. For John came to you in the way of righteousness and you did not believe him; but the tax-gatherers and harlots did believe him; and you, seeing this, did not even feel remorse afterward so as to believe him." (21:23-32)

Authority is a strong word, denoting power and privilege. A person with authority exercises control over the lives and welfare of other people. Society cannot operate without having some people in positions of authority; the alternative would be anarchy and chaos. In the family, parents have authority. In school, teachers and administrators have authority. In the community, the mayor, city council, police, and firemen all have spheres of authority. And so also in the larger bodies of government.

The conflict in this encounter between Jesus and the religious leaders was over the issue of authority, specifically Jesus' authority, which they questioned and which they feared would threaten their own positions of authority.

THE CONFRONTATION

And when He had come into the temple, the chief priests and the elders of the people came to Him as He was teaching, and said, "By what authority are You doing these things, and who gave You this authority?" (21:23)

It was still Wednesday morning of Passover week. After Jesus and the disciples had passed the fig tree He cursed the day before and found it completely withered (vv. 18-22; cf. Mark 11:20-21), **He had come** with them **into the temple**.

The group of **chief priests and elders** may have included the high priests Caiaphas and Annas, who served concurrently for several years (Luke 3:2). Because of the seriousness of their confrontation of Jesus, it is likely that at least the captain of the Temple, the second highest official, was present. **The elders** comprised a wide variety of religious leaders, which definitely included Pharisees (Matt. 21:45) and scribes (Luke 20:1), and possibly Sadducees, Herodians, and even some Zealots and Essenes. Although those groups had many differences from each other and were constantly disputing among themselves, they found common ground in opposing Jesus, because He threatened the authority of the entire religious establishment.

Every false religion has the common denominator of works righteousness, of salvation by human achievement, and is by nature offended by and opposed to the gospel of divine accomplishment by God in Christ. Although the religions of the world are divided by vast differences in theology and practice, they find common ground against the gospel of Jesus Christ, just as did the Jewish religionists in the Temple. They may presume to honor Christ as a prophet, a great teacher, or even as one among many gods, but they vehemently oppose the truth that He is the only Savior and that no person can come to God except through the merits of His sacrifice.

As He had the day before, when He so dramatically cleansed the Temple, Jesus now took center stage there again and **was teaching** as He walked about the courtyard (Mark 11:27). It seems certain that those whom He had driven out for making His Father's house a den of robbers (Matt. 21:13) had not returned, and the entire spacious Court of the Gentiles was now available for those who came to worship. Many of them had probably followed Jesus there when they saw Him come into the city that morning.

We are not told what Jesus was **teaching** on this occasion, but He was likely reiterating some of the more important truths He had taught many times before. We can be sure that whatever He said was related to His kingdom, the subject with which His ministry began (Matt. 4:17) and ended (Acts 1:3). In His parallel account, Luke reports that Jesus was "teaching daily in the temple, . . . preaching the gospel" (Luke 19:47; 20:1), which was sometimes called "the gospel of the kingdom" (Matt. 9:35). Whatever His specific theme, "all the people were hanging upon His words" (Luke 19:48).

The primary question the Jewish leaders now had for Jesus was the same as it had been from the beginning, **"By what authority are You doing these things, and who gave You this authority?"** (cf. John 2:18). By **these things**, they probably meant everything Jesus had been teaching and doing, but they particularly had in mind His abrupt and, in their eyes, utterly presumptuous cleansing of the Temple the day before. Except for His similar act at the beginning of His ministry, He had never done anything that more clearly, forcefully, and publicly devastated the religious establishment. While it was happening, they were powerless to stop Him and apparently were even speechless. But now that they had recovered from the initial shock, they were on the offensive and were demanding an explanation.

Rabbinical candidates originally had been ordained by a leading rabbi whom they respected and under whose teaching they served a kind of apprenticeship. And just as the teachings of the leading rabbis varied greatly, so did their ordinations. Because of widespread abuses, and probably also to centralize rabbinical authority, the Sanhedrin, or high Jewish council, had taken over all responsibility for ordination.

At his ordination a man was declared to be rabbi, elder, and judge, and was given corresponding authority to teach, to express his wisdom, and to make decisions and render verdicts in religious as well as many civil matters. During the service various discourses and readings were given and hymns sung. Once ordained, the man had official recognition as a credentialed teacher of Israel.

Jesus had had no such ordination and therefore had no such recognition. **By what authority,** then, the leaders asked, did He not only teach and preach but even heal the sick, cast out demons, and raise the dead? Most especially, why had He presumed to take upon Himself—an untrained, unrecognized, self-appointed rabbi—the task of casting the merchants and moneychangers out of the Temple? Although not themselves religious leaders, those men were operating their businesses under the auspices of the Temple authorities. **"Who gave You . . . authority** to throw them out?" those authorities asked Jesus.

Although they did not recognize the source and legitimacy of Jesus' power, they never questioned that He had it. That His authority was unprecedentedly powerful was incontestable. No one had ever healed as many sick people, cast out as many demons, or raised people from the dead as Jesus had done. The miracles were so obvious, numerous, and well attested that the religious leaders never doubted that Jesus performed them, having seen many of them with their own eyes.

Those leaders knew that power such as Jesus displayed had to be of supernatural origin, and they knew He claimed it was from God, whom He repeatedly called His heavenly Father. When He forgave a paralytic's sins, some of the scribes present "said to themselves, 'This fellow blasphemes.'" Knowing what they were thinking, Jesus accused them of having evil hearts and proceeded to heal the man's paralysis in order to show His critics that He, the Son of Man, had "authority on earth to forgive sins" (Matt. 9:2-6). The crowd of common people who witnessed what He did made the only sensible response: "They were filled with awe, and glorified God, who had given such authority to men" (v. 8). But the scribes refused to accept the obvious. No amount of evidence could penetrate their confirmed unbelief. And like the Pharisees on an earlier occasion (Matt. 12:24), the Temple authorities who now confronted Jesus no doubt preferred to believe that His power came from Satan rather than God.

The chief priests and elders in the Temple also knew, as the multitudes often acknowledged in amazement, that Jesus *taught* authoritatively, with a clarity, definitiveness, and certainty that was completely lacking in the pronouncements and interpretations of the scribes (Matt. 7:29; Mark 1:22). As in many liberal church circles today, a key qualification for acceptance was lack of dogmatism. Virtually every doctrine was open to reinterpretation and revision, and absolutes were shunned as presumptuous. Human wisdom had long since replaced divine revelation, and Old Testament Scripture was cited primarily to support their humanly-devised religious traditions. When Scripture conflicted with tradition, tradition prevailed (Matt. 16:6). In the minds of most Jewish religious leaders, there were many authorities but none that was exclusively authoritative, not even Scripture.

Yet Jesus' ministry was nothing if not authoritative. He demonstrated authority to grant those who believe in Him the right to become children of God (John 1:12). His heavenly Father "gave Him authority to execute judgment" (5:27) and "authority over all mankind" to give eternal life to those His Father has given Him (17:2). He had authority over His own life, "to lay it down," and over His own resurrection, "to take [His life] up again" (10:18).

In all the things He said and did, Jesus never sought approval or support from the recognized Jewish authorities. He completely ignored their system for ordaining rabbis and approving doctrines. He did not ask approval for His teachings, His healings, or His casting out of demons, and certainly not for His forgiving sins.

Jesus had both *dunamis* (power) and *exousia* (authority). *Dunamis* refers to ability, and *exousia* to right. Jesus not only had great power but the right to exercise that power, because both His power and His authority were from His heavenly Father. "Just as the Father raises the dead and gives them life," Jesus said, "even so the Son also gives life to whom He wishes," and "just as the Father has life in Himself, even so He gave to the Son also to have life in Himself" (John 5:21, 26). "For I have come down from heaven, not to do My own will, but the will of Him who sent Me" (6:38; cf. v. 44, 57; 7:16, 28; 8:18, 54).

And because Jesus had the Father's power and authority, He sought no human authority, accreditation, ordination, or credentials. By so doing, He pitted Himself directly against the Jewish religious system and incurred its unrelenting wrath. Its leaders were appalled and scandalized that He not only failed to consult the Sanhedrin and the Temple authorities but had the audacity to condemn them.

In asking Jesus to identify His authority, those leaders probably hoped He would say, as He had many times before, that He worked under the direct power and authority of God, His heavenly Father. That would give them another opportunity to charge Him with blasphemy, and perhaps to succeed in putting Him to death for it, as they had tried to do before without success (John 5:18; 10:31).

THE COUNTER QUESTION

And Jesus answered and said to them, "I will ask you one thing too, which if you tell Me, I will also tell you by what authority I do these things. The baptism of John was from what source, from heaven or from men?" And they began reasoning among themselves, saying, "If we say, 'From heaven,' He will say to us, 'Then why did you not believe him?' But if we say, 'From men,' we fear the multitude; for they all hold John to be a prophet." And answering Jesus, they said, "We do not know." He also said to them, "Neither will I tell you by what authority I do these things." (21:24-27)

Jesus answered the question of the chief priests and elders with a query of His own. He was not being evasive and had no reason to be, having given the answer to their question countless times before. And if they answered His question now, He would answer theirs, telling them again **by what authority** He did **these things.**

His question was simple: **"The baptism of John was from what source, from heaven or from men?"** Because **John** the Baptist had started his ministry first, the religious leaders had rejected him even before they began to reject Jesus. **The baptism of John** referred to His entire ministry, which was characterized by his baptizing those who repented of their sins (Matt. 3:6).

John was the last prophet of the Old Testament age and, like Jesus, became popular and admired by the masses. He was readying the people for the Messiah, and his demeanor and the content and power of his preaching had made a great impact throughout Israel. After Herod arrested John for condemning his adulterous marriage to his brother Philip's wife, Herodias, the king hesitated for a long time in putting John to death because the people considered him to be a prophet (Matt. 14:3-5).

As the chief priests and elders quickly realized, Jesus' question put them on the horns of a great dilemma. As **they began reasoning among themselves,** they saw they would be in trouble for whichever answer they gave. If they were to **say, "From heaven,"** Jesus would then say to them, **"Then why did you not believe him?"** It was not simply that they had rejected John himself but that they had also rejected John's clear testimony about Jesus, whom that prophet had openly acclaimed to be "the Lamb of God who takes away the sin of the world" and the very "Son of God" (John 1:29, 34). To have accepted John as a prophet **from heaven** would have required accepting Jesus as the Messiah; and that they absolutely would not do.

No amount of testimony from John or evidence from Jesus Himself would bring them to recognize Him as Messiah. They were trained to discount or explain away facts as well as scriptural truths that were not consistent with their humanly-devised religious beliefs and standards. The man born blind whom Jesus had healed told his Pharisee inquisitors, "We know that God does not hear sinners; but if anyone is God-fearing, and does His will, He hears him. Since the beginning of time it has never been heard that anyone opened the eyes of a person born blind. If this man were not from God, He could do nothing" (John 9:31-33). But the Pharisees were unmoved by those obvious truths. Instead, they lashed out at the man, resentful of his presumption in trying to teach the teachers of Israel (v. 34). When unbelief investigates spiritual truth, it is predisposed to reject it.

As the religious rulers continued to discuss Jesus' question, they realized that if they answered the opposite way they would also be in trouble. If they said John's ministry and message were **from men,** they would lose what little credibility they had with the people and would even incite their ire, because the **multitude** still considered **John to be a prophet.** They themselves firmly believed that **John** was not **a prophet,** but they did not dare state that belief in public. Their only recourse, therefore, was to confess with embarrassment, **We do not know.**

Consequently Jesus replied, **"Neither will I tell you by what authority I do these things."** As Jesus well knew, had He given them an answer, they would only have used it against Him. They were not interested in learning the truth about either John or Jesus. Their sole purpose was to induce Jesus to again claim messiahship and divinity so they would have grounds for putting Him to death for blasphemy (cf. John 5:18; Matt. 22:15).

The religious leaders persisted in rejecting the light Christ sent them, and He therefore turned it off. He had no more teaching for the scribes, Pharisees, chief priests, and others whose self-satisfaction blinded them to the truth of the gospel and their own need for it. For them there would only be further warning and condemnation. In a long series of woes, Jesus was about to declare judgment against them for doing their deeds to be seen of men, for refusing to enter the kingdom themselves and for hindering others from entering, for being blind religious guides, for being outwardly righteous but inwardly wicked, for honoring the ancient prophets in name but being of the same mind as their forefathers who killed the prophets, and for being a brood of vipers destined for hell (Matt. 23:5, 13, 16, 27, 30, 33).

When He was on trial before the high priest Caiaphas, "Jesus kept silent," refusing to give a single further word of testimony (Matt. 26:63). And when Pilate asked Him to respond to the accusations of the chief priests and elders, Jesus "did not answer him with regard to even a single charge" (27:14).

When a person steadfastly refuses to hear God's truth and to receive His grace, God may choose to withdraw Himself. In face of the unrelenting wickedness of mankind in Noah's day, the Lord declared, "My Spirit shall not strive with man forever" (Gen. 6:3). The Lord finally said of unrepentant Ephraim, "Ephraim is joined to idols; let him alone" (Hos. 4:17), and in relation to rebellious Judah, "He turned Himself to become their enemy, He fought against them" (Isa. 63:10).

Even as Jesus approached Jerusalem during His triumphal entry, He had wept over the city, saying, "If you had known in this day, even you, the things which make for peace! But now they have been hidden from your eyes. For the days shall come upon you when your enemies will throw up a bank before you, and surround you, and hem you in on every side, and will level you to the ground and your children within you, and they will not leave in you one stone upon another, because you did not recognize the time of your visitation" (Luke 19:41-44). And soon after Jesus' severe excoriation of the scribes and Pharisees, He lamented, "O Jerusalem, Jerusalem, who kills the prophets and stones those who are sent to her! How often I wanted to gather your children together, the way a hen gathers her chicks under her wings, and you were unwilling. Behold, your house is being left to you desolate! For I say to you, from now on you shall not see Me until you say, 'Blessed is He who comes in the name of the Lord!'" (Matt. 23:37-39).

THE CHARACTERIZATION

But what do you think? A man had two sons, and he came to the first and said, 'Son, go work today in the vineyard.' And he answered and said, 'I will, sir'; and he did not go. And he came to the second and said the same thing. But he answered and said, 'I will not'; yet he afterward regretted it and went. Which of the two did the will of his father?" They said, "The latter." (21:28-31a)

In this short parable Jesus characterizes two contrasting responses to the gospel. And once again He gives His opponents the opportunity to condemn themselves out of their own mouths.

In the first instance, the **son** who was asked to **work . . . in the vineyard** told his father, **"I will, sir,"** but he **did not go.** The implication is that he had never intended to go and lied to his father to give the false impression of obedience. The **second** son at first refused to go, saying, **"I will not,"** but he **afterward regretted it and went.**

When Jesus asked the chief priests and elders, **"Which of the two did the will of his father?"** they gave the obvious answer, **"The latter."**

Jesus' point in this story is that doing is more important than mere saying. It is, of course, best for a person to say he will do God's will and then do it. But it is immeasurably better to at first refuse His will and then repent and do it than to hypocritically agree to do it but not. In this context, the doing of God's will relates to acceptance of the gospel, of receiving Jesus as the Messiah and as Savior and Lord.

THE CONNECTION

Jesus said to them, "Truly I say to you that the tax-gatherers and harlots will get into the kingdom of God before you. For John came to you in the way of righteousness and you did not believe him; but the tax-gatherers and

harlots did believe him; and you, seeing this, did not even feel remorse afterward so as to believe him" (21:31b-32)

After His opponents gave the only possible answer to His question, **Jesus** showed them their connection to the parable. He informed them that, although their answer to His question was right, their response to Him and His ministry was wrong and wicked. Their own words condemned them. They did not correspond to "the latter" son, who did the father's will, but to the former, who did not do it. "They say things, and do not do them," Jesus said on a later occasion (Matt. 23:3). They claimed to obey God, but their actions denied that He had any place in their hearts. They claimed to be longing for the Messiah and lauded His name; but when He came, they would not have Him.

The Lord therefore **said to them, "Truly I say to you that the tax-gatherers and harlots will get into the kingdom of God before you."** No rebuke could have cut them deeper or infuriated them more, because in their eyes, **tax-gatherers and harlots** were the scum of society, perhaps even worse than Gentiles. **Tax-gatherers** not only were merciless extortioners but were traitors to their own people, Jews who bought franchises from the Romans to collect taxes from their own people to support the Roman occupation. **Harlots** were the epitome of gross immorality. If any people were totally outside the pale of God's mercy, the self-righteous Jewish leaders thought, it was those two groups.

The men who now stood before Jesus, on the other hand, were the religious elite, the interpreters of God's law and the keepers of God's Temple. They claimed to give their lives in obedience to God and lived under the self-serving illusion that, because of their exalted positions and their many religious works, they were of all men most pleasing to Him.

Yet Jesus declared to those proud leaders that **tax-gatherers and harlots** who chose to disobey God but later repented would **get into the kingdom of God before** they would. **Before you** does not mean that the unbelieving leaders would eventually enter the Kingdom, because no unbeliever will ever enter. Jesus simply used the expression to show God's reversal of man-made standards for salvation. The **tax-gatherers and harlots** were nearer the **kingdom** than the chief priests and elders, not because they were inherently more righteous or acceptable to God, but because they were more ready to acknowledge their need for God's grace than the self-satisfied priests and elders. Jesus' point was that claims to religion do not qualify a person to enter the kingdom, and even gross sin, when repented of, will not keep a person out.

"For John came to you in the way of righteousness," Jesus continued, giving the answer to the question His opponents had earlier refused to answer. To say that **John came . . . in the way of righteousness** was to say not only that his ministry was from God but that he was a godly man. He was a holy, righteous, virtuous, Spirit-filled man whom God had sent to prepare the way for His Son, the Messiah. He preached a righteous message and lived a righteous life. "Among those born of women," Jesus had affirmed, "there has not arisen anyone greater than John the Baptist" (Matt. 11:11).

"But **you did not believe him,**" Jesus told them. The Jewish leaders had been skeptical of John from the beginning, having sent a group of priests and Levites to question him (John 1:19-25). And when John "saw many of the Pharisees and Sadducees coming for baptism, he said to them, 'You brood of vipers, who warned you to flee from the wrath to come? Therefore bring forth fruit in keeping with repentance; and do not suppose that you can say to yourselves, "We have Abraham for our father"; for I say to you, that God is able from these stones to raise up children to Abraham'" (Matt. 3:7-9).

"**But the tax-gatherers and harlots did believe him,**" Jesus said. Some of **the tax-gatherers** had been open to the gospel even in its incomplete form taught by John the Baptist. As evidence of their sincerity in being baptized for the repentance of their sins, they asked John, "Teacher, what shall we do?" (Luke 3:12). Although no specific instance is mentioned in the gospels, Jesus makes clear that among the multitudes who were baptized by John there were also some **harlots** who **did believe him** and who, like those tax-gatherers, confessed their sins and were forgiven (see Matt. 3:5-6).

Concluding His indictment, Jesus said, "**And you, seeing this, did not even feel remorse afterward so as to believe him.**" They did not believe John's message when they heard it themselves and did not even **believe him** when they saw the transformed lives of the tax-gatherers and harlots who had believed. In other words, they would not be convicted either by the truth of the message or its power to transform sinners.

They had been exposed to the full light of the prophet of God and the even greater light of the Son of God, yet they refused to be enlightened. They had heard the message of the herald of the King and the message of the King Himself, yet they would not listen or believe. They had witnessed the power of John and the power of Christ, yet they would not be moved.

Judgment on Christ's Rejecters

28

(21:33-46)

"Listen to another parable. There was a landowner who planted a vineyard and put a wall around it and dug a wine press in it, and built a tower, and rented it out to vine-growers, and went on a journey. And when the harvest time approached, he sent his slaves to the vine-growers to receive his produce. And the vine-growers took his slaves and beat one, and killed another, and stoned a third. Again he sent another group of slaves larger than the first; and they did the same thing to them. But afterward he sent his son to them, saying, 'They will respect my son.' But when the vine-growers saw the son, they said among themselves, 'This is the heir; come, let us kill him, and seize his inheritance.' And they took him, and threw him out the vineyard, and killed him. Therefore when the owner of the vineyard comes, what will he do to those vine-growers?" They said to Him, "He will bring those wretches to a wretched end, and will rent out the vineyard to other vine-growers, who will pay him the proceeds at the proper seasons." Jesus said to them, "Did you never read in the Scriptures, 'The stone which the builders rejected, this became the chief cornerstone; this came about from the Lord, and it is marvelous in our eyes'? Therefore I say to you, the kingdom of God will be taken away from you, and be given to a nation producing the fruit of it. And he who falls on this stone will be broken to pieces; but on whomever it falls, it will scatter him like dust."

And when the chief priests and the Pharisees heard His parables, they understood that He was speaking about them. And when they sought to seize Him, they feared the multitudes, because they held Him to be a prophet. (21:33-46)

Jesus continued to respond to hostile retaliation by the hypocritical, threatened chief priests and elders, who had demanded that He tell them by what authority He carried on His ministry, and especially by what authority He had driven the merchants and moneychangers out of the Temple. After they had refused to say whether John the Baptist's ministry was from God or men, Jesus indicted them by means of the parable of the two sons and explained it by declaring that tax-gatherers and harlots would enter the kingdom before those religionists. He then threatened them further with **another parable,** the second in a trilogy of judgment parables (see also 22:1-14), which even more graphically illustrated their willful rejection of God.

The Illustration

"Listen to another parable. There was a landowner who planted a vineyard and put a wall around it and dug a wine press in it, and built a tower, and rented it out to vine-growers, and went on a journey. And when the harvest time approached, he sent his slaves to the vine-growers to receive produce. And the vine-growers took his slaves and beat one, and killed another, and stoned a third. Again he sent another group of slaves larger than the first; and they did the same thing to them. But afterward he sent his son to them, saying, 'They will respect my son.' But when the vine-growers saw the son, they said among themselves, 'This is the heir; come, let us kill him, and seize his inheritance.' And they took him, and threw him out the vineyard, and killed him. (21:33-39)

As always in parabolic teaching, Jesus told a simple and understandable story, often including a shocking element, to explain a profound truth that was unknown or generally misunderstood. The situation involved in the **parable** of the **landowner who planted a vineyard** was commonplace in that agrarian society and was easy for His hearers to identify with. In New Testament times, the hillsides of Palestine were covered with grape vineyards, which were a mainstay of the economy. It was not unusual for a wealthy man to buy a piece of land and develop it for **a vineyard.** He would first **put a wall** of stone or a hedge of briars **around it** to protect it from wild animals and thieves. He would then make **a wine press,** sometimes having to cut it out of bedrock. In the wide, shallow, upper basin, the grapes would be squeezed, and the juice would run down through a trough into a lower basin. From there the grape juice would be poured into wineskins or clay jars for storage. Often the owner would build **a tower,** which would be used as a lookout post against marauders, as shelter for the workers, and as a storage place for seed and implements.

Those details emphasized the owner's great care in developing the vineyard. And when everything was in order, he **rented it out to vine-growers** he thought were reliable caretakers, making an agreement with them to pay a certain percentage of the proceeds to him as rent. The rest would belong to them, as payment for their work in cultivating the vineyard. Satisfied that his business venture was in good hands, the owner **went on a journey.**

Some months later, **when the harvest time approached,** the owner **sent his slaves to the vine-growers to receive his** agreed-upon percentage of **produce.** But instead of paying what they owed the owner, the **vine-growers took his slaves and beat one, and killed another, and stoned a third.** As he did with the story of the fig tree (21:18-21; cf. Mark 11:12-14, 20-21), Matthew, under Holy Spirit inspiration, here condensed several episodes into one. From Mark's account we learn that Jesus said the first three slaves came separately, one after another (Mark 12:2-5). The wicked growers **beat,** or scourged, the first slave, leaving him bruised and bloody. The second slave they **killed** outright and then **stoned a third.** If the stoning referred to the kind used in Jewish executions, that slave was probably killed as well. After that, the owner **sent another group of slaves larger than the first, and they did the same thing to them,** "beating some and killing others" (Mark 12:5).

The tenant growers had a marvelous opportunity to develop a good living. They had an excellent vineyard to cultivate and were given the complete trust of the owner to operate it. But they were not content with merely a good living; they wanted the whole harvest for themselves and were merciless in achieving that end.

After the brutal rejection of his servants, the owner **sent his son to them, saying, "They will respect my son."** To the contrary, however, that act simply drove the growers to greater greed and more heinous treachery. **When the vine-growers saw the son, they said among themselves, "This is the heir; come, let us kill him, and seize his inheritance." And they took him, and threw him out of the vineyard, and killed him.** Originally, they had plotted simply to keep all the profits from the vineyard; now they planned to expropriate the entire vineyard.

The murder of **the son** was coldly premeditated. The growers did not mistake him for another slave but knew exactly who he was. It was for the very reason that he *was* the son that they planned his murder in order to **seize his inheritance.**

By the end of this startling and dramatic parable, the interest of the Jewish leaders and the many bystanders was thoroughly piqued. The story generated great pity for the betrayed, grieving owner and resentful rage at the heartless, brutal growers.

In fact, the patience of the owner and the brutality of the growers are so absolutely astounding, so unrealistic and abnormal, that some critics say Jesus overdrew the story or that the gospel writers exaggerated His original version. But those extremes are essential to the parable's point. It was the very uncommonness of the owner's patience and of the growers' wickedness that Jesus' wanted His hearers to notice.

THE CONCLUSION

Therefore when the owner of the vineyard comes, what will he do to those vine-growers?" They said to Him, "He will bring those wretches to a wretched end, and will rent out the vineyard to other vine-growers, who will pay him the proceeds at the proper seasons." (21:40-41)

In typical rabbinical fashion, Jesus led His hearers to finish the story themselves, asking, **"What will he do to those vine-growers?"** The chief priests and elders readily replied with moral indignation, **"He will bring those wretches to a wretched end, and will rent out the vineyard to other vine-growers, who will pay him the proceeds at the proper seasons."** They no doubt were highly pleased with this unusual opportunity to parade their self-righteousness before Jesus. They rightly assessed the proper ending of the parable, that the irate owner would first severely punish the wicked growers and then replace them with others who were reliable. They were completely unaware that, as they fed their pride on Jesus' baited question, they sprang the trap of their own condemnation.

THE EXPLANATION

Jesus said to them, "Did you never read in the Scriptures, 'The stone which the builders rejected, this became the chief cornerstone; this came about from the Lord, and it is marvelous in our eyes'? (21:42)

At first glance, this comment seems irrelevant to the parable. But the Lord was using a familiar passage from the Old Testament to reinforce the parable's point, and in doing so He changed metaphors. In a sarcastic query He asked the self-appointed authorities on the Old Testament, **"Did you never read in the Scriptures?"** and then cited the well-known words of Psalm 118:22.

Jesus quoted the same psalm from which were taken the acclamations of the multitude in His triumphal entry into Jerusalem, when He was hailed by the messianic title, Son of David (Matt. 21:9). And it was, in fact, for His accepting that messianic praise that Jesus was rebuked by the Pharisees (Luke 19:39). Now, from the same section of the psalm, Jesus reminded the religious leaders of **the stone which the builders rejected** that **became the chief cornerstone.**

A cornerstone was the most basic and essential part of a building, from which the proper placement and alignment of every other part was determined. If the cornerstone was imperfectly cut or placed, the symmetry and stability of the entire building would be adversely affected. Sometimes **the builders rejected** a number of stones before the right one was selected. In this account, one such rejected **stone** eventually **became the chief corner stone.**

For many centuries, Israel had been the **stone which the** empire **builders** of the world had rejected as insignificant and despised, fit only for exploiting and then discarding. But in the Lord's divine plan, Israel was chosen to be the **chief corner stone** in the redemptive history of the world, the nation through which salvation would come.

But the figure has an even greater significance than that. Peter declared in Jerusalem before the religious rulers shortly after Pentecost, "Let it be known to all of you, and to all the people of Israel, that by the name of Jesus Christ the Nazarene, whom you crucified, whom God raised from the dead . . . He is the stone which was rejected by you, the builders, but which became the very corner stone. And there is salvation in no one else; for there is no other name under heaven that has been given among men, by which we must be saved" (Acts 4:10-12). The greater **stone** than Israel is Jesus Christ, and **the builders** who **rejected** Him were the Jewish leaders, representing all Israel, and in a fuller sense the entire unbelieving world. The **stone . . . rejected** was the crucified Christ, and the restored **chief corner stone** is the resurrected Christ.

Jesus thereby tied the messianic psalm to the parable in order to reinforce His point. The rejected Son and the rejected stone both refer to Christ. The verse from Psalm 118 goes beyond the parable to allude also to the resurrection of the Son, something the parable could not cover and still maintain its simple naturalness.

Peter reiterated the same truth in his first letter: "Behold I lay in Zion a choice stone, a precious corner stone, and he who believes in Him shall not be disappointed. This precious value, then, is for you who believe. But for those who disbelieve, 'the stone which the builders rejected, this became the very corner stone,' and, 'a stone of stumbling and a rock of offense'; for they stumble because they are disobedient to the word, and to this doom they were also appointed" (1 Pet. 2:6-8). Paul declared to the Ephesian believers, "You are no longer strangers and aliens, but you are fellow citizens with the saints, and are of God's household, having been built upon the foundation of the apostles and prophets, Christ Jesus Himself being the corner stone" (Eph. 2:19-20).

When they told Jesus that the wretched vine-growers would be brought to a wretched end (v. 41), the Temple rulers judged themselves in the same way David had judged himself before Nathan. After hearing the prophet's touching parable about the rich man who took the poor man's only pet lamb to feed a visiting traveler, "David's anger burned greatly against the man, and he said to Nathan, 'As the Lord lives, surely the man who has done this deserves to die. And he must make restitution for the lamb fourfold, because he did this thing and had no compassion.' Nathan then said to David, 'You are the man!'" (2 Sam. 12:5-7).

Jesus, in effect, had said to the chief priests and elders, "You are the men! You are the wretched vine-growers who, by your own declaration, deserve a wretched end for beating and killing the vineyard owner's servants and then killing his son. Don't you realize that the owner is God, the vineyard is His kingdom, the servants were His prophets, and I am His Son? You have just judged yourselves guilty of condemning to death not only the prophets but even God's own Son."

With regard to killing the prophets, later the same day Jesus said to the unbelieving Jewish leaders, in particular the scribes and Pharisees, "You build the tombs of the prophets and adorn the monuments of the righteous, and say, 'If we had been living in the days of our fathers, we would not have been partners with them in shedding the blood of the prophets.' Consequently you bear witness against yourselves, that you are sons of those who murdered the prophets. Fill up then the measure of the guilt of your fathers" (Matt. 23:29-31).

God had prepared a place of great beauty and blessing and then graciously given stewardship of it to His people Israel. It was a place of promise, hope, deliverance, salvation, and security. But Israel misappropriated all those blessings for herself, robbing God of the gratitude, glory, and honor due Him. She persecuted the prophets He patiently and lovingly sent to call her to repentance and forgiveness. Jewish tradition held that Isaiah had been sawed in two with a wooden saw (cf. Heb. 11:37). From Scripture we know that Jeremiah was thrown into a pit of slime, and tradition held that he was eventually stoned to death. Ezekiel was rejected, Elijah and Amos had to run for their lives, Micah was smashed in the face by those who refused to hear his message (1 Kings 22:24), and Zechariah was actually murdered in God's own Temple (2 Chron. 24:20-22; cf. Matt. 23:35). Old Testament history bore witness to their murderous hearts, whose wickedness would culminate in killing the Son of God.

Through this parable and its explanation Jesus presented one of His clearest claims to divinity. The parable even alludes to the detail of His being crucified outside the city of Jerusalem (cf. Heb. 13:12), just as the vineyard owner's son was cast out of the vineyard before being murdered.

Jesus also made it clear that the Jewish leaders who rejected Him were without excuse, that, like the evil vine-growers, they knew He was God's Son but refused to accept and honor Him as such. They wanted Him dead not because He was evil and ungodly but because He threatened their evil and ungodly control of the Temple and of the entire Jewish religious system.

Throughout history, and still today, many people refuse to receive Jesus Christ as Savior and Lord not because of lack of evidence but because they refuse to believe the evidence. They do not believe simply because they do not *want* to believe.

The Application

Therefore I say to you, the kingdom of God will be taken away from you, and be given to a nation producing the fruit of it. And he who falls on this stone will be broken to pieces; but on whomever it falls, it will scatter him like dust." (21:43-44)

With those straightforward, unambiguous words, Jesus removed whatever uncertainty may have remained in the minds of the chief priests and elders about what He was saying to them. In the first half of verse 43 and in verse 44, the Lord reiterated the *judgment* on unbelieving Israel and her ungodly leaders; in the second half of verse 43 He reiterated their *replacement* by believing Gentiles.

"Therefore I say to you," the Lord declared, no doubt looking intently into the eyes of His adversaries, **"the kingdom of God will be taken away from you."** In their stead the kingdom would **be given to a nation producing the fruit of it.**

When he first began preaching the kingdom, John the Baptist demanded that the Pharisees and Sadducees who wanted to be baptized first "bring forth fruit in keeping with repentance" (Matt. 3:8). **The fruit of** the kingdom is the demonstrated righteousness produced out of a life turned from sin (see Phil 1:11; Col. 1:10). The unbelieving religious leaders would not turn from their sin and repent, and therefore they could not produce kingdom **fruit** (genuinely righteous behavior). They were spiritually barren, and because of that willful barrenness they were cursed, like the fig tree that had leaves but no figs (21:18-19).

By grace through God's unconditional promise, Israel will one day return to God and bear fruit for His kingdom. "God has not rejected His people whom He foreknew," Paul assured his fellow Jews. And when "the fulness of the Gentiles has come, . . . all Israel will be saved; just as it is written, 'The Deliverer will come from Zion, He will remove ungodliness from Jacob'" (Rom. 11:2, 25-26).

But in the meanwhile God has chosen another people to be His own witness. He had long ago declared "I will call those who were not My people, 'My people,' and her who was not beloved, 'Beloved.' And it shall be that in the place where it was said to them, 'You are not My people,' there they shall be called sons of the living God" (Rom. 9:25-26).

Ethnos (**nation**) has the basic meaning of "people" and seems best translated that way in this verse, as in Acts 8:9. The **nation,** or people, who produce the fruit of the kingdom is the church, "a chosen race, a royal priesthood, a holy nation, a people for God's own possession" (1 Pet. 2:9). As the only citizens of God's kingdom, only believers are equipped by the Holy Spirit to bear kingdom **fruit.** "I am the vine, you are the branches," Jesus said; "he who abides in Me, and I in him, he bears much fruit; for apart from Me you can do nothing" (John 15:5).

And he who falls on this rejected **stone,** that is, Jesus Himself, **will be broken to pieces.** The Jewish leaders who, as it were, fell on Jesus and put Him to death would themselves **be broken to pieces.** And on **whomever it,** Jesus the stone, **falls, it will scatter him like dust.** For those who will not have Jesus as Deliverer, He becomes Destroyer. Just as the Father has given all salvation to the Son (John 14:6), He has also "given all judgment to the Son" (John 5:22).

"If anyone does not love the Lord, let him be accursed," Paul declared (1 Cor. 16:22). To put that truth in the language of this text, let such a person **be broken to pieces,** crushed into powder and scattered **like dust,** just as the Lord Jesus Christ Himself had warned. God's enemies are destined to be pulverized into nothingness. To try to destroy Christ is to assure one's own destruction. Through Daniel the Lord predicted Christ's ultimate coming in judgment against the unbelieving peoples and nations of the world, represented by the magnificent and seemingly invulnerable statue of gold, silver, bronze, iron, and clay. As the "stone . . . cut out without hands," Jesus will one day strike the statue of unbelieving mankind, and "then the iron, the clay, the bronze, the silver and the gold [will be] crushed all at the same time, and [become] like chaff from the summer threshing floors; and the wind [will carry] them away so that not a trace of them [will be] found" (Dan. 2:32-35).

THE REACTION

And when the chief priests and the Pharisees heard His parables, they understood that He was speaking about them. And when they sought to seize Him, they feared the multitudes, because they held Him to be a prophet. (21:45-46)

There was no mistaking that these wicked religious leaders, typified by the **chief priests and Pharisees,** were the objects of Jesus' denunciation and condemnation. Beyond any doubt, **they understood that He was speaking about them.** They knew they were the son who falsely told his father he would work in the field but then did not go and that they were the wretched vine-growers who despised the vineyard owner and beat and killed his servants and eventually killed his son. They knew they were the builders who had rejected the stone that would become the chief corner stone and that, because of that rejection they themselves would be rejected by God and forbidden entrance into His kingdom.

But as always, in spite of what they understood, the Jewish leaders took nothing Jesus said to heart. They heard but refused to heed. They knew he spoke of their ungodliness and their condemnation, but they did not take even a moment to consider whether His charge against them was true. They would not be convinced, and hence could not be convicted. They would not repent, and therefore could not be forgiven. They knew the gracious truth about Jesus but would not follow Him, and they knew the damning truth about their own sin but would not turn from it.

Their only thoughts were of self-justification and revenge, so their reaction was **to seize** Jesus and put Him to death, just as they had been plotting since the beginning of His ministry. The hindrance to that happening was that **they feared the multitude, because they held** Jesus **to be a prophet.** The leaders had contempt for God but no fear of Him. They also had contempt for **the multitude** but *did* fear what they might do. They were not God-pleasers but men-pleasers. Consequently, they held off arresting Jesus until they were convinced they could turn the people against Him, which a few days later they succeeded in doing. Finally disillusioned with the Messiah who would not be their kind of savior and with the King who would not be their kind of lord, **the multitude** gave the rulers no more cause to fear them. When given the choice of releasing Jesus or the insurrectionist Barabbas, they chose Barabbas. And when Pilate asked what he should "do with Jesus who is called Christ," they cried, "Let Him be crucified!" (Matt. 27:21-22).

This amazing passage portrays God's gracious provision for men, His patience with their unbelief and rejection, and His love in sending even His only Son for their redemption. But it also displays His righteous judgment that will be executed when His divine patience has run its course.

The passage also portrays Jesus' deity as the Son of God, His obedience to His Father's will, His willingness to come to earth and die for man's redemption, and His resurrection. But it also displays His coming one day as the instrument of divine judgment, to destroy and break in pieces those who have rejected Him.

And the passage portrays sinful mankind, its great blessings and privileges from God, its opportunity to receive truth from His prophets and eternal life from the Son. It portrays their responsibility and their accountability before a loving but just God, before whom they will be either redeemed because of faith or condemned because of unbelief.

Responding to a Royal Invitation

29

(22:1-14)

And Jesus answered and spoke to them again in parables, saying, "The kingdom of heaven may be compared to a king, who gave a wedding feast for his son. And he sent out his slaves to call those who had been invited to the wedding feast, and they were unwilling to come. Again he sent out other slaves saying, 'Tell those who have been invited, "Behold, I have prepared my dinner; my oxen and my fattened livestock are all butchered and everything is ready; come to the wedding feast."' But they paid no attention and went their way, one to his own farm, another to his business, and the rest seized his slaves and mistreated them and killed them. But the king was enraged and sent his armies, and destroyed those murderers, and set their city on fire. Then he said to his slaves, 'The wedding is ready, but those who were invited were not worthy. Go therefore to the main highways, and as many as you find there, invite to the wedding feast.' And those slaves went out into the streets, and gathered together all they found, both evil and good; and the wedding hall was filled with dinner guests. But when the king came in to look over the dinner guests, he saw there a man not dressed in wedding clothes, and he said to him, 'Friend, how did you come in here without wedding clothes?' And he was speechless. Then the king said to the servants, 'Bind him hand and foot, and cast him into the outer darkness; in that place there shall be weeping and gnashing of teeth.' For many are called, but few are chosen." (22:1-14)

This parable is the third in Jesus' trilogy of judgment parables given in response to the Jewish religious leaders who maliciously challenged His authority (21:23, 28-30, 33-39). It is among the most dramatic and powerful of all His parables, which, though directed specifically at those leaders and all unbelieving Israel whom they represented, also has far-reaching significance and application for subsequent times, certainly including our own.

For three years Jesus had been preaching and teaching the gospel of the kingdom, which included proclaiming Himself as the Messiah, the Son of God and Savior of the world. He had been offering Himself and His kingdom to the people of Israel, His own people, the chosen people of God. But at the end of those three years, all but a handful of Jews had rejected Him. Although Jesus had always been popular with the masses wherever He ministered, their acceptance of Him was for the most part superficial and selfish.

The multitudes were awed by Jesus' straightforward, authoritative teaching, which was in refreshing contrast to the confusing, legalistic, and complicated tradition taught by their scribes and Pharisees. They were even more awed by His healing miracles, which had brought restored health, sanity, and even life to so many countless thousands of their friends and loved ones. They doubtlessly appreciated the fact that Jesus never took financial advantage of them, never taking payment for any supernatural good work He did. On the contrary, He was always giving to them freely, and had on several occasions miraculously fed thousands. They deeply admired Jesus for His humble, self-giving love and compassion, and they must have rejoiced when He rebuked and embarrassed their hypocritical, self-righteous leaders, who looked down on them in contemptuous superiority. How wonderful, they must have thought, that the Messiah not only is so powerful but also so compassionate.

But when the people finally realized the kind of Messiah Jesus was, and especially that He had no plans to deliver them from the Roman oppressors, their acclamation quickly turned to rejection—as is evident in their change of mood from Sunday to Thursday of this last Passover week of Jesus' ministry. Therefore, as He continued to respond to the Jewish leaders in the Temple, where He was teaching on Wednesday morning (21:23), it was also to the multitudes that the third judgment parable was directed.

THE INVITATION REJECTED

And Jesus answered and spoke to them again in parables, saying, "The kingdom of heaven may be compared to a king, who gave a wedding feast for his son. And he sent out his slaves to call those who had been invited to the wedding feast, and they were unwilling to come. Again he sent out other slaves saying, 'Tell those who have been invited, "Behold, I have prepared my dinner; my oxen and my fattened livestock are all butchered and everything is ready; come to the wedding feast."' But they paid no attention and went their way, one to his own farm, another to his business, and the rest seized his slaves and mistreated them and killed them." (22:1-6)

The parable contains four scenes, the first of which depicts the rejection of the invitation. Although none of His hearers may ever have attended a royal wedding feast, they were all familiar with wedding feasts in general and had some idea of the importance and magnificence of one that a king would prepare for his own son.

As **Jesus answered** the chief priests and elders (21:23), He was continuing to respond to their bitter challenge of His authority and **spoke to them again in parables** for the third time. It is likely they heard little of what He said, because their minds were by then singularly and unalterably bent on His arrest and execution. They had wanted to seize Him after He related the second parable but were still afraid of what the crowds might do (21:46).

In His first two parables Jesus gave no introduction, saving the explanation and application to the end. In this parable, however, He begins by stating that it illustrates **the kingdom of heaven.** Because most Jews believed that **the kingdom of heaven** was reserved exclusively for them, and possibly a few Gentile proselytes, the audience in the Temple immediately knew that what Jesus was going to say closely applied to them.

Although they had many perverted ideas about **the kingdom of heaven,** because the term **heaven** was so often used as a substitute for the covenant name of God (Yahweh, or Jehovah), most Jews would have understood that it was synonymous with the kingdom of God and represented the realm of God's sovereign rule. There are past, present, and future as well as temporal and eternal aspects of **the kingdom,** but it is not restricted to any era or period of redemptive history. It is the continuing, ongoing sphere of God's rule by grace. In a narrower sense, the phrase is also used in Scripture to refer to God's dominion of redemption, His divine program of gracious salvation. As Jesus uses the phrase here, it specifically represents the spiritual community of God's redeemed people, those who are under His lordship in a personal and unique way because of their trust in His Son.

In the ancient Near East, **a wedding feast** was inseparable from the wedding itself, which involved a week-long series of meals and festivities and was the highlight of all social life. For a royal **wedding** such as the one Jesus mentions here, the celebration often lasted for several weeks. Guests were invited to stay at the house of the groom's parents for the entire occasion, and the father would make as elaborate provisions as he could afford. A royal wedding, of course, would be held in the palace, and a king would be able to afford whatever he desired.

A **wedding feast** that a **king** prepared **for his son** would be a feast of all feasts, and Jesus was therefore picturing the most elaborate celebration imaginable. The fact that it was a **wedding** celebration was incidental to the purpose of the parable, the only mention of the groom being that of identifying him as the king's **son**. No mention at all is made of the bride or of any other aspect of a wedding. The point is that because the feast represents the greatest festivity imaginable, given by the greatest monarch imaginable, for the most-honored guests imaginable, a royal **wedding feast** was chosen as the illustration of the ultimate celebration.

When all the preparations were complete, the king **sent out his slaves to call those who had been invited to the wedding feast**. The fact that they **had been invited** indicates that the guests were invited earlier and already knew they were expected to attend the wedding. To be a pre-invited guest to the king's wedding was among the highest honors possible, and no doubt those who had received invitations were boasting to their neighbors and friends. It is therefore inconceivable that, when the actual **call** came to attend, **they were unwilling to come**.

As with the previous parable of the wicked vine-growers, it is the shockingly extreme and unthinkable nature of the events mentioned that are central to the story's point. Jesus' hearers already would have begun to think to themselves, "Who would do such a thing? The very idea is preposterous." Attending the royal wedding would be an even greater experience than receiving the invitation, and it would have provided the finest food and the most prestigious fellowship in the land. Not only that, but an invitation from one's king not only brought honor but obligation. It was a serious offense to spurn the king's favor.

The initial response of the king, like the initial response of the vineyard owner, is as amazing as the responses of the guests. Few monarchs were known for their humility and patience, especially in the face of open insult. But that king **sent out other slaves saying, "Tell those who have been invited, 'Behold, I have prepared my dinner; my oxen and my fattened livestock are all butchered and everything is ready; come to the wedding feast.'"**

The **dinner** was the first of many meals eaten during the feast, and it was ready to be served. "Remind the guests," the king said in effect, "of all the preparations that have been made. The **oxen and fattened livestock are all butchered** and waiting to be roasted, **and everything** else **is ready** also. Plead with the people to **come to the wedding feast** now."

But as before, the invited guests disregarded the call from the king, except that their refusal this time was even more crass and brutal. Many of the invitees were coldly indifferent, acting as if the wedding were of no consequence. They responded by carrying on business as usual. They **went their way**, doing the things they would normally have done in looking after their own interests, represented by the **farm** and **business**. They were so selfishly preoccupied with personal concerns for profit that the invitation and the repeated calls of the king to stop work and attend his son's wedding were altogether ignored. They willingly and purposely forfeited the beauty, grandeur, and honor of the wedding for the sake of their everyday, mundane, self-serving endeavors. They were not concerned about the king's honor but only about what they perceived as their own best interests.

But another group of guests were worse than indifferent. Rather than being concerned about offending the king, they were themselves offended at his persistence.

In an act of unbelievably brutal arrogance, they **seized** the king's **slaves and mistreated them and killed them.** Contempt for the king's **slaves** demonstrated contempt for the king himself, and in mistreating and killing his slaves they committed a flagrant act of rebellion.

As already noted, because Jesus had said that the parable was about the kingdom of heaven, its meaning needed no interpretation to any thinking hearer. The king obviously was God, and the invited guests were His chosen people, Israel, those who already had been called by Him.

God first called His chosen people through Abraham, whose descendants would be blessed and be a channel of blessing to the rest of the world (Gen. 12:2-3). After being captive in Egypt for 400 years, the chosen people were delivered through Moses. Through His prophets the Lord declared, "When Israel was a youth I loved him, and out of Egypt I called My son" (Hos. 11:1), and, "You only have I chosen among all the families of the earth" (Amos 3:2). In one of the most poignant accounts in Scripture, God described Israel as an abandoned newborn, with its umbilical cord untied and squirming in its own blood. To that hopeless infant He had said, "Live!" and it lived and prospered. The Lord bathed it, anointed it with oil, clothed and protected it, and adorned it with jewelry (Ezek 16:4-14).

The wedding feast represented God's promised blessing to Israel, a figure understood by everyone in the Temple that day. According to talmudic literature, the Messiah's coming would be accompanied by a grand banquet given for His chosen people.

The **slaves** God sent to call again and again those who had been invited were John the Baptist, Jesus Himself in His preaching-teaching ministry, and the New Testament apostles, prophets, and other preachers and teachers. It would seem that the **slaves** would also have to represent New Testament preachers, because their message pertained to the King's Son, Jesus Christ. God was saying to Israel, His already-invited guests, much the same as He had said from heaven at Jesus' baptism: "Here is My Son; come and give Him honor." But John the Baptist was rejected and beheaded, Jesus was rejected and crucified, and the apostles and prophets were rejected and persecuted, many being put to death.

The indifferent guests in the parable represent people who are preoccupied with daily living and personal pursuits. They are essentially the secular-minded, those who are interested in the here and now and have no interest in spiritual things. They are the materialists, whose primary interest is accumulating things, and the ambitious, whose main concern is "getting ahead." They are not usually antagonistic to the things of God but simply have no time for them.

Those who are actively hostile to the gospel invariably are people involved in false religion, including the many forms of humanistic religion that parade under a guise of philosophy, mysticism, or scientism. The history of persecution of God's people shows that the chief persecutor has been false religion. It is the purveyors of error who are the aggressive enemies of truth, and it is therefore inevitable that, as God's Word predicts, the final world system of the antichrist will be religious, not secular.

The fact that the king sent his messengers on two different occasions cannot be pressed to mean that only two calls were extended or that the first group consisted of John the Baptist and Jesus and the second consisted of the apostles. The parable makes no distinction in the types of slaves, or messengers. The point of the two callings of the invited guests was to illustrate God's gracious patience and forbearance with the rejecters, His willingness to call Israel again and again—as John the Baptist had done for perhaps a year, as Jesus did for three years, and as the apostles did for some forty years, until Jerusalem and the Temple were destroyed in A.D. 70.

THE REJECTERS PUNISHED

But the king was enraged and sent his armies, and destroyed those murderers, and set their city on fire. Then he said to his slaves, 'The wedding is ready, but those who were invited were not worthy. (22:7-8)

The second scene in the parable depicts the punishment of the rebellious subjects who rejected the king's call. As in the parable of the vineyard, God's patience is here shown to have its limit. **The king** would have been perfectly justified in punishing the offenders when they first ignored His call. After His repeated invitations and their repeated wicked responses, He finally became **enraged**. One is reminded of God's statement with regard to the antediluvian generation: "My Spirit shall not strive with man forever" (Gen. 6:3).

The term behind **armies** (*strateuma*) refers to any group of armed forces and is probably better translated "troops," since the king would hardly have needed his full military might to accomplish his purpose. According to the king's instructions, the troops both **destroyed** the **murderers** responsible for killing his emissaries **and set their city on fire.** The fulfillment of the second prophetic feature in the story occurred in A.D. 70.

When the Roman general Titus conquered Jerusalem in that year, he killed some 1,100,000 Jews, threw their bodies over the wall, and slaughtered countless thousands more throughout Palestine. In his *Jewish War*, the Jewish historian Flavius Josephus, who witnessed the destruction of Jerusalem, graphically chronicled the horrible scene:

> That building [the Temple at Jerusalem], however, God long ago had sentenced to the flames; but now in the revolution of the time periods the fateful day had arrived, the tenth of the month Lous, the very day on which previously it had been burned by the king of Babylon. . . . One of the soldiers, neither awaiting orders nor filled with horror of so dread an undertaking, but moved by some supernatural impulse, snatched a brand from the blazing timber and, hoisted up by one of his fellow soldiers, flung the fiery missile through a golden window. . . . When the flame arose, a scream, as poignant as the tragedy, went up from the Jews . . . now that the

object which before they had guarded so closely was going to ruin. . . . While the sanctuary was burning, . . . neither pity for age nor respect for rank was shown; on the contrary, children and old people, laity and priests alike were massacred. . . . The emperor ordered the entire city and sanctuary to be razed to the ground, except only the highest towers, Phasael, Hippicus, and Mariamne, and that part of the wall that enclosed the city on the west.

The king explained to **his slaves** that **the wedding** was **ready, but those who were invited were not worthy** to attend. Their unworthiness was not because in themselves they lacked the required righteousness. Neither the original invitation nor the subsequent calls were based on merit but solely on the king's gracious favor. Ironically and tragically, they were declared to be **not worthy** because they refused an invitation that was in no way based on worth. As the parable goes on to make clear (v. 10), "both evil and good" people were called.

That which makes a person worthy of receiving salvation is not any sort of human goodness or religious or spiritual accomplishment but simply his saying yes to God's invitation to receive His Son, Jesus Christ, as Lord. The people God here declared **not worthy** were His chosen people, Israel, who would not come to Him freely and without merit through His Son. And because they rejected the Son, God rejected them for a season. Because they rejected their own Messiah, they were temporarily cast off as a nation and as God's unique chosen people.

THE NEW GUESTS INVITED

Go therefore to the main highways, and as many as you find there, invite to the wedding feast.' And those slaves went out into the streets, and gathered together all they found, both evil and good; and the wedding hall was filled with dinner guests. (22:9-10)

The third scene in the parable depicts the guests who were finally invited to replace those who had repeatedly refused the king's call. The wedding feast for the king's son was ready, but there was no one to attend unless new guests were invited.

"Go therefore to the main highways," the king told His servants, **"and as many as you find there, invite to the wedding feast."** The plan was for them to go everywhere and find everyone they could and **invite** them to come. That is precisely what Jesus commanded in the Great Commission: "Go therefore and make disciples of all the nations" (Matt. 28:19). God had long beforehand predicted through Hosea, "I will call those who were not My people, 'My people,' and her who was not beloved, 'Beloved.' And it shall be that in the place where it was said to them, 'You are not My people,' there they shall be called sons of the living God" (Rom. 9:25-26; cf. Hos. 2:23; 1:10). By the Jews' "transgression," Paul wrote in that same letter, "salvation has come to the Gentiles" (11:11).

Just as their king commanded, **those slaves went out into the streets,**

and gathered together all they found, both evil and good. They called the morally **evil** and the morally **good** alike, their being equally unworthy in themselves to come to the king's feast. The original guests had not been invited because of their moral or spiritual superiority, and neither were the newly-invited guests. Among the ancient Jews were those who lived exemplary, upright lives, who were helpful to their neighbors, told the truth, never used the Lord's name in vain, never cheated in business, and never committed adultery or murder or theft. There were also those whose lives were a moral cesspool. But the first kind of person was no more acceptable to God in himself than the second. God has always extended His call for salvation to **both evil and good** people, because neither are righteous enough and both are equally in need of salvation.

Paul makes clear that "neither fornicators, nor idolaters, nor adulterers, nor effeminate, nor homosexuals, nor thieves, nor the covetous, nor drunkards, nor revilers, nor swindlers, shall inherit the kingdom of God" (1 Cor. 6:9-10). God will not allow those whose lives are characterized by such sins to have any part of His kingdom. But He will receive for salvation a person who is guilty of any or all of those and other sins and who desires to be cleansed from his sins by the redeeming work of Christ on the cross. Therefore Paul could continue to say to his Corinthian brothers in Christ, "And such were some of you; but you were washed, but you were sanctified" (v. 11).

What makes a person worthy of salvation today is exactly what has made a person worthy of salvation since the Fall, namely, personal faith in God's gracious provision in Christ. All who accept God's invitation to His Son's celebration, that is, who follow the Son as their saving Lord, will be **dinner guests** in His divine and eternally glorious **wedding hall.**

THE INTRUDER EXPELLED

But when the king came in to look over the dinner guests, he saw there a man not dressed in wedding clothes, and he said to him, 'Friend, how did you come in here without wedding clothes?' And he was speechless. Then the king said to the servants, 'Bind him hand and foot, and cast him into the outer darkness; in that place there shall be weeping and gnashing of teeth.' For many are called, but few are chosen." (22:11-14)

The fourth and last scene in the parable focuses on an intruder into the wedding feast, who did not belong because he was **not dressed in wedding clothes.** The man obviously had been included in the general invitation, because the king made no restrictions as to who was invited, having instructed his slaves to call both the evil and good wherever they might be found. He was not a party crasher who came without an invitation, but he had come improperly **dressed,** and he obviously stood out in the great wedding hall, in stark contrast to all the other **dinner guests.**

At first reading, one wonders how any of those who accepted the king's invitation could have been expected to come properly attired. They had been rounded up from every part of the land, and many had been taken off the streets. Even if they had time to dress properly, they had no clothes befitting such an occasion as the wedding of the king's son.

But the fact that all of **the dinner guests** except that one man were **dressed in wedding clothes** indicates that the king had made provision for such **clothes.** It would have been a moral mockery, especially for such an obviously kind and gracious ruler, to invite even the most wicked people in the land to come to the feast and then exclude one poor fellow because he had no proper clothes to wear.

That man was fully accountable for being improperly dressed, but the gracious king nevertheless gave him an opportunity to justify himself, asking with undeserved respect, **"Friend, how did you come in here without wedding clothes?"** Had the man had a good reason, he would certainly have mentioned it immediately. But **he was speechless,** unable to offer the king even the feeblest excuse. It is therefore obvious that he *could* have come in **wedding clothes** had he been willing.

Until that point the man had been utterly presumptuous, thinking he could come to the king's feast on his own terms, in any clothes he wanted. He was proud and self-willed, thoughtless of the others, and, worst of all, insulting to the king. Arrogantly defying royal protocol, he was determined to "be himself."

But his arrogance was short-lived. When, as the king knew in advance, the man could not excuse himself, **the king said to the servants, "Bind him hand and foot, and cast him into the outer darkness; in that place there shall be weeping and gnashing of teeth."** The binding of **hand and foot** probably represents prevention of the man's resisting as well as prevention of his returning. By that time it was night, and although the wedding hall would be well lighted, it was dark outside. The man was permanently expelled from the presence of the king and of the king's people **into the outer darkness.** He would have great regret and remorse, and, with everyone else **in that place,** he would experience perpetual **weeping and gnashing of teeth.** But though he had a great opportunity, he had never had, and did not now have, the godly sorrow that leads to repentance and salvation (2 Cor. 7:10).

Since Cain's first attempt to please God by offering his self-appointed sacrifice, men have been trying to come to the Lord on their own terms. They may fellowship with believers, join the church, become active in the leadership, give generously to its support, and speak of devotion to God. Like the tares among the wheat, they freely coexist for a while with God's people. But in the day of judgment their falsehood will become obvious and their removal certain. Some will dare to say to God "on that day, 'Lord, Lord, did we not prophesy in Your name, and in Your name cast out demons, and in Your name perform many miracles?' And then [Christ] will declare to them, 'I never knew you; depart from Me, you who practice lawlessness'" (Matt. 7:22-23).

The proper wedding garment of a true believer is God-imputed righteousness, without which no one can enter or live in the kingdom. Unless a person's righteousness exceeds the hypocritical self-righteousness that typified the scribes and Pharisees, he "shall not enter the kingdom of heaven" (Matt. 5:20). The only acceptable wedding garment is the genuine "sanctification without which no one will see the Lord" (Heb. 12:14).

Many of Jesus' Jewish hearers that day would have recalled the beautiful passage from Isaiah which declares, "I will rejoice greatly in the Lord, my soul will exult in my God; for He has clothed me with garments of salvation, He has wrapped me with a robe of righteousness" (Isa. 61:10). Sincere Jews knew that, contrary to the man-made, legalistic traditions of their rabbis, God not only requires inner righteousness of men but He also offers it as a gift.

God's eyes, of course, can see into men's hearts to know whether their righteousness is of their own making or His granting. But even outwardly a true believer's life will evidence right living and reflect right thinking. The Lord not only *imputes* but *imparts* righteousness to His children. Only *He* can see the internal righteousness that He imputes, but *everyone* can see the external righteousness that He imparts. A child of God is characterized by a holy life. Peter made that fact clear when he described salvation as "obedience to the truth" which has "purified your souls" (1 Pet. 1:22).

Just before Jesus declared that prophesying, casting out demons, and performing miracles in His name may be false evidence of salvation, He had said that true evidence of salvation will always be apparent. A person's spiritual condition will be manifested in the fruit of his living. "Grapes are not gathered from thorn bushes, nor figs from thistles, are they?" He had asked rhetorically. "Even so, every good tree bears good fruit; but the bad tree bears bad fruit" (Matt. 7:16-17, 21-23). A holy, godly life cannot help bearing righteous fruit, because it is the natural outgrowth of the work of the Spirit within (Gal. 5:22-23).

Jesus surely would have been pleased had one of His hearers interrupted and asked, "How can I be clothed in the proper garment? What can I do to keep from being cast into the outer darkness like that man?" He no doubt would have said to that person as He had said many times before in various ways, "Come to Me, that you may have life" (John 5:40). As Paul explained to the Corinthians, God made Christ "who knew no sin to be sin on our behalf, that we might become the righteousness of God in Him" (2 Cor. 5:21). That is the wedding garment that God demands and His Son provides.

Jesus did not ask the Jewish leaders to comment on this parable as He had done with the previous two, where in each case they condemned themselves by their answers (21:31-32, 40-45). He knew they would not be trapped again, because it was now obvious that the whole thrust of the parables was to condemn them. Their only purpose, now heating up to a fury, was to trap and condemn Him to death (22:15; cf. 21:46).

Consequently, the Lord closed with the simple but sobering statement, **Many are called, but few are chosen.** That phrase reflects the scriptural balance between God's sovereignty and man's will. The invitations to the wedding feast went out to

many, representative of everyone to whom the gospel message is sent. **But few** of those who heard the call were willing to accept it and thereby be among the **chosen.** The gospel invitation is sent to everyone, because it is not the Father's will that a single person be excluded from His kingdom and perish in the outer darkness of hell (2 Pet. 3:9). But not everyone wants God, and many who claim to want Him do not want Him on His terms. Those who are saved enter God's kingdom because of their willing acceptance of His sovereign, gracious provision. Those who are lost are excluded from the kingdom because of their willing rejection of that same sovereign grace.

Our Obligation to God and Government

30

(22:15-22)

Then the Pharisees went and counseled together how they might trap Him in what He said. And they sent their disciples to Him, along with the Herodians, saying, "Teacher, we know that You are truthful and teach the way of God in truth, and defer to no one; for You are not partial to any. Tell us therefore, what do You think? Is it lawful to give a poll-tax to Caesar, or not?" But Jesus perceived their malice, and said, "Why are you testing Me, you hypocrites? Show Me the coin used for the poll-tax." And they brought Him a denarius. And He said to them, "Whose likeness and inscription is this?" They said to Him, "Caesar's." Then He said to them, "Then render to Caesar the things that are Caesar's; and to God the things that are God's." And hearing this, they marveled, and leaving Him, they went away. (22:15-22)

Taxes are of major importance in any developed society, and without them government could not function. They are also a perennial point of contention for those citizens who wonder why their taxes are so high and why they are not spent more wisely.

From time to time certain Christian groups raise an organized protest against a given tax or a particular use of tax money they feel is contrary to biblical principles and the constitution. An outcry was raised some years ago when the United States government ordered churches and other religious organizations to withhold Social Security taxes from the payrolls of all employees except pastors. Some Christians vociferously argued that the law required the church to take money donated to the Lord's work and use it to pay the government.

It is with the ever-present issue of paying taxes that Jesus deals in the present passage.

It was still Wednesday of Passover week, and Jesus was teaching in the Temple, which He had violently cleansed the day before. He had just finished telling and explaining three judgment parables against unbelieving Israel, particularly directed against the Temple rulers who had challenged His authority (21:23). After the second parable the chief priests and Pharisees were so enraged that they would have had Him arrested on the spot had they not feared the multitudes (21:46). It was bad enough that He had devastated the physical domain of their concession booths in the Temple. Now He also devastated their religious domain, exposing their unbelief and ungodliness before all Israel.

The religious leaders resented Jesus because He exposed their pride, hypocrisy, and self-righteousness. They envied His great popularity with the people, especially in light of the fact that He had never sought or received official Sanhedrin certification as a rabbi. Most of all, they were incensed at His claim to be the Messiah and the Son of God, a claim which in their eyes was blatant blasphemy. He even dared to publicly humiliate them in the Temple, the one place where they thought their honor was sacrosanct and their authority incontestable. Now, after the third scathing parable, they were all the more determined to find a means of doing away with Him.

Following Jesus' series of three judgment parables against them, those religionists responded by confronting Him with a series of three questions, all designed to maneuver Him into condemning Himself either politically or religiously. The first question was devised by the Pharisees but asked of Jesus surreptitiously by their disciples (22:15-22), the second was asked by the Sadducees (vv. 23-33), and the third by the Pharisees directly (vv. 34-40). Instead of taking Jesus' warnings to heart and asking Him how they might avoid the judgment and receive mercy from God, the only word they wanted from Him was that which would bring about His own destruction.

THE ATTACK

Then the Pharisees went and counseled together how they might trap Him in what He said. And they sent their disciples to Him, along with the Herodians, saying, "Teacher, we know that You are truthful and teach the way of God in truth, and defer to no one; for You are not partial to any. Tell us therefore, what do You think? Is it lawful to give a poll-tax to Caesar, or not?" (22:15-17)

The Pharisees had always been Jesus' most vocal and vehement enemies, and at this moment, in response to His powerfully intimidating parables, they now **went and counseled together how they might trap** Jesus **in what He said.** While Jesus continued to teach the crowds in the Court of the Gentiles, **the Pharisees** gathered privately in another part of the Temple to plan their next move in private. Because they were still afraid to take action against Him directly, they cleverly planned to **trap** Him into making a subversive statement against Rome that would insure His arrest and execution as an insurrectionist. They wanted to "catch Him in some statement, so as to deliver Him up to the rule and the authority of the governor" (Luke 20:20), who at that time was Pilate. That way they would have Him out of the way without getting their own hands sullied or arousing the anger of the people.

Probably because the Pharisees were easily distinguished by their dress and many of them were known to Jesus by sight, they decided to send **their disciples to Him.** The Pharisees were Jesus' harshest critics and He theirs, and for them to flatter Him directly would have been ludicrous and self-defeating. Presumably **their disciples** would not be recognized as such and they could pretend simply to be a group of sincere admirers who wanted Jesus' advice about a question that burned in the minds of most Jews of that day. They hoped He would be caught off guard and entrap Himself before He realized what was happening.

The Herodians were not normal allies of the Pharisees. In fact, the two groups were usually at great odds with each other. Not much is known about **the Herodians** besides what can be inferred from their name. The Herod family was not Jewish but Idumean, descendants of Israel's ancient enemies the Edomites. Beginning with Herod the Great, they had received favors from Rome in the form of various high political appointments, including rulerships over parts of Palestine.

The Herodians had no love for Jesus and may even have been instructed by Herod Antipas to try to instigate His death or at least imprisonment. It was that tetrarch who had imprisoned and eventually beheaded Jesus' forerunner and friend, John the Baptist, and when Herod heard of Jesus' miraculous works, he was afraid that He was John risen from the dead. But he was also curious to see Jesus in order to witness His miracle-working power (Luke 9:7; cf. 23:8). Some time later, certain Pharisees who were friendly to Jesus warned Him to flee Perea because "Herod wants to kill you" (Luke 13:31). Consequently, during the latter part of His ministry Jesus had avoided the territory of Herod because of the hostility toward Him there, "for it cannot be that a prophet should perish outside of Jerusalem" (13:33).

Any **Herodians,** even if they were Jews as these men were, would have had strong allegiance to Rome, and it was doubtlessly for that reason that the Pharisees asked some of them to accompany their disciples as they confronted Jesus. Should Jesus fall into their trap and make the expected objection to paying Roman taxes, the Herodian Roman sympathizers would serve as credible witnesses. Although the Pharisees despised **the Herodians** as irreligious traitors, it well suited their purpose to enlist these men's help in entrapping Jesus.

Just as the Pharisees's praise of Jesus would not have been taken seriously, neither would anything they said in support of Rome. The Pharisees were highly religious and fiercely nationalistic, and some of them probably were Zealots. But they perhaps despised the Romans more for their paganism than for their military oppression. In any case, their hatred of Rome was no secret, and were they to report a seditious statement or activity to the governor, they would themselves have become suspect. **The Herodians** were therefore useful, even if dishonorable, co-conspirators, and they would make perfect pro-Roman witnesses against Jesus. Although the Pharisees and Herodians violently disagreed about religion and politics, they wholeheartedly agreed about Jesus and were not loath to make common cause against Him.

With the Herodians supporting them, the disciples of the Pharisees, whom Luke describes as "spies who pretended to be righteous" (Luke 20:20), flatteringly said to Jesus, **"Teacher, we know that You are truthful and teach the way of God in truth, and defer to no one: for You are not partial to any."** To address a Jewish man as **Teacher** was a high form of honor, reserved for rabbis who had distinguished themselves as astute students and interpreters of Jewish law and tradition. The Talmud said, "The one who teaches the law shall gain a seat in the academy on high."

The men outwardly praised Jesus' personal and doctrinal integrity by declaring that He was **truthful** and taught **the way of God in truth.** He was God's Man teaching God's truth, they affirmed. Neither did He **defer to** or become **partial to any,** they added. He would not be swayed by threats or opposition but was known for standing His ground with courage and conviction.

What those men said of Jesus could not have been more accurate, but they did not believe a word of it. Although flattery often involves lying, it is most deceptive and despicable when it employs the **truth** to achieve its wicked purposes.

Assuming that Jesus was inwardly reveling in their flattery, the men sprang their trap question: **"Tell us therefore, what do You think? Is it lawful to give a poll-tax to Caesar, or not?"** One of the highest forms of praise is to ask a person's advice on an important issue. Therefore, after Jesus' ego was, as they supposed, stimulated by the previous compliments, the questioners were certain that, like most men, He would be eager to display the wisdom for which He had just been praised. In doing so He would blurt out an unguarded answer that would become His death warrant.

Poll-tax translates *kēnsos,* taken from the Latin (i.e., Roman) *censēre,* from which is derived the English *census.* Of the many taxes the Romans exacted from occupied territories, none was more onerous to Jews than the **poll-tax,** a tax payable yearly by every individual and therefore sometimes called the head tax. Among other things, it was for the purpose of collecting the **poll-tax** that Rome took a periodic census, such as the one that had required Joseph and Mary to travel to Bethlehem just before Jesus was born (Luke 2:1-4).

Paying for the support of the occupying forces and providing the many beneficial services for which Rome was famous required an enormous amount of money, necessarily supplied by taxation. Consequently, a land tax of one tenth of the grain and one fifth of the wine and oil produced was assessed annually, as was a one percent income tax on wage earners. Customs taxes on merchandise were collected at all ports and major crossroads.

The Romans offered many services to conquered peoples, not the least beneficial of which was the Pax Romana, or Roman peace. Because of their strategic military and commercial locations, many countries of the Near East had had little respite from war for centuries. They fought one invader after another and were ruled by one conqueror after another. At least under Roman protection they were free from war and could travel in relative safety anywhere in the empire. The Romans also provided valuable roads and aqueducts, many ruins of which still exist today.

Although the **poll-tax** may not have been the most costly tax for most people, it was the most resented by Jews. Perhaps it was because they considered themselves as personally belonging to God rather than to Caesar. It was the census tax that incited the insurrection of Judas of Galilee in A.D. 6 that was instrumental in the deposing of Herod Archelaus and his replacement by a Roman governor. Judas's rallying cry was that, because God was their only God and Lord, the census tax would not be paid to Rome. As Gamaliel reminded the Sanhedrin when Peter and the other apostles were being questioned in Jerusalem, the rebel Judas "perished, and all those who followed him were scattered" (Acts 5:37). It was the nationalistic, anti-Roman sentiment of Judas on which the Zealot movement was built and that was behind the rebellion of A.D. 66 that eventuated in the Roman destruction of Jerusalem and the Temple four years later.

It was therefore not by accident that the Pharisees had instructed their disciples to induce Jesus to make a statement about the **poll-tax**. If He gave an answer favorable to the tax, He would become despised by the Jewish multitudes who until then highly admired Him. In that case, the Jewish leaders would then be free to arrest and have Him executed without interference from the populace. But they presumed He would answer otherwise and openly declare that the tax was both unjust and ungodly and should not be paid to the oppressive, pagan **Caesar,** thus incurring the wrath of Rome as an insurrectionist.

THE ACCUSATION

But Jesus perceived their malice, and said, "Why are you testing Me, you hypocrites? (22:18)

But by His divine discernment **Jesus perceived their malice.** It was not possible to blind-side Jesus, because "He Himself knew what was in man" (John 2:25). He omnisciently knew the question they would ask and the reason for asking it even before it came to the minds of the Pharisees who concocted it. He knew the men who posed the question were not the ones who devised it, and that the words of praise they had just showered on Him were not motivated by admiration but

malice. He knew their flattering tongues were tipped with poison. He also knew exactly the right answer.

Before answering their question, He threw a question of His own in their faces: **"Why are you testing Me, you hypocrites?"** He let them know that their wicked scheme was transparent to Him, that He knew their purpose was to test Him, not to seek His wisdom, and that He was hereby exposing them as the **hypocrites** they were. Although He had never seen them before, He knew they were emissaries of the Pharisees as surely as if He had overheard the plot. That demonstration of omniscience was in itself another marvelous testimony to His deity.

Not only the Old Testament but rabbinic tradition strongly condemned flattery and hypocrisy. Rabbi Eleazar had written in the Talmud, "Any community in which is flattery will finally go into exile. It is written [Job 15:34], 'For the community of flatterers is [barren]'" (*Sotah* 42a). Rabbi Jeremiah ben Abba had declared that four types of people do not deserve to be blessed by God: scorners, liars, tale-bearers, and hypocrites (*Sanhedrin* 103a).

THE ANALOGY

Show Me the coin used for the poll-tax." And they brought Him a denarius. And He said to them, "Whose likeness and inscription is this?" They said to Him, "Caesar's." (22:19-21a)

Jesus then said, **"Show Me the coin used for the poll-tax."** Disregarding Jesus' harsh accusations against them, the men readily **brought Him a denarius,** being more than glad to help Him fall into their snare. The specific **coin used for the poll-tax** was the **denarius,** which amounted to the daily wage for a soldier or common laborer in Palestine.

Although several coinages, including Greek and Hebrew, were used in Israel at the time, and exchange from one to the other was easy, only the Roman **denarius** could be used to pay the **poll-tax.** It was a silver coin, minted expressly by the emperor, who alone had the authority to issue coins in silver or gold. All such coins, including the **denarius,** bore an engraving of the emperor on one side and an identifying inscription on the other.

That fact made the coins especially offensive to Jews for several reasons. For one thing, the emperor's picture was a reminder of Roman oppression, and for another, the Mosaic law specifically forbade the making of images (Ex. 20:4). In modern Israel, certain extremely orthodox Jews strictly forbid the taking of their photographs, because the resulting picture is considered a graven image.

If the particular coin in Jesus' hand was minted by Tiberius, one side bore an engraving of his face and the reverse an engraving of him sitting on his throne in priestly robes, with an inscription designating him as the high priest. Several emperors, including Julius Caesar, had even accepted appellations of deity for themselves, thereby demanding religious as well as political homage. At the appearance of an unusual star in 17 B.C., Augustus Caesar had proclaimed a twelve-day celebration, at which the Roman college of priests, of which he was chief, granted mass absolution from sin for all the people of the empire. During that same year coins were minted claiming Augustus as the Son of God. And the idea of a divine emperor was inconceivably repulsive to Jews.

Although any child would have known the answer to His question, Jesus held up the coin and asked, **"Whose likeness and inscription is this?"** Thinking that He was at last about to speak the fatal words against Rome, the men eagerly replied, perhaps in unison, **Caesar's**. Because Jesus had claimed deity, calling Himself God's Son, the disciples of the Pharisees confidently expected Him to denounce as a false god and blasphemer the caesar whose **likeness and inscription** He was holding up before them.

THE ANSWER AND THE AFTERMATH

Then He said to them, "Then render to Caesar the things that are Caesar's; and to God the things that are God's." And hearing this, they marveled, and leaving Him, they went away. (22:21*b*-22)

But instead, Jesus **said to them, "Then render to Caesar the things that are Caesar's; and to God the things that are God's."** The profundity of that statement is often missed because of its simplicity. *Apodidōmi* (**render**) means to pay or give back, implying a debt. It carries the idea of obligation and responsibility for something that is not optional. Jesus' answer to the original question (v. 17) was therefore, "Yes, it is entirely lawful and right to pay the poll-tax to Caesar, because that tax is **Caesar's**, belonging to **the things** in his domain."

Jesus did not use the word *give,* as had the disciples of the Pharisees in asking the question. For them, as for most Jews, paying any tax to Rome was not considered a legitimate duty and was done only with the greatest reluctance. Now Jesus declared that the payment not only was perfectly legal but morally obligatory.

Jesus here declared the divinely-ordained obligation of citizens to pay taxes to whatever government is over them. Paying taxes is a legitimate duty of every person, but is specially binding on believers because they are specially bound to God's Word. Jesus made no qualifying exemptions or exceptions, even under rulers such as the blasphemous, pagan, idolatrous government that in a few days would nail Him to the cross. The government that executed the Son of God was to be paid taxes by God's people. The state has the divine right to assess taxes that are within its sphere of responsibility, and its citizens have the divine obligation to pay them.

Giving a universal command, but in the context of living under that same pagan Roman system, Paul wrote, "Let every person be in subjection to the governing authorities. For there is no authority except from God, and those which exist are established by God. . . . Wherefore it is necessary to be in subjection, not only because of wrath, but also for conscience' sake. For because of this you also pay taxes, for rulers are servants of God, devoting themselves to this very thing. Render to all what is due them: tax to whom tax is due; custom to whom custom; fear to whom fear; honor to whom honor" (Rom. 13:1, 5-7). We are not only to respect and submit to such rulers and leaders but also to pray for them. "I urge that entreaties and prayers, petitions and thanksgivings, be made on behalf of all men," Paul wrote to Timothy, "for kings and all who are in authority, in order that we may lead a tranquil and quiet life in all godliness and dignity. This is good and acceptable in the sight of God our Savior" (1 Tim. 2:1-3).

Teaching the same principle, Peter wrote, "Submit yourselves for the Lord's sake to every human institution, whether to a king as the one in authority, or to governors as sent by him for the punishment of evildoers and the praise of those who do right. For such is the will of God that by doing right you may silence the ignorance of foolish men" (1 Pet. 2:13-15).

By God's own sovereign decree, presidents, kings, prime ministers, governors, mayors, police, and all other governmental authorities stand in His place, as it were, for the preservation of society. To resist government is therefore to resist God. To refuse to pay taxes is to disobey God's command. By God's own declaration, to pay taxes to Caesar honors God.

If in an age of pagan despotism and open persecution of the church believers were obligated to pay taxes, how much more obligated are modern Christians who live in free and democratic societies? Regardless of the seemingly spiritual reasons that may be proposed for resisting the payment of taxes, there are none that the Lord recognizes. To argue that paying taxes to a worldly, humanistic government is ungodly and unjustified is spurious and contradicts what God Himself says on the subject. His own Word commands unequivocally that taxes are to be paid because, by His divine ordination, they are a part of **the things that are Caesar's.** All things belong to God, but He has decreed that a certain amount of that which He entrusts to each person is to be paid to human governments as taxes.

But even more importantly, Jesus went on to say, men must render **to God the things that are God's.** He was not separating secular human society from religion, saying, in effect, that one owes allegiance to human government in regard to material things and allegiance to God in regard to the spiritual. Scripture never makes such a dichotomy, because all things and every area of life belong to God. Jesus was still talking about Caesar, saying that **the things that are God's** do *not* belong to Caesar and should never be offered to him, but only **to God.**

As a representative of human government, Caesar had the right to assess taxes, but as a representative of human religion, as emperors frequently were, they had no right to command worship. Men are to pay taxes to the head of a government as a human ruler but never homage to him as a god. His realm is social and economic, and to the extent that he steps outside that realm, his authority ceases and men's obligation to him ceases. When the Sanhedrin, which had political as well religious authority in Jerusalem, gave the apostles "strict orders not to continue teaching in [Jesus'] name," Peter replied for all of them, saying, "We must obey God rather than men" (Acts 5:28-29).

The church in the Soviet Union and other communist countries is persecuted today because it refuses to give total allegiance to the state. Although the majority of Christians in those lands are good citizens in every way, including in the payment of taxes, they will not surrender their souls or the souls of their children to the government, because such homage is solely the prerogative of God.

Upon **hearing** Jesus' response, the disciples of the Pharisees were utterly astonished at His wisdom. **They marveled, and leaving Him, they went away.** They had nothing to say, and had the presence of mind to leave before exposing still more of their ignorance and wickedness.

The God of the Living
(22:23-33)

31

On that day some Sadducees (who say there is no resurrection) came to Him and questioned Him, saying, "Teacher, Moses said, 'If a man dies, having no children, his brother as next of kin shall marry his wife, and raise up an offspring to his brother.' Now there were seven brothers with us; and the first married and died, and having no offspring left his wife to his brother; so also the second, and the third, down to the seventh. And last of all, the woman died. In the resurrection therefore whose wife of the seven shall she be? For they all had her." But Jesus answered and said to them, "You are mistaken, not understanding the Scriptures, or the power of God. For in the resurrection they neither marry, nor are given in marriage, but are like angels in heaven. But regarding the resurrection of the dead, have you not read that which was spoken to you by God saying, 'I am the God of Abraham, and the God of Isaac, and the God of Jacob'? He is not the God of the dead but of the living." And when the multitudes heard this, they were astonished at His teaching. (22:23-33)

Mankind in general has always anticipated an afterlife of some sort. The idea is built into the heart of man that there must be a continuation of existence when the physical life is over. James Dwight Dana, a nineteenth-century professor at Yale

University, said that he could not believe that God would create man and then desert him at the grave. In that statement, Professor Dana summarized the hope that, to one degree or another, has captured virtually every heart in every culture in every time.

The ancient Egyptian *Book of the Dead* is filled with ideas and stories about life after death. In the tomb of the great pharaoh Cheops, who died some 5,000 years ago, archaeologists discovered a solar boat intended for him to use in sailing through the heavens during the next life. Ancient Greeks often placed a coin in the mouth of a corpse to pay his fare across the mystic river of death into the land of immortal life. Some American Indians buried a pony and bow and arrows with a dead warrior in order that he could ride and hunt in the happy hunting grounds. Norsemen buried a dead hero's horse with him so he could ride proudly in the next life. Eskimos of Greenland who died in childhood were customarily buried with a dog to help guide them through the cold wasteland of death.

Benjamin Franklin, who did not claim to be a Christian in the biblical sense, nevertheless had the following epitaph inscribed on his tombstone:

> The body of
> Benjamin Franklin, printer,
> (Like the cover of an old book,
> Its contents worn out,
> And stript of its lettering and gilding)
> Lies here, food for worms!
> Yet the work itself shall not be lost,
> For it will, as he believed, appear once more
> In a new
> And more beautiful edition,
> Corrected and amended
> By its Author!

Despite many strange and unbiblical aberrations regarding the subject, men feel the pull of the afterlife. The Jews of Jesus' day were certainly no exception. Belief in the resurrection of the body is taught throughout the Talmud, the ancient codification of Jewish oral and written tradition. The apocryphal book of 2 Maccabees, written about 100 B.C., describes a Jewish elder named Razis who greatly resented Greek oppression. Rather than be executed by the hated Greeks, he decided to take his own life. Standing on a rock in front of a large crowd, he disemboweled himself with his sword and threw his entrails into the crowd, in vain hope "calling upon the Lord of life and spirit to give [his discarded organs] back to him again" (14:46). In the Apocalypse of Baruch, written nearly 200 years later, the expectation is expressed that when a person dies he will come back to life in the same form in which he died.

> The earth shall then assuredly restore the dead, which it now receiveth in order to preserve them. It shall make no change in their form, but as it hath

received, so shall it preserve them, and as it delivered them unto it, so shall it restore them. . . . For then it will be necessary to show to the living that the dead have come to life again, and that those who had departed have returned. . . . They shall respectively be transformed . . . into the splendour of angels . . . and time shall no longer age them. For in the heights of that world shall they dwell, and they shall be made like unto the angels, and be made equal to the stars, and they shall be changed into every form they desire, from beauty into loveliness and from light into the splendour of glory. (50:2-51:10)

Much more important and reliable than those writings, of course, were the Old Testament statements regarding life after death. David wrote, "Therefore my heart is glad, and my glory rejoices; my flesh also will dwell securely. For Thou wilt not abandon my soul to Sheol; neither wilt Thou allow Thy Holy One to undergo decay" (Ps. 16:9-10). Another psalmist declared, "God will redeem my soul from the power of Sheol; for He will receive me" (Ps. 49:15), and still another that, "With Thy counsel Thou wilt guide me, and afterward receive me to glory" (Ps. 73:24). Hosea wrote, "Come, let us return to the Lord. For He has torn us, but He will heal us; He has wounded us, but He will bandage us. He will revive us after two days; He will raise us up on the third day that we may live before Him" (Hos. 6:1-2). In perhaps the clearest teaching of resurrection in the Old Testament, the Lord promised through Daniel that "many of those who sleep in the dust of the ground will awake, these to everlasting life, but the others to disgrace and everlasting contempt" (Dan. 12:2).

For the most part, therefore, Jews not only believed in life after death but in the resurrection of the body. The one exception were the Sadducees, who in that and other ways were at odds with the rest of Jewish theology and culture. It was representatives of that sect who asked Jesus the second in a series of three questions designed to entrap Him (see also 22:15-22; 34-40).

THE APPROACH

On that day some Sadducees (who say there is no resurrection) came to Him and questioned Him, (22:23)

It was still Wednesday, as Jesus continued to teach in the Temple after having driven the merchants out of it the previous day (21:12, 23). Sometime later **on that day,** after He had put to silence the disciples of the Pharisees and their Herodian co-conspirators (22:16), **some Sadducees** attempted to succeed where the others had failed.

The **Sadducees** were the smallest but by far the most wealthy and influential of the Jewish sects, which included the Pharisees, the Zealots, and the Essenes. The Pharisees were the most numerous, the most popular, the most outwardly religious. They held strongly to external customs and practices and were legalistic to the core, firmly believing that their works gained them acceptance with God. For them, the rabbinical traditions had become more authoritative than Scripture, although many of the traditions were devised simply as accommodations to their sinful desires.

The Zealots were political and often military activists, extremely nationalistic and resentful of Roman control of Israel.

The Essenes were a reclusive sect who spent much of their time copying the Old Testament. It was a group of Essenes living at Qumran, on the northwest shore of the Dead Sea, who produced what became known as the Dead Sea Scrolls.

The **Sadducees** were the aristocrats of Judaism, being largely in control of the Temple and the operation of the priesthood, and it was primarily through the Temple concessions of money changing and sacrifice selling (see 21:12) that they obtained their wealth. The high priest and chief priests were almost invariably Sadducees, as were most members of the Sanhedrin, the high Jewish council.

Despite their great power and influence, and partly because of it, the Sadducees were not respected by most Jews, especially by the Pharisees. They were aloof from the common people and acted superior to them. But they were also disliked for their theology, the most distinct teaching of which was that **there is no resurrection.**

Politically, the Sadducees were pro-Roman, because it was only by Roman permission that they exercised not only their religious but their considerable political control over the people. Because they were valuable in helping keep the people under control, the Sadducees were delegated limited authority by Rome, even to the extent of having their own police force in the form of a Temple guard. Because of their complete dependence on Rome for their power, they were understandably strongly supportive of their pagan rulers. And for that they were also hated by the people.

Because their power and wealth were founded in the Temple and its offerings, sacrificial system, and commercial enterprises, when the Temple was destroyed in A.D. 70, the Sadducees, like the entire priesthood, ceased to exist.

Religiously, the Sadducees were in some ways extreme fundamentalists. They interpreted Scripture with great literalism and consequently were even more absolutist and rigid on certain matters than the Pharisees. Josephus reported that in rendering judgments in behalf of the people they were more vicious than any other sect (*Antiquities*, XX.ix.i). They refused to acknowledge any worth, much less authority, in the oral or written interpretations of Scripture or in the rabbinical traditions. They were fastidious in Levitical purity and prided themselves as being the preservers of the true faith.

But for some reason they gave unique primacy to the Pentateuch, the first five books of the Old Testament, almost to the exclusion of the rest of Scripture. The other books were considered more or less as commentaries on the five books of Moses. It is therefore because Moses taught nothing directly about the resurrection that the Sadducees denied its reality.

But a person who does not believe in a life after this present life has little motive for living other than he pleases. After death he expects neither penalty nor reward, because he considers the end of this life to be the end of everything. And in spite of the many clear teachings in the Pentateuch about godly living, the Sadducees were perfectly comfortable in their proud and selfish worldliness.

The Sadducees and Pharisees were continually at odds with each other, and it was precisely for that reason that Paul declared his belief in the resurrection when he was on trial before the Sanhedrin. "Perceiving that one part were Sadducees and the other Pharisees, Paul began crying out in the Council, 'Brethren, I am a Pharisee, a son of Pharisees; I am on trial for the hope and resurrection of the dead!' And as he said this, there arose a dissension between the Pharisees and Sadducees; and the assembly was divided. For the Sadducees say that there is no resurrection, nor an angel, nor a spirit; but the Pharisees acknowledge them all" (Acts 23: 6-8).

When challenged by the Sadducees to prove that the resurrection was taught by Moses, the Pharisees apparently could muster only two or three obscure references. They argued that Numbers 18:28 implied resurrection, in that it spoke of giving "the Lord's offering to Aaron the priest," the present tense indicating that Aaron was still alive. An even more obscure text cited was Deuteronomy 31:16, which speaks of the people arising; but their arising was not to a future life but to harlotry. A third text was Deuteronomy 32:39, in which the Lord says, "It is I who put to death and give life," a reference simply to His sovereign authority over life and death.

The Pharisees and Sadducees had great social and political as well as theological animosity between them. Socially, the Sadducees were aristocratic and the Pharisees were commoners. Politically, the Sadducees were pro-Roman and the Pharisees anti-Roman.

There was one issue, however, that solidly united Pharisees and Sadducees: their intransigent opposition to Jesus.

Until the Lord's coming to Jerusalem on the previous Monday, the Sadducees had shown little interest in Jesus. The fact that He was popular with the people, believed in resurrection, and was opposed by the Pharisees was of little consequence to them as long as what He said and did had no direct, practical effect on them or their activities. Jesus' cleansing the Temple, however, immediately got their attention, because the merchants and moneychangers He drove out of the court of the Gentiles were the financial mainstay of Sadducee power. Jesus had now invaded their territory with a vengeance, disrupting their operation at the most lucrative time of the year, when all the Passover offerings and sacrifices were made.

Jesus' acclamation as the Son of David during His triumphal entry also no doubt had them worried, because any claim to kingship would evoke immediate and harsh repression by the Romans, who would not tolerate the smallest hint of rebellion. Any action against the Jews in general would necessarily threaten the Sadducees' own privileged position and power under the Romans, who expected those leaders to keep Jewish nationalism and resistance in check. Only a few days earlier, "the chief priests and the Pharisees convened a council, and were saying, 'What are we doing? For this man is performing many signs. If we let Him go on like this, all men will believe in Him, and the Romans will come and take away both our place and our nation.' But a certain one of them, Caiaphas, who was high priest that year, said to them, 'You know nothing at all, nor do you take into account that it is expedient for you that one man should die for the people, and that the whole nation should not perish'" (John 11:47-50; cf. Mark 14:1-2). "From that day on," John noted, "they planned together to kill Him" (v. 53).

After Pentecost, the Sadducees continued their strong opposition against Jesus by persecuting His followers. As the apostles "were speaking to the people, the priests and the captain of the temple guard, and the Sadducees, came upon them, being greatly disturbed because they were teaching the people and proclaiming in Jesus the resurrection from the dead" (Acts 4:1-2). According to Josephus, it was the Sadducees who murdered James, the brother of the Lord.

After the Pharisees had failed through their disciples to trick Jesus into making a traitorous statement against Rome, the Sadducees attempted to make Him discredit Himself in the eyes of the Jewish people. By asking Him what they thought was an unanswerable question, they planned to make Him look the fool, as they perhaps had succeeded, on occasion, in doing with the Pharisees.

THE ABSURDITY

saying, "Teacher, Moses said, 'If a man dies, having no children, his brother as next of kin shall marry his wife, and raise up an offspring to his brother.' Now there were seven brothers with us; and the first married and died, and having no offspring left his wife to his brother; so also the second, and the third, down to the seventh. And last of all, the woman died. In the resurrection therefore whose wife of the seven shall she be? For they all had her." (22:24-28)

Like the previous group (v. 16), by addressing Jesus as **Teacher**, the Sadducees thought to put Jesus off guard with condescending flattery, what one commentator has called "polished scoffing." Their choice of titles was especially duplicitous because it was as a Teacher that they intended to embarrass and discredit Him.

No higher appeal could be made than to **Moses**, not only for the Sadducees but for any Jew. He was the great lawgiver, the supreme spokesman for God in the Old Testament. Because the Sadducees were aware of Jesus' high regard for Scripture, they knew that He would not contest the validity of the teaching they were about to cite, namely, the provision for levirate marriage.

The term *levirate* is from *levir*, Latin for "husband's brother." The Mosaic provision is found in Deuteronomy 25:5-6, a summary of which the Sadducees here gave to Jesus. In order that tribal names, families, and inheritances might be kept intact, **If a man dies, having no children, his brother as next of kin shall marry his wife, and raise up an offspring to his brother.**

The custom of levirate marriage had been practiced for many centuries and was honored by God even before He directed Moses to place it in the law. When Judah's son Er was killed by the Lord for his wickedness, Judah told another son,

Onan, who was unmarried, "Go into your brother's wife, and perform your duty as a brother-in-law to her, and raise up offspring for your brother." But Onan resented the fact the children would not be considered his own and "he wasted his seed on the ground." That act was "displeasing in the sight of the Lord; so He took his life also" (Gen. 38:8-10).

It was in fulfillment of the levirate law that Boaz took Ruth as his wife because her first husband, Mahlon, had died. When a male relative closer to Ruth than Boaz was unable to redeem her, Boaz happily took her as his own bride (Ruth 4:1-10). That beautiful story not only depicts the human preservation of Mahlon's lineage but also the divine preservation of the lineage of Christ (Matt. 1:5).

Whether or not levirate marriage was still practiced in Jesus' day, the custom was well known to every Jew and recognized to be a divine provision. To the Sadducees it seemed the perfect means to prove the absurdity of the idea of resurrection.

In saying, **"Now there were seven brothers with us,"** the Sadducees may have meant they were reporting an actual story, but it is likely they custom-designed it for this occasion. When **the first** brother **married**, the six others were unmarried, and therefore when he **died . . . having no offspring**, he **left his wife to his brother**. The process was repeated with all seven brothers, and eventually everyone, including **the woman,** died.

It is not difficult to imagine the glint in the eyes and the smirks on the faces of the Sadducees as they looked at Jesus and propounded their supposedly unanswerable question: **"In the resurrection therefore whose wife of the seven shall she be?"** If all eight would appear in the resurrection exactly in the condition and circumstances in which they had died—as the Pharisees, and presumably Jesus, maintained—how could their marriage relationships possibly be reconciled? That dilemma proved the idea of resurrection to be patently absurd, as Jesus now would be forced to admit, by His silence if not His words.

The Answer

But Jesus answered and said to them, "You are mistaken, not understanding the Scriptures, or the power of God. For in the resurrection they neither marry, nor are given in marriage, but are like angels in heaven. But regarding the resurrection of the dead, have you not read that which was spoken to you by God saying, 'I am the God of Abraham, and the God of Isaac, and the God of Jacob'? He is not the God of the dead but of the living." (22:29-32)

The Sadducees probably expected Jesus to say nothing and to walk away in humiliation and disgrace, as they probably had caused the Pharisees to do at times.

But Jesus answered without hesitation and immediately put them on the defensive, saying **to them, "You are mistaken."** The Sadducees had succeeded only in putting their own ignorance on display for everyone in the Temple to see and hear. "You are dead wrong," Jesus said, in effect, "and have no idea what you are talking about."

Planaō, from which **are mistaken** is translated, means to go astray, wander off, or deceive. In its form here it means to lead oneself off course or to stray from the truth. It often carried the idea of being cut loose from reality. Like the false teachers condemned by Jude, the Sadducees were "wandering stars, for whom the black darkness has been reserved forever" (Jude 13).

Jesus next presented the two reasons *why* the Sadducees were **mistaken.** They erred in **not understanding the Scriptures** and in not understanding **the power of God.** Nothing could have cut them to the quick worse than to be accused of not understanding these two areas in which the proud Sadducees considered themselves most authoritative.

The Lord then explains, in reverse order, *how* they misunderstood God's Word and God's power.

IGNORANCE OF GOD'S POWER

For in the resurrection they neither marry, nor are given in marriage, but are like angels in heaven. (22:30)

In exposing the Sadducees' false notion about **the resurrection,** Jesus also exposed their false notion about **angels,** whose existence those religious leaders denied. In the heavenly state, He declared, men and women **neither marry, nor are given in marriage.** The relationship of **marriage** is beautiful and divinely ordained, but it is an entirely earthly and temporal institution.

Sexual relationships, reproduction, and childbirth have no place in heaven, because there is no death there and no new life born as there is on earth. Nor will there will be any exclusive relationships in heaven, because everyone will be perfectly and intimately related to everyone else, including to the living God Himself. **In heaven,** men will be **like angels,** equally spiritual in nature, equally deathless, equally glorified, and equally eternal. Luke reports Jesus' additional statement that resurrected believers "are sons of God, being sons of the resurrection" (Luke 20:36).

No doubt partly because of the influence of Pharisaic teaching about one's resurrection body being the same as his earthly body had been, the believers in Corinth were confused about the subject. Trying to explain in terms that those immature and misinformed Christians could understand, Paul pointed out that,

> all flesh is not the same flesh, but there is one flesh of men, and another flesh of beasts, and another flesh of birds, and another of fish. There are also heavenly bodies and earthly bodies, but the glory of the heavenly is one, and the glory of the earthly is another. There is one glory of the sun, and

another glory of the moon, and another glory of the stars; for star differs from star in glory. So also is the resurrection of the dead. It is sown a perishable body, it is raised an imperishable body; it is sown in dishonor, it is raised in glory; it is sown in weakness, it is raised in power; it is sown a natural body, it is raised a spiritual body. If there is a natural body, there is also a spiritual body. . . . As is the earthy, so also are those who are earthy, and as is the heavenly, so also are those who are heavenly. And just as we have borne the image of the earthy, we shall also bear the image of the heavenly. (1 Cor. 15:39-44, 48-49)

God's limitless power is easily able to transform the earthly into the heavenly. Why should anyone deny the resurrection because of the foolish idea that God is restricted to raising up bodies in the same form as that in which they died? Such a belief foolishly attacks the power of God.

IGNORANCE OF SCRIPTURE

But regarding the resurrection of the dead, have you not read that which was spoken to you by God saying, 'I am the God of Abraham, and the God of Isaac, and the God of Jacob'? He is not the God of the dead but of the living." (22:31-32)

Knowing that the Sadducees would not be convinced **regarding the resurrection** from any part of Scripture but the Pentateuch, Jesus reminded them of a statement **spoken . . . by God** that is recorded numerous times in the book of Exodus: **I am the God of Abraham, and the God of Isaac, and the God of Jacob.**

"That the dead are raised, even Moses showed," Jesus first told the doubting Sadducees (Luke 20:37). The words about His being the God of the patriarchs were first spoken to Moses by God when He appeared to him in the burning bush at Horeb and called him to lead His people out of bondage in Egypt to the Promised Land (Ex. 3:6). And the phrase was repeated many times after that (see, e.g., Ex. 3:15-16; 4:15). Hundreds of years earlier the Lord had declared to Jacob, "I am the Lord, the God of your father Abraham and the God of Isaac" (Gen. 28:13) long after Abraham had died.

Jesus' excellent exegetical argument is based on the emphatic present tense of the **I am** used in that passage from the Pentateuch. After **Abraham** and **Isaac** and **Jacob** were long dead, the Lord was still their **God** every bit as much as when they were alive—in fact, in many ways even more so, because they had become perfectly sinless and their souls were experiencing the fellowship of His eternal presence.

These three patriarchs are singled out, and each is specifically related to

333

God, suggesting His unique personal intimacy with each one. Whether the genitive preposition **of** refers to God's belonging to the patriarchs or to their belonging to God, both meanings are true.

The present tense is used because God **is not the God of the dead but of the living,** and if He is presently the God of Abraham, Isaac, and Jacob, then those men obviously are still alive in another realm. They would also still have to be **living** so that God could fulfill His promises to them which were not fulfilled during their lifetimes.

> All these died in faith, without receiving the promises, but having seen them and having welcomed them from a distance, and having confessed that they were strangers and exiles on the earth. For those who say such things make it clear that they are seeking a country of their own. And indeed if they had been thinking of that country from which they went out, they would have had opportunity to return. But as it is, they desire a better country, that is a heavenly one. Therefore God is not ashamed to be called their God; for He has prepared a city for them. (Heb. 11:13-16)

Jesus had accomplished what the wisest Pharisee or scribe had never been able to do: unequivocally prove the resurrection even from the Pentateuch. And in so doing, "He had put the Sadducees to silence" (Matt. 22:34).

THE ASTONISHMENT

And when the multitudes heard this, they were astonished at His teaching. (22:33)

The multitudes were accustomed to being **astonished at** Jesus' **teaching,** and Luke reports that even "some of the scribes answered and said, 'Teacher, You have spoken well'" (Luke 20:39). But the Sadducees "did not have courage to question Him any longer about anything" (v. 40). Tragically, Jesus had not convinced them, because they would not be convinced.

In the Temple that day Christ again magnificently demonstrated His deity, giving an answer to the unanswerable that could have come only from the omniscient mind of God. Christ demonstrated His absolute commitment to Scripture, an infinitely greater commitment than the biased and self-deceptive commitment of the Sadducees. And our Lord divinely affirmed the reality and glory of the resurrection that awaits those who belong to Him.

The Great Commandment

(22:34-40)

But when the Pharisees heard that He had put the Sadducees to silence, they gathered themselves together. And one of them, a lawyer, asked Him a question, testing Him, "Teacher, which is the great commandment in the Law?" And He said to him, "'You shall love the Lord your God with all your heart, and with all your soul, and with all your mind.' This is the great and foremost commandment. The second is like it, 'You shall love your neighbor as yourself.' On these two commandments depend the whole Law and the Prophets." (22:34-40)

Someone has said that love may not make the world go around but it makes the trip worthwhile.

Those words perhaps gather up the sentiment of the world that the sweetest and most exhilarating of all emotions and experiences is love. In whatever age or with whatever group of people, it has been the almost universal belief that love is the greatest thing in life, the summum bonum, the virtue par excellence. Consequently, volumes upon volumes of poems, songs, plays, novels, and films have been produced about love.

God's Word concurs that love is the greatest virtue, but the love which it elevates as supreme is of a much deeper and more substantive kind than that which the world understands and admires. In response to the third in a series of three questions posed by His adversaries for the purpose of discrediting and entrapping Him (see also 22:15-17, 23-28), Jesus declared that *agapē* love is the supreme divine requirement of men, both in regard to Himself and in regard to other men.

THE APPROACH OF THE PHARISEES

But when the Pharisees heard that He had put the Sadducees to silence, they gathered themselves together. And one of them, a lawyer, asked Him a question, testing Him, (22:34-35)

The first test of Jesus by the Pharisees, made through their disciples and the Herodians, was political, dealing with the payment of the despised poll-tax (v. 17). The second test, by the Sadducees, was theological, pertaining to the reality of the resurrection, which they denied (vv. 23, 28). Now **the Pharisees** were about to test Him again in the area of theology.

When Jesus answered the absurd question about the seven brothers by showing that even Moses taught the resurrection, **He had put the Sadducees to silence.** The verb *phimoō* (**put . . . to silence**) literally means to muzzle, to forcefully restrict the opening of the mouth. The term is used of the muzzling of an ox (1 Cor. 9:9) and of Jesus' silencing a demon (Mark 1:25) and a storm (Mark 4:39). The **Sadducees** were verbally incapacitated by the Lord, rendered utterly speechless, just like the man who was rebuked by the king for coming to the wedding feast without proper clothes (Matt. 22:12).

When the Pharisees heard about Jesus putting **the Sadducees to silence,** they decided to have another try themselves at entrapping Him, this time directly by one of their own number rather than through their less capable disciples. The Pharisees doubtlessly had mixed feelings when they **heard** the news. They must have been pleased that the Sadducees had been proved wrong about Moses not teaching resurrection. But that feeling was far outweighed by a sense of dismay and frustration at still another failure to discredit their common enemy, Jesus.

Consequently, **the Pharisees** again (see v. 15) **gathered themselves together** clandestinely somewhere in the Temple to plan their next strategy. In doing so, they unintentionally and unknowingly fulfilled prophecy by plotting together "against the Lord, and against His Christ" (Acts 4:26-28). Out of that conclave came the third and final question to test Jesus.

The particular **one of them** that they chose to confront Jesus was **a lawyer.** The man was a scribe (Mark 12:28) but was called **a lawyer** by Matthew to indicate his unusual expertise in the Mosaic law and perhaps also his renown in adjudicating religious and social disputes. He was probably the most learned and astute expert on scriptural and rabbinical law in their ranks, and if anyone would be a match for Jesus, they thought, this man would be.

This **lawyer,** however, also seems to have been a cut above his fellow religious leaders in honesty and humility. Like that of a few of the other scribes, his acknowledgment that Jesus had answered the Sadducees wisely seems to have been genuine (Mark 12:28; cf. Luke 20:39). Obviously the man was not totally straightforward, because he allowed himself to be used in **testing** Jesus in order to discredit Him. But apparently his duplicity was mixed with a measure of sincere concern for what Jesus would say in response to the test **question.**

THE QUESTION BY THE LAWYER

"Teacher, which is the great commandment in the Law?" (22:36)

In his addressing Jesus as **Teacher,** the lawyer was probably not being scornful, as the previous questioners had been (see vv. 16, 24). As already noted, he seems to have had respect for Jesus and may have felt somewhat guilty at being used to ensnare Him.

In asking, **"Which is the great commandment in the Law?"** the lawyer was asking what was the greatest commandment of Moses. Although the scribes and Pharisees considered the whole Old Testament to be authoritative, and not just the five books of Moses as did the Sadducees, they nevertheless considered Moses to be the supreme human figure in Scripture. Moses had spoken with God face to face, was the humblest man on earth, and had taken the engraved tablets of the law directly from the hand of God, as it were. He was also the great deliverer whom God called to lead Israel out of Egypt to the Promised Land. He was therefore without peer among those the Lord chose to be human instruments of His divine revelation and activity.

The scribes and Pharisees were said to sit in Moses' seat (Matt. 23:2) because that represented the ultimate authority in Judaism. One rabbi said that by referring to Moses as "faithful in all My household" (Num. 12:7), the Lord ranked Moses above the angels. From the beginning of His ministry, Jesus assured His hearers that, far from seeking "to abolish the Law or the Prophets," He had come to fulfill them, and that "until heaven and earth pass away, not the smallest letter or stroke shall pass away from the Law, until all is accomplished" (Matt. 5:17-18). He made clear that, although He was the Messiah and God's own Son, He was not preaching and teaching anything that obviated the law of Moses or any other part of Scripture.

But because Jesus' teaching of Scripture was so utterly contrary to theirs, which for centuries had been encrusted by thousands of humanly-devised rabbinical interpretations, the Pharisees were convinced that He must be teaching a message He considered to be greater than that of Moses. And it was evidence to that effect that they now hoped Jesus would disclose, because to contradict Moses was to contradict God and be guilty of heresy. Their purpose was to expose Him as an apostate and thereby turn the people against Him.

Over the years, the rabbis had supposedly determined that, just as there were 613 separate letters in the Hebrew text of the Decalogue, or Ten Commandments, in the book of Numbers, there were also 613 separate laws in the Pentateuch, the five books of Moses. Such letterism, as it is sometimes called, was extremely popular and was considered to be a valuable exegetical tool for interpreting Scripture. The rabbis had divided those 613 laws into affirmative and negative groups, holding that there were 248 affirmative laws, one for every part of the human body, as they supposed, and 365 negative laws, one for each day of the year. The laws were also divided into heavy and light, the heavy ones being absolutely binding and the light ones less binding.

There had never been unanimity, however, as to which laws were heavy and which were light, and the rabbis and scribes spent countless hours proudly debating the merits of their particular divisions and the ranking of laws within the divisions.

It was doubtlessly that superficial and fanciful orientation to the law that led them to think Jesus had his own scheme. Because He considered Himself to be the Messiah, they assumed that surely Jesus had devised a system to display His erudition in the law just as they were accustomed to doing. And judging by the lawyer's single and extremely simple question, they assumed that His naming the *one* **great commandment in the Law** would be sufficiently unorthodox to condemn Him.

THE RESPONSE OF THE LORD

And He said to him, "'You shall love the Lord your God with all your heart, and with all your soul, and with all your mind.' This is the great and foremost commandment. The second is like it, 'You shall love your neighbor as yourself.' On these two commandments depend the whole Law and the Prophets." (22:37-40)

Jesus responded without hesitation, and the answer He gave was in total accord not only with Mosaic law but with an ancient Jewish custom based on that law. The command, **You shall love the Lord your God with all your heart, and with all your soul, and with all your mind,** was part of the Shema (Hebrew for "Hear"), so named because it began with, "Hear, O Israel!" The Shema comprised the texts of Deuteronomy 6:4-9; 11:13-21; and Numbers 15:37-41—by far the most familiar, most quoted, and most copied Scripture passages in Judaism. In Jesus' day, every faithful Jew recited the Shema twice a day.

Deuteronomy 6:4-9 and 11:13-21 were two of the four Scripture texts (with Ex. 13:1-10 and 13:11-16) that were copied on small pieces of parchment and placed in phylacteries that were worn on the foreheads and left arms of Jewish men during prayer. The practice was based on the admonition of Deuteronomy 6:8, "You shall bind them as a sign on your hand and they shall be as frontals on your forehead" (cf. 11:18). It was for the ostentatious display of phylacteries that Jesus rebuked the scribes and Pharisees only a short while later, while He was still teaching in the Temple (Matt. 23:5). In a similar way, copies of Deuteronomy 6:4-9 and 11:13-21 were placed in mezuzahs, small boxes that Jews attached to their doorposts, following the instruction of Deuteronomy 6:9 and 11:20. Both phylacteries and mezuzahs are still used by many orthodox Jews today.

"I am declaring to you," Jesus was therefore saying, "that **the great commandment** is the commandment of Moses that all of you recite every day and that many of you bind on your arms and foreheads every day."

Aheb, the Hebrew word for **love** used in Deuteronomy 6:5, refers primarily to an act of mind and will, the determined care for the welfare of something or someone. It might well include strong emotion, but its distinguishing characteristics were the dedication and commitment of choice. It is the **love** that recognizes and chooses to follow that which is righteous, noble, and true, regardless of what one's feelings in a matter might be. It is the Hebrew equivalent of the Greek *agapaō* in the New Testament, the verb of intelligent, purposeful, and committed **love** that is an act of the will. This love is in contrast to the emotion and tender affection of *phileō* and the physical, sensual love of *eros* (which is not used in the New Testament).

To **love the Lord with all** one's **heart, . . . soul, and . . . mind** (Mark's account adds "strength," 12:30) does not express separate and technical definitions of each element of human nature or a compartmentalizing of love into three or four categories, but rather connotes comprehensiveness. We are to **love the Lord** our **God** with every part of our being.

On the other hand, the areas are listed distinctly, each one preceded by its own **with all your.** It is therefore helpful to look at some distinctions in each of them in order to understand the fullness of what **love** for God should include.

To the ancient Hebrews, **heart** referred to the core of one's personal being. The book of Proverbs counsels, "Watch over your heart with all diligence, for from it flow the springs of life" (4:23). The term **soul** is closest to what we would call emotion and is the word Jesus used when He cried out in the Garden of Gethsemane the night He was arrested: "My soul is deeply grieved, to the point of death" (Matt. 26:38). **Mind** corresponds to what is usually translated "might" in Deuteronomy 6:5. The Hebrew term had a broad connotation and carried the general idea of moving ahead with energy and strength. **Mind** is used here in the sense of intellectual, willful vigor and determination, carrying both the meaning of mental endeavor and of strength.

Genuine **love of the Lord** is intelligent, feeling, willing, and serving. It involves thought, sensitivity, intent, and even action where that is possible and appropriate. God has never sought either empty words or empty ritual. His desire is for the person himself, not simply what the person possesses. If He truly has the person, He inevitably has all that the person possesses as well. And just as God loves us with His whole being, we are to return His love with our whole being. His love for mankind was so great "that He gave His only begotten Son" for their redemption (John 3:16). Godly love, whether as His love for man or man's love for Him, is measured by what it gives, not by what it might gain. It does not love because love is beneficial but because love is right and good.

God requires more than bare belief. James reminds us that even the demons believe that God exists; but instead of rejoicing in that belief, they shudder (James

2:19). The distinguishing mark of saving belief in God is love of God. Faith in Jesus Christ that is not characterized by a consuming love for Him is not saving faith but simply an acknowledgement of His divinity such as even the demons make.

I believe that the transforming new creation that takes place at salvation produces a new will, desire, and attitude deep within the person that can best be described as love for God. John makes love for God the true mark of the believer (see John 14:23-24; 1 John 2:5; 3:17; 4:12-13, 16-21). Peter declares that God is precious to those who believe (1 Pet. 2:7), pointing to the same truth that love for God and Christ characterize a true Christian.

The Ten Commandments themselves make clear that love for and obedience to God are inseparable. The Lord shows His "lovingkindness to thousands, to those who love [Him] and keep [His] commandments" (Ex. 20:6; cf. Deut. 7:9; Neh. 1:5). Jesus declared, "If you love Me, you will keep My commandments" (John 14:15), and John wrote, "And by this we know that we have come to know Him, if we keep His commandments. The one who says, 'I have come to know Him,' and does not keep His commandments, is a liar, and the truth is not in him; but whoever keeps His word, in him the love of God has truly been perfected. By this we know that we are in Him" (1 John 2:3-5). A person who belongs to God loves God and therefore obeys God. One of the most beautiful descriptions of a Christian is one who loves "our Lord Jesus Christ with a love incorruptible" (Eph. 6:24). And one of the most sobering descriptions of an unbeliever is "anyone [who] does not love the Lord" (1 Cor. 16:22).

True love of God declares with Paul, "For that which I am doing, I do not understand; for I am not practicing what I would like to do, but I am doing the very thing I hate" (Rom. 7:15). In essence he was saying that, even though he did not always do what was right, he always loved what was right and longed to do what was honoring to God. That was the opposite attitude of the scribes and Pharisees, whom Jesus repeatedly condemned for making great pretense of love for God on the outside while having no inward love for Him at all. They were interested only in the outward religious ceremonies and actions that fed their self-righteousness, self-satisfaction, and hypocrisy. Although they recited the Shema with meticulous regularity, that verbal declaration of love for God was hollow and meaningless.

Just as belonging to God is loving God, not belonging to Him is hating Him (Ex. 20:5). God's people are those who love Him, and the unsaved are those who hate Him and are His adversaries (Deut. 32:41; Prov. 8:36).

The person who truly loves **the Lord** with all his **heart** and **soul** and **mind** is the person who trusts Him and obeys Him. That person demonstrates his love by meditating on God's glory (Ps. 18:1-3), trusting in God's divine power (Ps. 31:23), seeking fellowship with God (Ps. 63:1-8), loving God's law (Ps. 119:165), being sensitive to how God feels (Ps. 69:9), loving what God loves (Ps. 119:72, 97, 103), loving whom God loves (1 John 5:1), hating what God hates (Ps. 97:10), grieving over sin (Matt. 26:75), rejecting the world (1 John 2:15), longing to be with Christ (2 Tim. 4:8), and obeying God wholeheartedly (John 14:21).

Above all, the one who truly loves God is the one who truly obeys God. Like

Paul, he knows his love is imperfect and his obedience is imperfect, but he presses "on in order that [he] may lay hold of that for which also [he] was laid hold of by Christ Jesus," pressing "on toward the goal for the prize of the upward call of God in Christ Jesus" (Phil. 3:12, 14).

To say that Jesus died for man's sin is to say that He died for man's hatred of God, which is the essence of all sin. Christ died for man's lack of love for God. And just as He offers forgiveness for past lack of love for God, Christ also provides for future love for God. The great Forgiver is also the great Enabler, because through Christ, "the love of God has been poured out within our hearts through the Holy Spirit who was given to us" (Rom. 5:5).

Even before Christ came to earth, God's way was the way of love, which was the way of obedience. The Jews of Jesus' day should have been convicted of their lovelessness and their disobedience, because the Old Testament was clear—and nowhere more clear than in the Shema—that the person without obedience for God was without love for God and was therefore without God Himself.

After stating the first and greatest commandment, Jesus did the Pharisees one better and added **the second** as well: **You shall love your neighbor as yourself.** Not surprisingly, **the second** greatest commandment involves the same virtue as the first, namely, **love.** The command for genuine love of God, Jesus declared, is next followed in importance by the command for a **love** of **your neighbor** that is of the same order as the love you already have for **yourself.**

Just as the Pharisees had no genuine love for God, neither did they have genuine love even for their Jewish **neighbor,** not to mention their Gentile **neighbor.** Instead, as Jesus reminded the multitudes a short while later, the scribes and Pharisees "tie up heavy loads, and lay them on men's shoulders; but they themselves are unwilling to move them with so much as a finger" (Matt. 23:4). Like the mercenary Sadducees who extorted the Temple worshipers in the selling of sacrifices and exchanging of money, the scribes and Pharisees also abused and made religious merchandise of their fellow Jews.

Genuine **love** for one's **neighbor** is of the same kind as genuine love for God. It is by choice purposeful, intentional, and active, not merely sentimental and emotional. And it is measured, Jesus said, by your love for **yourself.** When a person is hungry, he feeds himself; when he is thirsty, he gets himself a drink; and when he is sick, he takes medicine or sees a doctor—all because he is so consumed with caring for himself. He does not simply think or talk about food or water or medicine but does whatever is necessary to provide those things for himself. A person never simply says to himself, "Go in peace, be warmed and be filled," without doing anything to secure his needed clothing and food (see James 2:16).

Contrary to some contemporary interpretations of this passage, Jesus was not commanding that a person love himself but assumed he already does love himself. "No one ever hated his own flesh," Paul states, "but nourishes and cherishes it" (Eph. 5:29). And just as a person looks out for his own welfare, both by the legitimacy of natural design as well as because of sinful selfishness, he will also look out for the welfare of others if he truly loves them.

The basic requirements both of Judaism and of Christianity are summed up in the same dual command: to love God and to love one's fellow man. **"On these two commandments,"** Jesus said, **"depend the whole Law and the Prophets."** Everything else in the Old Testament that God required of believers hung on those two commands. Likewise, every New Testament requirement of believers is based on them. "Beloved, let us love one another, for love is from God," John declares; "and everyone who loves is born of God and knows God. The one who does not love does not know God, for God is love" (1 John 4:7-8). "He who loves his neighbor," Paul says, "has fulfilled the law. For this, 'You shall not commit adultery, You shall not murder, You shall not steal, You shall not covet,' and if there is any other commandment, it is summed up in this saying, 'You shall love your neighbor as yourself.' Love does no wrong to a neighbor; love therefore is the fulfillment of the law" (Rom. 13:8-10).

If people loved perfectly there would be no need for law, because the person who loves others will never do them harm. In the same way, the believer who loves God with all his being will never take His name in vain, will never worship idols, and will never fail to obey, worship, honor, and glorify Him as Lord.

The lawyer was favorably, and no doubt surprisingly, impressed by Jesus' answer. "Right, Teacher," he said; "'You have truly stated that . . . to love Him with all the heart and with all the understanding and with all the strength, and to love one's neighbor as himself, is much more than all burnt offerings and sacrifices.' And when Jesus saw that he had answered intelligently, He said to him, 'You are not far from the kingdom of God'" (Mark 12:32-34).

Whose Son Is Christ?

(22:41-46)

33

Now while the Pharisees were gathered together, Jesus asked them a question, saying, "What do you think about the Christ, whose son is He?" They said to Him, "The Son of David." He said to them, "Then how does David in the Spirit call him 'Lord,' saying, 'The Lord said to my lord, "Sit at My right hand, until I put Thine enemies beneath Thy feet"'? If David then calls Him 'Lord,' how is He his son?" And no one was able to answer Him a word, nor did anyone dare from that day on to ask Him another question. (22:41-46)

The most important question in the world is, "Who is Jesus Christ?" And the world has never lacked for ideas and opinions about the answer. Certain Pharisees in Jesus' own day accused Him of casting "out demons only by Beelzebul the ruler of the demons" (Matt. 12:24). A second-century A.D. comment in the Talmud said Jesus practiced magic and led Israel astray (*Sanhedrin* 43a). Julian the Apostate, emperor of Rome from A.D. 361-363, declared, "Jesus has now been celebrated about three hundred years; having done nothing in his lifetime worthy of fame, unless anyone thinks it a very great work to heal lame and blind people and exorcise demoniacs in villages of Bethsaida and Bethany" (quoted by Cyril, a fifth-century

343

bishop of Alexandria, in *Contra Julian,* lib. vi., p. 191).

In modern times, most people have tended to be complimentary of Jesus, although their opinions are frequently condescending and naive. The radical French philosopher Jean-Jacques Rousseau wrote, "When Plato describes his imaginary righteous man loaded with all the punishments of guilt, yet meriting the highest rewards of virtue, he describes exactly the character of Jesus Christ. . . . The life and death of Jesus are those of a God" (*Oeuvres complétes* [Paris, 1839], tome iii, pp. 365-67). The famous poet Ralph Waldo Emerson held Jesus to be the most perfect of all men who have appeared on earth, and Napoleon said, "I know men, and I tell you that Jesus Christ was not a man."

The English philosopher and economist John Stuart Mill said Jesus was "the pattern of perfection for humanity," and the Irish historian and essayist William E. Lecky said Jesus was "the highest pattern of virtue." French philologist and historian Ernest Renan said Jesus "will never be surpassed," and American Unitarian clergyman Theodore Parker called Jesus the youth with God in His heart. German theologian and philosopher David Strauss, a staunch critic of biblical Christianity, said Jesus is the "highest model of religion within the reach of [human] thought." English novelist H. G. Wells wrote, "When I was asked which single individual has left the most permanent impression on the world, the manner of the questioner almost carried the implication that it was Jesus of Nazareth. I agreed. . . . Jesus stands first."

As those testimonies give evidence, many people who do not trust in Jesus Christ as their Lord and Savior still rank Him as the highest model of humanity. But beneath most such compliments is the incipient, if not specific, denial that He was anything more than a man. And many of those who highly praise Him nevertheless deny much of what He taught, especially what He taught about Himself and His work.

Christianity has always found its most violent detractors and enemies in those who deny the divinity of Jesus Christ. Many of those detractors presume to go under the name of Christian. Some years ago a Washington State newspaper reported that the minister of a liberal church had begun a sermon series emphasizing that Jesus Christ was merely a man and not God. He said that the reason there is any controversy at all on this issue is because "there is always a bunch of people who say Jesus is God." The minister suggested that Jesus was simply like Mother Teresa or Caesar Chavez.

Many religions and cults teach that Jesus was a prophet of God, or at least a great religious teacher, but that He was not the Savior of the world and was not divine to any greater degree than they consider all men to be divine.

The battle lines of biblical Christianity are inevitably drawn at the issue of Jesus' divinity. That is the one doctrine apart from which all others are meaningless, because if He were not divine He could not be the Savior of the world, and men would have no way of becoming reconciled to God.

It is that supreme issue of Jesus' full identity with which Matthew 22:41-46 deals.

Now while the Pharisees were gathered together, Jesus asked them a question, saying, "What do you think about the Christ, whose son is He?" (22:41-42a)

After irrefutably answering the three questions the Jewish leaders had designed to entrap Him (Matt. 22:15-40), Jesus continued teaching in the Temple, where He had been since early that Wednesday morning (21:23). **The Pharisees were gathered together** by themselves, no doubt more perplexed than ever as to what they could do to discredit and eliminate **Jesus.** They were obviously standing nearby, and while they were pondering what to do next, Jesus **asked them a question** about **the Christ.**

He did not, however, ask directly about Himself. Although He often had declared His messiahship and His divinity, He now wanted the Pharisees to focus on what they already believed about the identity of the Messiah, **the Christ,** God's promised Anointed One. Specifically, He asked, **"Whose son is He?"** That is, from what Jewish line was He to be descended?

THE INADEQUATE ANSWER

They said to Him, "The Son of David." (22:42b)

To the Pharisees, as well as to most other Jews, the answer was obvious and simple. Because they were convinced the Messiah was no more than a man, the only identity of the Messiah they took seriously was that of his being **the Son of David.** The scribes had long taught that "the Christ is the son of David" (Mark 12:35), a teaching that was perfectly true. Through the prophet Nathan, the Lord had promised David, "When your days are complete and you lie down with your fathers, I will raise up your descendant after you, who will come forth from you, and I will establish his kingdom. He shall build a house for My name, and I will establish the throne of his kingdom forever. . . . My lovingkindness shall not depart from him, as I took it away from Saul, whom I removed from before you. And your house and your kingdom shall endure before Me forever; your throne shall be established forever" (2 Sam. 7:12-13, 15-16).

That promise could not have applied to Solomon. He did build a house for God in the form of the Temple, but his kingdom did not last forever. Nor could any other descendant (note the singular in 2 Sam. 7:12) of David claim an everlasting throne. After Solomon, the Davidic kingdom was divided and has never been restored.

Psalm 89 makes repeated references to the Messiah as the unique descendant of David: "I have made a covenant with My chosen; I have sworn to David My servant, I will establish your seed forever, and build up your throne to all generations. . . . I have found David My servant; with My holy oil I have anointed him, with whom My hand will be established; My arm also will strengthen him. . . . And My faithfulness and My lovingkindness will be with him, and in My name his horn will be exalted. . . . I also shall make him My first-born, the highest of the kings of the earth. My lovingkindness I will keep for him forever, and My covenant shall be confirmed to him. So I will establish his descendants forever, and his throne as the days of heaven" (vv. 3-4, 20-21, 24, 27-29).

Amos prophesied, "In that day I will raise up the fallen booth of David, and wall up its breaches; I will also raise up its ruins, and rebuild it as in the days of old" (Amos 9:11). Through Micah the Lord declared, "As for you, Bethlehem Ephrathah, too little to be among the clans of Judah, from you One will go forth for Me to be ruler in Israel. His goings forth are from long ago, from the days of eternity" (Mic. 5:2).

God commanded Ezekiel to write,

> Thus says the Lord God, "Behold, I will take the sons of Israel from among the nations where they have gone, and I will gather them from every side and bring them into their own land; and I will make them one nation in the land, on the mountains of Israel; and one king will be king for all of them; and they will no longer be two nations, and they will no longer be divided into two kingdoms. . . . I will deliver them from all their dwelling places in which they have sinned, and will cleanse them. And they will be My people, and I will be their God.
>
> "And My servant David will be king over them, and they will all have one shepherd; and they will walk in My ordinances, and keep My statutes, and observe them. And they shall live on the land that I gave to Jacob My servant, in which your fathers lived; and they will live on it, they, and their sons, and their sons' sons, forever; and David My servant shall be their prince forever." (Ezek. 37:21-25)

Starting at the millennial kingdom and sweeping into eternity, David's greater Son, often called David by extension of the ancestral name, will rule an everlasting kingdom. "When I shall raise up for David a righteous Branch," the Lord said, "He will reign as king and act wisely and do justice and righteousness in the land. In His days Judah will be saved, and Israel will dwell securely; and this is His name by which He will be called, 'The Lord our righteousness'" (Jer. 23:5-6).

Throughout his gospel, Matthew focuses on Jesus' being the Son of David. He begins with an abbreviated genealogy that establishes Jesus' direct lineage from David (1:6; cf. Luke 3:31). He reports Jesus' frequently being hailed by various individuals and groups as the Son of David. The two blind men in Galilee cried out to Him, "Have mercy on us, Son of David" (9:27), clearly acknowledging Him as the promised Messiah, the Christ. The two blind men of Jericho made the same plea: "Lord, have mercy on us, Son of David" (20:30). After Jesus healed the demon-possessed man who was also blind and dumb, "all the multitudes were amazed, and began to say, 'This man cannot be the Son of David, can he?'" (12:23), a question equivalent to, "He cannot be the Messiah, can he?" And it was the fact the multitudes had acclaimed Jesus as the Son of David that the religious leaders were so indignant, because He was being hailed as the Messiah and would not renounce the acclaim (21:9, 15-16).

It was partly because Jesus' lineage from David was incontestable that the Jewish authorities were so distressed. Until the Temple was destroyed in A.D. 70, meticulous genealogical records of all Jews were kept there. That information not only was essential to establish levitical and priestly lineage, for the men as well as for their wives, but for many other purposes as well. No one could hold a position of responsibility in Israel whose genealogy was unverified. It is therefore certain that the authorities had carefully checked Jesus' genealogy and discovered that His descent from David was legitimate. Otherwise, they would simply have exposed Him as having no claim to Davidic heritage and all discussion about His possible messiahship would have ended.

Yet true as it was that the Christ would be **the Son of David,** that answer was partial and inadequate. Rather than that title's being too great for Jesus, as the Jewish leaders contended, it was much too limited. As He proceeded to explain, the Messiah had a claim to greatness that far exceeded His descent from David.

The Infinite Reality

He said to them, "Then how does David in the Spirit call him 'Lord,' saying, 'The Lord said to my lord, "Sit at My right hand, until I put Thine enemies beneath Thy feet"'? If David then calls Him 'Lord,' how is He his son?" (22:43-45)

The terms *kurios* (**Lord**) and its corresponding Hebrew word *ădōnāy* are among the most common designations for deity in the New and Old Testaments, respectively. Because God's covenant name, Yahweh, or Jehovah, was considered too holy to be spoken, the Jews always substituted the word *Ădōnāy*. In many English translations that unique use of "Lord" is indicated by its being printed in large and small capital letters (Lord), meaning that the Hebrew text actually reads *Yahweh*. When God is called "Lord" as a title, rather than as a substitute for His covenant name, the word is printed simply with capital and lower case letters (Lord), meaning that the Hebrew text reads *Ădōnāy*.

Jesus' argument, therefore, was this: "If the Messiah, the Christ, is no more than a man, the human the son of David, **Then how does David in the Spirit call him 'Lord,' saying, 'The Lord said to my lord.'"**

First of all, Jesus declared that **David** was speaking under the inspiration of God's **Spirit** when he wrote those words of Psalm 110:1. The Greek phrase behind **in the Spirit** is identical to that used by John of his vision on Patmos, when he "was in the Spirit on the Lord's day" (Rev. 1:10; cf. 4:2). It refers to being under the control of the Holy Spirit in a unique and powerful way. And as Mark makes clear in his account of this incident, Jesus' full statement was, "David himself said in the Holy Spirit" (Mark 12:36), ruling out the possibility that Jesus was referring to David's human spirit.

Second, every Jew recognized Psalm 110 as being written by David and as being one of the clearest messianic passages in the Old Testament. Consequently, there could be no argument—and there was none by Jesus' opponents—that David was speaking here about the Messiah, the second **lord** mentioned in verse 1. The first **Lord** in the Hebrew text is *Yahweh*, whereas the second is *Ădōnāy*. The idea is: **the Lord** (*Yahweh*) **said to** David's **lord** (*Ădōnāy*), **"Sit at My right hand, until I put Thine enemies beneath Thy feet."** In other words, David addressed the Messiah as his **Lord.**

Third, and most importantly, Jesus was declaring the Messiah's deity. Under the guidance of the Holy Spirit, David had declared that God told the Messiah to **sit at** His (God's) **right hand,** a place recognized by Jews to be a designation of coequal rank and authority. The verb behind **sit** in the original text indicates continuous sitting in the place of exaltation. God was going to bring the Messiah to a place of equality with Himself in honor, power, and glory.

At God's **right hand,** the Messiah would be invincible, because God would **put** His **enemies beneath** His **feet,** a figure of abject, helpless subjugation. When a defeated enemy was brought before an ancient oriental monarch, the ruler would make the prisoner prostrate himself at his feet. The king would then place his foot on the neck of the vanquished enemy as if he were a footstool (see Josh. 10:24). All the detractors, deniers, and other **enemies** of the Messiah are doomed to subjugation beneath His control.

Liberal critics have long maintained that David could not have written Psalm 110, arguing that the Hebrew language in David's time had not developed to the level found in the psalm and that David would not have been familiar with the priest-king relationship expressed in verse 4. But historical and archaeological discoveries have proved both of those assumptions to be unfounded. Some critics also deny the messianic character of the psalm, largely because they discount all supernatural revelation and consequently all predictive prophecy. If a "prediction" came true, they argue, it was obviously written after the fact. But that humanistic approach not only makes Scripture out to be intentionally deceptive but makes Jesus Himself a liar or a dupe. He could hardly have been the model for the highest level of human virtue, as many of those same critics claim, if He declared Himself to be divine but was not. Or if the gospel writers misrepresented what He said about Himself, how can anything else they reported about Him be considered reliable?

If David then calls Him "Lord," Jesus asked the Pharisees, **how is He his son?** Jesus' point was that the title "Son of David" alone was not sufficient for the Messiah, that He is also the Son of God. **David** would not have addressed a merely human descendent as **"Lord."** Jesus was saying, in effect, "I am not giving you any new teaching or revelation. You should have been able to figure it out for yourselves, and would have done so if you truly believed Scripture." The religious elite of Judaism had never seen that obvious truth, because, like many people today, they did not look to Scripture for truth. When they looked to it at all, it was for the purpose of trying to shore up their humanly devised religious traditions and personal preferences.

Jesus did not mention the most important conclusion the Pharisees should have made from what He had just said: that He Himself was the divine Messiah, the Son of David and Son of God. It was unnecessary for Him to do that, because He had been presenting His divine messianic credentials for three years. He had done so many things to prove He was the Son of God that unbelievers had to deny the obvious to conclude anything else. The signs and miracles recorded in the gospels are but a part of the countless others than He performed. "Many other signs therefore Jesus also performed in the presence of the disciples, which are not written in this book," John tells us; "but these have been written that you may believe that Jesus is the Christ, the Son of God; and that believing you may have life in His name" (John 20:30-31; cf. 21:25).

Although Jesus was correcting the Pharisees' incomplete concept of who He was, He also seems to have been giving them still another invitation to believe in Him. Several of the scribes, including the lawyer who had asked Jesus about the greatest commandment, commended Him for His wise answers to the questions given to test Him (Mark 12:32; Luke 20:39). Jesus even told the lawyer that he was not far from the kingdom (Mark 12:34). There doubtlessly were others in the Temple that day who were tender-hearted and open to God's truth and who might be led to trust in Him and follow Him as Lord if they were convinced He were truly God's Son.

Jesus was obviously no phantom, as some heretics in the early church proposed. He ate, drank, slept, felt pain, bled, and died. He was even "tempted in all things as we are, yet without sin" (Heb. 4:15). He was the Son of Man in every way. That He was specifically the Son of David was obvious and provable by the Temple records. And that He was the divine Son of God was obvious from the miracles that He performed without number for everyone to see.

Jesus shares with God all the attributes of omnipotence. He is the Creator, the controller of the heavens and the earth and all its creatures. He is the provider of food, the healer of the sick, the raiser of the dead, the forgiver of sin, the giver of eternal life, and the judge of all men and angels.

Jesus shares with God all the attributes of omnipresence. Wherever "two or three have gathered together in My name," He declared, "there I am in their midst" (Matt. 18:20).

Jesus shares with God all the attributes of omniscience. He knew what His disciples were thinking and what His enemies were thinking. "He did not need anyone to bear witness concerning man for He Himself knew what was in man" (John 2:25).

The New Testament consistently presents Christ as Son of David and Son of God. The gospel message Paul preached and wrote about was promised by God "beforehand through His prophets in the holy Scriptures, concerning His Son, who was born of a descendant of David according to the flesh, who was declared the Son of God with power by the resurrection from the dead, according to the spirit of holiness, Jesus Christ our Lord" (Rom. 1:2-4). Paul admonished Timothy to "remember Jesus Christ, risen from the dead, descendant of David" (2 Tim. 2:8).

In his letter to believers at Philippi, Paul wrote,

> Have this attitude in yourselves which was also in Christ Jesus, who, although He existed in the form of God, did not regard equality with God a thing to be grasped, but emptied Himself, taking the form of a bond-servant, and being made in the likeness of men. And being found in appearance as a man, He humbled Himself by becoming obedient to the point of death, even death on a cross. Therefore also God highly exalted Him, and bestowed on Him the name which is above every name, that at the name of Jesus every knee should bow, of those who are in heaven, and on earth, and under the earth, and that every tongue should confess that Jesus Christ is Lord, to the glory of God the Father." (Phil. 2:5-11)

"The Word became flesh, and dwelt among us," John declared, "and we beheld His glory, glory as of the only begotten from the Father, full of grace and truth" (John 1:14).

In his classic apologetics work *Protestant Christian Evidences,* Bernard Ramm gives a series of incisive answers to the question he himself propounds: "If God became incarnate, what kind of man would He be?" In abbreviated form, six of the answers are: we would expect Him to be sinless; we would expect him to be holy; we would expect His words to be the greatest words ever spoken; we would expect Him to exert a profound power over human personality; we would expect Him to perform supernatural doings; and we would expect Him to manifest the love of God. Of all human beings who have ever lived, Jesus Christ alone met all of those criteria ([Chicago; Moody, 1953], pp. 166-75).

The Inappropriate Response

And no one was able to answer Him a word, nor did anyone dare from that day on to ask Him another question. (22:46)

It is probable that some of the leaders who heard Jesus that day eventually believed in Him. But when Jesus finished His short but irrefutable proof of the Messiah's divinity, there is no indication that anyone profited from that great truth.

Mark reports that "the great crowd enjoyed listening to Him" (Mark 12:37); but that sentiment was far from saving trust. The initial response of the people was favorable, but in two days many of them would cry out with the chief priests and elders who incited them, "Let Him be crucified!" (Matt. 27:22).

The Pharisees and other religious leaders there that day were dumbfounded but not convinced, silenced but not convicted, humiliated but not humbled, reluctantly impressed but still unbelieving. Doubtlessly they were thinking that they had been intimidated and embarrassed for the last time by the uneducated, unordained, and in their minds unorthodox rabbi from Nazareth.

Self-righteous religion has always been and will always be the greatest enemy of the gospel. Secularism generally is indifferent, whereas human religion invariably is hostile.

The Samaritan woman whom Jesus met at the well outside Sychar was the first person to whom He directly revealed His messiahship. After she commented "that Messiah is coming (He who is called Christ)," Jesus then "said to her, 'I who speak to you am He'" (John 4:25-26). That woman trusted in Christ herself and immediately went into her village and witnessed to others, many of whom also believed (vv. 39-42). But most of the Samaritans did not believe and down through the centuries have not believed. Today they number perhaps fewer than 500, and, like their Jewish counterparts, they are still looking for a Messiah who has already come. Like so many people, they failed to believe the truth, though the testimony of Scripture is overwhelmingly convincing.

The Character of False Spiritual Leaders

34

(23:1-12)

Then Jesus spoke to the multitudes and to His disciples, saying, "The scribes and the Pharisees have seated themselves in the chair of Moses; therefore all that they tell you, do and observe, but do not do according to their deeds; for they say things, and do not do them. And they tie up heavy loads, and lay them on men's shoulders; but they themselves are unwilling to move them with so much as a finger. But they do all their deeds to be noticed by men; for they broaden their phylacteries, and lengthen the tassels of their garments. And they love the place of honor at banquets, and the chief seats in the synagogues, and respectful greetings in the market places, and being called by men, Rabbi. But do not be called Rabbi; for One is your Teacher, and you are all brothers. And do not call anyone on earth your father; for One is your Father, He who is in heaven. And do not be called leaders; for One is your Leader, that is, Christ. But the greatest among you shall be your servant. And whoever exalts himself shall be humbled; and whoever humbles himself shall be exalted. (23:1-12)

Matthew 23 records Jesus' last public sermon. It was not a sermon on salvation, on the resurrection, or on principles for living the kingdom life but rather a vital and sobering message of condemnation against false teachers. In verses 1-7

353

He warns the people about false religious leaders in Israel, and in verses 8-12 He admonishes the disciples and other true spiritual leaders not to emulate them. He then turns His attention directly to the false leaders themselves, epitomized by the scribes and Pharisees, and gives them His final and most scathing denunciation (vv. 13-36). In His closing comments (vv. 37-39) He expresses His intense compassion for unbelieving Israel and gives the assurance that one day, in fulfillment of God's sovereign promise, His chosen people will turn back to Him in faith.

Since the Fall, the world has always had false religious leaders, pretending to represent God but representing only themselves. False leaders were active in the rebellious scheme to erect the tower of Babel. Moses came into serious conflict with the religious sorcerers and magicians of Egypt when he demanded the release of God's people by pharaoh, who probably considered himself to be a god (see Ex. 7:11-12, 22; 8:7). Ezekiel faced the false prophets in Israel, whom God called "foolish prophets who are following their own spirit and have seen nothing" (Ezek. 13:3).

Jesus referred to spurious religious leaders as "false Christs and false prophets [who] will arise and will show great signs and wonders, so as to mislead, if possible, even the elect" (Matt. 24:24). Paul called them preachers of a perverted gospel (Gal. 1:8) and purveyors of the doctrines of demons (1 Tim. 4:1). Peter spoke of them as those who "secretly introduce destructive heresies, even denying the Master who bought them" (2 Pet. 2:1). John called them antichrists who deny that Jesus is the Messiah, the Christ (1 John 2:18, 22). Jude called them dreamers who "defile the flesh, and reject authority, and revile angelic majesties" (Jude 8). As Paul declared to the Ephesian elders in his brief and touching reunion with them on the beach near Miletus, false religious leaders are "savage wolves" of the spirit world whose purpose is to corrupt and destroy God's people (Acts 20:29).

The religion pages of major newspapers in our day are filled with advertisements for every kind of sect and false religion, including deviant forms of Christianity as well as cults and the occult. Many of those groups masquerade as forms of Christianity and claim to teach a new and better gospel. But while purporting to offer spiritual life and help, they instead teach the way of spiritual death and damnation. While claiming to lead people to heaven, they usher them directly into hell.

Scripture makes clear that as the second coming of Christ comes near, counterfeiters of the gospel will proliferate and amass to themselves great followings and immense influence (see, e.g., 2 Thess. 2:3-4; 1 Tim. 4:1-3; 2 Tim. 3:1-9; 2 Pet. 2:1-3;). The only time in history equal to what that future demon-inspired age will be like was the time of our Lord's ministry on earth. At that time all hell garnered its forces in a three-year assault against the Son of God in a desperate effort to contradict what He taught and to counteract what He did. It is against the human instruments of that satanic attack that Jesus addresses this last public and permanently instructive message, given near the end of a long and grueling day of teaching and confrontation in the Temple.

Dialogue between Jesus and the Temple authorities had ended, because "no one was able to answer [Jesus] a word, nor did anyone dare from that day on to ask Him another question" (Matt. 22:46). Although the Lord had frequently spoken against the unbelieving religious leaders (see Matt. 5:20; 15:1-9; 16:6-12; John 8:44), it was necessary to give a final word, a last comprehensive warning, to them and to everyone else, about the eternal danger of their perverse teachings. Jesus also no doubt wanted to give those unbelieving leaders themselves opportunity to turn from their falsehood and follow Him to forgiveness and salvation.

It seems evident that many hearts were softened to the gospel that day, including the hearts of some of the leaders. On the day of Pentecost alone some three thousand souls came to the Lord (Acts 2:41), and it may well have been that eight or ten times that number believed within a few more months, as the apostles "filled Jerusalem with [their] teaching" (Acts 5:28). We can be certain that many, and perhaps most, of the converts in those early days had seen and heard Jesus personally and been drawn by the Holy Spirit to His truth and grace. Perhaps for some, this message was the point of initial attraction to Jesus Christ.

THE DESCRIPTION OF FALSE SPIRITUAL LEADERS

Then Jesus spoke to the multitudes and to His disciples, saying, "The scribes and the Pharisees have seated themselves in the chair of Moses; therefore all that they tell you, do and observe, but do not do according to their deeds; for they say things, and do not do them. And they tie up heavy loads, and lay them on men's shoulders; but they themselves are unwilling to move them with so much as a finger. But they do all their deeds to be noticed by men; for they broaden their phylacteries, and lengthen the tassels of their garments. And they love the place of honor at banquets, and the chief seats in the synagogues, and respectful greetings in the market places, and being called by men, Rabbi. (23:1-7)

At this time **Jesus spoke** directly **to the multitudes and to His disciples,** but the religious leaders, most particularly **the scribes and the Pharisees,** were within earshot nearby (see v. 13).

When the Jews returned to Palestine after the seventy years of captivity in Babylon, the Scriptures for a while regained their central place in Israel's life and worship, humanly speaking due largely to revival under the godly leaders Nehemiah and Ezra (see Neh. 8:1-8). Ezra was one of the first Jewish scribes in the sense in which the title was used in Jesus' day.

An ancient Jewish saying held that God gave the law to angels, angels gave it to Moses, Moses gave it to Joshua, Joshua gave it to the elders, the elders gave it to the prophets, and the prophets gave it to the men of the synagogue who were later called **scribes.** Over the course of the years, those synagogue scribes became responsible not only for copying and preserving but also for teaching and interpreting God's law. There were no more prophets after the Exile, and the scribes inherited the primary role of spiritual leadership in Israel. In Jesus' day **scribes** were found among both the Pharisees and Sadducees but were more commonly associated with the Pharisees.

Although the precise origin of **the Pharisees** is unknown, they appeared sometime before the middle of the second century B.C. Numbering perhaps as many as six thousand, many of them were also scribes, authorities in Jewish law, both scriptural and traditional. As has been noted many times in this study of Matthew, **the Pharisees** were by far the dominant religious group in Israel in Jesus' day and the most popular with the masses. The other major party, the Sadducees, were largely in charge of the Temple, but their driving concern was not for religion but for money and power. As their name suggests, the Herodians were a political party loyal to the Herod family. The Essenes, which are not mentioned in Scripture, were a reclusive sect who devoted much of their efforts to copying the Scriptures, and the Zealots were radical nationalists who sought to overthrow Rome militarily. Like the Sadducees, the Herodians' and Zealots' interest in religion was motivated primarily by desire for personal and political gain. Consequently, it was to **the scribes and the Pharisees** that the people looked for religious guidance and authority, a role those leaders greatly cherished.

William Barclay, who devoted many years to biblical research in Palestine, reports that the Talmud (*Sotah,* 22*b*) speaks of seven kinds of Pharisees.

The first group Barclay calls "shoulder Pharisees," so named because of their custom of displaying accounts of their good deeds on their shoulders for other people to see and admire. When they prayed, they put ashes on their heads as an act of humility and wore sad expressions on their faces to suggest piousness.

The second group he calls "wait a little," due to their cleaver ability to come up with a fabricated spiritual reason for putting off doing something good. Pious excuses were their stock in trade.

The third group were the "bruised and bleeding." In order not to commit the sin of looking at a woman lustfully, those Pharisees closed their eyes whenever women were around. Understandably, they received many bruises and abrasions from bumping into walls, posts, and other objects. They measured their piousness by the number and severity of their injuries.

The fourth group were the "humpback tumbling." In order to show off their supposed humility, they slouched over with bent backs and shuffled their feet instead of taking normal steps, leading to frequent stumbles and tumbles.

The fifth group were the "ever-seeking," named because of the meticulous record keeping of their good deeds in order to determine how much reward God owed them.

The sixth group were the "fearing" Pharisees, whose terror over the prospect of hell motivated everything they did.

The seventh and last group were the "God-fearing," those whose lives were motivated out of genuine love for God and a desire to please Him. The Pharisee Nicodemus (see John 3:1; 19:39) would doubtlessly have been classed in this group.

But Nicodemus and the few other Pharisees who believed in Jesus were very much the exceptions. For the most part, the Pharisees were the Lord's most strident critics and implacable enemies. In Matthew 23:2-7, Jesus presents five characteristics of the unbelieving **scribes and the Pharisees,** characteristics that typify all false spiritual leaders.

FALSE LEADERS LACK AUTHORITY

[they] **have seated themselves in the chair of Moses;** (23:2b)

The initial characteristic describing false religious leaders is lack of divine authority. The key to our Lord's point is the fact that the scribes and Pharisees had **seated themselves.** They were not appointed by God to sit **in the chair of Moses** and had not even been elected by the people. They had simply arrogated to **themselves** that position of authority, which was therefore spurious.

Chair is from *kathedra,* the Greek term from which we get *cathedral,* which originally referred to a place, or seat, of ecclesiastical authority. The same idea is found today in such expressions as "chair of philosophy" or "chair of history," which refer to the most esteemed professorships in a college or university. When the pope of the Roman Catholic church speaks in his full ecclesiastical authority, he is said to be speaking *ex cathedra.*

For Jews, **Moses** was the supreme law giver, the supreme spokesman for God. Therefore to sit **in the chair of Moses** was tantamount to being God's authoritative spokesman, and it was that very claim that many of the scribes and Pharisees made for **themselves.**

It was for that reason they were envious of Jesus and so determined to undermine Him. They were infuriated because the people discerned that Jesus taught with an authority that seemed genuine (Matt. 7:29). Even to the uneducated masses, something about the teaching of the scribes and Pharisees did not ring true, whereas Jesus' teaching did. Jesus was therefore a threat to those leaders and to their heretofore unchallenged religious authority.

Jeremiah was confronted by false prophets in his day, prophets the Lord repeatedly said were not sent by Him and were not preaching His word. "I have neither sent them nor commanded them nor spoken to them," God declared to the prophet; "they are prophesying to you a false vision, divination, futility and the deception of their own minds" (Jer. 14:14). "I did not send these prophets, but they ran," the Lord later said to Jeremiah. "I did not speak to them, but they prophesied. . . . 'Behold, I am against those who have prophesied false dreams,' declares the Lord, 'and related them, and led My people astray by their falsehoods and reckless boasting; yet I did not send them or command them, nor do they furnish this people the slightest benefit,' declares the Lord" (23:21, 32; cf. 27:15; 28:15; 29:9).

God told Isaiah that many of the people would not listen to his words. "For this is a rebellious people," He said, "false sons, sons who refuse to listen to the instruction of the Lord; who say to the seers, 'You must not see visions'; and to the prophets, 'You must not prophesy to us what is right, speak to us pleasant words, prophesy illusions'" (Isa. 30:9-10). Sinful people resist God's truth because it is a rebuke to them, and they just as naturally turn to false religions and philosophies because those systems in one way or another approve and indulge their wicked inclinations and desires. They are therefore easy prey for false teachers who appeal to their base natures.

Jesus warned that such teachers and leaders are lying shepherds who do not enter the sheepfold by the door but climb in surreptitiously over the fence to wreak havoc among the flock. They are thieves who come "only to steal, and kill, and destroy" (John 10:1, 10). They do not represent God or speak in His name or in His authority but are deceivers, usurpers, and destroyers of God's Word, God's work, and God's people.

They are in marked contrast to those who are genuinely sent by the Lord as ministers of His gospel, which He has committed to them (Gal. 1:15). Like Timothy, they have been called and set apart by God by the laying on of hands as confirmation of their divine commission and authority (1 Tim. 4:14). They are like the apostles, on whom the Lord breathed, saying, "Receive the Holy Spirit" (John 20:22) and to whom He later said, "All authority has been given to Me in heaven and on earth. Go therefore and make disciples of all the nations" (Matt. 28:18-19).

False leaders, on the other hand, lack divine authority in what they say and do. They are self-appointed ministers of human ideas and traditions, and as they promote their false notions they obscure God's truth and pervert God's righteousness for their own selfish purposes.

As in the prophets' times and in Jesus' time, the world still abounds with teachers who claim to speak in God's name and power but do not. They usurp the place of the Lord's true shepherds with lies, false promises, delusions, dreams, visions, and usually are guilty of immoral living.

FALSE LEADERS LACK INTEGRITY

therefore all that they tell you, do and observe, but do not do according to their deeds; for they say things, and do not do them. (23:3)

Second, false religious leaders are characterized by lack of integrity, hypocritically demanding of others many things they never do themselves.

In exhorting His followers, **"All that they tell you, do and observe,"** Jesus obviously was not speaking comprehensively of the lies and errors they taught but only of their instructions that conformed to Scripture. He had made clear that the righteousness acceptable to God must exceed the hypocritical, works-oriented self-righteousness the scribes and Pharisees advocated and practiced (Matt. 5:20). In His following comments He also made clear that their countless man-made traditions, many of which actually contradicted God's law, were absolutely worthless and led people away from God rather than to Him. They were wrong about murder, fornication, divorce, adultery, swearing, praying, worship, and virtually every other area of living (see 5:21-48). They "invalidated the word of God for the sake of [their] tradition" (15:6).

Jesus was not giving blanket approval for following the teachings of the scribes and Pharisees but was rather warning against throwing the baby out with the dirty bath water. In other words, if they speak God's truth, you should **do and observe** it, Jesus was saying. The Word of God is still the Word of God, even in the mouth of a false teacher. Insofar as the scribes and Pharisees accurately taught the law and the prophets, their teaching was to be heeded.

The verb *poieō* (**do**) is an aorist imperative and demands an immediate response. *Tēreō* (**observe**) is a present imperative and carries the idea of continuing action. Jesus was therefore saying, "Immediately obey and keep on obeying whatever the scribes and Pharisees teach if it follows God's Word."

But do not do according to their deeds. When the scribes and Pharisees did occasionally teach God's truth, they did not obey it themselves. **"They say things, and do not do them,"** Jesus declared. They were religious phonies, consummate hypocrites who did not practice what they preached.

The unbelieving religious leaders did not have the ability to keep God's law even had they genuinely wanted to, because they possessed no spiritual resources to make such obedience possible. Being unredeemed, they lived only in the flesh and by the flesh's power, and the flesh is not capable of fulfilling God's law (Rom. 3:20). It has no power either to restrain evil or to do good. It can develop impressive and sophisticated systems of external morality and ethical codes of conduct, but it cannot empower men to live up to them. It may talk much about God's love and about His will for man to live in love, but it cannot produce love in a sinful heart. It may talk much about serving the poor and living in peace, but it cannot produce genuine love for the poor or genuine peace in the heart, much less in the world. Many religions, sects, and cults have high moral standards, promote close family ties, and advocate generosity, neighborliness, and good citizenship. But because all such systems are man-made, they work entirely in the power of the flesh, which can only produce the works of the flesh. Only the new person in Christ can "joyfully concur with the law of God in the inner man" (Rom. 7:22), and only the redeemed life, the life "created in Christ Jesus for good works" (Eph. 2:10) is able to do good works.

Later in this diatribe against the scribes and Pharisees the Lord speaks of their carefully tithing "mint and dill and cummin" but neglecting "the weightier provisions of the law: justice and mercy and faithfulness" (Matt. 23:23). Mint, dill, and cummin were not farm crops grown for profit but were garden spices used in cooking, and a tithe of those herbs was therefore worth very little. But whereas those leaders were meticulous in giving every tenth herb seed to the synagogue or Temple, they were totally unconcerned about fulfilling the moral demands of God's law, represented by justice, mercy, and faithfulness. They were adroit at making good appearances of right living, of cleaning the outside of the cup. But inside, Jesus declared, they were nothing but self-indulgent thieves, the decaying carcasses of spiritually dead men. You "outwardly appear righteous to men, but inwardly you are full of hypocrisy and lawlessness" (vv. 25-28).

The false religious leader tries, often unsuccessfully, to put a cap on his wicked behavior to keep it out of view, but in so doing he merely traps it underneath the surface, where it festers, putrefies, and becomes still more corrupt. Paul speaks of such hypocrites as being "seared in their own conscience as with a branding iron" (1 Tim. 4:2). They have sinned so long and so willfully that their consciences have lost all sensitivity to truth and holiness, just as scar tissue loses sensitivity to pain.

Peter vividly portrays the nature of false prophets and teachers, about whom he solemnly warns believers. They "secretly introduce destructive heresies, even denying the Master who bought them," he said, "bringing swift destruction upon themselves." They "follow their sensuality and because of them the way of the truth [is] maligned; and in their greed they will exploit you with false words" (2 Pet. 2:1-3). He further describes them as,

> those who indulge the flesh in its corrupt desires and despise authority. Daring, self-willed, . . . unreasoning animals, born as creatures of instinct to be captured and killed, reviling where they have no knowledge, . . . stains and blemishes, reveling in their deceptions, . . . having eyes full of adultery and that never cease from sin, enticing unstable souls, having a heart trained in greed, accursed children, . . . springs without water, and mists driven by a storm, . . . speaking out arrogant words of vanity they entice by fleshly desires, by sensuality, those who barely escape from the ones who live in error, promising them freedom while they themselves are slaves of corruption. (vv. 10, 12-14, 17-19)

As noted earlier, Jude refers to them in similar terms, calling them dreamers of wicked dreams, defilers of the flesh, rejecters of authority, and revilers of angelic majesties, unreasoning animals, hidden reefs, clouds without water, "trees without fruit, doubly dead, uprooted; wild waves of the sea, casting up their own shame like foam; wandering stars, for whom the black darkness has been reserved forever" (Jude 8, 10, 12-13).

In the unregenerate heart, vice cannot be restrained and virtue cannot be produced. That is why even the best man-made system, even one that espouses many standards that Scripture itself espouses, cannot keep its followers from doing wrong or empower them to do what is truly right—for the simple reason that it cannot change their hearts. That is also why every system that gives man the duty to make himself right before God is doomed to hypocrisy and sham, because the best it can produce is outward righteousness, outward good works, outward love, outward peace, while the depraved inner person remains unchanged.

FALSE LEADERS LACK SYMPATHY

And they tie up heavy loads, and lay them on men's shoulders; but they themselves are unwilling to move them with so much as a finger. (23:4)

Third, false religious leaders are characterized by lack of sympathy. They not only are usurpers and hypocrites but are loveless and uncaring.

The picture Jesus gives here reflects the common custom of that day, and of people in many underdeveloped countries today, of loading up a donkey, camel, or other beast of burden to the point where it can hardly move. As they traveled down the road, the owner would walk alongside, carrying nothing himself, berating and beating the animal if it happened to stumble or balk, with no concern for the animal's feelings or welfare.

That, Jesus said, is exactly the way the scribes and Pharisees treated their fellow Jews. They piled **up heavy loads** of religious regulations, rules, and rituals **on men's shoulders** until they were unbearable and impossible to carry. And when the people failed to keep all of the requirements, as they were doomed to do, they were chided and rebuked by the leaders, who thereby added the burden of guilt to those of weariness and frustration.

The people were taught that it was only by their own good works they could please God. If at the end of life the good works outweighed the bad, then God would grant entrance into heaven. But the scribes and Pharisees offered the people no help in achieving even those fleshly goals, much less any spiritual ones. **They themselves** were **unwilling to** help **move** those unbearable burdens **with so much as a finger.** Consequently, Judaism had become insufferably depressing and debilitating.

The good news that Jesus brought, on the other hand, was that He would take away the load of sin that always outweighed their good works. That is why Paul was infuriated with the Judaizers, who tried to draw the Galatian believers back into legalism. He did not care who they were or claimed to be. "Even though we, or an angel from heaven, should preach to you a gospel contrary to that which we have preached to you, let him be accursed. As we have said before, so I say again now, if any man is preaching to you a gospel contrary to that which you received, let him be accursed" (Gal. 1:8-9). "It was for freedom that Christ set us free," he said later in the same letter; "therefore keep standing firm and do not be subject again to a yoke of slavery" (5:1).

The scribes and Pharisees had no interest in God's grace, forgiveness, and mercy, because those divine provisions make no allowance for human merit or good works. They could not comprehend and were utterly offended by a gospel that did not credit their own goodness. And they were scandalized by a gospel that declared, "Humble yourselves, therefore, under the mighty hand of God" (1 Pet. 5:6).

They did not feel they needed God's grace for themselves and did not want it preached to others, because that liberating truth undercut the entire system of works-righteousness by which they kept the people in subjection to their own human authority.

Certain false leaders in the early church forbad marriage and the eating of particular foods, which Paul declared "God has created to be gratefully shared in by those who believe and know the truth" (1 Tim. 4:3). Under the name of

Christ, Roman Catholicism still forbids marriage of their clergy and teaches abstinence from certain foods on certain days and other legalistic and unscriptural doctrines.

Peter declared of false teachers that "in their greed they will exploit you with false words" (2 Pet. 2:3). Those under the care of such a fleshly, ungodly leader are no more than merchandise to be exploited to feed his ego and his wallet.

For centuries Israel had been stumbling and falling under the burden of unscrupulous, hardened religious leaders who, although they claimed to minister in God's name, had love neither for God nor for His people. Long before the time of Christ, the Lord spoke to Ezekiel about such men, saying,

> Son of Man, prophesy against the shepherds of Israel. Prophesy and say to those shepherds, "Thus says the Lord God, 'Woe, shepherds of Israel who have been feeding themselves! Should not the shepherds feed the flock? You eat the fat and cloth yourselves with the wool, you slaughter the fat sheep without feeding the flock. Those who are sickly you have not strengthened, the diseased you have not healed, the broken you have not bound up, the scattered you have not brought back, nor have you sought for the lost; but with force and with severity you have dominated them. And they were scattered for lack of a shepherd, and they became food for every beast of the field and were scattered.'" (Ezek. 34:2-5)

False religious leaders today are still building empires and amassing fortunes by fleecing those they pretend to serve. It would be impossible to determine the millions of believers and unbelievers alike who are misled spiritually, abused emotionally, and bilked financially in the name of Christ. Like the false shepherds of ancient Israel, they feed on their own sheep.

Earlier in His ministry, as He looked out over the multitudes who had so long been exploited by the corrupt religious leaders of Israel, Jesus "felt compassion for them, because they were distressed and downcast like sheep without a shepherd" (Matt. 9:36). It must have been gloriously refreshing for those people to hear Jesus say, "Come to Me, all who are weary and heavy-laden, and I will give you rest. Take My yoke upon you, and learn from Me, for I am gentle and humble in heart; and you shall find rest for your souls. For My yoke is easy, and My load is light" (Matt. 11:28-30).

Following the spirit and example of his Master, the apostle Paul always ministered to those under his care like the gentlest of shepherds, even like the most caring of mothers. "We proved to be gentle among you," he reminded the Thessalonians, "as a nursing mother tenderly cares for her own children. Having thus a fond affection for you, we were well-pleased to impart to you not only the gospel of God but also our own lives, because you had become very dear to us. For you recall, brethren, our labor and hardship, how working night and day so as not to be a burden to any of you, we proclaimed to the gospel of God" (1 Thess. 2:7-9).

FALSE LEADERS LACK SPIRITUALITY

But they do all their deeds to be noticed by men; for they broaden their phylacteries, and lengthen the tassels of their garments. (23:5)

Fourth, false religious leaders are characterized by lack of spirituality, by the absence of a genuine desire to please God. Like the scribes and Pharisees, the motivation for all their pretentious religious activities and **deeds** is **to be noticed by men.** Everything is done for outward show rather than from the heart, for fleshly gratification of ego rather than selfless service to God and to others in His name. The issue for them is not godly character but fleshly appearance, the making of "a good showing in the flesh" (Gal. 6:12). Their purpose is to glorify themselves, not God.

The Jewish religious leaders paraded their piosity everywhere they went. The center of their living was "practicing [their] righteousness before Men to be noticed by them" (Matt. 6:1). When they prayed in the synagogue or on the street corner, they did so with great ostentation (v. 5), and when they fasted, they went out of their way to call attention to the sacrifice they were making (v. 16).

Such people, Jude says, are "worldly-minded, devoid of the Spirit" (Jude 19). They follow their natural appetites and ambitions without restraint or shame, considering themselves to be the spiritually elite with a favored status before God as well as before men.

Hundreds of such fleshly frauds without the Holy Spirit still proclaim themselves as representatives of God and are followed by millions of gullible people who support them with hundreds of millions of dollars every year. In order to feed their egos and to amass wealth and power, these false leaders sometimes pastor huge churches, head colleges and seminaries, direct radio and television empires, and promote many other personally-oriented activities in the name of the gospel.

In Jesus' day, the means for being **noticed by men** were much more limited and less sophisticated, but false leaders then reflected the same fleshly desire to elevate self. Everything they did was to advance themselves and to foster the admiration of men.

To flaunt their religiosity, the scribes and Pharisees would **broaden their phylacteries, and lengthen the tassels of their garments.**

Four times in the Pentateuch (Ex. 13:9, 16; Deut. 6:8; 11:18) the Lord commanded that His law was to be upon the hands and foreheads of His people as a reminder of Him. The ancient Jews understood that command as it was given, not to be taken literally but as symbolic of God's law being the controlling factor in their lives, not only in what they did, represented by the hand, but in what they thought, represented by the forehead. Both their thoughts and their actions were to be directed by God's Word. Far from having the purpose of promoting external human pretense and pride, that instruction was meant to elevate the Lord and to draw His people closer to Himself.

As the centuries passed, many Jews came to look on the injunction not as a means of making God's Word dominant in their lives but of making themselves dominant in the eyes of their fellow Jews. They literalized and externalized the command and turned it into a means of feeding their own egos.

Phylacteries were sometimes called *tephillin,* a name derived from the Hebrew word translated "frontals" in Deuteronomy 6:8 and 11:18 (cf. Ex. 13:16). Phylacteries were small square boxes made of leather from a ceremonially clean animal. After being dyed black, the leather was sewn into a box using twelve stitches, each stitch representing one of the twelve tribes of Israel. Placed into each phylactery were copies of Exodus 13:1-10 and 13:11-16 and of Deuteronomy 6:4-9 and 11:13-21. The phylactery worn on the head had four compartments, each containing one of the texts on a small piece of parchment. The phylactery worn on the hand contained a single piece of parchment on which all four texts were written. The Hebrew letter shin (y) was inscribed on both sides of the box worn on the head, and the head strap was tied to form the letter daleth (d) and the hand strap to form the letter yodh (j). The three letters together formed *Shaddai,* one of the ancient names of God usually translated "Almighty." Long leather straps were used to bind one box to the forehead and the other to the arm and left hand, because the left side was considered to be closer to the heart.

In Orthodox Judaism still today, every boy is given a set of phylacteries when he comes of age on his thirteenth birthday. Like the other Jewish men, he then wears his phylacteries at morning prayer, as was the general custom in Jesus' day.

There is no record of the use of **phylacteries** until about 400 B.C. during the intertestamental period. Relics of them were found in the Essene community at Qumran near the Dead Sea. **Phylacteries** is a transliteration of the Greek *phulaktēria,* which referred to a means of protection or a safeguard. In pagan societies it was sometimes used as a synonym for amulet or charm. Although trust in such magical protection was clearly condemned in the Old Testament, as apostate Jews drifted away from God's Word—the very Word of which the phylactery was meant to remind them—they invariably picked up pagan beliefs. Consequently, some Jews came to look on their phylacteries as magical charms for warding off evil spirits and other dangers.

The story is told in rabbinical literature of a rabbi who had an audience with a king. Ancient custom dictated that a person who left the king's presence always walked away backwards while bowing, since it was considered a mark of great dishonor to turn one's back on a monarch. That particular rabbi, however, simply turned around and walked away, apparently to demonstrate his conviction that, because of their high standing before God, rabbis were superior to royalty. When the irate king ordered his soldiers to kill the man for his effrontery, the straps of his phylacteries were said to blaze with fire, putting fear into the hearts of the soldiers and the king and thus saving the rabbi from death.

Some scribes and Pharisees held the phylacteries to be even more sacred than the golden head plate worn by the high priest, because God's name was written twenty-three times in the phylacteries but only once on the golden head plate. God had been so made over into their own image that many Pharisees believed the Lord

Himself wore phylacteries. Some Jewish writings from intertestamental and New Testament times give the impression that God was often thought of as little more than a glorified rabbi who studied the law three hours a day.

Rather than wearing their phylacteries only at prayer time, as the custom was for most Jewish men, the Pharisees wore them continually as a sign of superior spirituality. They also would **broaden their phylacteries,** making them larger than normal to signify supposed greater devotion to God. In a similar way and for the same purpose, they would **lengthen the tassels of their garments.**

As with phylacteries, the use of **tassels** had its origin in Scripture. The Lord instructed Moses to tell the sons of Israel "that they shall make for themselves tassels on the corners of their garments throughout their generations, and that they shall put on the tassel of each corner a cord of blue. And it shall be a tassel for you to look at and remember all the commandments of the Lord, so as to do them and not follow after your own heart and your own eyes, after which you played the harlot, in order that you may remember to do all My commandments, and be holy to your God" (Num. 15:38-40).

Jesus Himself wore **tassels,** and it was these tassels, or fringes, on His cloak that the woman with the hemorrhage touched (Matt. 9:20). In later Judaism the tassels were worn on the man's inner garments, and today the remnant of the tassel tradition is seen in the prayer shawls, called tallithim, worn by Orthodox Jewish men.

The purpose of both the **phylacteries** and **the tassels** was ostensibly to remind the people of God and His Word and to set them apart as His people (cf. Zech. 8:23). Both of those outward symbols were intended to be inward reminders and motivators. They were given a means of calling attention to God, but the scribes and Pharisees turned them into a means of calling attention to themselves. Because of their misuse, the broadened phylacteries and lengthened tassels became marks of carnality rather than spirituality.

FALSE LEADERS LACK HUMILITY

And they love the place of honor at banquets, and the chief seats in the synagogues, and respectful greetings in the market places, and being called by men, Rabbi. (23:6-7)

Fifth, false religious leaders are characterized by lack of humility. As with their modern counterparts, the scribes and Pharisees loved **the place of honor at banquets.** They vied with each other for a place at the host's table in order to be in the center of attention. They gloried in being given places of prestige and eminence. It was that ego-centered spirit that led James and John to ask their mother to request of Jesus that they be appointed to sit at His right and left hands in the kingdom (Matt. 20:20-21).

Out of the same motivation the scribes and Pharisees prized **the chief seats**

in the synagogues. As in most churches today, synagogues typically had a raised platform in front where the worship leaders would sit. Visiting rabbis and other religious dignitaries were often asked to participate by reading Scripture and giving a homily. It was on the basis of that custom that Jesus was asked to read and expound the text from Isaiah 61:1-2 in His home synagogue in Nazareth (Luke 4:16-21). Far from having Jesus' humble spirit, however, the religious leaders often used such opportunities to ostentatiously display themselves before the congregation.

Christian pastors are tempted at times to use their positions and the Christian activities in which they are involved for their own gratification and glory. Unfortunately, many congregations encourage ostentation and show by providing elaborate and ornate pulpits and other platform furnishings and by treating their pastors with unjustified distinction.

In addition to having seats of honor, the scribes and Pharisees also loved to have **respectful greetings in the market places, and being called by men, Rabbi.** As they traveled through town they doted on being treated with special honor. Rabbinical writings report that a certain pagan governor in Caesarea flatteringly spoke of the rabbis' faces as faces of angels.

They especially loved the formal and respectful title **Rabbi,** which was used in that day much as "doctor" is today. In fact, the Latin equivalent of rabbi comes from *docēre,* which means to teach and is the term from which the English word *doctor* is derived. In Jesus' day, the title **Rabbi** carried the exalted ideas of "supreme one, excellency, most knowledgeable one, great one," and such. One rabbi insisted that he be buried in white garments when he died, because he wanted the world to know how worthy he was to appear before the presence of God.

Rabbinical writings included detailed systems of protocol for such things as addressing, consulting with, and entertaining rabbis and scribes. They were held in such high regard that, according to one passage in the Talmud (*Sanhedrin,* 88*b*), it was considered more punishable to act against the words of the scribes than against the words of the Scripture.

THE DECLARATION TO TRUE SPIRITUAL LEADERS

But do not be called Rabbi; for One is your Teacher, and you are all brothers. And do not call anyone on earth your father; for One is your Father, He who is in heaven. And do not be called leaders; for One is your Leader, that is, Christ. But the greatest among you shall be your servant. And whoever exalts himself shall be humbled; and whoever humbles himself shall be exalted. (23:8-12)

Contrary to the proud and ostentatious practices of the scribes and Pharisees, Jesus declared, true spiritual leaders are to avoid elevated titles and be willing to accept lowly service.

But do not be called Rabbi; for One is your Teacher, and you are all brothers. And do not call anyone on earth your father; for One is your Father, He who is in heaven. And do not be called leaders; for One is your Leader, that is, Christ. (23:8-10)

Godly spiritual leaders are to shun pretentious titles such as **Rabbi,** which carried the basic idea of teacher but had come to signify much more than that. Jesus Himself is the believer's only true **Teacher** in the elevated sense in which rabbis and scribes were commonly addressed and treated in Jesus' day. He is the supreme and only source of divine truth, for which human teachers are but channels of communication.

Human teachers who faithfully proclaim and interpret God's Word are to be appreciated, loved, and highly esteemed by those they serve (1 Thess. 5:12-13). But they are not to seek honor, much less demand it or glory in it. They need to remember that they are neither the source of truth, which is God's Word, nor the illumination of truth, which is God's Spirit. Human teachers, including the apostles whom Jesus addressed on this occasion, **are all brothers** with every other believer. No man's calling, however unique, justifies his being given a title intended to portray him as being spiritually superior.

Consequently, the Lord went on to command, **"Do not call anyone on earth your father."** Jesus was of course using the sense of spiritual **father,** indicating a superior spiritual position and even suggesting one's being a source of spiritual life. Members of the Sanhedrin, the high Jewish council, loved to be called by the title **father,** especially when acting in official capacities.

In direct contradiction of Jesus' prohibition, the Roman Catholic Church and even some formal Protestant churches use the term father as an official form of address for their clergy. Even the titles *abbot* and *pope* are forms of father.

"For One is your Father, He who is in heaven," Jesus said. The title of **Father** in a spiritual sense is to be reserved for God, who alone is the source of all spiritual life and blessing. To call any human being by that name is a clear violation of Scripture.

And do not be called leaders; for One is your Leader, that is, Christ. As with the other titles, this one is forbidden when used in the formal, exalted sense that was common in ancient Judaism and is still common today in many religious circles. When wrongly used, such titles can place barriers between those in leadership positions and others in the church but, even worse, they arrogate for God's human instruments the honor and glory that belong only to Him.

TRUE LEADERS ACCEPT LOWLY SERVICE

But the greatest among you shall be your servant. And whoever exalts

himself shall be humbled; and whoever humbles himself shall be exalted.
(23:11-12)

Godly leaders not only avoid elevated titles but also willingly accept lowly service in their Lord's name, following their Lord's example.

As Jesus Himself beautifully exemplified, **the greatest** person is the one who is a willing **servant.** Jesus' human greatness not only was manifested in His perfect sinlessness and love but in His being the perfect **servant.** In His humanity He was the Servant of servants just as in His divinity He is the Lord of lords and the King of kings. His mission on earth was not to be served but to serve, He said, "and to give His life a ransom for many" (Matt. 20:28).

During His last time alone with the disciples in the Upper Room, Jesus reiterated the lesson of servanthood He had taught and demonstrated so often. In the midst of the supper He arose,

> and laid aside His garments; and taking a towel, He girded Himself about. Then He poured water into the basin, and began to wash the disciples' feet, and to wipe them with the towel with which He was girded. . . . And so when He had washed their feet, and taken His garments, and reclined at the table again, He said to them, "Do you know what I have done to you? You call Me Teacher and Lord; and you are right, for so I am. If I then, the Lord and the Teacher, washed your feet, you also ought to wash one another's feet. For I gave you an example that you also should do as I did to you. Truly, truly, I say to you, a slave is not greater than his master; neither is one who is sent greater than the one who sent him. If you know these things, you are blessed if you do them." (John 13:4-5, 12-17)

The greatest person in God's sight is not the one with the most degrees or titles or awards but the one who serves in genuine humility as a selfless **servant.**

Jesus sums up the teaching about true and false teachers by declaring, **"And whoever exalts himself shall be humbled; and whoever humbles himself shall be exalted."** That is the opposite of the world's standard for exaltation. The world teaches that it is the one who **exalts himself** who gets ahead and the one who **humbles himself** who loses out and gets pushed aside. Looking out for number one is the accepted principle for success.

But in His sovereign wisdom God has decreed otherwise, and self-exaltation has no place in those who represent Christ. The paradox Jesus teaches here represents God's absolute truth, and a life that does not conform to that truth is doomed to failure and insignificance, no matter what human accomplishments, titles, and recognition may be achieved. The proud, ostentatious, arrogant, self-serving person ultimately **shall be humbled.** And just as assuredly, the humble, unpretentious, self-giving, serving person ultimately **shall be exalted.**

Peter exhorted elders in the church: "Shepherd the flock of God among you, exercising oversight not under compulsion, but voluntarily, according to the will of God; and not for sordid gain, but with eagerness; nor yet as lording it over those allotted to your charge, but proving to be examples to the flock" (1 Pet. 5:2-3). To all leaders in the church, both young and old, he then gave the admonition: "Clothe yourselves with humility toward one another, for God is opposed to the proud, but gives grace to the humble. Humble yourselves, therefore, under the mighty hand of God, that He may exalt you at the proper time" (vv. 5-6).

The nineteenth-century Scottish preacher and author Andrew Bonar said he knew a Christian was growing when he talked more of Christ than of himself. The maturing Christian, Bonar said, sees himself growing smaller and smaller until, like the morning star, he gives way to the rising sun. Thomas Shepherd, founder and first president of Harvard University, wrote in his diary for November 10, 1642, "Today I kept a private fast to see the full glory of the gospel and to seek the conquest of the remaining pride in my heart."

Unlike the proud and arrogant scribes and Pharisees, the true spiritual leader works in God's authority, and he lives in integrity, sympathy, spirituality, humility, and lowly service. He is filled with grace, mercy, love, and willing self-giving. Like his Master, the Lord Jesus Christ, he manifests the heart of a servant who humbles himself and exalts God.

The Condemnation of False Spiritual Leaders—part 1
Expressing the Condemnation
(23:13-33)

But woe to you, scribes and Pharisees, hypocrites, because you shut off the kingdom of heaven from men; for you do not enter in yourselves, nor do you allow those who are entering to go in. [Woe to you, scribes and Pharisees, hypocrites, because you devour widows' houses, even while for a pretense you make long prayers; therefore you shall receive greater condemnation.]

Woe to you, scribes and Pharisees, hypocrites, because you travel about on sea and land to make one proselyte; and when he becomes one, you make him twice as much a son of hell as yourselves.

Woe to you, blind guides, who say, 'Whoever swears by the temple, that is nothing; but whoever swears by the gold of the temple, he is obligated.' You fools and blind men; which is more important, the gold, or the temple that sanctified the gold? And, 'Whoever swears by the altar, that is nothing, but whoever swears by the offering upon it, he is obligated.' You blind men, which is more important, the offering or the altar that sanctifies the offering? Therefore he who swears, swears both by the altar and by everything on it. And he who swears by the temple, swears both by the temple and by Him who dwells within it. And he who swears by heaven, swears both by the throne of God and by Him who sits upon it.

Woe to you, scribes and Pharisees, hypocrites! For you tithe mint and dill and cummin, and have neglected the weightier provisions of the law: justice and mercy and faithfulness; but these are the things you should have done without neglecting the others. You blind guides, who strain out a gnat and swallow a camel!

Woe to you, scribes and Pharisees, hypocrites! For you clean the outside of the cup and of the dish, but inside they are full of robbery and self-indulgence. You blind Pharisee, first clean the inside of the cup and of the dish, so that the outside of it may become clean also.

Woe to you, scribes and Pharisees, hypocrites! For you are like whitewashed tombs which on the outside appear beautiful, but inside they are full of dead men's bones and all uncleanness. Even so you too outwardly appear righteous to men, but inwardly you are full of hypocrisy and lawlessness.

Woe to you, scribes and Pharisees, hypocrites! For you build the tombs of the prophets and adorn the monuments of the righteous, and say, 'If we had been living in the days of our fathers, we would not have been partners with them in shedding the blood of the prophets.' Consequently you bear witness against yourselves, that you are sons of those who murdered the prophets. Fill up then the measure of the guilt of your fathers. You serpents, you brood of vipers, how shall you escape the sentence of hell? (23:13-33)

Throughout its pages, Scripture highly honors genuine spiritual leaders who rightly and faithfully represent God and seek no self-glory. God lifts up His true servants and presents them as examples for others to follow and respect. The Christians of Galatia must have greatly pleased God's heart when they received the apostle Paul "as an angel of God, as Christ Jesus Himself" (Gal. 4:14). Paul called upon the Philippian church to receive Epaphroditus "in the Lord with all joy, and hold men like him in high regard; because he came close to death for the work of Christ" (Phil. 2:29-30). He implored the Thessalonians: "Appreciate those who diligently labor among you, and have charge over you in the Lord and give you instruction, and . . . esteem them very highly in love because of their work" (1 Thess. 5:12-13). He advised Timothy, "Let the elders who rule well be considered worthy of double honor, especially those who work hard at preaching and teaching" (1 Tim. 5:17). The writer of Hebrews exhorts believers: "Obey your leaders, and submit to them; for they keep watch over your souls, as those who will give an account. Let them do this with joy and not with grief, for this would be unprofitable for you" (Heb. 13:17).

On the other hand, no one in Scripture is more condemned than the religious charlatan who teaches and practices falsehood. God's most furious wrath is reserved for those men who parade themselves as His servants but who are servants only of evil and falsehood, liars and deceivers whose own spiritual father is Satan himself (John 8:44).

The seventeenth-century Puritan preacher Richard Baxter wrote, "Many a tailor can go in rags while making costly clothes for others. Many a cook may scarcely lick his fingers when he has prepared the most sumptuous dishes for others to eat" (*The Reformed Pastor* [Portland. Ore.: Multnomah, 1982], p. 28). His point was that many religious leaders supposedly offer spiritual provision for those in their care but are themselves spiritually shabby and starving. Such were most of the Jewish religious leaders in New Testament times.

Many Christians today are greatly concerned about the rising influences of communism, humanism, secularism, and social injustice. Yet those evils, great as they are, do not together pose the threat to Christianity that false shepherds and pastors do. Throughout the history of redemption, the greatest threat to God's truth and God's work has been false prophets and teachers, because they propose to speak in His name. That is why the Lord's most scathing denunciations were reserved for the false teachers of Israel, who claimed to speak and act for God but were liars.

Yet for some reason, evangelical Christianity is often hesitant to confront false teachers with the seriousness and severity that Jesus and the apostles did, and that the godly prophets before them had done. Today, more than at any time in modern history and perhaps more than at any time in the history of the church, pagan religions and cults are seriously encroaching on societies that for centuries have been nominally Christian. Even within the church, many ideas, teachings, and philosophies that are little more than thinly veiled paganism have become popular and influential. As in ancient Israel, the further God's people move away from the foundation of His Word, the more false religion flourishes in the world and even in their own midst. At no time have Christians had greater need to be discerning. They need to recognize and respect true godly shepherds who feed them God's Word and build them up in the faith, and they also must recognize and denounce those who twist and undermine God's Word, who corrupt the church and who lead lost people still further away from God's truth and from salvation.

The godly prophets of the Old Testament were constantly opposed and often persecuted by ungodly prophets, who invariably drew many of the people after them. Isaiah declared, "the people will be like the priest" (Isa. 24:2). Jeremiah wrote, "The prophets prophecy falsely, and the priests rule on their own authority; and My people love it so!" (Jer. 5:31) and "Many shepherds have ruined My vineyard, they have trampled down My field; they have made My pleasant field a desolate wilderness" (12:10).

In Matthew 23:13-33 Jesus relentlessly condemned the false spiritual leaders of Israel, in particular the scribes and Pharisees, who then held the dominant power and influence in Judaism. Jesus warned about them in His first sermon, the Sermon on the Mount (see, e.g., 5:20; 7:15), and His last sermon (Matt. 23) consists almost entirely of warnings about them and to them. In this final public message, the Lord wanted to draw the people away from those false leaders and turn them to the true teaching and the godly examples of His apostles, who would become His uniquely commissioned and endowed representatives on earth during the early years of the church. He also gave the apostles themselves a final example of the confrontational stance they would soon find it necessary to take in their proclamation and defense of the gospel.

The unbelieving scribes and Pharisees whom Jesus addressed in the Temple stood alone in their sin and were condemned alone in their guilt for misappropriating and perverting God's law and for leading Israel into heresy, just as the false prophets among their forefathers had done (vv. 30-32). But they also stood as models of all false spiritual leaders who would come after them. Therefore what Jesus said about them and to them is of much more than historical significance. It is essential instruction for dealing with the false leaders who abound in our own day.

In the first twelve verses of chapter 23, Jesus had declared that the scribes and Pharisees, typical of all false spiritual leaders, were without authority, without integrity, without sympathy, without spirituality, without humility, and therefore without God's approval or blessing. Now speaking to them directly, He asserts they are under God's harshest condemnation.

In verses 13-33 Jesus pronounces seven curses, or woes, on those wicked leaders. If verse 14 were included there would be eight woes, but that verse is not found in the best early manuscripts of Matthew (as indicated by its being set off by brackets in the NASB text). It was probably added later by a well-meaning copyist who picked it up from Mark 12:40 or Luke 20:47. Although the statement is genuine, it will not be discussed here, because originally it was not likely a part of this passage.

The scene in the Temple that day had become volatile in the extreme, in some ways more volatile than when Jesus had cast out the merchants and money-changers the day before. At that time Jesus' anger was vented against what the religious leaders were doing outwardly, and that attack had outraged them (21:16, 23). Now, however, He attacked what they were inwardly, and that infuriated them even more.

In our day of tolerance and eclecticism, the kind of confrontation Jesus had with the scribes and Pharisees seems foreign and uncharitable. A person who speaks too harshly against a false religion or unbiblical teaching or movement is considered unkind, ungracious, and judgmental. Jesus' indictments in Matthew 23, as well as in other parts of the gospels, are so inconsistent with the idea of Christian love held by some liberal theologians and Bible scholars, for example, that they conclude He could not have spoken them. What Jesus really said, they maintain, was modified and intensified either by the gospel writers or the sources from whom they received their information.

But the nature of Jesus' condemnation of those corrupt religious leaders is perfectly consistent with the rest of Scripture, both the Old Testament and the New. Not only that, but Jesus' words in this passage fly from His lips, as someone has said, like claps of thunder and spears of lightning. Out of His mouth on this occasion came the most fearful and dreadful statements that Jesus uttered on earth. They do not give the least impression of being the afterthought of an overzealous writer or copyist.

Matthew 23 is one of the most serious passages in Scripture. Jesus here makes the word *hypocrite* a synonym for scribe and for Pharisee. He calls them sons of hell, blind guides, fools, robbers, self-indulgent, whitewashed tombs, full of hypocrisy and lawlessness, serpents, vipers, and persecutors and murderers of God's people. He uttered every syllable with absolute self-control but with devastating intensity.

Yet Jesus was never cold or indifferent, even toward His enemies, and on this occasion His judgment is mingled with sorrow and deep pathos. It is not the Son's will any more than the Father's that a single person perish, because it is the gracious divine desire that everyone would come to repentance and salvation (2 Pet. 3:9). At the end of His denunciation, Jesus extended by implication another last invitation for belief, suggesting that He would still gladly gather any unbelievers under His wings as a mother hen gathers her chicks, if only they would be willing (Matt. 23:37).

As Jesus had approached Jerusalem during His triumphal entry, "He saw the city and wept over it, saying, 'If you had known in this day, even you the things which make for peace! But now they have been hidden from your eyes'" (Luke 19:41-42). He knew of the coming judgment on Israel and its leaders, and He was deeply grieved. There was therefore much pain involved in the curses He would soon pronounce. On the one hand is the fiery righteousness of God that yearns for rectification, and on the other is His sympathetic love, as His heart aches over the doom of His people.

In His castigation of the false Jewish leaders, Jesus repeatedly used two words, **woe** and **hypocrites**, that are keys to understanding Matthew 23:13-33. **Woe** is from *ouai*, which is not so much a word in the ordinary sense as an onomatopoeic interjection, suggesting a guttural outcry of anger, pain, or both. It is used in the Septuagint (Greek Old Testament) to express grief, despair, sorrow, dissatisfaction, pain, and fear of losing one's life. In the New Testament it is used to speak of sorrow and of judgment, carrying the mingled ideas of punishment and pity, cursing and compassion.

But Jesus used **woe** against the scribes and Pharisees not as an exclamation but as a declaration, a divine pronouncement of judgment from God. He did not use the term in the sense of the profane phrase "Damn you!" He was not wishing for the damnation of those false leaders but certifying it. As already noted, it was not His desire that they be condemned but rather that they repent and come to salvation. But He knew that if they did not repent and believe they were doomed to hell under God's righteous and just wrath. When God utters **woe** against evil men He sets divine judgment in motion.

Hypocrites is from *hupokritēs*, whose original meaning was that of answering or replying. It later came to refer to actors, who answered one another back and forth in dialogue, and from there it came to mean deceitful pretense, the putting on of a false front. It was used to describe what might be called theatrical goodness— pretended goodness that is simply for show.

In His series of seven curses, or woes, against the scribes and Pharisees, Jesus condemned by extension all false spiritual teachers. He condemns them for their exclusion of people from God's kingdom, for their subversion of the people, for their perversion of truth, for their inversion of God's priorities, for their extortion and self-indulgence, for their contamination, and for their pretension.

FALSE LEADERS ARE CURSED FOR THEIR EXCLUSION

But woe to you, scribes and Pharisees, hypocrites, because you shut off the kingdom of heaven from men; for you do not enter in yourselves, nor do you allow those who are entering to go in. (23:13)

First Jesus cursed the **scribes and Pharisees** for their exclusion of **men** from **the kingdom of heaven.** The chief evil of every false religion is that it shuts people out of God's kingdom.

Regardless of the appealing, benign, and promising front that a false system of religion or philosophy may have, its ultimate accomplishment is to **shut off the kingdom of heaven from men.** It may feed their bodies, stimulate their minds, and calm their emotions, but it will inevitably damn their souls. It may raise their moral standards, increase their worldly success, overcome practical problems, and improve their outward relationships with other people, but it will not remove their sin or improve their relationship to God. It may promise heaven, but it can only deliver hell.

"You do not enter the kingdom **yourselves,"** Jesus said, **"nor do you allow those who are entering to go in."** In their hypocrisy, the unbelieving scribes and Pharisees pretended to know God but did not, pretended to be His spokesmen but were not, pretended to be in His kingdom but were not. In their boundless pride they even believed they themselves were the doorkeepers of the kingdom.

In his letter to the Roman church, Paul said:

> If you bear the name "Jew," and rely upon the Law, and boast in God, and know His will, and approve the things that are essential, being instructed out of the Law, and are confident that you yourself are a guide to the blind, a light to those who are in darkness, a corrector of the foolish, a teacher of the immature, having in the Law the embodiment of knowledge and of the truth, you, therefore, who teach another, do you not teach yourself? . . . You who boast in the Law, through your breaking the Law, do you dishonor God? For the name of God is blasphemed among the Gentiles because of you. (Rom. 2:17-21, 23-24)

The scribes and Pharisees, and all other Jews who followed their hypocritical traditions, lived under the delusion that, because they were His called People and the receivers and human custodians of God's law (Rom. 3:2; 9:4-5), they were somehow automatically destined to live under God's approval. In their spiritual darkness they confused merely knowing the law with keeping it, and merely knowing about the light with living in it.

But Jesus declared that they had no part in God's **kingdom,** which is the sphere of His reign and power and, in this context, especially refers to the sphere of salvation in which His redeemed people live.

The picture Jesus gives here suggests the idea of the scribes and Pharisees standing just outside the gates of the **kingdom** and slamming them shut in the faces of those who were about **to go in.** People who came to those religious leaders for direction and help in finding God were actually being **shut off** from Him even while they were on the verge of salvation.

In the immediate historical context, Jesus was saying that He had come to Israel to proclaim the kingdom of God and to provide entrance for all who would believe in Him. But as soon as a Jew showed interest in the gospel, the scribes and Pharisees would step between that person and Christ, as it were. Tragically, they succeeded in turning many seekers away. They had done the same thing to those who were drawn to God through the preaching of John the Baptist, and they would soon do the same thing to those who were drawn to God through the preaching of the apostles.

As soon as men and women from Jerusalem and from "all Judea, and all the district around the Jordan" went out to hear John the Baptist and "were being baptized by him in the Jordan River, as they confessed their sins," the unbelieving and unrepentant Pharisees and Sadducees showed up, attempting to corrupt John's work and confuse the people by pretentiously submitting to baptism but without genuine confession of their sins. Discerning their hypocrisy, John called them a "brood of vipers" who were under the judgment of God's fiery wrath (Matt. 3:5-8; cf. vv. 10, 12), using virtually the same words Jesus was now about to use against them in the Temple (23:33).

It is painful to consider—and was immeasurably more painful for Jesus to consider—the countless thousands who had been **shut off** from His **kingdom** by Israel's false religious leaders. In his parallel passage Luke reports Jesus as saying, "Woe to you lawyers! For you have taken away the key of knowledge; you did not enter in yourselves, and those who were entering in you hindered" (Luke 11:52).

The false leaders took away the key of knowledge by misinterpreting the Word of God, by denying the Messiah, by denying the need for repentance, and by denying salvation by grace. Their work-righteous system had no place for the gospel of grace, which is the only way into the kingdom. By drawing people away from Jesus Christ, those leaders thwarted their salvation and confirmed their damnation.

That is why the greatest battle in the world is not against communism or humanism or secularism or social injustice. The greatest battle by far is the battle for men's souls, a battle which could be lost even if somehow all those other battles were won. The great challenge of the church in our day is to clearly and boldly articulate God's truth and just as clearly and boldly to expose Satan's falsehoods.

The great need of the world today is to turn from its falsehoods and to hear and heed God's truth and be saved.

When men's eternal souls are at stake, the church cannot be passive and indifferent. Nor can it hide behind false humility that fears being judgmental or behind false love that fears offending. Christ was supremely humble, yet He never called evil anything but what it was. Christ was supremely loving, yet He never withheld a warning that might save His hearers from hell. And He had nothing but intense anger for those who by their false teachings led men away from God and directly toward hell.

Nowhere is the Pharisees's hardness of heart more graphically portrayed than in the account of the blind man Jesus healed on the Sabbath. When the healed man was brought to the Pharisees and they heard he had been healed on the Sabbath, their sole concern was for Jesus' breaking one of their Sabbath traditions (John 9:16). The fact that this man who had lived all his life in blindness and despair had now been given sight was of no consequence to them. Nor was the fact that Jesus had obviously performed the healing by divine power of any consequence to them. They were utterly devoid of compassion and blind to the truth. They were indifferent to the confirmation by the man's parents that their son was indeed born blind (v. 20) and impervious to the man's own astute arguments about the divine source of his healing (vv. 30-33). The factualness of his healing was not a consideration to them. They had made up their minds that Jesus was not the Christ (see v. 22), and no evidence to the contrary carried any weight with them. In this one incident the Pharisees conclusively demonstrated their rejection of Jesus as the Messiah, their rejection of His divine nature and power, and their contempt for His divine grace and for the souls of men.

When the church began to move with great force after Pentecost, proclaiming Christ's power to save men's souls and demonstrating His power to heal men's bodies, the Jewish religious leaders again demonstrated their hardness of heart. "What shall we do with these men?" they said of Peter and John after the healing of the lame man outside the Temple. "For the fact that a noteworthy miracle has taken place through them is apparent to all who live in Jerusalem, and we cannot deny it. But in order that it may not spread any further among the people, let us warn them to speak no more to any man in this name" (Acts 4:16-17). In their minds, neither the power the apostles manifested nor the truth they proclaimed was of any relevance. They themselves had rejected the kingdom and, just as during Jesus' ministry, they were determined to prevent others from **entering.**

Paul reminded the Thessalonian believers that they suffered persecution at the hands of their own unbelieving countrymen just as the believing Jews in Judea had suffered at the hands of theirs. Those Jewish leaders "both killed the Lord Jesus and the prophets, and drove us out. They are not pleasing to God, but hostile to all men, hindering us from speaking to the Gentiles that they might be saved; with the result that they always fill up the measure of their sins" (1 Thess. 2:14-16).

Some years ago, a young man called and informed me that he was planning to leave our church and join Mormonism, two workers from which were going to visit him again shortly. I immediately drove to his house and confronted him with the extreme peril of what he was about to do. I told him that if he was not now a true Christian, they would damn his soul by leading him away from Christ and that if he were a Christian they would make a shambles of his spiritual life. When the workers arrived I refused to discuss doctrine with them but rather in the spirit of Matthew 23 presented the true gospel of Christ and denounced the unbiblical and damning errors that their sect taught. However, the young man fell into the cult and was not able to escape for a number of years.

Every non-Christian religion is a works-righteous religion, and works righteousness is inherently at mortal enmity with the gospel of God's grace. By their very nature such belief systems exclude people from God's kingdom.

False Leaders Are Cursed for Their Subversion

Woe to you, scribes and Pharisees, hypocrites, because you travel about on sea and land to make one proselyte; and when he becomes one, you make him twice as much a son of hell as yourselves. (23:15)

Second, Jesus cursed the **scribes and Pharisees** for their subversion of the people. They not only excluded them from the true faith but subverted them with false faith.

In New Testament times a great effort was being made to convert Gentiles to Judaism. They worked aggressively, traveling **about on sea and land to make one proselyte.** The word **proselyte** had the basic meaning of a person who has arrived, and came to be commonly used of an outsider who was brought into a religion.

Had that Jewish effort been made in the right way and for the right reasons, it would have been commendable, because Israel had been called to be God's channel for reaching the world for Himself. In His covenant with Abraham the Lord promised that through him and his descendants "all the families of the earth shall be blessed" (Gen. 12:3). In the covenant at Sinai the Lord set Israel apart as a "kingdom of priests and a holy nation" (Ex. 19:6), who, like her Messiah, was meant to be a light to the nations (Isa. 49:6).

But for most of her history, Israel aspired to do anything but bring Gentiles to God. Like Jonah, they loathed the idea of pagans repenting, being saved, and thereby gaining the same standing before God that they enjoyed. By his own admission, it was for the purpose of forestalling, and no doubt if possible preventing, the repentance and forgiveness of Nineveh that Jonah tried to flee to Tarshish (Jonah 4:2).

By the time Jesus began preaching, however, a different spirit had arisen among some of the Jews, and they were zealously trying to win converts. As the result of those efforts, many synagogues had regular Gentile worshipers who had turned from paganism. Partly because Jews had such an unsavory reputation for exclusiveness and bigotry, Gentile proselytes were not easy to make, and when one of them converted he was considered something of a prize.

There were two kinds of proselytes in the synagogues. One was called "a proselyte of the gate," a Gentile who only attended the services. He now worshiped the true God, but he had not committed himself to full ritualistic and legalistic Judaism. Such proselytes are referred to in the book of Acts as a person who was devout (10:2, 7; 13:50), as "God-fearing" (10:2, 22, 35; 17:4, 17), or as "a worshiper of God" (16:14; 18:7).

The other kind was referred to as "a proselyte of righteousness," so called because he became as religiously Jewish as a Gentile could become. They participated in all the ceremonies, rituals, and feasts; they observed all the cleansing and other rites, both biblical and traditional; and if males, they were circumcised. Those converts were even given Jewish names in order to separate them as much as possible from their pagan past. Contrary to their popular appellation, however, they became anything but righteous. Like the scribes and Pharisees who instructed them, they became paragons of self-righteousness.

For obvious reasons there were many more proselytes of the gate than proselytes of righteousness. It was the latter kind in which the scribes and Pharisees delighted, and it was considered a great achievement to initiate a Gentile into all their legalistic practices.

As is often the case with new converts, including true converts to Christ, many of the proselytes of righteousness became extremely zealous for their new faith, some of them even more zealous than those who converted them. But because they were brought into a false religious system that had replaced biblical Judaism, such a **proselyte** became **twice as much a son of hell as** the scribes and Pharisees themselves. They sometimes surpassed their mentors in fanatical zeal, but because their zeal was not godly it simply led them more certainly to **hell.**

Of hell translates a Greek genitive that refers to belonging to or being characterized by. **Son of hell** referred to a person who was especially characterized by hellishness. **Twice . . . a son hell** would be person who was doubly hellish and doubly damned.

Hell is from *geenna,* derived from the name of a valley just outside Jerusalem called Hinnom where refuse was burned. It was considered an accursed place because it was the site where ancient worshipers of the pagan deity Moloch offered their children as live burnt sacrifices, a hideous practice taken up even by some Israelites (see 2 Chron. 28:3; Jer. 7:31). When King Josiah declared the place unclean (2 Kings 23:10), it became a garbage dump, and because flames and smoke arose from the valley continually, it also became a vivid picture of the eternal fires of hell.

How grateful every believer should be that at some time in His life he was confronted by a spiritual door-opener rather than a spiritual door-closer, someone who shows the way to the kingdom rather than shuts people out of it. And how grateful every believer should be who has the opportunity to hear and study the Word of God in truth. Even a dull presentation of the true gospel is immeasurably superior to the most exciting presentation of a false gospel that damns to hell.

As a citizen of God's kingdom, every believer ought to be one who opens the door of the kingdom to others. All saints have the keys of the kingdom, which is the saving gospel of Jesus Christ (Matt. 16:19), and every false teacher takes away the key of knowledge that leads to the kingdom (Luke 11:52). When Christians are confronted by a representative of a false cult, sect, or religion, they should offer to explain the way of salvation in Christ to him, hoping to snatch him out of the fire, as it were (Jude 23). But they should not debate theology or the merits of various sacred writings or interpretations of the Bible, thereby "casting pearls before swine," but firmly denounce the teachings of that group as ungodly and damning—just as their Lord did with the scribes and Pharisees.

FALSE LEADERS ARE CURSED FOR THEIR PERVERSION

Woe to you, blind guides, who say, 'Whoever swears by the temple, that is nothing; but whoever swears by the gold of the temple, he is obligated.' You fools and blind men; which is more important, the gold, or the temple that sanctified the gold? And, 'Whoever swears by the altar, that is nothing, but whoever swears by the offering upon it, he is obligated.' You blind men, which is more important, the offering or the altar that sanctifies the offering? Therefore he who swears, swears both by the altar and by everything on it. And he who swears by the temple, swears both by the temple and by Him who dwells within it. And he who swears by heaven, swears both by the throne of God and by Him who sits upon it. (23:16-22)

Third, Jesus cursed the scribes and Pharisees for their perversion of truth. God is the God of truth and cannot lie (Titus 1:2; Heb. 6:18), and His people are therefore to be people of truth. On the other hand, there is no truth at all in Satan. "Whenever he speaks a lie, he speaks from his own nature," Jesus says; "for he is a liar, and the father of lies" (John 8:44). His followers are also skilled in lying, and perversion of truth is the hallmark of every false religious system. From the beginning, those who have rejected God have rejected His truth. They have "exchanged the truth of God for a lie, and worshiped and served the creature rather than the Creator" (Rom. 1:25).

In this particular indictment, Jesus did not call His opponents hypocrites but **blind guides,** emphasizing their unawareness that they were ignorant of the truth. As God's chosen people who were entrusted with His revelation, the Jews had long considered themselves as guides to the blind, lights to those in darkness, correctors of the foolish, and teachers of the immature (Rom. 2:19-20; cf. 3:2). But as Jesus had declared earlier in His ministry, they were "blind guides of the blind. And if a blind man guides a blind man, both will fall into a pit" (Matt. 15:14). The scribes and Pharisees prided themselves in their superior religious knowledge and under-standing, but they were blind leaders trying to lead blind Israel, and together they were doomed to judgment if they would not come to the light.

Among their many perversions of truth was the teaching that **Whoever swears by the temple, that is nothing; but whoever swears by the gold of the temple, he is obligated.** The very fact that they had developed such a double standard for swearing gives evidence that their concern was not for truth but for the evasion of it when it did not suit their selfish interests. The underlying purpose behind the first part of the standard was to provide sanctimonious justification for lying with impunity. A person could lie all he wanted, provided he swore **by the temple** and not **by the gold of the temple.** Since no society can survive without some provision for verifying and guaranteeing such things as promises and contracts, the second part of the standard was developed as a necessary expediency. If a person wanted to make absolutely certain that someone was telling the truth or would live up to an agreement, he would make him swear **by the gold of the temple,** which supposedly made his word binding. A person who broke his word after taking such an oath was subject to penalties under Jewish law.

Societies have had various means of trying to make its people keep their word. In some, the most sacred and binding vow was sealed with the blood of the parties involved. In others, an agreement is written in a contract, which each party signs and which often specifies penalties for defaulting. Until recent years, many western courts of law required those giving testimony to swear to tell the truth by placing their right hand on a copy of the Bible and invoking God's help.

The use of oaths had become so perverse in Israel that they were used even to renege on promises made to God. If a person, for example, vowed to give a certain amount to the Lord's work, he would often swear to his vow **by the temple.** If he later decided he had pledged too much, or if he never intended to give the full amount, he had an out, because that vow was considered to be **nothing.**

In the Sermon on the Mount, Jesus condemned all swearing of vows. "But I say to you, make no oath at all, either by heaven, for it is the throne of God, or by the earth, for it is the footstool of His feet, or by Jerusalem, for it is the city of the great King. Nor shall you make an oath by your head, for you cannot make one hair white or black. But let your statement be, 'Yes, yes,' or 'No, no'; and anything beyond these is of evil" (Matt. 5:34-37). A godly person will always tell the truth, and for him a simple yes or no is sufficient, because his virtuous character is his bond.

Jesus was not teaching a new principle. The psalmist declared, "Offer to God a sacrifice of thanksgiving, and pay your vows to the Most High" (Ps. 50:14). In other words, a vow made is a vow to be kept. David testified, "Thy vows are binding upon me, O God; I will render thank offerings to Thee" (Ps. 56:12), and again, "I will sing praise to Thy name forever, that I may pay my vows day by day" (Ps. 61:8; cf. 66:13; 76:11). It is significant that in each of those quotations the keeping of vows to God is directly related to praise and thankfulness to Him.

The great offense of Ananias and Sapphira was not in giving less to the Lord's work than they were able to give but in lying about it. When Peter confronted them, he charged them with lying to the Holy Spirit and putting God to the test. The Lord takes lying very seriously, and for their deception those two believers lost their lives.

It is not surprising that, as a result, "great fear came upon the whole church, and upon all who heard of these things" (Acts 5:1-11).

The idea that swearing by the gold in the Temple was binding but swearing by the Temple itself was not binding was moral chicanery and logical absurdity. **"You fools and blind men,"** Jesus said; **"which is more important, the gold, or the temple that sanctified the gold?"** In other words, by what perverted logic had it been determined that making a vow on something lesser was more binding than one made on something greater? The only reason **the gold** could be thought of as sacred, and thereby make the vow supposedly more obligatory, was **the temple that sanctified the gold.**

The religious leaders applied the same twisted logic to swearing **by the altar,** which was considered to be **nothing,** that is, nonobligatory, and to swearing by **the offering upon it,** which was thought to make a person **obligated** to keep his vow. **"You blind men,"** Jesus said, **"which is more important, the offering or the altar that sanctifies the offering?"** The whole idea was both theologically and logically preposterous. Those standards were nothing more than wicked pretenses for using holy things to disguise their unholy propensity to lie.

As Jesus went on to point out, to swear **by the altar** was to swear **by everything on it;** to swear **by the temple** was to swear **by Him who dwells within it,** namely, God Himself; and to swear **by heaven** was to swear **both by the throne of God and by Him who sits upon it.** In other words, everything involved with **the temple** and everything involved with **heaven** involved God. In fact, since God is the creator of everything, to swear by anything at all involves God.

FALSE LEADERS ARE CURSED FOR THEIR INVERSION

Woe to you, scribes and Pharisees, hypocrites! For you tithe mint and dill and cummin, and have neglected the weightier provisions of the law: justice and mercy and faithfulness; but these are the things you should have done without neglecting the others. You blind guides, who strain out a gnat and swallow a camel! (23:23-24)

Fourth, Jesus cursed the **scribes and Pharisees** for inverting divine priorities. They magnified the insignificant and minimized the essential.

Mint and dill and cummin were garden herbs used as kitchen spices, and were not generally considered farm produce, of which the Mosaic law required a **tithe** be paid to the treasury in Israel (Lev. 27:30). Because it helped support the government, which was a theocracy operated to a great extent by the priesthood, the tithe was a form of taxation. A second tenth was to be paid each year for support of the various worship ceremonies and national festivals (Deut. 12:11, 17). Another tithe was to be paid every three years for a type of welfare, to support the Levites, aliens, orphans, and widows (Deut. 14:28-29), which amounted to an additional 3.3

percent a year. Israelites were therefore required to pay just over 23 percent of their income a year in taxes to fund the theocracy.

The instructions for tithing produce (see also Deut. 14:22) related to marketable farm crops such as grains, olive oil, wine, fruits, and vegetables. But the legalistic scribes and Pharisees extended the provision to include the smallest potted plant grown in a kitchen window. As today, herbs then were grown mostly for their leaves and seeds, and when the scribes and Pharisees picked leaves from a **mint** plant or gathered seeds from the **dill and cummin** plants, they would carefully count out the leaves and seeds, separating out one for God from each ten counted. They gloried in the self-righteousness of subscribing to such minutiae.

But with all their carefulness in such insignificant and often noncompulsory matters, they **neglected the weightier provisions of the law: justice and mercy and faithfulness.** They were obsessed with counting leaves and seeds but indifferent to basic ethics.

Jesus borrowed the word **weightier** from the rabbinical tradition, which had divided the law into light and heavy categories. In their inverted priorities the scribes and Pharisees had reduced such matters as **justice and mercy and faithfulness** to the light category, and elevated the tithing of garden herbs to the **weightier** category. In His reference to the truly **weightier** matters, Jesus paraphrased the words of Micah. Some 700 years earlier that prophet had declared, "[The Lord] has told you, O man, what is good; and what does the Lord require of you but to do justice, to love kindness, and to walk humbly with your God?" (Mic. 6:8).

The scribes and Pharisees were inequitable, unfair, unjust, unmerciful, brutal, unforgiving, unkind, greedy, and abusive of others. They were everything that is contrary to the **weightier provisions of the law.** Worst of all, they walked by sight rather than faith, trusting in their own works rather than God's grace.

Jesus did not denounce the tithing of herbs, which would have been perfectly acceptable if done in sincerity and faith. And because tithing was at that time still a valid requirement under the Old Covenant, He certainly did not reprove tithing in general. **"These are the things you should have done,"** He said, **"without neglecting the others."** In light of the fact that such garden plants had not generally been considered covered under the Mosaic laws of tithing until rabbinical times, it seems likely that by **these . . . things** Jesus was referring to tithing in general. In other words, while being faithful to tithe according to scriptural instruction, they should not have **neglected** the Lord's much **weightier** demands.

The tithe, however, was strictly a requirement of the Old Covenant. It is mentioned only six times in the New Testament, three times each in the gospels and in the book of Hebrews. In the gospels it is always used, as here, in regard to its abuse by the scribes and Pharisees (see also Luke 11:42; 18:12). In the book of Hebrews the Mosaic tithe is mentioned only in regard to its use in ancient Israel (Heb. 7:8-9; vv. 5-6). At no time in the New Testament is tithing mentioned as binding on the church or even recommended as the standard for Christian giving. This is easy to understand if one recognizes that tithes were a form of taxation to support the national life of Israel (see the author's *1 Corinthians* [Chicago: Moody, 1984], pp. 454-55). The closest New Testament parallel is the requirement to pay taxes indicated in Romans 13:6-7.

Almost without exception, false religions strongly magnify the insignificant and minimize or entirely ignore the truly spiritual. The worldly is idolized; the spiritual is disregarded.

It is also possible for true believers to become caught up in minutiae. Some Bible students, for instance, claim to have ascertained the meaning of virtually every obscure sign and symbol in Scripture yet give scant attention in their lives to the Bible's clear and unambiguous moral truths.

Jesus graphically illustrated the scribes' and Pharisees' inversion of priorities by saying that they would **strain out a gnat and swallow a camel.** The **gnat** and the **camel** represented the smallest and the largest, respectively, of the ceremonially unclean animals (see Lev. 11:4, 42). Fastidious Pharisees would drink their wine through clenched teeth in order to filter out any small insects that might have gotten into the wine. In their typical reversal of values, those Jewish religious leaders were more concerned about being contaminated by a tiny **gnat** than by a huge **camel.** They were painstaking about formal, ceremonial trivialities but were unconcerned about their hypocrisy, dishonesty, cruelty, greed, self-worship, and a host of other serious sins. They substituted outward acts of religion for the essential virtues of the heart.

FALSE LEADERS ARE CURSED FOR THEIR EXTORTION AND SELF-INDULGENCE

Woe to you, scribes and Pharisees, hypocrites! For you clean the outside of the cup and of the dish, but inside they are full of robbery and self-indulgence. You blind Pharisee, first clean the inside of the cup and of the dish, so that the outside of it may become clean also. (23:25-26)

Fifth, Jesus cursed the **scribes and Pharisees** for their extortion of others and indulgence of themselves.

To illustrate again their hypocrisy, Jesus used the figure of cleaning the **outside of** a **cup and . . . dish, but** not the **inside.** The Greek phrase behind **dish** was often used of a platter on which exquisite delicacies were served. The idea is of a person who offers a guest a seemingly lovely meal served with the best wine. But it turns out that, although the utensils are beautiful and ceremonially purified, the food served on them was putrid.

Outwardly, the religious leaders gave the appearance of pious devotion to the Lord, but inwardly they were **full of** the moral and spiritual filth of **robbery and self-indulgence.** They were ceremonially immaculate and attractive but spiritually squalid and repulsive.

Harpagē (**robbery**) carries the ideas of plundering, pillaging, and extortion, and *akrasia* (**self-indulgence**) has the basic meaning of lack of self-control and was often used to denote unrestrained self-gratification. The unscrupulous religious leaders robbed the people they were supposed to serve in order to satisfy their own greed. They plundered both the souls and the wallets of the people and used the ill-gotten gains to serve themselves.

Making the accusation more personal and direct, Jesus said, "**You blind Pharisee, first clean the inside of the cup and of the dish, so that the outside of it may become clean also.**" No utensil is clean that holds ill-gotten food or drink.

Throughout history, false religious leaders have become rich and fat by fleecing those they pretend to serve. Outwardly they appear righteous, caring, and exemplary, but inwardly they are rapacious wolves.

FALSE LEADERS ARE CURSED FOR THEIR CONTAMINATION

Woe to you, scribes and Pharisees, hypocrites! For you are like whitewashed tombs which on the outside appear beautiful, but inside they are full of dead men's bones and all uncleanness. Even so you too outwardly appear righteous to men, but inwardly you are full of hypocrisy and lawlessness. (23:27-28)

Sixth, Jesus cursed the **scribes and Pharisees** for spiritually contaminating everyone they touched.

After the spring rains had ceased, Palestinian Jews in New Testament times had the custom of whitewashing houses, walls, and particularly **tombs.** They began this task on the fifteenth of Adar, which roughly corresponds to March, in order to make their communities more attractive for Passover pilgrims. They had an additional purpose for whitewashing grave sites, however, especially those in and near Jerusalem. Because a person became ceremonially unclean for seven days if he touched a dead body or even a grave (Num. 19:16), all **tombs** were carefully whitewashed to identify them to unwary travelers. They would be prevented from inadvertently touching the tombs and becoming defiled and thereby disqualified to participate in many of the Passover activities, including the offering of sacrifices. In some cases the entire tomb was painted, and in others drawings of bones were painted on it to mark it as a sepulcher. Because of all the whitewash, Jerusalem and its environs glistened in the sunlight during the Passover season.

Like the **whitewashed tombs,** the scribes and Pharisees **on the outside** appeared **beautiful, but inside they** were also like the tombs, **full of dead men's bones and all uncleanness.** They were spiritually dead and had no genuine regard for God's law, despite their outward praise of it and claim to be its true interpreters and teachers. In an infinitely worse way than the tombs ceremonially defiled those who touched them, the scribes and Pharisees spiritually defiled those whom they touched.

FALSE LEADERS ARE CURSED FOR THEIR PRETENSION

Woe to you, scribes and Pharisees, hypocrites! For you build the tombs of the prophets and adorn the monuments of the righteous, and say, 'If we had been living in the days of our fathers, we would not have been partners with them in shedding the blood of the prophets.' Consequently you bear witness against yourselves, that you are sons of those who murdered the prophets. Fill up then the measure of the guilt of your fathers. You serpents, you brood of vipers, how shall you escape the sentence of hell? (23:29-33)

Seventh and last, Jesus cursed the **scribes and Pharisees** for their pretension in presuming to be superior to others, including their forefathers.

For many hundreds of years these leaders had been in the vanguard of ventures to **build the tombs of the prophets and adorn the monuments of the righteous** saints and heroes of Israel. They would have been on the speaker's platform in ceremonies honoring the great men of the past and would have voiced the loudest adulations.

Realizing that many of those saints had been persecuted and martyred by their own forefathers, the scribes and Pharisees made vehement disclaimers for themselves, asserting self-righteously: **"If we had been living in the days of our fathers, we would not have been partners with them in shedding the blood of the prophets."**

But Jesus repudiated their pretension and exposed their true character, declaring that **"consequently you bear witness against yourselves, that you are sons of those who murdered the prophets."** At that very moment they were plotting to kill Jesus, their Messiah and the Prophet of prophets, proving they were even more wicked than their ungodly ancestors. They were so consumed by hatred of the truth and righteousness of God that they were totally blinded to the fact that they were about to crucify the very Son of God.

"Fill up then the measure of the guilt of your fathers," Jesus said. "Your scheming to put to death the greatest prophet of all," He declared in effect, "will be the final **measure** of the murderous conspiracies of your **fathers** against God's messengers." They were about to culminate all the guilt of those in the past who killed God's messengers. This was the supreme act of sin against God's prophets, as they murdered the Prophet-Messiah.

In a final curse Jesus exclaimed, **"You serpents, you brood of vipers, how shall you escape the sentence of hell?"** The question was rhetorical, meaning that they could not possibly **escape the sentence of hell** if they carried out the evil intent that now poisoned their hearts.

Ophis (**serpents**) was a general word for snakes, but *echidna* (**vipers**) referred to small poisonous snakes that lived primarily in the desert regions of Palestine and other parts of the eastern Mediterranean. Because they looked like a dried twig when they were still, a person collecting wood for a fire would often pick one up inadvertently and be bitten, as happened to Paul on the island of Malta. That particular viper was deadly, and when Paul suffered no harm from the bite, the superstitious islanders thought he was a god (Acts 28:3, 6). **Vipers** therefore had the understandable reputation for being both deadly and deceitful.

At the beginning of his ministry John the Baptist had called the unbelieving and unrepentant Pharisees and Sadducees who came to him for baptism a "brood of vipers" (Matt. 3:7), using exactly the same phrase used now by Jesus at the end of His ministry to describe those same false leaders. Neither the messages of John the Baptist nor of Jesus had any positive effect on those men, but served only to harden them in their unbelief and in their opposition to the gospel and to God's righteous messengers.

In pagan Greek culture, the *echidna* had long been associated with evil. In their mythology the name was given to a monster deity that was half snake and half woman and that gave birth to other monsters, including the murderous sphinx of Thebes.

By the time of Christ, *echidna* was universally associated with extreme wickedness and danger. Therefore when Jesus called the scribes and Pharisees a **brood of vipers,** He was declaring them to be both evil and deadly.

As explained earlier in this chapter, the term *geenna* (**hell**) was derived from the name of a valley near Jerusalem where trash and garbage continually burned. Jesus' relating **vipers** to **the sentence of hell** suggests the common practice of a farmer's burning the dried stubble in his field to prepare the land for the next planting. As the flames approached their dens, **vipers** would try to scurry away but were usually unsuccessful and consumed by the fire. Jesus said, in effect, "You wicked, deceitful men, do you really think you can outrun God's fire of judgment?"

As Jesus had just reminded them, those false leaders were guilty of keeping people out of the kingdom, guilty of subverting the people, guilty of perverting God's truth, guilty of inverting God's priorities, guilty of extorting God's people, guilty of spiritually contaminating everyone they touched, guilty of pretending to be righteous while being malevolent, and worst of all guilty of preparing to execute God's own Son.

The Condemnation of False Spiritual Leaders—part 2
Proclaiming the Judgment
(23:34-36)

Therefore, behold, I am sending you prophets and wise men and scribes; some of them you will kill and crucify, and some of them you will scourge in your synagogues, and persecute from city to city, that upon you may fall the guilt of all the righteous blood shed on earth, from the blood of righteous Abel to the blood of Zechariah, the son of Berechiah, whom you murdered between the temple and the altar. Truly I say to you, all these things shall come upon this generation. (23:34-36)

For centuries the Jews had awaited the arrival of their Messiah. The abiding hope in the heart of the Jew was that the day would soon come when the Messiah's arrival and establishment of His kingdom would usher in the enduring age of promised blessing for God's people. Every Jewish woman longed to be mother of that Messiah, and every Jewish man thought of rising to that place of prominence, honor, and service.

Yet when the Messiah did come and did offer His kingdom and did promise blessing and hope and salvation, instead of receiving Him in faith and love His people rejected Him in unbelief and abhorrence. They so despised Him that they murdered Him and persecuted and often murdered His followers.

In that grievous epoch in the history of Israel, God's uniquely chosen and blessed people confirmed that they preferred falsehood above truth, darkness above light, iniquity above righteousness, their own worthless works above God's divine grace, damnation above salvation, Satan's way above God's. They were called out by God's grace and given His promises and covenants and laws. Yet when those blessings came to perfect consummation in the coming of their long-promised Messiah, the Lord and Savior, they rebelled against Him and put Him to death.

Leading that rejection were the scribes and Pharisees, the epitome of false spiritual leaders. Those self-righteous, legalistic, hypocritical haters of God hungered and thirsted not for righteousness but for the blood of the righteous. At the very moment Jesus addressed them face to face in the Temple, they were plotting His arrest and murder. In so doing, they were, as Jesus had just declared, filling "up then the measure of the guilt of [their] fathers" (Matt. 23:32).

The phrase "fill up" is often used in Scripture in relation to sin, wrath, and judgment when those have reached their full limit. It depicts a cup filled to the brim with sin, which becomes a cup of condemnation. The cup that is full of sin is full of punishment to the same level. When sin is full it brings wrath, which when full brings judgment, which when full brings eternal destruction. Isaiah exclaimed, "Arise, O Jerusalem, you who have drunk from the Lord's hand the cup of His anger; the chalice of reeling you have drained to the dregs" (Isa. 51:17). Jeremiah declared, "For thus the Lord, the God of Israel, says to me, 'Take this cup of the wine of wrath from My hand, and cause all the nations, to whom I send you, to drink it'" (Jer. 25:15). Habakkuk warned Judah that "the cup in the Lord's right hand will come around to you, and utter disgrace will come upon your glory" (Hab. 2:16). In the seventh bowl judgment in the final days, God will give Babylon, the paradigm of false religion, "the cup of the wine of His fierce wrath" (Rev. 16:19).

The scribes and Pharisees, and with them most of Israel, were about to fill up the limit of their sin. When man irrevocably rejects God, God irrevocably rejects him, giving him over to his own willful wickedness. When men "did not see fit to acknowledge God any longer," Paul says, "God gave them over to a depraved mind, to do those things which are not proper, . . . and, although they know the ordinance of God, that those who practice such things are worthy of death, they not only do the same, but also give hearty approval to those who practice them" (Rom. 1:28, 32). Because Pharaoh had irrevocably hardened his heart against God, God confirmed that hardening (Ex. 9:34-35; cf. 4:21; 7:3, 13; 10:1). When Judas had irrevocably committed himself to betraying Christ, Jesus told him, "What you do, do quickly" (John 13:27), not approving what Judas had determined to do but divinely confirming that decision.

Ever since there have been righteous men there have been persecutors and murderers of righteous men, who are a rebuke to unrighteousness. Whenever a society has the opportunity to express its hatred of righteousness, which reflects its hatred of God, it will abuse and, if possible, destroy the righteous people who belong to God.

After Jesus finished His series of seven curses against the scribes and Pharisees (vv. 13-33), He added another word of warning, declaring that their judgment was both inevitable and imminent.

JUDGMENT WAS INEVITABLE

Therefore, behold, I am sending you prophets and wise men and scribes; some of them you will kill and crucify, and some of them you will scourge in your synagogues, and persecute from city to city, that upon you may fall the guilt of all the righteous blood shed on earth, from the blood of righteous Abel to the blood of Zechariah, the son of Berechiah, whom you murdered between the temple and the altar. (23:34-35)

Because the cup of their sin and the cup of God's wrath would very shortly be filled up (vv. 32-33), **therefore** the judgment of the scribes and Pharisees was inevitable.

"As evidence and verification of that judgment," Jesus said, "**Behold, I am sending you prophets and wise men and scribes; some of them you will kill and crucify, and some of them you will scourge in your synagogues, and persecute from city to city.**" In other words, after they crucified Him, their Messiah, they would proceed to **kill and crucify** His followers, especially the godly men He would send as His emissaries—the New Testament **prophets and wise men and scribes.**

In mentioning both **kill** and **crucify,** Jesus was probably referring to Jewish and Roman means of execution, respectively. Jesus was crucified, of course, as also was Peter according to tradition. Stephen was stoned, and James was put to death by the sword (Acts 7:58-60; 12:2). Other believers in the early church were murdered by those and countless other methods.

"**Some** of My followers," Jesus predicted, "**you will scourge in your synagogues, and persecute from city to city.**" All of the apostles experienced abuses for their faith, as did most other believers. "Five times I received from the Jews thirty-nine lashes," Paul recounted. "Three times I was beaten with rods, once I was stoned" (2 Cor. 11:24-25). Before his conversion, Paul had himself been in the vanguard of those who persecuted Christians **from city to city** (Acts 8:1-4; 9:1-2), and after his conversion he was the recipient of such persecution. He was opposed in and frequently driven out of many cities, including Pisidian Antioch (Acts 13:45, 50), Iconium (14:1-2), Lystra (14:19-20), Thessalonica (17:5-10), Berea (17:13-14), Corinth (18:12-18), Jerusalem (21:27; 23:12), and Caesarea (24:1-9). Believers in the early church were continually hounded by the false spiritual leaders of Israel, who sought to stamp out the gospel of Christ.

Characteristic of Matthew's gospel, the three titles **prophets and wise men and scribes** were uniquely Jewish. Although He was speaking of the apostles and other teachers, preachers, and writers of the New Testament age, Jesus used Old Testament terms His hearers would be sure to understand. Those Spirit-endowed leaders would be used of God to minister His gospel to the world and to complete His written Word in order that men might accurately hear the full message of His grace and be saved.

But those men would also fulfill another purpose, less consciously but as divinely ordained as that positive one. Just as they would be ministers of salvation they would also be ministers of judgment. Just as they would lead many to accept Jesus as Savior and Lord, they would also lead others to confirm their rejection of Him as Savior and Lord. **"I am sending them to you,"** Jesus said to the unbelieving scribes and Pharisees, **"that upon you may fall the guilt of all the righteous blood shed on earth."** While others were having the opportunity to receive Him, they would have further opportunity to reject Him—which they would do. They would have additional chances to reject Him in order that they might pile upon themselves an even greater weight of guilt, which would earn them even more severe judgment (cf. Rom. 2:5).

Hopōs **(that)** relates to purpose, meaning "in order that" or "for the purpose of." It was fully within God's purpose that the wicked leaders of Israel, along with all other Jews who rejected Christ, have **the guilt of all the righteous blood shed on earth** come down on their heads. As far as the hardened scribes and Pharisees were concerned, the only gain they would receive from hearing more of the gospel would be more **guilt** and greater judgment.

It is not that God desires for men to reject His grace and be condemned (2 Pet. 3:9) but that when they persist in rejecting Him, they bring upon themselves the righteous outpouring of His wrath. The more they hear of His truth, the more accountable and guilty they become if they continue to reject it.

The scribes and Pharisees had all the accumulated revelation of the Old Testament, and for three years they had even received the perfect revelation of God's own Son. And the more they accumulated God's revelation without believing and following it, the more they accumulated God's wrath and judgment in direct proportion. They and their generation could be held guilty for **all the righteous blood shed on earth,** because no generation in history has had or will ever have more of God's light. They had God incarnate in their midst, who was Himself all truth and all light, yet they would not have Him.

The western world today is in a similar situation. The church has not always witnessed to Christ as clearly, fully, or lovingly as it might, but no generation in history, outside of that of Jesus' own day, has had more access to God's truth and the way of salvation than twentieth century western man. In addition to having great light, we have had benefit of the accumulated light, power, and blessing of the gospel for 2,000 years. Yet each successive generation seems to reject the gospel more vehemently, amassing for itself greater guilt and therefore greater judgment.

Paul testified, "For we are a fragrance of Christ to God among those who are being saved and among those who are perishing." The great difference, he went on to explain, was that to the saved they were "an aroma from life to life," whereas to the lost they were "an aroma from death to death" (2 Cor. 2:15-16). In other words, every time the gospel is proclaimed, it either draws men to Christ or drives them further away. Because it runs so contrary to popular notions about God, that truth is difficult for many Christians to accept. But the New Testament makes abundantly clear that the purpose of the gospel is not always to bring salvation; it has the equally divine purpose of bringing judgment. As the saying goes, the same sun that softens the wax hardens the clay. God not only is a God of love, mercy, and grace but of holiness, wrath, and judgment; and Scripture is equally emphatic about both aspects of His nature.

When men receive God's Son and are saved, He is glorified because His grace is vindicated; and when they refuse His Son and are condemned, He is glorified because His holiness is vindicated. Knowing how troublesome the second part of that truth is even for many believers to accept, Paul went on to assert that he was "not like many, peddling the word of God" in ways that were pleasing to men, "but as from sincerity, but as from God, [he spoke] in Christ in the sight of God" (2 Cor. 2:17). Lest any of his readers think he was simply expressing personal fanaticism, the apostle categorically asserted that he was speaking not only sincerely but from God and in God's sight.

In his letter to the Romans, Paul presents the same truth in a somewhat different light. He anticipated that some people would object to his teaching that God "has mercy on whom He desires, and He hardens whom He desires," and would ask, "Why does He still find fault? For who resists His will?" (Rom. 9:18-19). In reply the apostle said,

> On the contrary, who are you, O man, who answers back to God? The thing molded will not say to the molder, "Why did you make me like this," will it? Or does not the potter have a right over the clay, to make from the same lump one vessel for honorable use, and another for common use? What if God, although willing to demonstrate His wrath and to make His power known, endured with much patience vessels of wrath prepared for destruction? And He did so in order that He might make known the riches of His glory upon vessels of mercy, which He prepared beforehand for glory. (vv. 20-23)

God is God, and whatever He does is right by definition, because He is both the source and the measure of what is right.

In God's final word to mankind in Scripture, He declared, "Let the one who does wrong, still do wrong; and let the one who is filthy, still be filthy; and let the one who is righteous, still practice righteousness; and let the one who is holy, still keep himself holy" (Rev. 22:11). As men are in the end, so they will be forever. And whether in His gracious saving of those who receive His Son or in His holy judgment of those who do not, He will be glorified forever.

From the blood of righteous Abel to the blood of Zechariah, the Jews had been killing God's people and storing up greater and greater wrath and judgment.

Unrighteous Cain slew **righteous Abel,** his brother. He could not tolerate his brother's purity and godliness, because righteousness itself is a type of judgment on sin, exposing it for what it is.

The identity of **Zechariah, the son of Berechiah,** has long been debated among Bible students. According to 2 Chronicles 24:20-21, Zechariah the son of Jehoiada was stoned to death by order of King Joash for his relentless stand against idolatry. His murder "in the court of the house of the Lord" occurred about 800 B.C., long before the end of the writing of the Old Testament.

Over twenty men by the name of **Zechariah** are mentioned in Scripture, indicating that it was a very popular name. Among the hundreds or perhaps thousands of Zechariahs who had lived before Christ it would not be surprising if more than one had been killed in the Temple. Because Jesus was pointing out the extensiveness of persecution of righteous people, beginning with **Abel** and ending with **Zechariah,** it would suggest that He was covering the whole of Old Testament history, from creation to the end of the prophetic period. It is also significant that **Zechariah** wrote more of the coming Messiah than did any other prophet except Isaiah.

The prophet **Zechariah,** whose father's name was **Berechiah** (Zech. 1:1), was among the last prophets of Israel and apparently the last to be martyred. And although the Old Testament does not report his being **murdered between the temple and the altar,** it seems certain he was the **Zechariah** to whom Jesus referred.

It is significant that Jesus said, **whom you murdered,** speaking directly to the scribes and Pharisees but including all unbelieving Israel (v. 36). Although the murder of the prophet had been over 500 years earlier, the wicked leaders the Lord now addressed had participated in it. By their murdering Jesus, the incarnation of righteousness, they proved their complicity in and solidarity with the persecution and murder of every righteous person who has ever suffered at the hands of evil men.

JUDGMENT WAS IMMINENT

Truly I say to you, all these things shall come upon this generation. (23:36)

All these things—that is, the multiplied guilt and judgment that unbelieving mankind had been accumulating since the Fall—was about to **come** down **upon** the head of **this generation.** There is no reason to believe Jesus was speaking any way but historically when He spoke of **this generation.** It would be that generation who would experience the total destruction of Jerusalem and the Temple less than forty years later, in A.D. 70., a time Jesus called the "days of vengeance" (Luke 21:22). He had in mind not only those to whom He was then speaking but all other false leaders and unbelieving Jews living at that time—in other words, the nation of

Israel as a whole. In a tragic chronicle, its people have continued in suffering from then until now.

In the year 66, Jewish revolution again broke out against Rome. Having taken as much as they could tolerate of Roman oppression, injustice, and pagan ways, the Jews turned against their rulers. Largely inspired by the Zealots, the party of radical nationalists known for their guerilla tactics and frequent terrorism, many Palestinian Jews took up whatever arms they could find and joined in rebellion. Rome struck back by slaughtering thousands of Jews in northern Galilee, and eventually Titus came down to Jerusalem with an army in excess of 80,000 men. After stationing his army throughout the city as well as all around it, the general demanded its immediate surrender. When the Jews replied with mocking laughter and attacks on the soldiers, the troops began a massacre that almost defies description. (See chapter 29 of this volume for a vivid eye-witness account by the famed Jewish historian Josephus.)

About that same time, the Gentile inhabitants of Damascus are said to have slit the throats of ten thousand Jews living among them. Several centuries later, the Roman emperor Theodosius II enacted a legal code that declared Jews were inherently inferior and did not deserve the same legal protection and privileges as other people. Tragically, those anti-Semitic views came to permeate subsequent western culture and law. In A.D. 630, the Byzantine emperor Heraclitus banished from Jerusalem the Jews who had begun to resettle there.

During the first crusade, which began in 1096, the established church in Europe instigated what was declared to be a holy war to deliver the Holy Land from the Muslim Turks who had ruled it for many centuries. Fearing Jews would want to resettle and reclaim the land for themselves, many crusaders engaged in brutal massacres of European Jews, supposedly in the name of Christ, as they marched toward Palestine. Sometimes the soldiers would herd all the Jews in a town or city together and give them an ultimatum to confess Christ and be publicly baptized or else be killed. Some Jews made a verbal profession merely to save their lives, while others refused and were slain where they stood. The atrocities included trampling Jews under their horses' hooves as well as other means of execution too brutal to mention. Rather than face such humiliation and horror, many Jews committed suicide when they were informed that crusaders were approaching.

For many years Jews had experienced a relatively safe and untroubled asylum in England. But when a Dominican monk in the thirteenth century began to study the Hebrew Scriptures in order to be better able to witness to Jews, he himself converted to Judaism and was circumcised. In an irate reaction, the Roman Catholic Church had all Jews expelled from Cambridge.

In other parts of Europe Jews were falsely accused of counterfeiting coins and other serious crimes. After sham trials or no trial at all, the accused would be tortured, imprisoned, exiled, or executed. Sometimes all Jews in a community would be required to wear identifying arm bands or badges to set them apart. In London a group of Jews had their arms and legs tied to horses that were then driven off in opposite directions, and after the bodies were ripped apart, the remains were draped on gallows for the townspeople to see.

When the black plague swept across Europe in the fourteenth century, killing hundreds of thousands, many people blamed the Jews. In France they were accused of poisoning water wells, and in one town a synagogue filled with worshipers was burned to the ground. In desperation, many Jews fled to Poland and Russia in the farthest reaches of Europe, where many of their descendants still live today.

Having considerable freedom in Poland, they established several outstanding Talmudic schools and seminaries. They were later oppressed by the church for a while, but nevertheless joined the government and the church in fighting the Russian Cossacks. When the Cossacks were victorious, they vengefully massacred thousands of Jews.

Jews who fled to Spain found poor refuge. Among their worst persecutors were King Ferdinand and Queen Isabella, the two monarchs who commissioned Christopher Columbus's first ventures to the new world. That country was described by one Jewish poet as the hell of the Jews. During the Spanish Inquisition, the graves of those who had converted to Judaism were dug up and the bodies desecrated. The heirs of those proselytes had their property confiscated as a warning to others who might consider converting. Every Jew was made to wear a symbol of burning crosses, and in 1492, the year Columbus began his first voyage, most of them were expelled from the country. A large number emigrated to Russia, where persecution in varying degrees has persisted to this day.

In medieval Germany, Jews were accused of using the blood of Christian children in their Passover rites. Some were even charged with stabbing the host (the bread served in the Catholic mass and believed to turn into the actual body of Christ) to make it bleed—thereby reenacting His crucifixion. Those accused of such things were tortured and killed in a variety of cruel ways.

For many centuries anti-Semitism polluted most of western civilization. In 1894 a Jewish army officer named Alfred Dreyfus was falsely accused and convicted of treason simply because he was Jewish. His conviction precipitated the removal of all high-ranking Jews from the French army.

Despite the continued persecution, twenty million Jews still lived in Europe at the outbreak of World War II. In what has come to be termed "The Holocaust," Adolph Hitler hideously exterminated at least six million Jews in Germany and Nazi-occupied territories. Those demon-inspired atrocities were not grounded so much in religious as racial prejudice, with Jews being declared racially inferior.

With little respite, for two thousand years the Jews have endured persecution after persecution, being maligned, falsely accused, treated unjustly, denied dignity and jobs and schooling and citizenship, driven out of country after country, and not infrequently massacred without mercy—for no other reason than being Jewish.

The modern state of Israel bears the marks of much of that persecution, including Titus's destruction of the Temple, the excavated partial western wall of which is now called the wailing wall. There are also more modern relics there, such as tanks and other armored vehicles intentionally left to rust in public view as reminders of the costly battles Israelis have fought and continue to fight in defense of their new nation since it was founded in 1948.

Through all those horrors and systematic attempts at their extermination, the Jews remain. They remain because the holy God who preserves them will not be thwarted by the evil hosts of both men and demons who seek to destroy them.

Yet as Jesus gravely declares in this passage, the divine preservation of the Jews is not only for God's purpose of ultimately redeeming His chosen people but is also a perpetuation of their punishment. It is a continuing chastening that they will endure until Israel declares in faith, "Blessed is He who comes in the name of the Lord" (Matt. 23:39; cf. Ps. 118:26).

Jesus' Last Words to Israel

(23:37-39)

"O Jerusalem, Jerusalem, who kills the prophets and stones those who are sent to her! How often I wanted to gather your children together, the way a hen gathers her chicks under her wings, and you were unwilling. Behold, your house is being left to you desolate! For I say to you, from now on your shall not see Me until you say, 'Blessed is He who comes in the name of the Lord!'" (23:37-39)

Since the call of Abraham, the Jews have been God's special people, and a Christian who truly loves God cannot help loving the Jewish people. He has deep concern for their plight in our day and a heavy burden for their salvation in Christ, their Messiah.

Throughout all the centuries of their oppression, including attempts to exterminate them, as in the Nazi holocaust, they have survived and been divinely preserved in their racial identity. Although they have been scattered to every part of the world, have become citizens in countless different countries, have intermarried with Gentiles, and even have differing opinions among themselves as to who a real Jew is, they continue as a distinct people.

To those who know and believe Scripture, their perpetuation is not surprising, because, since He made His covenant with Abraham some four thousand years ago,

God has pledged to preserve His chosen people and one day to call them permanently back to Himself.

In the meanwhile, they cry out to a God who never answers. They wonder why, if they are indeed His chosen people, they have suffered so much at the hands of the world's most wicked people? Why, if their Scriptures are truly the oracles of God, have they been so abandoned by God, who in those oracles so often promised to be their Provider and Deliverer? Why, if He called all of His holy prophets from among them, has He since deserted them to the prejudice and malice of ungodly men? If they are the apple of God's eye, why has so much hatred arisen specifically against them and caused them incalculable misery and anguish?

In the close of this His last public message, Jesus gave the sobering answer to such questions, yet He gave it with intense compassion and with the assurance of Israel's ultimate conversion.

THE INTENSE COMPASSION

O Jerusalem, Jerusalem, who kills the prophets and stones those who are sent to her! How often I wanted to gather your children together, the way a hen gathers her chicks under her wings, and you were unwilling. Behold, your house is being left to you desolate! (23:37-38)

As Jesus had entered Jerusalem the morning before, "He saw the city and wept over it, saying, 'If you had known in this day, even you, the things which make for Peace! But now they have been hidden from your eyes'" (Luke 19:41-42). Jeremiah expressed similar grief when He considered the prospect of Judah's being taken captive by Babylon because of her defiance of God: "My soul will sob in secret for such pride; and my eyes will bitterly weep and flow down with tears" (Jer. 13:17).

Now Jesus expresses grief at the hardness of His people. There was great pathos as well as rebuke in His repeating the name, **Jerusalem, Jerusalem.** It was much as when He had said, "Martha, Martha, you are worried and bothered about so many things" (Luke 10:41); and when He had said, "Simon, Simon, behold, Satan has demanded permission to sift you like wheat" (Luke 22:31); and when He would say some years later, "Saul, Saul, why are you persecuting Me?" (Acts 9:4). The name **Jerusalem** means "city of peace," and it was often called the holy city. But over many centuries it had become the city of violence and of unholiness. In the book of Revelation it is called, "the great city which mystically is called Sodom and Egypt" (11:8), Sodom representing moral perversion and Egypt representing pagan religion. The city of God had become the city of Satan.

Using **Jerusalem** as representative of all Israel, the Lord again reminded the people of their rebellion against Him, manifested in their killing **the prophets** and stoning the other messengers He **sent to her.** The verbs **kills** and **stones** translate two Greek present active participles and could be rendered, "who are killing . . . and stoning," indicating a process that was still continuing. Unbelieving, rebellious

Israel had been killing God's righteous people from Abel to Zechariah (v. 35), and they would soon kill God's Son and then continue to kill the "prophets and wise men and scribes" that the Son Himself would send to them (v. 34). In the parable of the vineyard grower, Jesus described them as tenants who beat and killed the servants the owner sent to them and even killed the son and heir when he came (Matt. 21:33-39).

It was never God's ultimate plan and desire for His people to be punished but for them to return to Him in faithfulness and devotion. **"How often I wanted to gather your children together, the way a hen gathers her chicks under her wings,"** Jesus lamented. He longed to draw Israel to Himself and protect her just as a mother **hen gathers her chicks under her wings** to protect them from a storm that would batter them or a hawk that would devour them. There was a beautiful intimacy and tenderness in Jesus' words and no doubt in His voice as He mourned over His people. He had come "to His own, and those who were His own did not receive Him" (John 1:11).

David exulted, "How precious is Thy lovingkindness, O God! And the children of men take refuge in the shadow of Thy wings" (Ps. 36:7). It was God's great desire that all men, especially His beloved **children** Israel, would take refuge under His **wings.** At many times and in many forms Jesus had **often** given invitations such as, "Come to Me, all who are weary and heavy-laden, and I will give you rest. Take My yoke upon you, and learn from Me, for I am gentle and humble in heart; and you shall find rest for your souls" (Matt. 11:28-29).

But **you were unwilling,** He said. He came to His people in truth and light and love and offered them the kingdom God had long promised, but they rejected the King and forfeited the kingdom. Instead of inheriting the blessing God proffered for their faith, they inherited the judgment He promised for their unbelief.

Nothing in Scripture is more certain than the truth that God is sovereign over all things; but God's Word nowhere teaches determinism, as this verse makes clear. God was abundantly willing for Israel and all men to receive and follow His Son, but most of them **were unwilling.** They did not turn from Christ because of fate but solely because of their own unwillingness. When a person rejects Christ, it is never God's desire or God's fault but always his own.

A privilege was given to Israel that is absolutely unique in the history of mankind, and with that privilege came great opportunity and responsibility. The incarnate Son of God came into her midst as the Son of David, her own Messiah, Lord, and Savior. He taught and healed and exhorted and entreated. In His unparalleled truth and love He demonstrated God so perfectly that He could say, "He who has seen Me has seen the Father" (John 14:9; cf. 12:45). Yet Israel rejected that revelation and forsook that opportunity, and in so doing brought upon herself God's wrath and judgment.

Because Jews are God's chosen people they are the objects of Satan's fiercest hatred. Therefore when God removed His protective hand from Israel it was to expose her to the worst furies that Satan could bring upon a people. It is Satan's continual desire to eliminate them, because they are specially beloved by God and because to destroy them would be to frustrate God's promise of bringing them back to Himself (Rom. 11:26) and giving them to Christ as an inheritance.

Yet although Israel as a people has suffered because God withdrew His blessing from them, many individual Jews have come and continue to come to Christ in saving faith. God has never been without a chosen remnant (Isa. 10:22; Jer. 23:3; Ezek. 6:8; Zech. 8:12; Rom. 9:27).

During the days of Isaiah the Lord reminded Israel of His great love and care in calling them out and building them up as a people, using the figure of a grower who carefully planted and cultivated a vineyard only to find that it produced worthless grapes. Because of their unfaithfulness and unfruitfulness, the Lord declared that He would remove the protective hedge around the vineyard, break down its wall, and lay it waste. God went on to explain through the prophet, "For the vineyard of the Lord of hosts is the house of Israel, and the men of Judah His delightful plant. Thus He looked for justice, but behold, bloodshed; for righteousness, but behold, a cry of distress" (Isa. 5:1-7). That prediction was fulfilled when Judah was conquered by Babylon in 586 B.C. and had many of its inhabitants, including three of its kings, taken into exile by Nebuchadnezzar over a period of years.

In declaring, **"Behold, your house is being left to you desolate!"** Jesus was saying that, much as in that earlier time of judgment, Israel would be **left** devastated and **desolate.** Only a few days earlier Jesus had referred to the Temple as His Father's house (Matt. 21:13; cf. 12:4), but it had been so long profaned and desecrated that He now called it **your house,** a reference also to the nation as a whole, the house of Israel. Like the son of Phinehas's widow (1 Sam. 4:21), the Temple and all Israel could soon be called Ichabod, because God's glory would depart from them. In the present age, while God's glory and protective hand are withdrawn from Israel, the house of God is Christ's church, "the church of the living God, the pillar and support of the truth" (1 Tim. 3:15).

Early in her history God had warned Israel that if she would not obey Him, "to observe to do all His commandments and His statutes," that the curses He was about to enumerate would come upon her (Deut. 28:15-68). Because she not only had forsaken God's commandments but even His own Son, Israel would now be left **desolate,** subject to the vagaries of an ungodly world that would mock her, despise her, and persecute her people from city to city just as she would soon do with the prophets, wise men, and scribes Christ would send to her (v. 34).

In the end times the persecution of Jews will escalate into a holocaust like no other they have experienced. That suffering will occur in a period called the time of Jacob's distress (Jer. 30:7) and the Great Tribulation, a time "such as has not occurred since the beginning of the world until now, nor ever shall" (Matt. 24:21).

The Insured Conversion

For I say to you, from now on you shall not see Me until you say, "Blessed is He who comes in the name of the Lord!" (23:39)

Jesus' farewell words to Israel were, **"From now on you shall not see Me."** For the unbelieving Jews listening to Him that day and for all the other unbelieving Jews of that generation (v. 37) and for countless generations to come, those words were final. Because they rejected God, God rejected them. He would no longer be their God, and they would no longer be His people.

Were it not for Jesus' qualifying word **until,** that would have been their final moment in history, and the theology of the Bible, both in the Old and New Testaments, would be radically altered. In addition to that, men would have had good reason never to trust God's word again, because He repeatedly promised that His chosen people would ultimately be saved, restored, and blessed (see, e.g., Jer. 23:5-6; Isa. 66:10-22; Zech. 14:1-11).

Jesus did not say "unless," making Israel's restoration only a possibility, but **until,** making it a certainty. Even in the context of His most severe curses upon unbelieving Israel and her false leaders, that word offered hope. One day Israel will finally say in faith, **"Blessed is He who comes in the name of the Lord,"** and in that day she will be forever redeemed, restored, and blessed.

Only a few days earlier those very words from Psalm 118:26 had been shouted at Jesus by the multitudes as He came into Jerusalem seated on the donkey (Matt. 21:9). They were words that all Jews associated with acclamation of the Messiah when He came to establish His kingdom on earth. But true and appropriate as those words were on the occasion of His triumphal entry, they were not spoken in faith by most of the people who uttered them. The Messiah they wanted was not God's kind of Messiah but their own, and when Jesus soon demonstrated that He had not come to remove the Roman yoke as they expected, the cries for His coronation turned to cries for His crucifixion.

But one day with those same words Israel will hail her Messiah in faith, and the Lord's hand of blessing and protection will once again be upon her. "In that day the Lord will defend the inhabitants of Jerusalem," declared Zechariah, the prophet whom the forefathers of those inhabitants had "murdered between the temple and the altar" (Matt. 23:35). Continuing to describe that great reversal in the last days, He said,

> And the one who is feeble among them in that day will be like David, and the house of David will be like God, like the angel of the Lord before them. And it will come about in that day that I will set about to destroy all the nations that come against Jerusalem. And I will pour out on the house of David and on the inhabitants of Jerusalem, the Spirit of grace and of supplication, so that they will look on Me whom they have pierced; and they will mourn for Him, as one mourns for an only son, and they will weep bitterly over Him, like the bitter weeping over a first-born. (Zech. 12:8-10)

When the cup of God's wrath is empty, He will sovereignly overturn and destroy the evil world system of Satan that He has given temporary rein to tyrannize

His people. When Israel turns back to Him, He will turn back to them and pour out upon them His Holy Spirit of grace and blessing, and they will both rejoice and weep. They will rejoice in thanksgiving for their new-found Savior and Lord, but they will weep in penitence as they remember what they had done to Him. "In that day there will be great mourning in Jerusalem, . . . And the land will mourn, every family by itself" (Zech. 12:11-12). Their grief will be overwhelming and their sense of sin totally consuming.

In gracious response to that penitential grief, the Lord will pick them up and take them once again to Himself. "'In that day a fountain will be opened for the house of David and for the inhabitants of Jerusalem, for sin and for impurity. And it will come about in that day,' declares the Lord of hosts, 'That I will cut off the names of the idols from the land, and they will no longer be remembered; and I will also remove the [false] prophets and the unclean spirit from the land" (Zech. 13:1-2). "Then the Lord will go forth and fight against those nations, as when He fights on a day of battle. . . . And it will come about in that day that living waters will flow out of Jerusalem, half of them toward the eastern sea and the other half toward the western sea; it will be in summer as well as in winter. And the Lord will be king over all the earth; in that day the Lord will be the only one, and His name the only one" (14:3, 8-9).

Speaking of the Jews, who were his own people, the apostle Paul wrote, "I say then, they did not stumble so as to fall, did they? May it never be! But by their transgression salvation has come to the Gentiles, to make them jealous. Now if their transgression be riches for the world and their failure be riches for the Gentiles, how much more will their fulfillment be!" (Rom. 11:11-12).

Israel has not permanently fallen away from God. "They also, if they do not continue in their unbelief," Paul says, "will be grafted in; for God is able to graft them in again. . . . For I do not want you, brethren, to be uninformed of this mystery, lest you be wise in your own estimation, that a partial hardening has happened to Israel until the fulness of the Gentiles has come in; and thus all Israel will be saved" (vv. 23, 25-26).

Bibliography

Barclay, William. *The Gospel of Matthew.* Philadelphia: Westminster, 1959.

Broadus, John A. *Commentary on the Gospel of Matthew.* Valley Forge, Pa.: Judson, 1886.

Eerdman, Charles R. *The Gospel of Matthew.* Philadelphia: Westminster, 1966.

Gaebelein, Arno C. *The Gospel of Matthew.* Neptune, N.J.: Loizeaux, 1961.

Hendriksen, William. *New Testament Commentary: Exposition of the Gospel According to Matthew.* Grand Rapids: Baker, 1973.

Lange, John Peter. *Commentary on the Holy Scriptures: Matthew.* Grand Rapids: Zondervan, n.d.

Lenski, R.C.H. *The Interpretation of St. Matthew's Gospel.* Minneapolis: Augsburg, 1964.

Lloyd-Jones, D. Martyn. *Studies in the Sermon on the Mount.* Grand Rapids: Eerdmans, 1977.

Lovelace, Richard. *Dynamics of Spiritual Life.* Downers Grove, Ill.: InterVarsity, 1979.

Morgan, G. Campbell. *The Gospel According to Matthew.* Old Tappan, N.J.: Revell, 1939.

Pentecost, J. Dwight. *The Sermon on the Mount.* Portland, Ore.: Multnomah, 1980.

Pink, Arthur W. *An Exposition of the Sermon on the Mount.* Grand Rapids: Baker, 1953.

Plummer, Alfred. *An Exegetical Commentary on the Gospel According to St. Matthew.* Grand Rapids: Eerdmans, 1963.

Sanders, J. Oswald. *Bible Studies in Matthew's Gospel.* Grand Rapids: Zondervan, 1973.

Tasker, R.V.G. *The Gospel According to St. Matthew.* Grand Rapids: Eerdmans, 1977.

Indexes

Index of Greek Words

Index of Hebrew/Aramaic Words

Index of Scripture

Index of Subjects

Unforgiveness, 152, 154
Unity
  forgiveness and, 143
  with Christ, 103
Universalism, 130
Unrepentance, 135

Vengeance, 152

Wealth, spiritual, 200
Wisdom
  limitations of human, 42
  worldly, 6

Works, good
  divinely provided, 57
  evidence of salvation, 57
Works righteousness
  basis of human religion , 201
  futility of, 192, 202
Worship, God's presence in, 139

Yahweh. *See also* Jehovah, 96, 137, 198, 305, 347, 348

Zeal, discipline and, 131
Zealots, description of, 328

Moody Press, a ministry of the Moody Bible Institute, is designed for education, evangelization, and edification. If we may assist you in knowing more about Christ and the Christian life, please write us without obligation: Moody Press, c/o MLM, Chicago, Illinois 60610